HABITS OF THE ANTHROPOCENE: SCARCITY AND ABUNDANCE IN A POST-MATERIAL ECONOMY
PROCEEDINGS OF THE 43RD ANNUAL CONFERENCE OF THE ASSOCIATION FOR COMPUTER AIDED DESIGN IN ARCHITECTURE
VOLUME III: PROCEEDINGS BOOK TWO

Editors
Assia Crawford, Nancy Diniz, Richard Beckett, Jamie Vanucchi, Marc Swackhamer

Copy Editing
Lynne Campbell

Graphic Identity
Luke Bulman

Graphic Design
Luke Bulman

Layout
Dilan Ozkan

Printer
IngramSpark

© Copyright 2023
Association for Computer Aided Design in Architecture (ACADIA)

All rights reserved by individual project authors who are solely responsible for their content.

No part of this work covered by copyright may be reproduced or used in any form, or by any means graphic, electronic or mechanical, including recording, taping or information storage and retrieval systems without prior permission from the copyright owner.

ISBN 979-8-9891764-1-0

HABITS OF THE ANTHROPOCENE

PROCEEDINGS OF THE 43RD ANNUAL CONFERENCE OF THE ASSOCIATION FOR COMPUTER AIDED DESIGN IN ARCHITECTURE

VOLUME III: PROCEEDINGS BOOK TWO

Editors
Assia Crawford, Nancy Diniz, Richard Beckett, Jamie Vanucchi, Marc Swackhamer

acadia

HABITS OF THE ANTHROPOCENE
CONTENTS

INTRODUCTION

10 Shelby Elizabeth Doyle
Foreword: Computational Habits For The Chthulucene

14 Assia Crawford
Conference Introduction: Beyond Normal

16 Assia Crawford
Contribution Statement

FIELD NOTES

19 Rachel Dickey
Material Interfaces

27 Vasiliki Bakomichali, Mathilde Marengo, Julia Thomas, Hiranya Ganatra, Iacopo Neri
Fostering Symbiosis for Ecosystem Revival

33 Nikoletta Karastathi
Textile Narratives: Rhythmic Tactile Architectures

39 Jonathan A. Scelsa, Kyriaki Goti, Natalia Rossi, Wei Wang, Arthur Palaci Zani
Bric(k)olage: Spoliated Masonry C+D Waste

45 Christina Doumpioti
Artificial Images of Environmental Sensibility: A Manifesto

49 Vernelle A. A. Noel, Hayri Dortdivanlioglu
Text-to-Image Generators: Semiotics, Semantics, Syntax, and Society

55 Tatiana Estrina
The Yamal Conspiracy: A Geo-Engineered Fabulation

63 Kristof Crolla, Garvin Goepel
Kepiting Bambu: Mixed-Reality-Aided Bamboo Construction

69 Chenoe Hart
Elevators, Hard Drives and Teleportation

71 Shahin Vassigh, Biayna Bogosian
Envisioning an Open Knowledge Network (OKN) for AEC Roboticists

77 Nima Zahiri
Height-active Wood: Elasticity, Anisotropicity, and Hygroscopicity in Timber High-Rises

AWARDS

84 Awardees Biography

87 Kathy Velikov
Society Award for Leadership

91 Terry Knight
Teaching Award of Excellence

95 Joseph Choma
Innovative Research Award of Excellence

99 Odile Decq
Design Excellence Award

103 Nader Tehrani
Digital Practice Award of Excellence

KEYNOTE SPEACHES 1

110 Speakers Bioraphy

111 Areti Markopoulou
Urban Mining: Material Resources for Circular Construction

115 Martyn Dade-Robertson
Designing with Agential Matter

121 Panel Discussion

KEYNOTE SPEACHES 2

128 Speakers Bioraphy

129 Phil Ayres
Sensitive Scaffolds

131 Joyce Hwang
In Consideration of Neighbors

135 Orkan Telhan
Growing Towards Mycelium

145 Panel Discussion

KEYNOTE SPEACHES 3

154 Speakers Bioraphy

157 Simone C Niquille
Model Home

163 Chris Cornelius
Relatives

169 **AM Kanngieser**
Ethics and Ecocidal Listening: Oceanic Refractions as an Artistic Case Study

173 **Panel Discussion**

WORKSHOPS

179 **Wassim Jabi, David Andres Leon, Abdulrahman Alymani, Solda Pourali Behzad, Michelle Salamoun**
Exploring Building Topology Through Graph Machine Learning

185 **Haottian Zhang**
Today Once More: Filmmaking with Photogrammetry and Neural Radiance Fields

189 **Pok Yin Victor Leung, Yijiang Huang**
Task and Motion Planning for Robotic Assembly

193 **Kristof Crolla, Abdullah Tahir Sheikh**
Immersive Realities

195 **Augusto Gandia, Aileen Iverson**
Hybrid Making: Physical Explorations with Computational Matter

201 **DART, XTreeE, SIKA**
Towards a Low Carbon Additive Manufacturing

203 **Nic Bao, Xin Yan**
Habitat Formation

ACADIA CULTURAL, HISTORY FELLOWSHIP, AUTODESK ACADIA BIPOC SCHOLARSHIP

207 **Shelby Doyle, Biayna Bogosian, Melissa Goldman**
ACADIA Cultural/History Fellowship

211 **Hanan Kataw**
ACADIA's Open Call: Expanding the Narrative of Diversity and Inclusion in Computational Design

221 **Hayri Dortdivanlioglu**
Word Webs: Bridging the Gap between Theory and Practice

229 **Constantinos Miltiadis**
An Open Living Archive for ACADIA

233 **Jenny Sabin, Biayna Bogosian, Sabina Poole, Cesar Escalante, Zach Kron**
Inaugural Autodesk ACADIA BIPOC Student Scholarship and Workshop

THE EVENT

241 **Leyuan Li**
Wall-Table-Bed

247 **Luke Bulman**
Notes on a Visual Identity

249 **Sarah Miller**
An Ocean of Coffee, A Sea of Red: ACADIA Conferences are Worth It

253 **Marc Swackhamer**
CU Denver and Impact

ACADIA CREDITS

256 **Conference Chairs**
260 **Session Chairs**
266 **ACADIA Organization**
268 **Conference Management**
270 **ACADIA 2023 Sponsors**

Computational Habits for the Chthulucene

Shelby Elizabeth Doyle
AIA, ACADIA President 2022-23
Associate Professor of Architecture
Stan G. Thurston Professor of Design-Build
Iowa State University College of Design
Director, ISU Computation & Construction Lab

"Unlike either the Anthropocene or the Capitalocene, the Chthulucene is made up of ongoing multispecies stories and practices of becoming-with in times that remain at stake, in precarious times, in which the world is not finished and the sky has not fallen—yet. We are at stake to each other. Unlike the dominant dramas of Anthropocene and Capitalocene discourse, human beings are not the only important actors in the Chthulucene, with all other beings able simply to react. The order is re-knitted: human beings are with and of the Earth, and the biotic and abiotic powers of this Earth are the main story."[1] - Donna Haraway

Habits of The Anthropocene: Scarcity and Abundance in a Post-Material Economy was organized during the hottest summer in recorded history, marked by now routine floods, heatwaves, wildfires, and storms.[2] Climate catastrophe and the intertwined crises of social and racial justice are the direct result of human "habits" of designing, constructing, and occupying the Earth.

Habits are settled tendencies or practices, especially ones that are difficult to relinquish and the term implies repetition, perhaps unconscious, that becomes normalized through its reiteration. Within the ACADIA community, computational habits can be found in our ways of thinking and making: in our pedagogies, our programming, our processes, and our practices. Given the stakes of the ongoing ecological crisis, what habits does the ACADIA community want to reveal and relinquish? What are the computational habits we need to identify, recall, question, break, and replace with new (or perhaps old) ways of thinking and working?

The 2023 conference themes offer a few methods for consideration: Digital Materiality, Feminist Thinking, Craft and the Digital, Damaged Grounds, Indigenous Voices, New Ecologies, Virtual Scapes, Bio-Digital Hybrids, and Chimeras & Cyborgs. These themes find resonance between 6 pre-conference workshops and 90 research contributions: Project, Paper, and Field Notes organized across 16 sessions. Five award winners will share their exceptional contributions to the teaching and practice of architectural computing: Joseph Choma, Odile Decq, Terry Knight, Nader Tehrani and Kathy Velikov.

Bracketing these conversations will be by a series of keynotes and panel discussions by Phil Ayres, Chris Cornelius, Martyn Dade-Robertson, Joyce Hwang, Amer Kanngieser, Areti Markopoulou, Simone C. Niquille, and Orkan Telhan. These computational designers, artists, and theorists are working on a range of topics including biomaterials, ecological design, ethical practices, indigenous knowledge, gender equity, anti-racism, and social responsibility. These are not extra-disciplinary anxieties; architecture, computational design, and their allied disciplines are exceptionally powerful technologies capable of both magnifying and reducing vast inequalities.

Each contribution to the conference offers a piece of how we might find a way out of the "Habits of the Anthropocene" and become re-knitted into Haraway's Chthulucene through the integration of non-human actors - plants, animals, lichens, fungi, bacteria, viruses - into computational design coupled with more capacious and inclusive ways of creating community. This year marked the introduction of the Inaugural Autodesk ACADIA BIPOC Scholarship promoting participation from Black, Indigenous, People of Color, and the continuation of the Student Conference Attendance Scholarship and Workshop Scholarship directed to support students from The National Organization of Minority Architecture Students (NOMAS), architecture students from Mexico, and international students from developing countries, as identified by the United Nations Development Programme.

The 2023 ACADIA conference marks the 42nd anniversary of the organization: forty-two times the community has remade itself around an evolving set of questions. Our habits were radically short-circuited in 2020 and required reconsidering nearly every aspect of running a conference and an organization. One outcome is the ongoing ACADIA Cultural History Project[3] (CHP) which is "a promise to the future that the present will make itself accountable". This began with making public a complete digital archive of ACADIA proceedings and quarterlies to make the history of the organization visible as a means for considering its future. The CHP then began documenting gender disparities in keynotes, awardees, and attendees as a method to reconsider how we value and promote forms of computational knowledge - this led to the first female majority keynote lineup in 2020 in the organization's history as well as live-streaming the conference for free to increase global student access. The project was documented in the 2021 proceedings and became an exhibition at the 2022 conference. In 2023, the inaugural ACADIA Cultural History Fellowship was launched to facilitate research projects that advance the histories, theories, and practices of underrepresented voices or reveal uncelebrated cultural trends in the computational design community.[4]

Each year is an opportunity to reflect on whether the community's research on computational design is "contributing to the construction of humane physical environments" as ACADIA's second bylaw pledges. In the context of immediate and imminent socio-political and environmental crises, how do we even begin to think about the built environment - digital or physical - as humane?[5] We construct computational habits for the Chthulucene and we remain at stake to each other.

Thank You

The annual conference would not be possible without incredible amounts of volunteer time from the Conference Chairs and the ACADIA Board, significant in-kind support from the host institution, and the financial support of our sponsors.

On behalf of the ACADIA membership and the Board, I would like to thank the 2023 Conference Site-Chairs from University of Denver Colorado, Assia Crawford and Marc Swackhamer, for the incredible work they have done to conceive of, plan, and execute the Annual Conference. Thank you also to 2023 Conference Co-Chairs Nancy Diniz, Richard Beckett, Jamie Vanhucchi, Thora Arnardottir, Leyuan Li, Cynthia Fishman, Dilan Ozkan, Andrew Adamatzky, and Joern Langhorst.

I would also like to extend many thanks to University of Colorado – Denver College of Architecture and Planning - for hosting ACADIA, and to the staff and students who have worked behind the scenes.

In addition to the team, I want to recognize and thank Biayna Bogosian for her work as Steering Chair collaborating with the 2023 team and Cameron Nelson for their dedication and tireless efforts as conference manager.

I would also like to acknowledge and thank the dedicated members of the ACADIA Board and Officers, who volunteer countless hours to the organization and the annual conference. In particular, the leadership and contributions of Vice President Jenny Sabin, Treasurer Philip Anzalone, Communications Officer Melissa Goldman, Secretary Katie MacDonald, Membership Officer Vernelle A.A. Noel, Technology Officer Jose Luis García del Castillo y López, and Development Officer Sina Mostafavi have been invaluable.

ACADIA Development Committee: Sina Mostafavi (chair) with Daniel Bolojan, and Robert Stuart-Smith.

ACADIA Awards Committee: Leslie Lok (chair) with Maria Yablonina, Stefana Parascho, and Shermeen Yousif.

ACADIA Scholarships Committee: Kathrin Dörfler (chair) with Daniel Bolojan, Vernelle A. A. Noel, and Felicia Davis

ACADIA Elections Committee: Behnaz Farahi (chair) with Leslie Lok, Leighton Beaman, and Robert Stuart-Smith.

ACADIA Steering Committee: Biayna Bogosian (chair) with Vernelle A. A. Noel, Katie MacDonald, Jenny Sabin, and Shelby Doyle (ex officio).

ACADIA Scientific Committee: Stefana Parascho (chair) with Kathrin Dorfler, Daniel Bolojan, and Shermeen Yousif.

ACADIA Website Committee: Leighton Beaman (chair) with Melissa Goldman, Behnaz Farahi, Katie MacDonald, and Jose Luis García del Castillo y López.

ACADIA Ethics Committee: Vernelle A. A. Noel (chair) with Leighton Beaman, Jenny Sabin, and Shelby Doyle (ex officio).

Diversity Committee: Daniel Bolojan with Felecia Davis, Jenny Sabin, and Shelby Doyle (ex officio).

ACADIA IJAC Editors Dana Cupkova, Maria Yablonina, Sina Mostafavi, Tsz Yan Ng, Kyle Steinfeld, Ehsan Baharlou, Adam Marcus, Mollie Claypool, Matias del Campo, and Andrew John Wit.

REFERENCES

[1] https://www.e-flux.com/journal/75/67125/tentacular-thinking-anthropocene-capitalocene-chthulucene/

[2] https://www.scientificamerican.com/article/july-2023-is-hottest-month-ever-recorded-on-earth/

[3] Reflections on the Past 40+ Years of ACADIA Shelby Doyle, Melissa Goldman, and Biayna Bogosian K. Dörfler, S. Parascho, J. Scott, B. Bogosian, B. Farahi, J. del Castillo y López, J. Grant, V. Noel. (Eds) ACADIA 2021: Realignments Toward Critical Computation [Proceedings of the 41st Annual Conference of the Association of Computer Aided Design in Architecture. Online and Global. 3-6 November 2021. (pp. 650-657)

[4] http://acadia.org/news/MA4V63

[5] http://assets.acadia.org/doc/ACADIA%20Bylaws_Version%2010-15-11.pdf

HABITS OF THE ANTHROPOCENE
CONFERENCE INTRODUCTION

Beyond Normal

Introduction to the Proceedings of the 43rd Annual ACADIA Conference

Assia Crawford
University of Colorado Denver

As we slowly stumbled back into old pre-pandemic modes of work, and carried forward the lessons and burdens of the global lockdown, we embarked on assembling a post-pandemic conference. This entailed acknowledging the traumas, disruptions, and potentials of practices that venture beyond established norms. By now, we are under no illusions of a "Normal", yet norms and prescribed forms of being still govern our society. This prompted a new look at the fields of design and computation so as to generate a platform for new types of discourse surrounding our making practices.

Our team was comprised of academics from North America and Europe, and spanned the fields of Architecture, Landscape Architecture, and Computer Science. It was a collaboration between the University of Colorado Denver, Cornell University, University College London, Central Saint Martins, and Newcastle University in the United Kingdom. This international array of scholars and institutions reflects the reshaped landscape of the profession and the opportunities that came about following the global COVID-19 crisis. It was our hope to help further dissolve boundaries and promote a more permeable academic environment. In this vein of thought, we also promoted diversity within our peer review team that represented institutions from across the world and through a highly rigorous review process. This year's conference had a 30% acceptance rate and showcased-cutting-edge research from across the world. The papers showcased in this volume illustrate new forms of making, processes, and critical reflections that underpin the final manifestations of the work. In many instances, they are as much a product as a provocation.

The event was split into full-length and work-in-progress paper presentations, project panel discussions, and exhibitions, as well as field notes that were peer reviewed by a panel of experts assembled by the designated chairs. There were a series of workshops and exhibitions organized and curated by the Workshop and Exhibitions Chairs that took place in the days leading up to the conference, as well as throughout the event.

In the spirit of international collaboration, we partnered with our sister organization, The Association for Computer-Aided Architectural Design Research in Asia (CAADRIA) and the Department of Architecture at the University of Hong Kong. The collaboration resulted in a satellite exhibition in Hong Kong featuring the projects in this book, along with selected CAADRIA contributions. The keynote speeches were livestreamed at the Department of Architecture at the University of Hong Kong. In the months that led up to the conference, discussions took place concerning the role of international collaboration, hybrid modes of dissemination of work, and the new prospects of conference organization.

The conference made use of the digital modes of disseminating the content of the conference through a livestream available to audiences across the world. Furthermore, the livestream was made available free of charge to students across the globe. This was done in the hope of promoting equal access to the future generation of designers and thinkers, who will inevitably be faced with great challenges, and who we hope will renegotiate a better future for our planet.

These challenges, some deeply engrained in today's society, with others emerging as recent byproducts of past decisions, inspired the theme of the conference. The theme is based on the rather brief, yet profound period of the Anthropocene that brings about the uncertainty of unstable and unprecedented conditions that incite a paralysis born of the inability to challenge the existing systems, as well as an exciting landscape of opportunities. These new prospects bring about questions of how humanity can renegotiate its position within multispecies networks and artificial intelligence. The ecology of our planet involves more-than-human actors, and this becomes a key focus in an age of disturbed ecologies and eroded human/non-human boundaries. Our role in these negotiations with the natural and the artificial as well as the human drive for growth, has come to the forefront during the COVID-19 pandemic. With these contemporary uncertainties it becomes increasingly challenging to define, quantify, or separate nature, the human and the digital. Therefore, there is an emergence of chimeras, holobionts, cyborgs, and grotesque, and sublime creatures. Whether caused by self-indulgence or brought about by necessity, these new ecologies are a direct product of the Anthropocene. The emerging pressures of environmental decline, along with political and social unrest, accelerate humanity towards unknown ground that calls for new mythologies. We looked to, among others, fictional narratives, animism, and tribal identities to inform making and give value beyond consumer-driven mass production. Our keynote speakers took part in panel discussions that looked at these topics, both on a local and a global, scale across various modes of practice.

The conference examined suppressed voices, indigenous and feminist thinking, and queer theory, all of which bring a new dimension to utopianism, capitalism and consumerism. We ask scholars to embrace uncertainty through digital and manual forms of making, engagement with virtual and physical spaces, and artistic and scientific endeavors that span multiple disciplines and weave together old and new knowledge. Although we often look to the digital and the emergent, we recognize that it is critical to reconnect with lost knowledge and spiritual practices that seek to amplify our humanity and enforce our stewardship of nature and fellow humans. Ways of repairing the damaged and grieving the lost in a digital world become a challenge that the conference explored. Practitioners were asked to offer disruptive making practices, experimental computation and ways of growing and emotionally connecting with the non-human, be it biological or artificial, as well as theoretical thinking surrounding the challenges created by the human species. The conference recognized that critically examining these ideas is an essential component of imagining a future beyond the status quo.

These new modes of thinking and making bring forth questions of how such experiments will be embraced and what aspects of everyday life, the built environment, and manufacture they are likely to challenge. Speculative and artistic endeavors pave the way for potential futures and shine light upon the pitfalls of accelerated growth, techno-fixes, and declining ecosystems. As we face new global challenges, we asked contributors to explore local and place-specific making that carries its own unique signature through the systems, species, constraints, and folklore that inform their practice. This is a direct attempt to think globally while acting locally, sensitively and with a sense of responsibility, not only for our own species' survival, but towards planetary interests. The call asked thinkers and makers to consider what new local ecologies shall emerge through environmental displacement of people, gradual migration of species, and unprecedented environmental changes. What forensic landscapes shall emerge from the byproducts of our contemporary society, and how can we scavenge and repurpose the leftovers of civilization? How do our mind and body interface with the bio-digital, and how do we approach bioengineered chimeras?

It is our sincere hope that we continue to stray from established norms and continue to search for diversity of though, plurality of practice, and a multiplicity of creative problem solving. We hope that the practices featured in this volume inspire and cultivate a sense of hope against the backdrop of ever-growing uncertainty.

Contribution Statement

Assia Crawford
University of Colorado Denver

Richard Becket
University College London

Jamie Vanucchi
Cornell University

Marc Swackhamer
University of Colorado Denver

Nancy Morgado Diniz
University of the Arts London

Leyuan Li
University of Colorado Denver

Luke Bulman
Office of Luke Bulman

Lynne Campbell
ACADIA

Dilan Ozkan
Newcastle University

Thora Arnardottir
Newcastle University

In support of transparency in authorial attribution, the conference chairs wish to briefly highlight the specific contributions of each member of the team to both the conference and this publication, in addition to their roles in the general overall planning for the ACADIA 2023 Conference. These categories are adapted from and expanded upon the CRediT (Contributor Roles Taxonomy) promoted and administered as an informal standard at CASRAI (https://casrai.org/credit/). Names are listed here in order of contribution to this volume.

Assia Crawford: Conceptualization (Conference Themes and Conference Platform), Writing - Original Draft, Writing - Review and Editing, Visualization, Supervision, Project Administration (Technical Papers, Projects and Field Notes Peer Review Process, Conference Budget, Conference Program Organization, Keynotes Organization, Session Chairs Organization, Exhibitions, Workshops Call, Peer Review and Graphics, Projects and Proceedings Books Writing).

Richard Becket: Project Administration (Technical Papers, Projects and Field Notes Peer Review Process, Conference Program Organization, Projects and Proceedings Books Writing), Supervision.

Jamie Vanucchi: Project Administration (Technical Papers, Projects and Field Notes Peer Review Process, Conference Program Organization, Projects and Proceedings Books Writing).

Marc Swackhamer: Conceptualization (Conference Themes), Writing - Review and Editing, Supervision, Project Administration (AIA CEUs Administration, Technical Papers, Projects and Field Notes Peer Review Process), Funding Acquisition, Communication.

Nancy Morgado Diniz: Supervision, Project Administration (Proceedings Books Volume 2 and 3).

Leyuan Li: Visualization, Supervision, Project Administration (Projects and Field Notes Peer Review Process, Conference Program Organization, Curated Projects, Exhibitions, CADRIA Collaboration Organization), Communication.

Luke Bulman: Visualization (Graphic Identity, Graphic Design of Website, Design of Book Volumes and All Associated Merchandise).

Lynne Campbell: Project Administration (Copy Editing of Proceedings and Projects Books).

Dilan Ozkan: Project Administration (Proceedings and Projects Books), Communication.

Cynthia Fishman: Project Administration (Conference Logistics), Supervision.

Thora Arnardottir: Conceptualization (Conference Platform Workshops Section), Visualization, Supervision, Project Administration (Workshops).

General Statement Regarding Attribution

Attribution order for work submitted to ACADIA and published in this volume is determined by level of contribution, with the first author listed considered the principal author and subsequent authors listed in order of contribution to the work. If authors have contributed equally, those names are indicated with an asterisk. The only exception to this convention is that lab/studio leaders' names (if applicable) appear last on the list of authors.

HABITS OF THE ANTHROPOCENE
FIELD NOTES

Material Interfaces

Rachel Dickey
University of North Carolina
Charlotte

1 Covid Confessionals project providing protective barriers producing fields of color and light (Dickey, 2020, © Studio Dickey).

Disembodied Experiences

Based on our current daily rate, 85,410 hours is the average amount of time that an adult in the United States will spend on their phone in a lifetime (Howarth 2023). This is time spent texting, tweeting, emailing, snapping, chatting, posting, and interacting with an interface which each of us carry in our pocket. Kelly Dobson explains, "We psychologically view the cell phone as an extension of our bodies, which is why when you accidentally forget it or leave it behind you feel you have lost apart of yourself" (2013). In reality, this device is just one of many technologies which affect our relationship with our bodies and the physical world. Additionally, Zoom meetings, social media networks, on-line shopping, and delivery robots, all increasingly detach our bodies and our senses from our everyday experiences and interactions. In response to digital culture, Liam Young writes, "Perhaps the day will come when we turn off our target ads, navigational prompts, Tinder match notifications, and status updates to find a world stripped bare, where nothing is left but scaffolds and screens" (2015). Make no mistake; the collection of projects shared in these field notes is intended to be a counterpoint to such a prophesied future. However, the intent is not to try to compete with technology, but rather, to consider the built environment itself as an interface, encouraging interaction through feedback and responsivity directly related to human factors, finding ways to re-engage the body through design.

A Collection of Material Interfaces

This line of inquiry started with a series of sketches and prototypes involving the design of family of furniture, more specifically a collection of responsive chairs that encourage

2   Family of Furniture that synchronizes with rhythms of the body.

synchronized and conscious breathing (Figures 2 and 3). These studies investigate the possibilities of using technology to mediate psychological and physiological states in spaces for therapeutic, and otherwise, beneficial ends. It emerged from a goal similar to what Nicholas Negroponte describes as the desire to "conjure a world where buildings are [...] animate, thinking, and emotive beings, which actively house and protect us physically as well as psychologically" (1975).

Such early work was a starting point grounding the next set of experiments. Similar to the breathing chair, the Air Hugs installation offers a deliberate, gracious, and delicate hug (Figure 4). The installation is a responsive environment that uses color tracking for proximity detection to control a network of pneumatic membranes that reconfigure space (Figure 5). As the title suggests, it explores the use of air as a material and the hug, which offers an awareness of one's body and other bodies, and of the space between, or lack thereof, recalibrating human scale and social interactions.

In the midst of a global pandemic, questions about the intimate space around the body became even more prevalent. Designed and built within two months in 2020, the Covid Confessionals installation is as a rapid response, public intervention that provides spaces for interaction during a time of distressing social isolation (Figures 1 and 6). It architecturally manifests distancing measures using the Center for Disease Control's (CDC) six-foot metric of separation as the modular basis of its parametric design. Its dichroic walls cast caustic patterns and fields of color and light (Figures 7 and 8). Physically, it provides an analog filter upon which to view the city, oneself, and each other, much like the digital filters used on our cameras today. Overall, its various configurations provide conditions for social exchange and playful interactions, colorfully reminding us of our capacity for resilience.

Similar to the invisible boundaries defined with social distancing, the Sound Pavilion project delineates space through non-visual sensations involving the design of subtle acoustical variations in the environment (Figure 9). It examines the experience of sound by way of the entire body whereby acoustic perception not only takes place

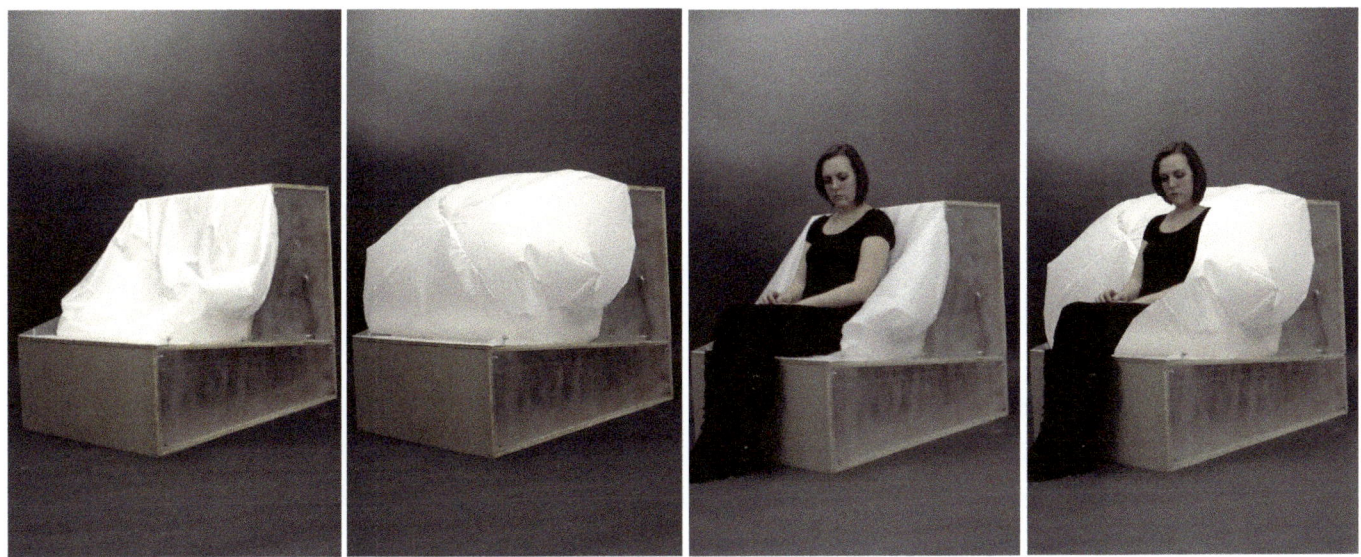

3   Prototype chair that synchronizes with the breath of the user through inflation and deflation (Dickey).

4   Air Hugs responsive environment that reconfigures space around the body based on proximity of visitor (Dickey).

5   Air Hugs installation responds with inflation (right) and deflation (left).

through the ears, since the entire body is exposed to sound waves (Figure 10). The pavilion manipulates sound through surface diffusion with its texture, while also preserving and intensifying sound through form-based reflection. It includes multi-channel speakers embedded in key geometrically altering sound panels playing compositions produced in collaboration with a composer. Sound then plays at various levels and heights in the pavilion to define boundaries of auditory space in and around it.

So, what about material interfaces for public use? The last project outlined here transforms a median into a linear park housing a series of rocking chairs that activate public space (Figures 11 and 12). While the project steers away momentarily from digital interfaces, it considers analog forms of feedback, taking body movement as input from either a single user or multiple users, then outputting a rocking path of motion, generating a playful exchange between the user and the interface.

Materiality and Human Experience

This collection of work invites us to interact with the material conditions of our physical world and with each other. It examines how architectural bodies become more responsive to human bodies by channeling essential environmental ingredients like air, light, sound, and movement. Antoine Picon describes similar relationships to experience and materiality when he writes, "Materiality usually designates the material dimension of a phenomenon, a thing, an object, or a system in relation to human thought and practice. [...] It characterizes the type of rapport that we, humans, maintain with materials, and, more broadly with the physical world around us with the phenomena, things, and objects that we perceive through our senses as fundamentally material" (2020). Materiality moves ideas to a physical reality where people interact with our imaginaries, experiences and practices (Picon 2020).

The material interfaces outlined here attempt to encourage alternative forms of interactivity with the built environment, mediating between our bodies and the world around us and acknowledging that with all things we create, they shape us. The work tries to ask critical

6   Covid Confessionals installation built as a rapid response intervention.
7   Covid Confessionals shields producing fields of color and light.

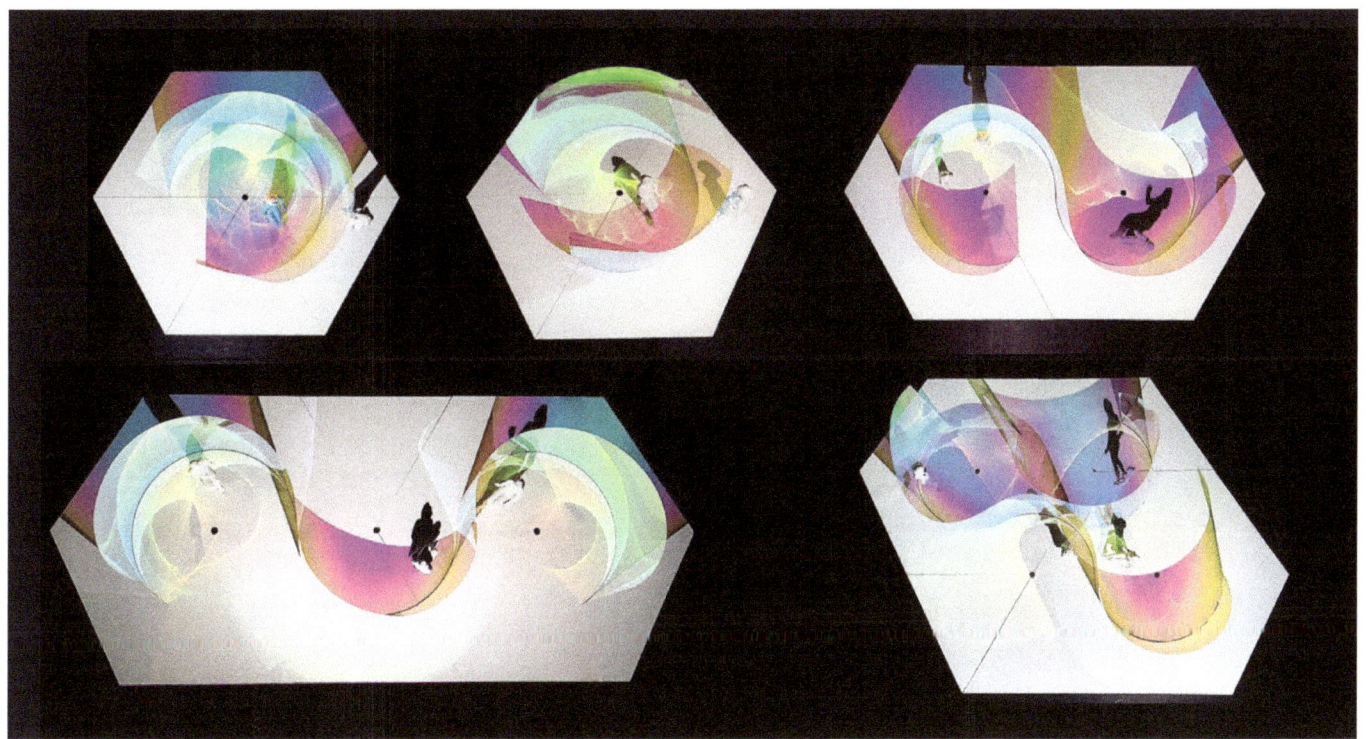

8   Covid Confessionals physical models design based on six-foot social distancing radius.

9   Sound Pavilion alters sound through form-based reflection.

questions, and responds by appropriating computation as a way of thinking, designing, making, and operating, considering a world of inputs and outputs, exploring alternative ways we, as humans, relate to our built world.

ACKNOWLEDGMENTS

All projects included in this publication were produced by Studio Dickey, a practice which uniquely involves students and professionals collaborating on the design and production of creative work. The Air Hugs installation team included: Noushin Radnia, Alireza Karduni, William Hutchins, Sara Shamloo, Hunter Sigmon, Swathi Sreedharan, and Lina Taheri. The Covid Confessionals installation team included: Noushin Radnia, Alex Cabral, Sierra Grant, Will Hutchins, Alex Casar Rodriguez, Robby Sachs, and Elvie Sumner The Sound Pavilion team included: Alexander Cabral, Drake Cecil, Hana Maleki, Margaret Martin, Jarrod Norris, Robert Sachs, and Hunter Sigmon. The Rocking Chairs and design of the Bleachery Heritage Plaza were produced in collaboration with TGR Landscape Group and team members included: Sierra Grant, Sheriyth Cain, Hunter Sigmon, Drake Cecil, Will Hutchins, Alex Casar Rodriguez, and Robby Sachs.
Project Title: Covid Confessionals

Client: Charlotte City Center Partners
Designer: Studio Dickey
Event: Rail Trail Light Festival
Date: 2021

Project Title: Sound Pavilion
Funding Source: David Ravin School of Architecture Faculty Research Grant
Year: 2018

Project Title: Bleachery Heritage Plaza and Rocking Chairs
Client: Rock Hill Economic and Urban Development
Designer: Studio Dickey with TGR Landscape Group
Location: Rock Hill, South Carolina
Date: 2023

REFERENCES

Dobson, Kelly. 2013. "Cultural Prosthetics," lecture in Project, Installation, Intervention. Cambridge, MA. March 2013.

Howarth, Josh. 2023. "Time Spent Using Smartphones," Exploding Topics. Website. Accessed May 25, 2023. https://explodingtopics.com/blog/smartphone-usage-stats.

10 Sound Pavilion produces unique auditory experiences as the visitor moves in and around it.

11 Multi-occupant rocking chairs along a median transformed into a linear park.

12 Interactive street furniture that rocks based on the movement of the user(s).

Negroponte, Nicholas. 1975. Soft Architecture Machines. Cambridge: MIT Press. 12-13.

Picon, Antoine. 2020. The Materiality of Architecture, Minneapolis: University of Minnesota Press. 9-20.

Young, Liam 2015. "Atlas of Fiducial Landscapes," in RoboLog. Winter 2016. Cambridge: MIT Press. 125-145.

IMAGE CREDITS

All images by the author.

Rachel Dickey is the founding principal of Studio Dickey and is an Associate Professor of Architecture at the University of North Carolina Charlotte. Studio Dickey, a Charlotte-based art and design practice, uniquely consists of students and professionals collaboratively working on the design and production of creative work. Dickey's work is characterized by the synthesis of architecture, digital art, and design appropriated towards innovative material interfaces for the built environment. Dickey holds a Master of Design Studies from Harvard University and a Bachelor of Science in Architecture and a Master of Architecture from Georgia Institute of Technology.

Fostering Symbiosis for Ecosystem Revival

Vasiliki Bakomichali
Institute for Advanced
Architecture of Catalonia

Mathilde Marengo
Institute for Advanced
Architecture of Catalonia

Julia Thomas
Institute for Advanced
Architecture of Catalonia

Hiranya Ganatra
Institute for Advanced
Architecture of Catalonia

Iacopo Neri
Institute for Advanced
Architecture of Catalonia

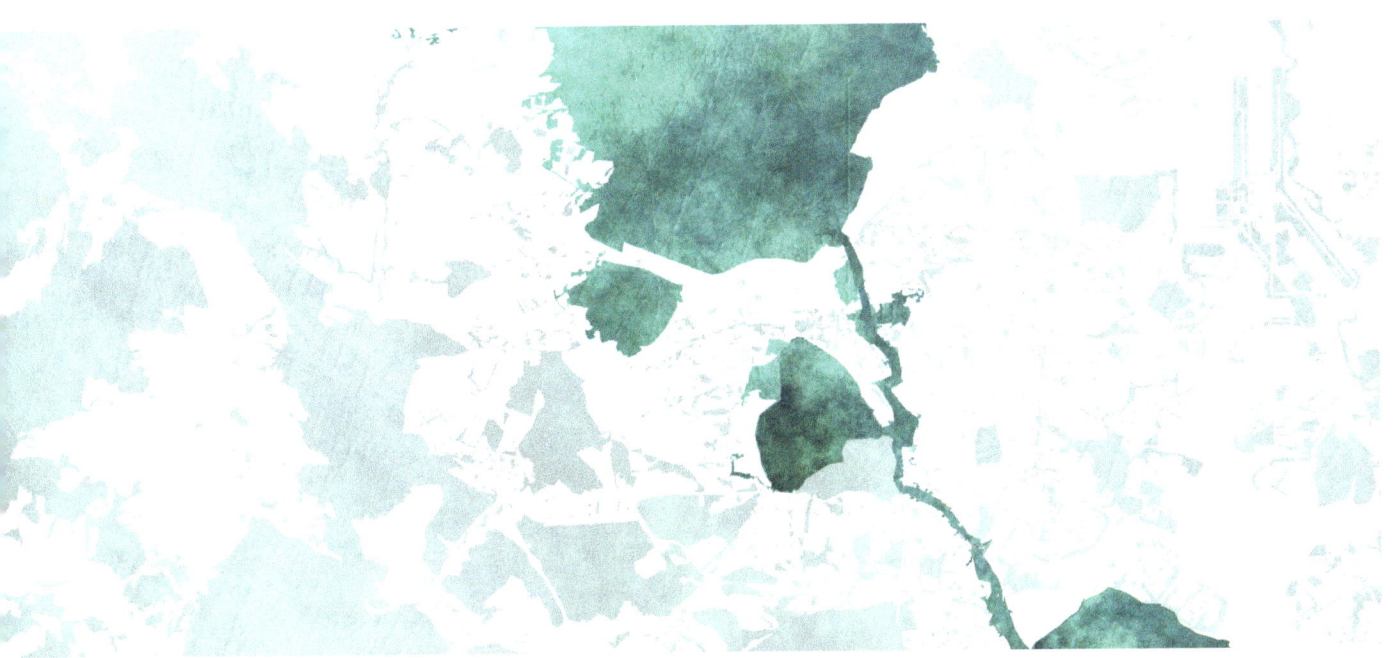

1   Forest Patches and Green Areas - Ecological Corridor in Madrid, Spain (The Green Ally, Developed by students Hiranya Ganatra, Julia Thomas, Vasiliki Bakomichali, Internet of Cities Studio, Master in City & Technology, IAAC, Barcelona, 2023, ©).

Abstract
The impact of human activity on natural landscapes has been so profound that scientists defined a new era to characterize the trajectory shift of the planet's ecosystem. Interference with the operation of planetary mechanisms that support the life cycles of 8.7 million species (Ritchie 2022), for the sole benefit of one, has inevitably created a crisis. The data-informed approach presented in these field notes helps to integrate ecological needs within the design process, and develop more precise design strategies to mitigate this impact.

By forging the synergy between red squirrels and humans for ecosystem regeneration and defragmentation, a computational design methodology is introduced, extracting information from the remote sensing geospatial datasets of Google Earth Engine (GEE), filtering and analyzing them in Grasshopper3D (Neri 2023) in order to identify urban areas in Madrid, Spain, that that are susceptible to the Urban Heat Island (UHI) effect. By analyzing the urban conditions and utilizing the Circuitscape connectivity analysis software (McRae et al. 2008), pathways for multispecies rehabilitation of degraded landscapes are detected (Figure 1).

Over the last several years, Spain has experienced record-challenging heat waves, which have led to severe droughts and wildfires, causing immense landscape degradation. To further enhance this condition, and in reference to the case study city, the Hansen Global Forest Change dataset from GEE (Hansen et al. 2013) portrays the stark loss of forest cover in Madrid over the last two decades (Figure 2).

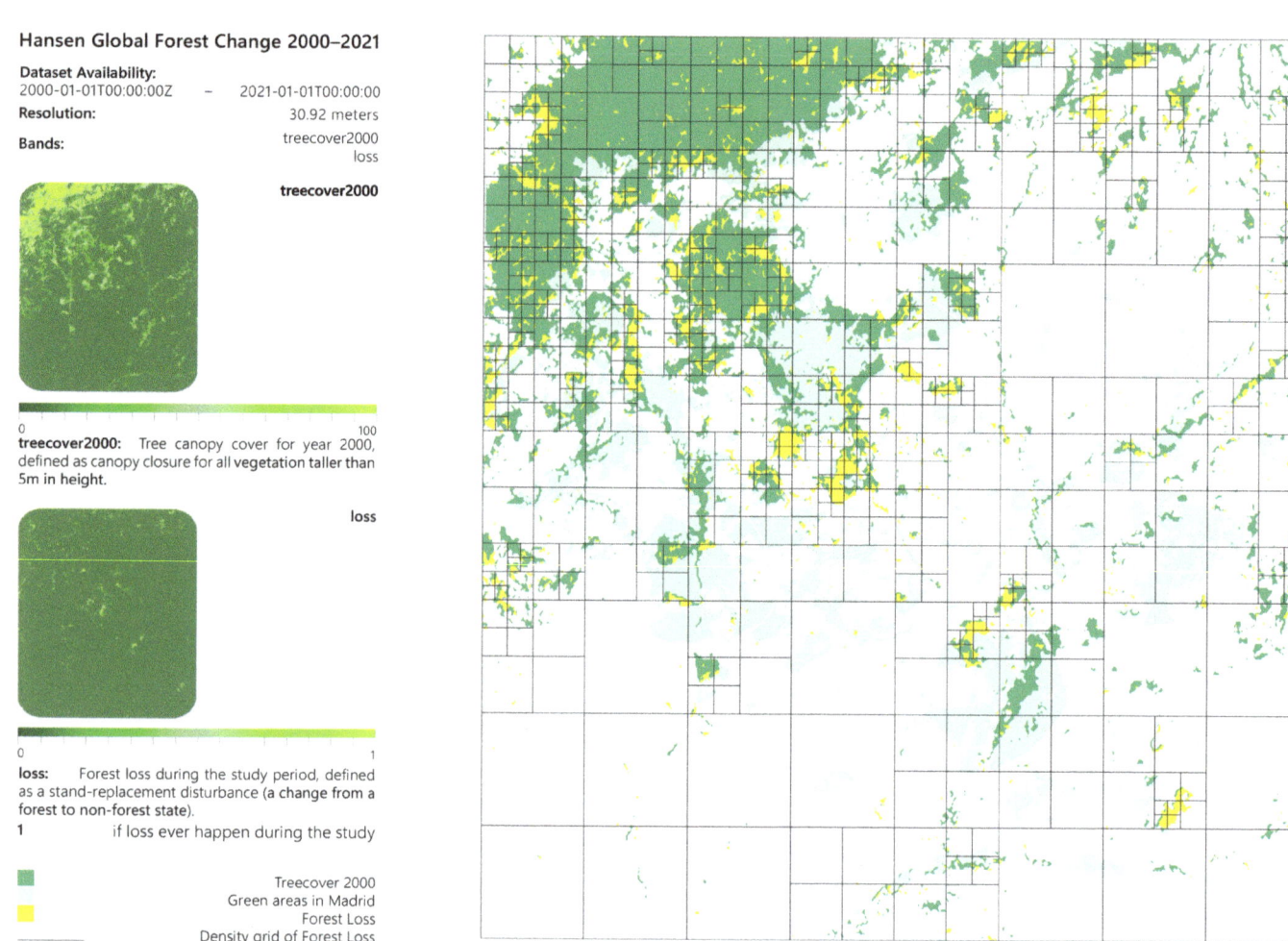

2   Forest Change Analysis in Madrid, Spain (The Green Ally, Developed by students Hiranya Ganatra, Julia Thomas, Vasiliki Bakomichali, Internet of Cities Studio, Master in City & Technology, IAAC, Barcelona, 2023, ©).

Additionally, land transformation, due to the rapid pace of urbanization, has led to a significant change in localized urban microclimates, exacerbating the already burdened conditions in cities. In particular, urbanization modifies surface materials and, due to vegetation suppression, albedo variation, and soil sealing, influences the local energy balance, finally contributing to the emergence of the UHI effect (Almeida et al. 2021). The most adverse effects of UHI are related to increased temperatures in urban territories and higher risks associated with heat waves, as they do not only affect human health (Hsieh and Huang 2016), posing a potential heat-stress risk to city dwellers and biodiversity by altering species' interactions, but also minimize and fragment natural habitats.(Ke et al. 2021).

To gain a more comprehensive understanding of the impact of both loss and fragmentation of green cover, as well as the collateral heat build-up in the city, a study was conducted to test the applicability of geospatial data as a tool to explore the interrelationship between the presence of natural vegetation and UHI. Leveraging the datasets of Yale Center for Earth Observation (YCEO) Surface Urban Heat Islands (Chakraborty and Lee 2019) and Landsat 7, 5-year, TOA-percentile composites from GEE, a data-driven analytical methodology was developed to compare, combine, and filter the UHI and the Normalized Difference Vegetation Index (NDVI) to discern the different urban conditions within greater Madrid (Figure 3).

A decreasing temperature gradient was shown as we moved from the dense vegetation cover in the north, through the city centre with fragmented green spaces, and finally to the quasi-barren peripheral area in the south. More precisely, we define three areas of incremenental risk. The best-case scenario (Figure 4) in the northwest of the city partly surrounded by forest patches; followed by the route of action, the densely populated city centre of Madrid in which the dense tree canopy in the streets substantially minimizes the urban temperature; and finally the area of concern (Figure 5) in the southeast of the city, that experiences the highest temperatures of the

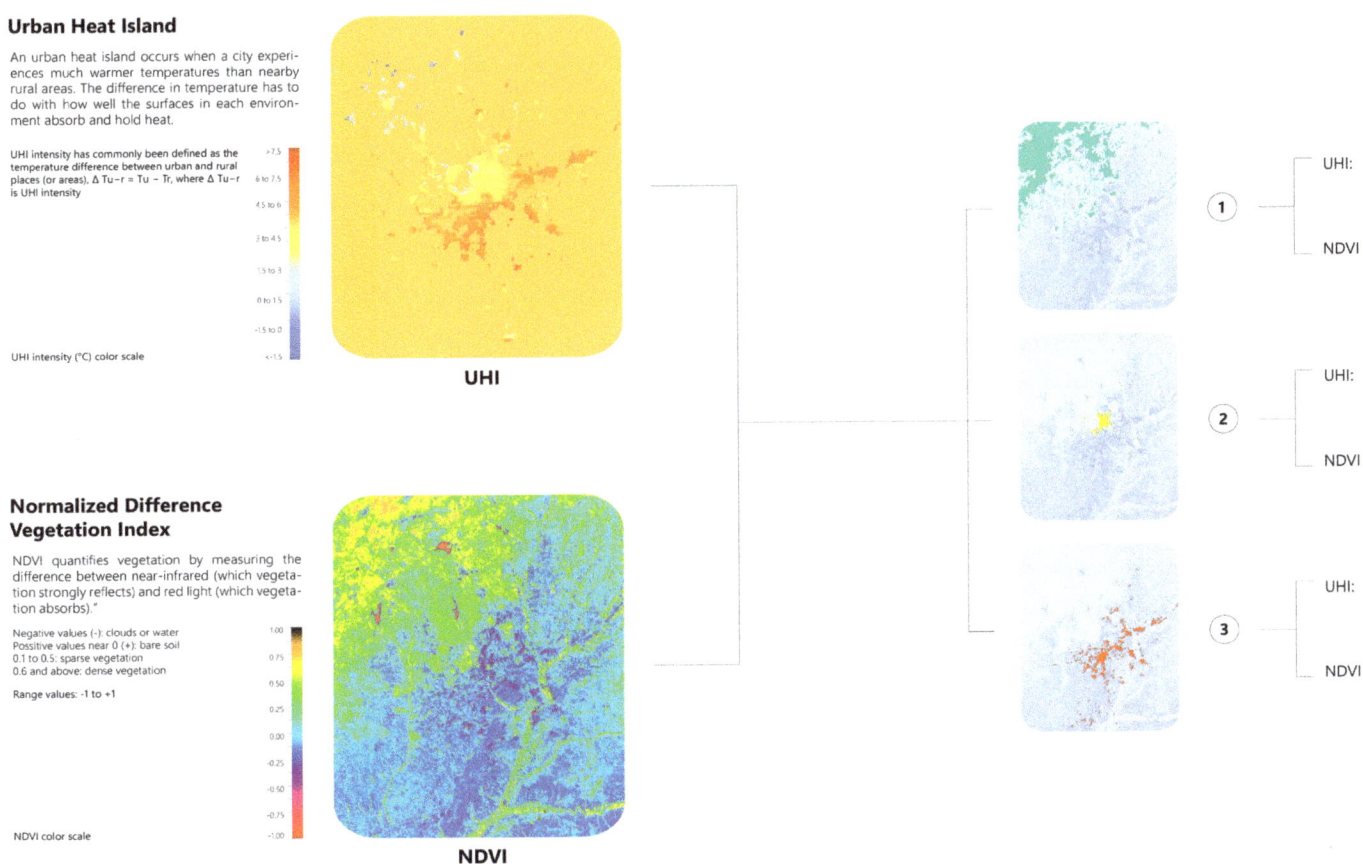

3   Analysis of UHI-NDVI utilizing the geospatial dataset of GEE (The Green Ally, Developed by students Hiranya Ganatra, Julia Thomas, Vasiliki Bakomichali, Internet of Cities Studio, Master in City & Technology, IAAC, Barcelona, 2023, ©).

entire study area due to the combination of a dense urban fabric, with fragmented green spaces and underutilized or degraded land. Consequently, a land use analysis was carried out focusing on the unbuilt areas of each zone to finally reveal the physical potentials and challenges of the city. The correlation between the severity of disconnect between green spaces and the temperature gradient unveiled the importance of defragmentation to mitigate the UHI effect.

In order to identify the most performative ecoloical corridor for multispecies collaboration, deeper research was conducted on the role of species in habitat regeneration. Red squirrels are native species in Madrid, and their degree of ecological specialization - the capacity to inhabit many or few environments - is one of the most important factors in their evolutionary success in the face of climate change (Menendez et al. 2021). Moreover, squirrels play a significant ecological role, especially in the forest ecosystems: while foraging for food, they gather seeds, bury them, and when they return to retrieve them, they are often unable to remember the location, therefore leaving the seeds to flourish unintentionally having planted the seeds. Over time, this caching behavior not only changes the composition of a forest, but can also be fostered for ecological regeneration purposes.

The study culminates in the synergy between red squirrels and humans fostered by an ecological corridor that connects the green nodes in the city, and activates the previously identified underutilized spaces. In order to identify the area of intervention, the Circuitscape software was employed, and a connectivity analysis (Figure 6) was run by assigning different resistance values for the red squirrels to each land use of the Corine Land Cover 2018 GeoTIFF. A connectivity simulation was performed between the two focal points derived within the best-case scenario and the area of concern. The objective was to identify the squirrels' movements, define the connectivity intensities between the two areas, and generate the new ecological map. By filtering it through a second connectivity analysis and extracting the highest connectivity values, the ecological corridor with the least resistance, and therefore greater potential, was identified.

While the first connectivity simulation aimed to replicate

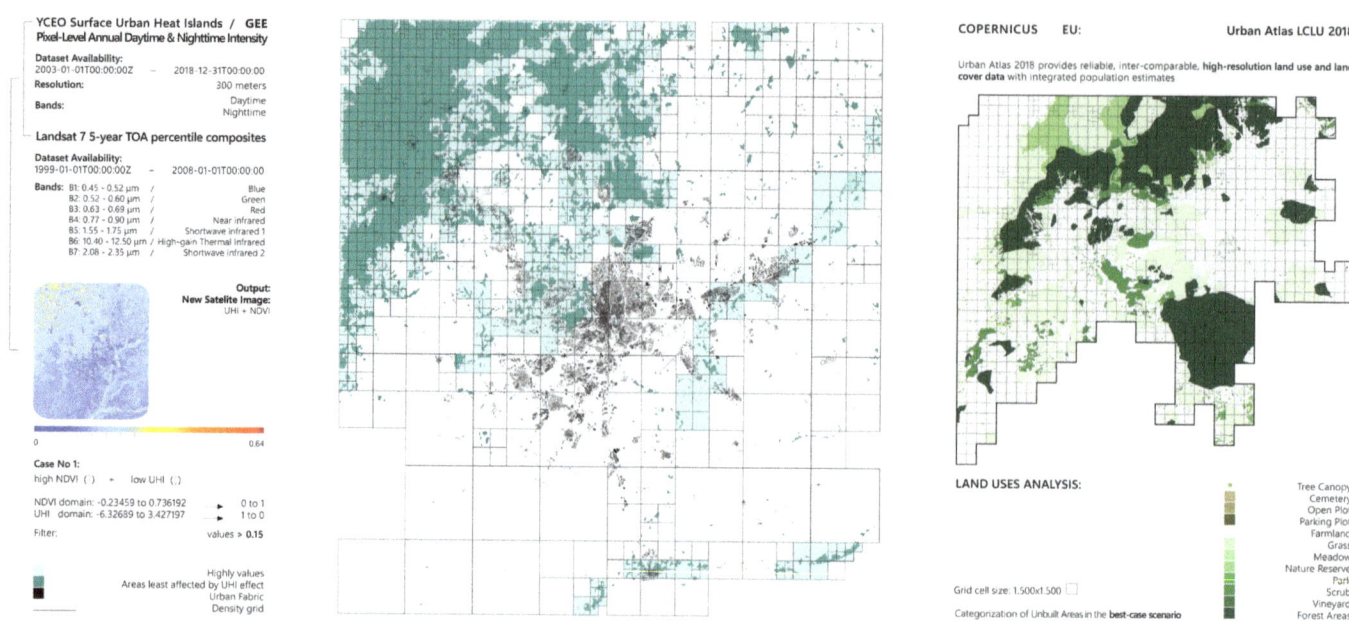

4   CASE 01 | The best case scenario: High NDVI, Low UHI (The Green Ally, Developed by students Hiranya Ganatra, Julia Thomas, Vasiliki Bakomichali, Internet of Cities Studio, Master in City & Technology, IAAC, Barcelona, 2023, ©).

the best-case scenario in the area of concern, the second connectivity analysis was conducted focusing primarily on the area with significant UHI. In particular, the ecological corridor originates from Casa de Campo, the breeding ground of squirrels located close to the city centre, towards the underutilized land in Villa de Vallecas. Along the identified ecological corridor, an edge condition analysis was conducted in order to formulate a design framework that would determine the performance and physicality of each condition. With computational design methods, the ecological corridor identified not only pays heed to defragmentation by opening safe paths for red squirrels to contribute to ecological restoration, but also takes into account barren lands that aggravate UHI effect and revive them, resulting in a restructured urban fabric that facilitates a flourishing ecosystem.

ACKNOWLEDGMENTS

The project discussed in these field notes is *The Green Ally* that was developed at the Institute for Advanced Architecture of Catalonia (IAAC) in the framework of the Master in City & Technology program (MaCT) by the students Vasiliki Bakomichali, Julia Thomas, and Hiranya Ganatra during the Internet of Cities Studio (2022/23) directed by Mathilde Marengo, Eduardo Rico, and Iacopo Neri.

REFERENCES

Almeida Catarina R. Ana Cláudia Teodoro and Mário A. Gonçalves. 2021. Study of the urban heat island (UHI) using Remote Sensing data/techniques: A systematic review. Environments, 8(10): 105.

Chakraborty Tirthankar and Lee Xuhui. 2019. A simplified urban-extent algorithm to characterize surface urban heat islands on a global scale and examine vegetation control on their spatiotemporal variability. International Journal of Applied Earth Observation and Geoinformation: ITC Journal, 74: 269–280.

Hansen, Matthew C . Peter Potapov. et al. 2013. High-resolution global maps of 21st-century forest cover change. In: Science. Vol. 342, No. 6160. pp. 850-853.

Hsieh Chun-Ming and Huang Hsin-Chiao. 2016. Mitigating Urban Heat Islands: A Method to Identify Potential Wind Corridor for Cooling and Ventilation. Computers, Environment and Urban Systems, 57, 130-143.

Ke Xinli. Hongling Men. Ting Zhou. Zhuoyang Li and Fengkai Zhu. 2021. Variance of the impact of urban green space on the urban heat island effect among different urban functional zones: A case study in Wuhan. Urban Forestry & Urban Greening, 62(127159), 127159.

McRae Brad. Brett G Dickson. Timothy H Keitt. and Viral Shah. 2008. Using circuit theory to model connectivity in ecology, evolution, and conservation. Ecology 89: 2712-2724.

Menéndez Iris. Ana Rosa Gómez Cano. Juan L. CantalapiedraL. Pablo Peláez-Campomanes. María Ángeles Álvarez-Sierra and Manuel Hernández Fernández. 2021. A multi-layered approach to the diversification of squirrels. Mammal Review,

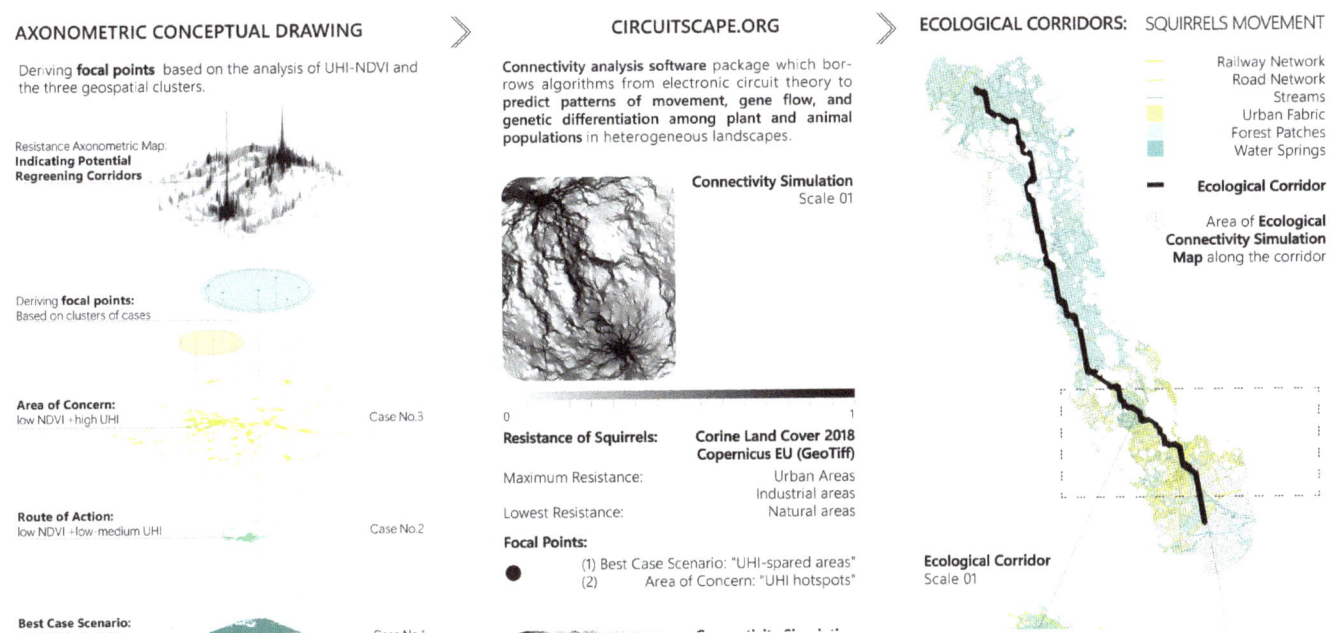

5 **CASE 03 | The area of concern: Low NDVI , High UHI** (The Green Ally, Developed by students Hiranya Ganatra, Julia Thomas, Vasiliki Bakomichali, Internet of Cities Studio, Master in City & Technology, IAAC, Barcelona, 2023, ©).

51(1): 66–81.

Neri Iacopo 2023. Expanding Digital Design Workflows with Geospatial Analytics: Linking Grasshopper3D with Google Earth Engine. *DE: Wichmann Verlag*.443-444.

Ritchie Hannah. 2022. "How many species are there?" Our World in Data. April 28, 2023. https://ourworldindata.org/how-many-species-are-there.

IMAGE CREDITS

Figures 1 through 6: © The Green Ally project, IAAC, MaCT, Internet of Cities Studio, 2022-23.
All drawings and images by the authors.

Vasiliki Bakomichali is a licensed architect whose interest lies on the intersection of urbanism and data science. She holds a MSc from the Department of Architecture at the University of Patras in Greece, and she is currently pursuing a Master in City and Technology (MaCT02) degree at the Institute for Advanced Architecture of Catalonia (IAAC), Spain. Through her studies, she explores how data analytics, artificial intelligence, and generative design can reshape urban planning, thereby converting cities into sustainable and human-centric built environments.

Mathilde Marengo is a PhD Architect, Head of Studies, MaCT Co-director, Faculty and PhD Supervisor at the IAAC. whose research focuses on the Contemporary Urban Phenomenon, its integration with technology, and its implications on the future of our planet. Mathilde develops her research at IAAC's Advanced Architecture Group (AAG) investigating designs, and experimenting with innovative educational formats based on holistic, multi-disciplinary and multi-scalar design approaches, oriented towards materialization. Her investigation is also actuated through her role in several National and EU-funded research projects, among these URBiNAT, InnoChain ETN, Knowledge Alliance for Advanced Urbanism, BUILD Solutions, and more. Her work has been published and exhibited internationally.

Julia Thomas is pursuing a master's degree in City and Technology at the Institute for Advanced Architecture of Catalonia. She received a bachelor's degree in architecture from Manipal University, India. She possesses a profound interest in research pertaining to environmental issues and ecologically responsible design solutions. She focuses on climate data analysis and its socio-economic impacts to develop interdisciplinary solutions.

Hiranya Ganatra is an aspiring urban technologist with a Bachelor's in Architecture from Mumbai University, who delves into urban-tech synergy, exploring how spatial data and data-driven policies can shape vibrant, efficient cities. Through pursuing a Master's degree in City and Technology at the Institute for Advanced Architecture of Catalonia, Hiranya focuses on gaining insights into into urban planning strategies that harmonize human needs with technological advancements, aiming to create sustainable and resilient cities for future generations.

Iacopo Neri explores the intersection of architecture, computer science, and urban planning through his research. He has been involved in teaching activities since 2015 at the University of

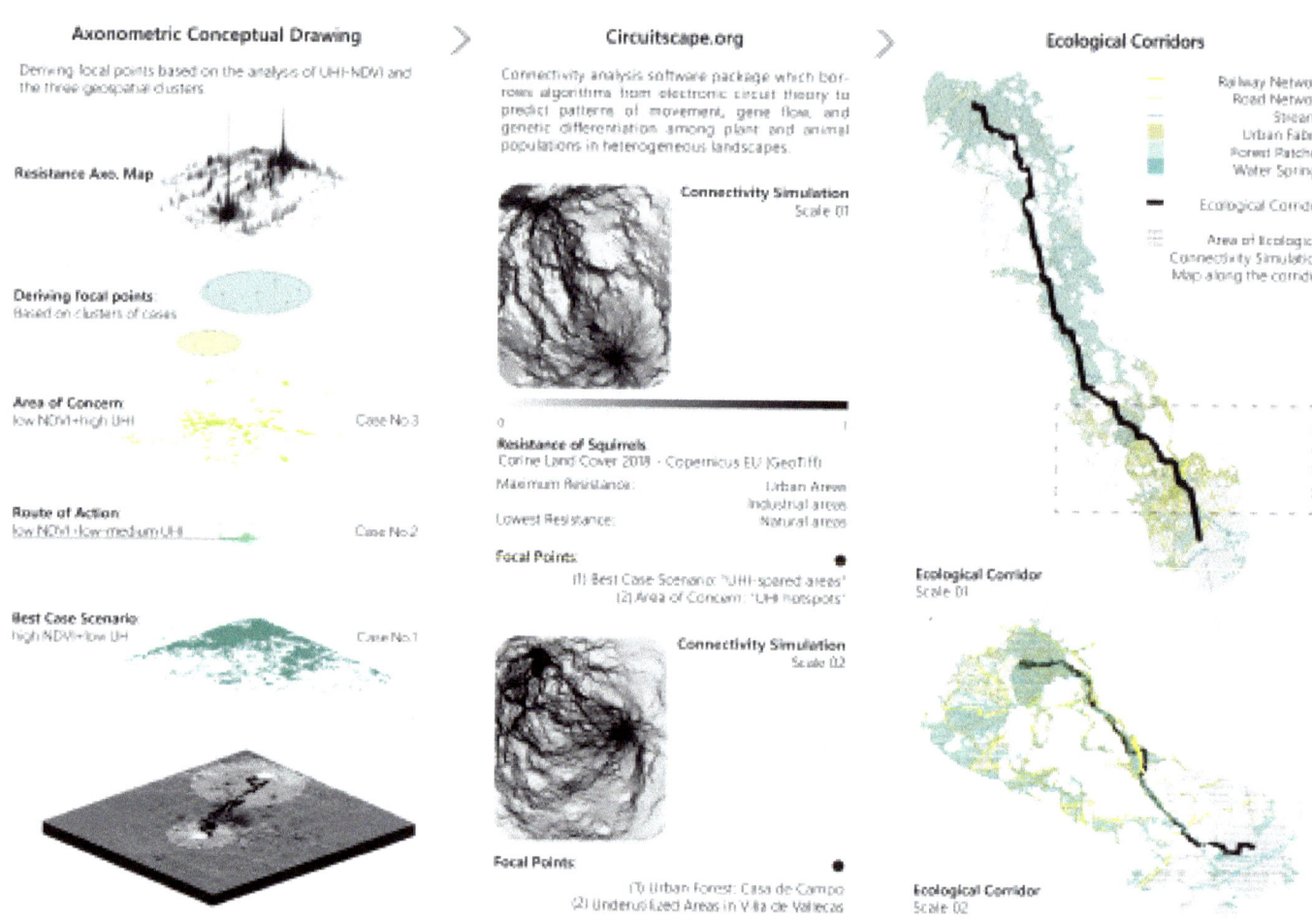

6   Methodology of Connectivity Analysis and Regeneration of the Ecologival Corridors (The Green Ally, Developed by students Hiranya Ganatra, Julia Thomas, Vasiliki Bakomichali, Internet of Cities Studio, Master in City & Technology, IAAC, Barcelona, 2023, ©).

Florence, the Polytechnic University of Milan, the Ecole des Ponts - ParisTech, the Harbin Institute of Technology, and at the IAAC - Institute for Advanced Architecture of Catalonia, where he is now computational Lead. In parallel, he serves as scientific collaborator for the Department of Digital Visual Studies (DVS) at the University of Zurich UZH, and as front-end developer at Noumena, Barcelona.

Textile Narratives: Rhythmic Tactile Architectures

Nikoletta Karastathi
Bartlett School of Architecture, University College London

1   Gathering narratives from the burnt forest.

Abstract
The work investigates the reinterpretation of ancient textile practices, examining the development of visually and tactile architectures that incorporate coding and rhythmic elements. It aims to recode textile configurations by using traditional techniques to create hybrid storytelling textiles. By intertwining multiple narratives within soft architecture, a story of environmental disaster unfolds, showcasing the intersection of computational methods and environmental storytelling. Additionally, it highlights the convergence of traditional practices with contemporary computational methods, expanding the horizons of textiles and providing a platform for diverse voices and cultural perspectives to be woven into a tapestry of storytelling tectonics.

Cultural Significance of Textiles in Storytelling
Textiles have played a significant role in conveying narratives throughout various historical periods. One of the examples can be seen in ancient Greece, where they understood and used the transformative power of textiles. People have effectively shared stories, made connections, and preserved cultural values through successive generations by using patterns and myths (Barber 1992). Greek mythology showcased ample examples of weavers, fibers, patterns, and looms being utilized to communicate untold stories and amplify the voices of women during significant events. Female characters, such as Philomena, skillfully incorporated their personal narratives of suffering and betrayal into the fabric, utilizing textiles as a means of seeking justice and raising awareness about the injustices they experienced (Kruger 1994 p.66). In a similar way, the weaving techniques employed by Penelope and Arachne served as a means of conveying notions of defiance,

2 Rhythmic pixels.

autonomy, and dissatisfaction with divine authority (Kruger 1994 p.98 -106). In addition to mythology, research has demonstrated that textiles have incorporated not just mythical narratives, but also historical events, social contexts, and notable individuals into their woven fabric (Barber 1992). This intricate fusion of myth and reality reinforces the profound connection between textiles, storytelling, and the preservation of cultural memory.

Interweaving Rhythm and Code

The relationship between patterns, storytelling, and fabric in textile creation has been widely explored (Nosch 2014 p. 92). Studies have emphasized the interplay between narrative, song, rhythm, pattern, and textile fabrication (Tuck 2009; Nosch 2014). An example of this can be observed in the practices of weavers coming from Northern India and Central Asia, who skillfully integrate rhythmic chants into their textile production, seamlessly interweaving them with the art of storytelling (Tuck 2006; Howells 2015, p. 67). Woven patterns were synthesized through repetitive phrases, considering the interrelationship between elements (Tuck 2006).

One example of a cloth that exhibits these qualities is the Navajo saddle blankets, which include a weaving method that is deeply rooted in rhythmic songs and prayers. Those familiar with the songs and prayers can visually discern the rhythmic variations interwoven into the blankets, amplifying their significance (Willink 1996 p.70). Weavers who have examined these pieces possess the ability to recognize and appreciate the rhythmic patterns intricately integrated within the fabric (Willink 1996 p.70). Additionally, Navajo weavers employ weaving to create a sense of place, establish balance and order from disorder, and explore the fusion of mythological and historical associations. They maintain a close connection with their environment and draw inspiration and techniques from neighboring cultures. Notably, variation is intentionally embraced in Navajo textiles, as none are perfectly symmetrical or identical.

Within the contemporary practices of textile design and fabrication, there exists a clear link between textile patterns and the digital realm. This connection is evident due to the ability to translate each individual knot into a

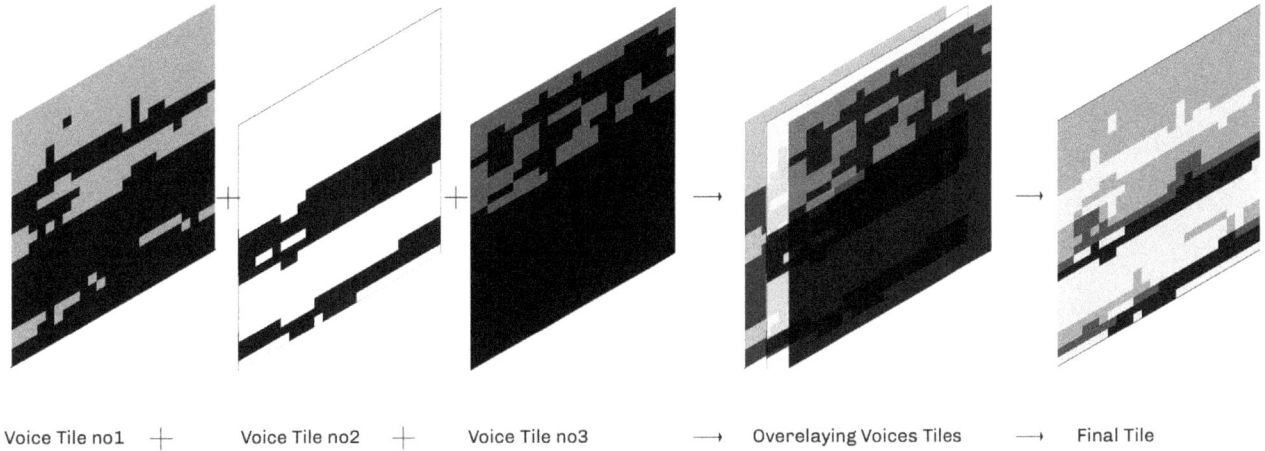

3 Overlaying voice tiles.

digital environment (Popescu et all. 2018). By combining the physical and digital worlds, and using rhythm as a basic building block for making patterns, traditional practices can be re-coded and expanded using modern computational methods.

Creating a Storytelling Cloth through the Multiplicity of Voices

To investigate the translation and recording of rhythms and patterns as a means of storytelling and data synthesis in a contemporary context, a narrative of ecological crisis was deliberately selected as a starting point. The primary context of this study revolved around the devastating wildfires that occurred in the Mediterranean region in the summer of 2021 (Figure 1). The aim of the prototype was to incorporate, express, and translate multiple voices and storylines into one cloth, exploring the intricate interconnection and dynamics of the multiple involved agents. The cloth becomes a testing ground for looking into storing, retelling, and expressing multiple narratives.

To document the events of the summer of 2021, three distinct voices were chosen: one narrated through a computer, conveying the factual aspects; another as a self-recorded voice, recounting the experiential elements while visiting the site; and a third as a non-human voice, symbolizing the trees. The process of designing and manufacturing the multi-voice fabric involves the following steps:

a) Recording and translating the voices:

To facilitate the translation from rhythm to pattern to fabrication, Houdini (a 3D animation software application) is used as the computational tool. Sentences are recorded and translated into grid patterns, with each voice having its own unique pattern (Figure 2). The rhythmic pattern is visualized using extracted stilts (Karastathi 2022), and patterns are overlaid to create the final storytelling cloth (Figure 3 and 4).

b) Fabrication from pattern to cloth:

In order for the knitting machine's software to interpret the visual representation, it is converted into a bitmap format, where each pixel represents a single stitch. The final prototype is manufactured by Kniterate, a medium-sized computerized knitting machine (Figure 5,6, and 7).

Conclusions

In conclusion, this project exemplifies the potential of computerized knitting to create vibrant story-data cloths that weave together multiple voices and narratives. By infusing the textiles with diverse potentials, and intertwining cultural realities, it reflects the interconnectedness of human experiences. Through the seamless translation of rhythm and pattern into the digital realm, it showcases the convergence of physical and virtual worlds, pushing the boundaries of textile tectonics. This project expands the scope of textile storytelling by offering a platform for the integration of many voices, cultural viewpoints, computational methods, and architectural narratives into soft data-driven narratives.

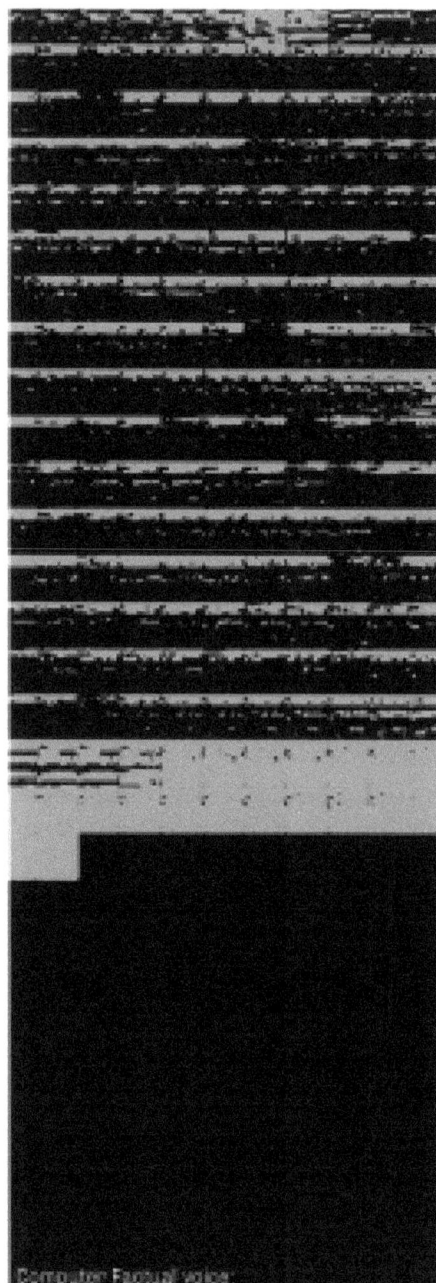 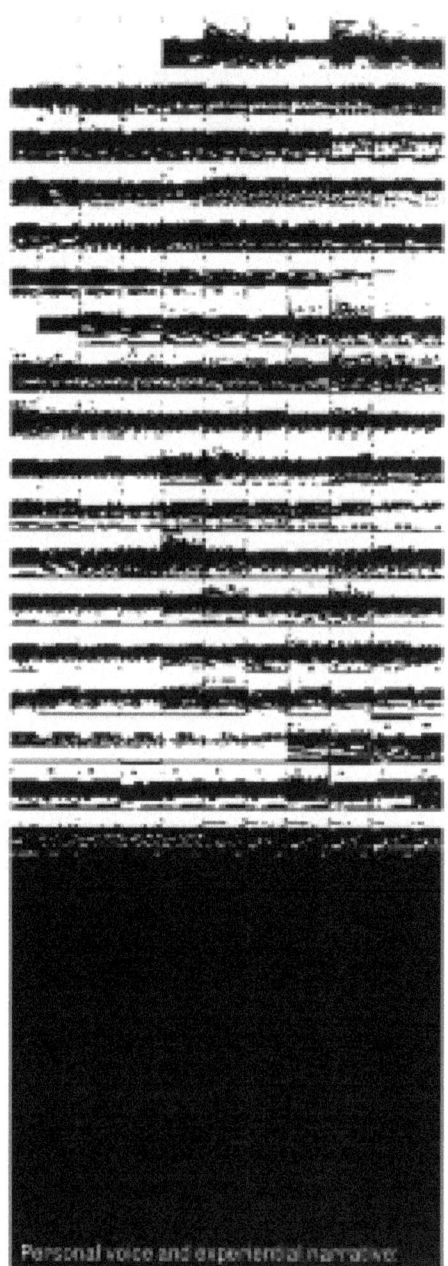 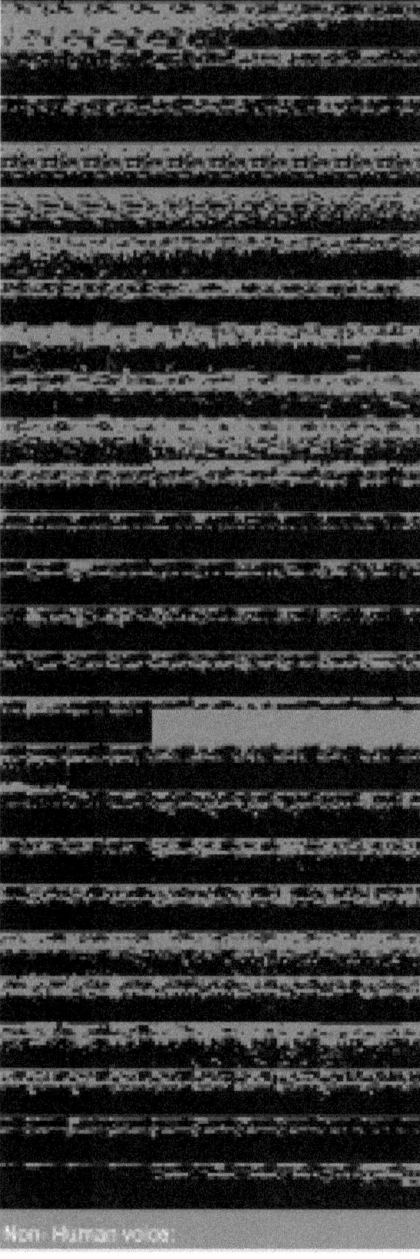

Computer Factual voice:

The summer of 2021 has been a catastrophe due to the wildfires raging through the Mediterranean forests. Only in Greece, over a million square meters of area were burned, with most of this turning into ashes within two weeks. The area burned in 2021 is estimated to be 4.5 folds more than the total areas burned during 2008 to 2020.

[ref: European Forest Fire Information System (EFFIS)].

Personal voice and experiential narrative:

The smell proceeds the sight
The air is heavy and dense, and it smells of smoke
I am alone
I walk into the forest
The smell is overwhelming, I can hear my footsteps and the wind
I pause – I touch the ground
And then I can hear it
I am listening to the crackling noises coming from the trees ,
I cannot tell from which trees they are coming from,
It is symphony of mourning
I am back to the ground gathering ashes
My skin turns to the colour of the ashes

Non-Human voice:

Tree crackling voice.

Recorded the sound of the crackling trees in the forest a few days after the fires.

4   Multiple voices translated to rhythmic pixels.

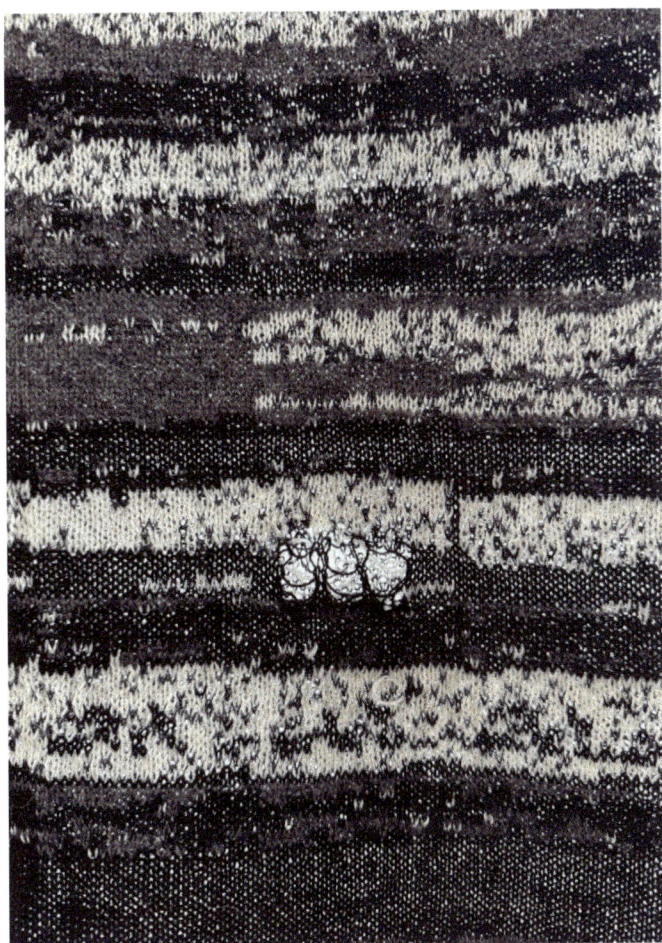

5   Fabrication of the textile with Kniterate.

6   Textile close-up detail.

REFERENCES

Barber, Elizabeth Jane Wayland. 1992. "The Peplos of Athena." In Goddess and Polis: The Panathenaic Festival in Ancient Athens, edited by J. Neils, 102–16. Hanover.

European Forest Fire Information System (EFFIS). n.d. "EFFIS - European Forest Fire Information System." September 20, 2021. https://effis.jrc.ec.europa.eu/#:~:text=EFFIS%20%2D%20European%20Forest%20Fire%20Information,on%20wildland%20fires%20in%20Europe.

Howells, Richard. 2015. *A Critical Theory of Creativity: Utopia, Aesthetics, Atheism and Design.* Houndmills, Basingstoke, Hampshire: Palgrave Macmillan.

Karastathi, Nikoletta. 2022. "RE-coding and multiplying ancient textile practices through Neo–Baroque 'folding'. " Paper presented at TRAITS of Postdigital Neobaroque Conference, Obergurgl Austria.

Kruger, Kathryn Sullivan. 1994. "Weaving the Word: The Metaphorics of Weaving and Female Textual Production." PhD diss, University of Miami.

Nosch, Marie-Louise B. 2014. "Voicing the Loom: Women, Weaving, and Plotting." In KE-RA-ME-JA. Studies Presented to Cynthia W. Shelmerdine, edited by D. Nakassis, J. Gulizio, and S. A. James, 91-101. United States: INSTAP.

Popescu, Mariana, Matthias Rippmann, Tom Van Mele, and Philippe Block. 2018. "Automated Generation of Knit Patterns for Non-Developable Surfaces." In Humanizing Digital Reality Design Modelling Symposium Paris 2017 , edited by Rycke.K, Gengnagel.C, Baverel.O, Mueller, Rahm.P, Burry.J, Nguyen.M.M, Thomsen.M.R , 271–84 , Springer Singapore : Imprint : Springer.

Tuck, Anthony. 2006. "Singing the Rug: Patterned Textiles and the Origins of Indo-European Metrical Poetry." American journal of archaeology 110, no. 4: 539–550.

Tuck, Anthony. 2009. "Stories at the loom: Patterned textiles and the recitation of myth in Euripides." Arethusa 42, no.2: 151–159.

Willink, Roseann S. 1996. *Weaving a World: Textiles and the Navajo Way of Seeing.* Santa Fe, NM: Museum of New Mexico Press.

7   Knitted narrative cloth (Alberto Fernandez Gonzalez, February 2022).

IMAGE CREDITS

Figure 7: © Alberto Fernandez Gonzalez, February 2022.
All other drawings and images by the author.

Nikoletta Karastathi is an architect, a PhD candidate funded by the LAHP, and a Lecturer at UCL's Bartlett School of Architecture. She has worked as an architect for Napper Architects and Chapman and Taylor, as well as a design tutor at Bristol, Cardiff, Newcastle, and Edinburgh. Nikoletta's work has been exhibited at the London Design Festival, Dutch Design Week, the Baltic Centre for Contemporary Arts, and the Lakeside Arts Center, among others. Her research interests include architecture, textiles, computation, storytelling, and material programmability.

Bric(k)olage
Spoliated Masonry C+D Waste

Kyriaki Goti
Pratt Institute

Jonathan A. Scelsa
Pratt Institute

Natalia Rossi
Pratt Institute

Wei Wang
Pratt Institute

Arthur Palaci Zani
Pratt Institute

1   Detail photography of the interlocking nature of the spolia blocks and 3d printed composite collage aggregate.

INTRODUCTION

The 2016 US Environmental Protection Agency reported that 23.1 million tons of broken pieces of concrete waste are annually discarded from new construction sites (EPA -2) and in example states in the north american context only 6.6% of C&D concrete is recycled; the rest is thrown out in landfills as it is labeled "contaminated or too hard to process on a large scale." (CT DOE 25) Relatively little investigation has occurred in how this material could reappear in the architectural project that might honor its intrinsic broken quality as a part of its materiality within a life-cycle of continual usage. This project speaks towards a problematic Habit of the Anthropocene in how we construct buildings placing intrinsic cultural value on new parts over the broken and old due to economic efficiencies.

BACKGROUND

The Roman late republic between the years 123 - 23 BCE, showcases a period where scavenging for building materials was a thriving business. Examples from this time particularly those for adaptive re-use, where a building itself is expanded upon, often use Spolia, or stolen (recycled) bits of buildings as a construction material in a primary sense. Historian Hans-Rudolf Meier points our attention to the idea that "In material-poor pre-modern eras, the reuse of building elements was more the rule than the exception." (Meier 225) Herein, the concept of Spolia inherently requires sustainable reuse, within the locality the building material is found, as our aging buildings in cities reach the point of demolition it could be understood that this stock is itself the marketplace for future construction.

2   Researcher's using physical drop process to create material for test matter. The generated pieces were measured, weighed and catalogued by volumetric size, and shape grammar.

Several recent paradigmatic changes in digital technology have prompted the use of C+D waste in the building process more viable (Carpo – 5). LIDAR scanning or Light Detection and Range based scanners are the critical technological advance that provides new access to this modality. This technology has been used successfully in archaeological object excavation where Ahmed, Carter, and Ferris explain how "Laser pulse/radar technologies operate much like radar and sonar, relying on a 'bounce back' and the calculated time taken to return a sample to the scanning sensor."(Ahmed 3). This technology has already been explored in recent design scholarship by Matter Design Studio, who's "Cyclopean Cannibalism, has leveraged digital scanning, stacking, and carving techniques to achieve geometric intricate interlocking between salvaged site-cast concrete (Clifford 410). CMU Spolia Composites in a similar yet different vein utilize the scanning process to register the intricacy of masonry block parts, with clay paste extrusion as a means of unique infill bondwork to create a complete envelope solution.

PROOF OF CONCEPT

As a proof of concept, the researchers chose to work with a common CMU Block typical to North American construction, measuring nominally 7.625"x7-6.25"x11.625". The research team began by simulating a cache of CMU Block waste, as might be found on a typical construction or landfill, through the process of dropping (Figure 2). Each piece of CMU block Spolia was scanned using a FARO scanning arm into a 3D point-cloud model, which in turn was triangulated into a 3D mesh model water-tight model with 40,000-50,000 polygons.

The design team constructed a digital scene, into which the broken pieces could be inserted as mesh objects, and then dropped into a constraining bounding box using a rigid body simulation native to the Unreal Engine 5.1. The bounding box was constrained on the X and Y axis with a plan of 24 x 7.75". The mesh objects are arranged in a cartesian grid above the boundary and a collision box is programmed for each mesh object. The physics simulation is enabled, wherein each mesh object is provided with a load along the Z-axis akin to gravity. Several trials were conducted including arranging the mesh objects from largest Spolia to smallest, vice-versa, as well as the programming of rigid body apertures into the bounding box around which the meshes would fall to inform potential inscribed fenestration. (figure 5) A prototypical solution was chosen and exported into Rhino 3d, for the generation of infill blocks. Herein an XZ plane was inserted that intersects through the stacked assembly of mesh spolia objects generating a figure -ground network. Each contour is then offset by 5 mm to provide an infill ring which is then extruded the width of the assembly. 2.5 mm vertical bars are added at 5mm spacing to strengthen the blocks along the vertical axis of load. Each infill block geometry in the digitally modeling environment was contoured in third dimension with a 2mm separation between contours to allow for interlayer adhesion for a 3mm paste extruder nozzle. (Figure 4)

The figural infill blocks were then first prototyped at full scale as XPS foam pieces extracted from a sheet utilizing a 3 axis CNC router. The original cataloged CMU block detritus along with these brick inserts were then stacked to test whether the geometric bond-work aggregate would perform at full-scale. Following the success of this test, the foam blocks were re-fabricated into 3d print files for a 3mm nozzle clay paste extruder. The pieces were printed utilizing Stoneware Amaco 38 clay, on a 3d potter paste extruder mounted to a 6 axis IRB 2600, and then fired to cone 04 as bisqueware. The final pieces were assembled with type S mortar mix, which for its high strength capacity and high density mixture to infill between the textural nature of the 3d-printed infill. (figure 1 + 6)

CONCLUSION

This process that utilizes simulated physics for modeling different bondwork patterns of found material refuse demonstrates its facility for adapting to many

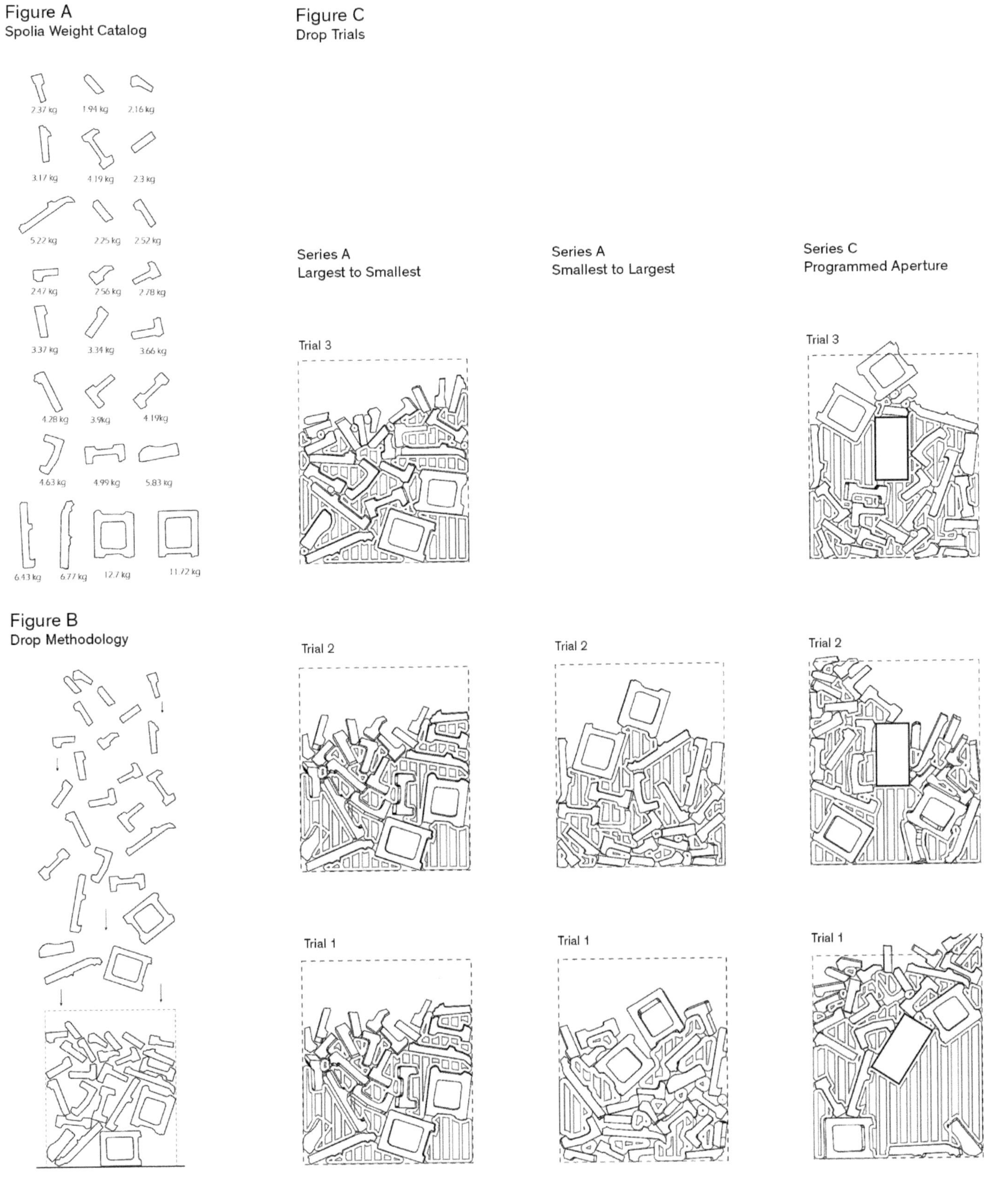

Figure A
Spolia Weight Catalog

Figure C
Drop Trials

Series A
Largest to Smallest

Series A
Smallest to Largest

Series C
Programmed Aperture

Trial 3

Trial 2

Trial 1

Figure B
Drop Methodology

3   The figure depicts the catalog of salvaged masonry parts by organized by mass, 2.B depicts the drop methodology. 2.C shows a matrix of various drop trials as shown at point of rest equilibrium.

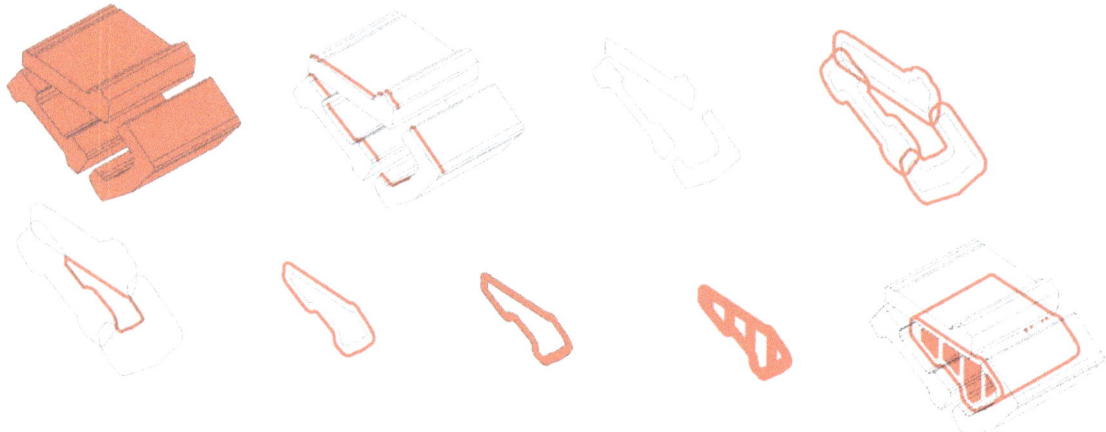

4   The 3d printed infill blocks and their 3d print files for the figure-ground pattern with spoliated masonry bond-work was programmed for auto-generation in grasshopper 3d.

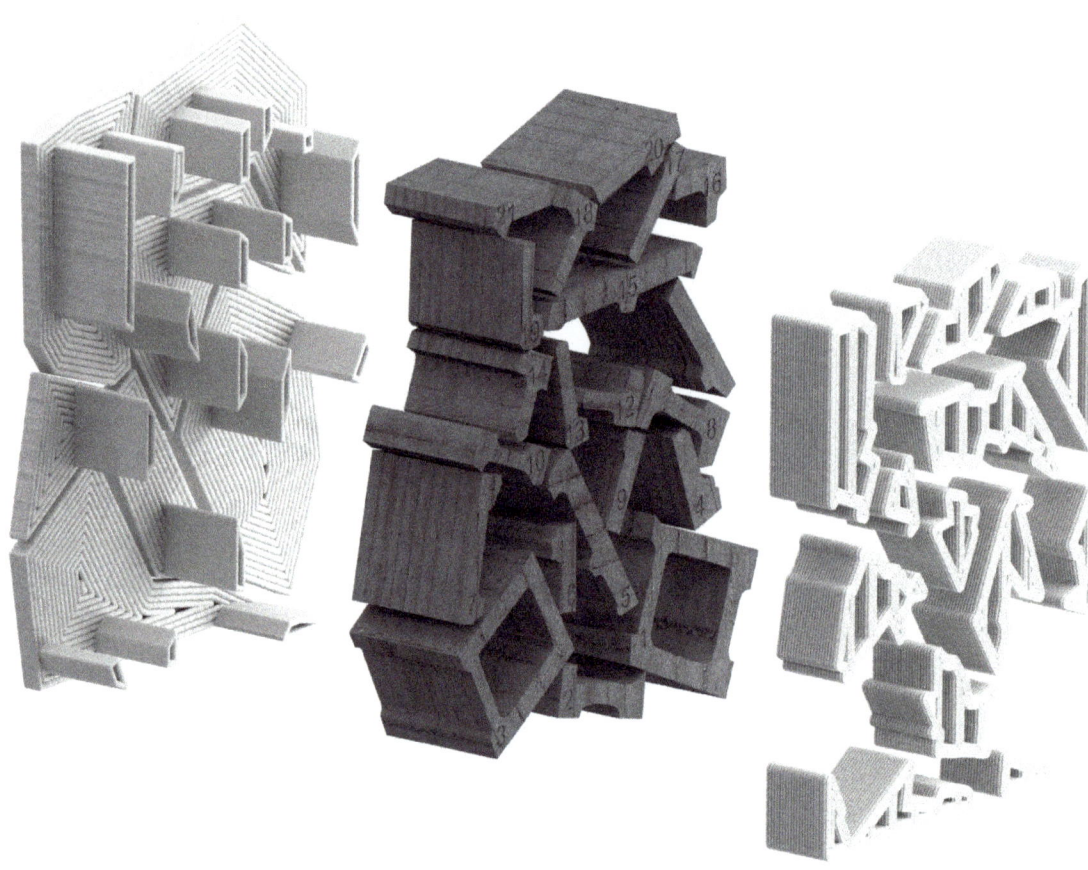

5   The Diagram depicts the figure-ground relationship between the network of dropped masonry spolia parts and the auto-generated infill pieces. A possible 3rd layer is shown to create an elevational infill for interior exterior dichotomy.

configurations. The assembled concrete masonry clusters have the potential for deployment in many situations in terms of both new and old construction, both creating capacity to lower our intake of new materials in local conditions but also to suggest the life-cylce of material waste can be a continuous form of new aesthetic matter in envelope construction.

ACKNOWLEDGMENTS

Funding for this research was made possible through the support of a Westchester Arts Grant obtained by Jonathan A. Scelsa with the Haverstraw Brick Museum of New York as well as through funded support from Pratt Institute's Provost Office.

6 The figure ground network of 3d printed bisque stoneware clay, and pre-cast concrete spolia blocks was mortared using type s mortar for assembly.

REFERENCES

Ahmed Namir, et al. "Sustainable Archaeology through Progressive Assembly 3D Digitization." (World Archaeology, 2014), 3.

Brandon Clifford, and Wes McGee. 2018. "Cyclopean Cannibalism." In ACADIA 2018 RECALIBRATION: on imprecision and infidelity: Mexico City, 2018, 404 – 413

Connecticut Department of Energy and Environmental Protection (DEEP) (2014) Construction and Demolition Waste Characterization and Market Analysis. The Department of Energy and Environmental Protection Bureau of Materials Management and Compliance Assurance , CT: The Department of Energy and Environmental Protection Bureau of Materials Management and Compliance Assurance, 25

Carpo, Mario." The Second Digital Turn: Design beyond Intelligence"(Cambridge, MA: The MIT Press, 2017).

Meier, Hans-Rudolf. "Spolia in Contemporary Architecture: Searching for Ornament and Place," Reuse Value: Spolia and Appropriation in Art and Architecture from Constantine to Sherrie Levine, eds. Richard Brilliant and Dale Kinney (New York: Ashgate Publisher, 2011), 225.

U.S. Environmental Protection Agency. 2016. Construction and Demolition Debris Generation in the United States: Facts and figures.

IMAGE CREDITS

All drawings and images by the authors.

Kyriaki Goti is the founder of the design and innovation studio SomePeople. Her work focuses on the integration of cutting edge technologies, such as robotic fabrication and innovative material techniques, in architectural design and construction. Her projects have received several international awards such as the AZ Awards 2018, the Fast Company 2018 Innovation by Design Awards, the YouFab Global Creative Awards 2017 and the MAD Travel Fellowship 2017.

Jonathan A. Scelsa is an Architect, Urbanist, and Educator. He is a founding partner of the New York based practice, OP – Architecture Landscape, which operates in between the oppositions of Architecture and Landscape resulting in design solutions that strive to dis-integrate the subject-object relationship conventionally established between the two disciplines. He is a co-director of the Digital Masonry Group, at Pratt Institute where his research explores robotic production of component-based construction.

Natalia Rossi is a dedicated and forward-thinking fifth-year undergraduate student at Pratt with a Concentration in Morphology where she maintains research in the correlations between structure and forms. Her projects combine historical preservation, sustainability, material exploration, and robotic fabrications, demonstrating a thoughtful approach to design that considers the past and the future

---

Wei Wang Wei Wang is a fifth-year undergraduate student at Pratt Institute. By looking into the digital side of architecture, structure and manufacturing, Wei has experiences in BIM, parametric design, and manufacture automation. His projects include advanced structures, design optimization automation, and executed with sustainability and regional development in mind.

Arthur Palaci Zani a fifth-year architecture undergraduate student with an entrepreneurship minor, embodies a fusion of design and innovation. While pursuing his studies, he concurrently holds a position at an architectural office specializing in public sector projects, His journey epitomizes a relentless pursuit of innovation in an attempt to redefine the boundaries of architectural possibility

Artificial Images of Environmental Sensibility: A Manifesto

Christina Doumpioti
École Polytechnique Fédérale de Lausanne

Artificial images are created through models that learn from vast datasets of text, images, or a combination of both. By assimilating and understanding this substantial information, the models acquire the ability to generate new images based on provided inputs or descriptions.

Artificial images change how we approach and conceptualize design by extending human intuition and connecting it to the archived knowledge of others before us (relating it both to wise and obsolete traditions of humanity). They redefine the role of the architect, transforming them into curators and co-designers operating within a network of interconnected human and non-human agencies.

They serve as new design tools that enhance our cognitive abilities, expanding our repertoire in communicating and visualizing ideas in an automated manner. Their rapid generation enables us to shift our focus from the demands of notational design communication to the more meaningful task of reflecting on urgent matters and pressing issues.

Imagery is a cognitive resource that people can use for inventive thinking (Finke 1990). Architects have used sketch, reference images, and models as catalysts, igniting creativity and discovery. With the emergence of artificial images, the process of continuously modifying and refining imagery takes on a new dimension, enabling the development and organization of ideas within the image itself. Artificial images come to life through the power of words, offering a unique cognitive experience that diverges from, or blends

1   Close-up of an artificial image translated from pixels to material traits.

PRODUCTION NOTES

Architect: Christina Doumpioti
Supervisor: Jeffrey Huang
Status: ongoing
Workflow tools: Midas (depth map), Grasshopper (pointcloud to mesh), Midjourney (image generation), Ladybug (simulation)
Date: 2023

2 Embodied energy and carbon footprint analysis of a façade of a residential building

3 Visualization of radiation on the façade of a mid-rise residential building.

together, conventional modes of reasoning and thinking (inductive, deductive, and abductive).

Artificial images bring nuances that expand our imagination, rather than imposing the inherent (to a software) logic of modeling and thinking. They allow us to conceptualize unanticipated outcomes through insightful imagery, beyond finite, linear, and rational modeling spaces.

Artificial images of embedded environmental sensibility is a text-to-image-to-data model we propose as a new tool for connecting computational creativity (text-to-image) to environmental and material realms through analysis and simulation (to-data).

Artificial images of embedded environmental sensibility are generated by a design pipeline that starts from images, and progresses to multi-modal data extraction, consisting of depth map generation, point cloud and mesh creation, semantic segmentation, and finally, analysis and simulation to incorporate quantifiable data and microclimatic dimensions into the image (Doumpioti 2023).

Artificial images are overlaid hidden information maps representing virtual states of potential actualizations. Their translation from bits to atoms (Figure 1), and consequent form acquisition, is a materialized snapshot of a virtual state. Each artificial image carries the embodied energy and carbon footprint of an actualization. It brings the physical sentiency of an environment yet to be.

Artificial architectural images manifest the extensive attributes of virtual architectures, offering glimpses into their unrealized potential. Yet, their interplay with information on environmental sensibility unveils the "intensive differences" mediated by material morphologies. By creating new images and imaginative representations of possible futures, we continually assess metrics that bind us to our climate and the world at large. In this peculiar twist, what was once considered intensive becomes quantitative, while the "extensive" realm becomes imbued with nuanced qualities, shaping the selection of potential actualities (De Landa 2005).

Artificial images with environmental sensibility convey information on each represented bit's embodied energy and carbon footprint (Figure 2) through computer vision of material recognitions, and show the operational performance of solar radiation (Figure 3) and sunlight distribution visualized as heatmaps on the automatically simulated geometry.

Artificial images of embedded environmental sensibility are a means of acting responsibly by understanding the complexity of non-human physical entities and their interactions, employing a collective human and non-human intelligence system.

Artificial images at present are often connected to scenarios of dystopian futures, linked to the presence of bias (and outdated notions) in datasets, the extensive energy requirements, or the potential to exacerbate inequitable systems of exploitation. However, by acknowledging and addressing these issues, we can reimagine and redefine their role, aligning it with ecological and social practices through collective engagement and embedded environmental sensibilities.

We can initiate the education of different forms of intelligence by imparting foundational knowledge and subsequently allowing them to gain insights through experiential learning. By guiding their engagement with the complexity of real-world situations, we may witness a growth of ideas as they intermingle with data obtained from the physical world.

Through this combination of teaching and experiential acquisition, we can create a symbiotic relationship between machines and the environment. As hyper-dimensional intelligence that engages with complex, dynamic, and local real-time data, it will gain profound insights into the implications and potentials of various material structures within their physical milieu. Khan : "Speaking about super-intelligence in non-anthropomorphic terms seems like a crucial, precious practice to start right away. The ability to anticipate and think outside ourselves will only help us in future encounters. We will have to rely on our speculative strengths. We must reorient outwards" (Khan 2020).

ACKNOWLEDGMENTS

This study is part of a PhD research conducted at the Media x Design lab of the Swiss Federal Institute of Technology Lausanne (EPFL) under the supervision of Professor Jeffrey Huang.

REFERENCES

DeLanda, Manuel. 2005. "Space: Extensive and Intensive, Actual and Virtual." In Deleuze and Space, edited by I. Buchanan and G. Lambert, 80–87. Edinburgh: Edinburgh University Press.

Doumpioti, Christina. 2023. "Artificial Images of Environmental Sensibility: the Workflow." Adobe. Accessed [August 2023]. https://indd.adobe.com/view/c862dfc9-bd8c-4bf8-ab3e-ad83ac1d2f3c.

Finke, Ronald A. 1990. Creative Imagery: Discoveries and Inventions in Visualization. New York: Psychology Press.

Khan, Nora. 2020. "Towards a Poetics of Artificial Superintelligence." In Atlas of Anomalous AI, edited by Kenric McDowell and Ben Vickers. London: Ignota Books.

Christina Doumpioti [Dip. Arch.Eng, MArch] is an architect and educator. She is a member of OCEAN net, an experimental design practice, and researcher at EPFL. Her PhD research in Media x Design Lab focuses on the integration of generative and analytical design, with emphasis on environmental sensibilities. Her teaching experience includes the Architectural Association, Brighton University, and the Royal College of Art. In addition, she has worked at Arup Associates, London. Her work on computational form-finding and AI-embedded practices has been published in CumInCAD journals, TAD, Arch+, and AD.

Text-to-Image Generators: Semiotics, Semantics, and Society

Vernelle A. A. Noel
Carnegie Mellon University

Hayri Dortdivanlioglu
Georgia Institute of Technology

1 Images generated by Midjourney from prompts related to the built environment in six different languages.

Introduction

Text-to-image generators, such as Midjourney, DALL-E, and Stable Diffusion, are becoming increasingly popular. These generators, whose models are trained on large datasets of text-image pairs, often scraped from the web, take text prompts as input, and use them to generate images—text-to-image prompting. In this visual essay, we raise questions about the entanglement of semiotics, semantics, syntax, and society in these text-to-image generator tools. We are intrigued by how these technologies are "intrawoven" with social and cultural contexts. How are their constructions and presentations reconfigurations? How do, or might they, inform pedagogy, theory, methods, and our publics?

To explore these questions, we entered six prompts related to the built environment in six different languages, eight months apart in Midjourney ("Midjourney" n.d.). The generated images (Figure 1), require that we ask deep questions of each image, in comparison with each other, across each group of four, and across time (eight months apart). We argue that text-to-image generators call for a rigorous exploration of semiotics, semantics, syntax, and the society, with implications for pedagogy, theory-building, methodologies, and public enlightenment. Furthermore, we assert that these tools can facilitate pertinent questions about the relationships between technology and society. This is just the beginning. For now, we have questions.

Language and Meaning: Same words in different languages.
We entered six prompts related to the built environment: architecture, city, buildings, nature, urban, and light in six languages, including English, Amharic (Latin alphabet and

Variable: Language (September 2022)

English
architecture
city
buildings
nature
urban
light

Amharic
kine hinsa,
ketema,
hinsa,
tefetero,
ketema,
berhan

Chinese
jianzhu,
chengshi,
jianzhuwu,
ziran,
chengshide,
dengguang

Variable: Language (May 2023)

English
architecture
city
buildings
nature
urban
light

Amharic
kine hinsa,
ketema,
hinsa,
tefetero,
ketema,
berhan

Chinese
jianzhu,
chengshi,
jianzhuwu,
ziran,
chengshide,
dengguang

2   Images generated in Midjourney with prompts in English, Amharic, and Chinese Mandarin using Latin alphabet as input in September 2022 and May 2023.

script), Chinese (pinyin and characters), Turkish, Italian, and Hindi (Latin and Sanskrit) in September 2022, and again in May 2023. Each figure in this essay presents the generated images in four-tile format, grouped according to the language and time of prompts.

Latin alphabet: English, Amharic, Chinese
Upon examining Figure 2, we ask a series of questions: What is lost in translation? What does it mean that people and faces show up for some and not for others? Who is erased? Whose imaginaries are depicted in these images? How is time understood when images generated months apart are so vastly different? What does it mean when buildings are generated only in English? What does it mean when people are absent from images generated with English prompts? What does it mean when people are present in most images generated with Amharic and Chinese prompts in May 2023?

Latin alphabet: Turkish, Italian, Hindi
Some questions we ask about the Figure 3 are: What does it mean when images generated from Italian

Variable: Language (September 2022)

Turkish
mimarlık,
şehir,
binalar,
doğa,
kent,
ışık

Italian
architettura,
citta,
edifici
natura,
urbano,
luce

Hindi
vaastukala,
shahar,
imaaraten,
kudrat,
shahari,
roshanee

Variable: Language (May 2023)

Turkish
mimarlık,
şehir,
binalar,
doğa,
kent,
ışık

Italian
architettura,
citta,
edifici
natura,
urbano,
luce

Hindi
vaastukala,
shahar,
imaaraten,
kudrat,
shahari,
roshanee

3 Images generated in Midjourney with prompts in Turkish, Italian, and Hindi as input in September 2022 and May 2023.

prompts—another Western language—display modern forms and aesthetics? What does it mean when images generated with Turkish prompts reflect a historical period resembling an Ottoman era? What does "nature" mean to Midjourney such that representations differ from 2022 to 2023? What does it mean when images have modern, technological aesthetics in English, but orientalist aesthetics for Turkish and Hindi? What does it mean when Italian prompts conjure up images without people? What does it mean when images generated from Hindi mostly show humans, human-like figures, and deities? Whose views are being represented here? Who and what is being erased or stereotyped?

Language, Meaning and Place: Country + Same words, different languages, and alphabets.

Some questions we ask regarding the Figure 4 are: What does it mean when images generated from English text generate modern forms and aesthetics? What does it mean when prompts in Amharic text and script result in images of people? What does it mean when English prompts do not

Variable: Language, Characters, and Country (September 2022)

English	Amharic	Amharic
Ethiopia		
architecture	kine hinsa,	ኪነ-ህንፃ,
city	ketema,	ከተማ,
buildings	hinsa,	ህንፃ,
nature	tefetero,	ተፈጥሮ,
urban	ketema,	ከተማ,
light	berhan	ብርሃን

Variable: Language, Characters, and Country (May 2023)

English	Amharic	Amharic
Ethiopia		
architecture	kine hinsa,	ኪነ-ህንፃ,
city	ketema,	ከተማ,
buildings	hinsa,	ህንፃ,
nature	tefetero,	ተፈጥሮ,
urban	ketema,	ከተማ,
light	berhan	ብርሃን

4   Images generated using prompts associated with Ethiopia. In the first instance we use English words and add "Ethiopia." In the second and third, Amharic (Latin alphabet) and Amharic (script) are, respectively, used as input in September 2022 and May 2023.

result in people? What does it mean when signs of flags and colors that showed up in 2022, no longer show up in 2023?

Some questions that we ask regarding the Figure 5 are: What does it mean when humans take primacy in images generated with Hindi and Sanskrit prompts, but not in the ones with English prompts? What does it mean when English prompts seem to erase humans?

Some questions regarding the Figure 6 are: What does it mean when English prompts in 2023 generate images of traditional architypes of Chinese architecture, but when Chinese characters are used, images of a dense, contemporary urbanity are presented? What does it mean when architecture and buildings take prominence when English and Chinese character prompts are used, but no architecture shows up with Chinese pinyin? What does it mean when the images generated with Chinese pinyin are of a traditional time and representation?

Variable: Language, Characters, and Country (September 2022)

English
India
architecture
city
buildings
nature
urban
light

Hindi
vaastukala,
shahar,
imaaraten,
kudrat,
shahari,
roshanee

Hindi
वास्तुकला
शहर,
इमारतें,
कुदरत,
शहरी,
रोशनी

Variable: Language, Characters, and Country (May 2023)

English
India
architecture
city
buildings
nature
urban
light

Hindi
vaastukala,
shahar,
imaaraten,
kudrat,
shahari,
roshanee

Hindi
वास्तुकला
शहर,
इमारतें,
कुदरत,
शहरी,
रोशनी

5 Images generated using prompts associated with India. In the first instance we use English words and add "India." In the second and third, Hindi (Latin alphabet) and Hindi (script) are, respectively, used as input in September 2022 and May 2023.

But what does this mean fundamentally?

What does this mean for computational design pedagogy; what and how do we teach? What does this mean for design methods? What does it mean for human-machine conversations? What does this mean for new courses, faculty, and expertise that institutions would need to hire? What does this mean for the development of new theories? What theoretical frameworks might explain design's relation with these technologies? What does this mean for how architecture might interface with our publics?

REFERENCES

"Midjourney." n.d. Midjourney. https://www.midjourney.com

IMAGE CREDITS

All images by the authors.

Vernelle A.A. Noel is a design scholar, founder of the Situated Computation + Design Lab (Sit.Co.De), and Assistant Professor in Computational Design in the School of Architecture at Carnegie Mellon University. She investigates traditional and

Variable: Language, Characters, and Country (September 2022)

English
China
architecture
city
buildings
nature
urban
light

Chinese
jianzhu,
chengshi,
jianzhuwu,
ziran,
chengshide,
dengguang

Chinese
建筑
城市，
建筑物，
自然，
城市的，
灯光

Variable: Language, Characters, and Country (May 2023)

English
China
architecture
city
buildings
nature
urban
light

Chinese
jianzhu,
chengshi,
jianzhuwu,
ziran,
chengshide,
dengguang

Chinese
建筑
城市，
建筑物，
自然，
城市的，
灯光

6 Images generated using prompts associated with China. In the first instance we use English words and add "China." In the second and third, Chinese pinyin and Chinese characters are, respectively, used as input in September 2022 and May 2023.

digital practices, and their intersections with society. Using interdisciplinary approaches, she builds new frameworks, methodologies, expressions, and tools to explore social, cultural, and political aspects of craft, design, and computation for new reconfigurations of practice, pedagogy, and publics. Noel has received awards from the Graham Foundation for Advanced Studies in the Fine Arts, the Mozilla Foundation, and ideas2innovation (i2i), among others.

Hayri Dortdivanlioglu is a Ph.D. candidate in architecture and a Fulbright Scholar at the Georgia Institute of Technology. His dissertation research revisits Vitruvian theory and challenges canonic dichotomy between practice and theory in architecture through a counter-canonical reading of Vitruvius's foundational treatise, De Architectura. In a broader sense, his research interest includes the interaction between technology and design, architectural theories, mapping, and data visualization. Besides his concentration in architecture, Dortdivanlioglu received the Science, Technology, and Society certificate from Ivan Allen College of Liberal Arts at the Georgia Institute of Technology.

The Yamal Conspiracy:
A Geo-Engineered Fabulation

Tatiana Estrina
Massachusetts Institute of Technology

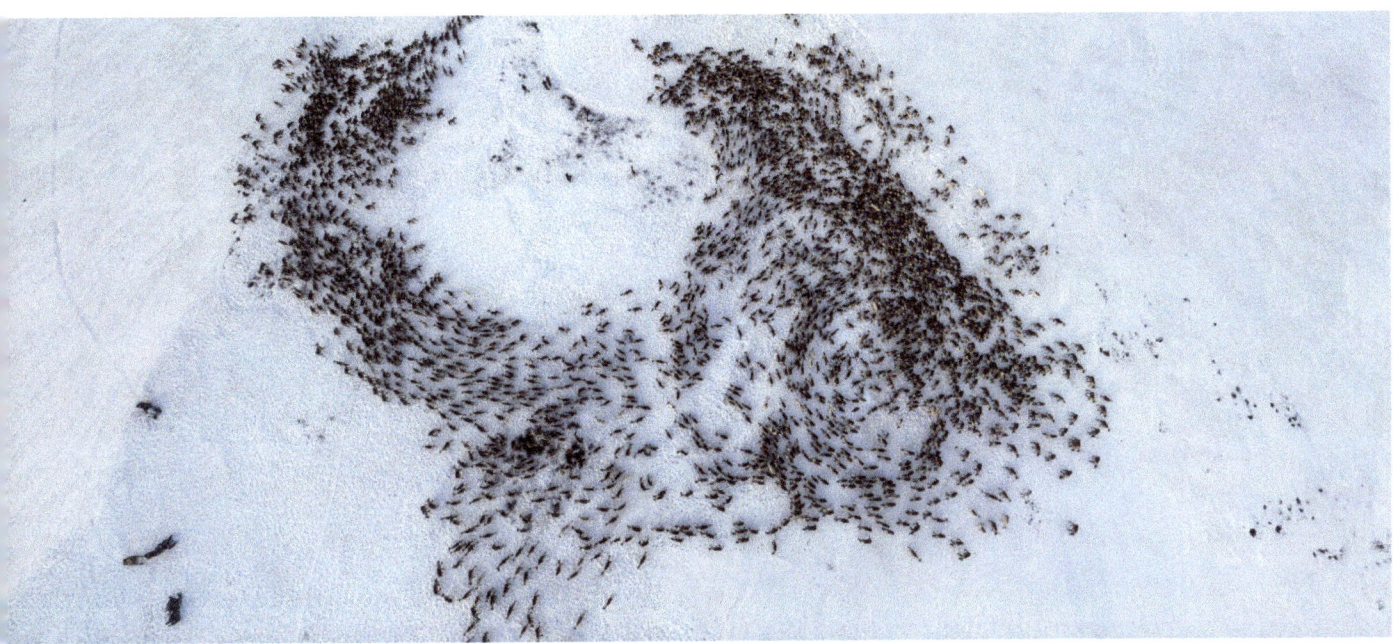

1   Aerial view of reindeer herd on the Yamal Peninsula (Dmitry Moiseenko © www.airpano.com).

INTRODUCTION
In the Neret language, 'Yamal' denotes "the land's end", which is precisely what the peninsula is – an arctic lowland in Northwestern Russia, sparsely populatedwith burgeoning, oil-based infrastructure. This land is the site of a multi-front war between ice and oil (Figure 1).
Behind closed doors, the Arctic Consortium took on the challenge of geo-engineering the Yamal Peninsula. This document contains evidence of their interventions within the Yamal Peninsula, specifically as this anonymous group of individuals got to work, as a speculation on the possibilities of geo-engineering of the shifting environment (Figure 2).

CHAPTER 1: $C_{17}H_9ClF_3NO_4S_2$
Mediator: The Yamal Peninsula's land coverage is a 'hot spot' for shifting dynamics, due to development, warming, and increased plant growth (Qin Yu, Epstein, and Walker, 2010).
Climate change reduces the sun's reflectivity, accelerating UV absorption and warming the earth. Nitrogen availability in the warming atmosphere allows tundra plants to grow larger, requiring grazing to regulate their size (Q Yu et al. 2011).
Director (UNICEF): Reindeer need to consume more vegetation on the peninsula at higher rates to combat climate change (Molloy 2016).
Introducing grazing animals to restore ecosystems, as done in Pleistocene Park, located in Russia, has shown positive effects on land after 20 years (Zimov 2005). However, it jeopardizes existing ecologies (Rubenstein et al. 2006). Maintaining the ecosystem and supporting native species is recommended.
Sergey Zimov (founder of Pleistocene Park): It is unwise to introduce species unfamiliar with the arctic circle climate. Native creatures should be used.

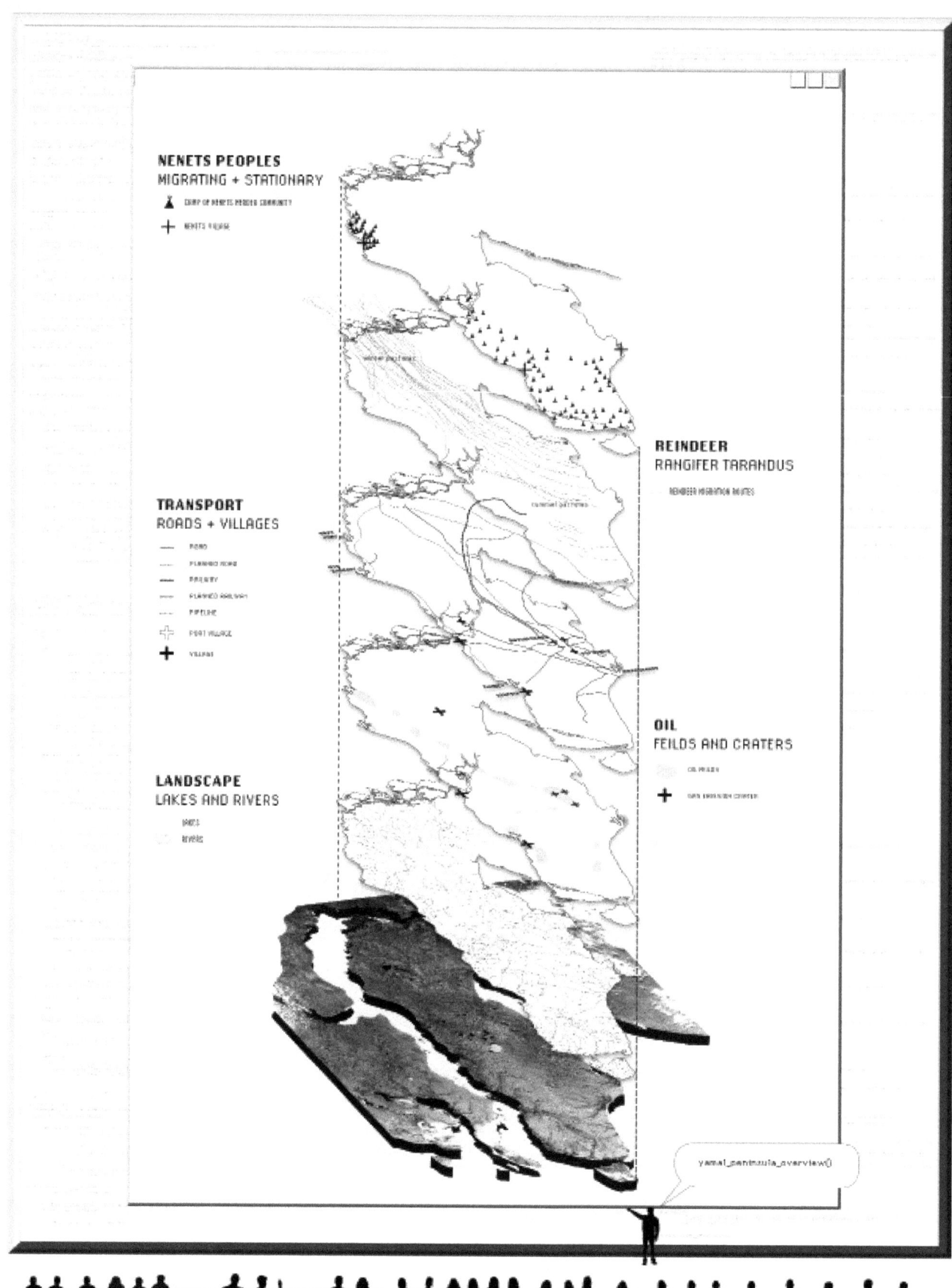

2 The numerous layers of complexity that the Arctic Consortium attempts to address.

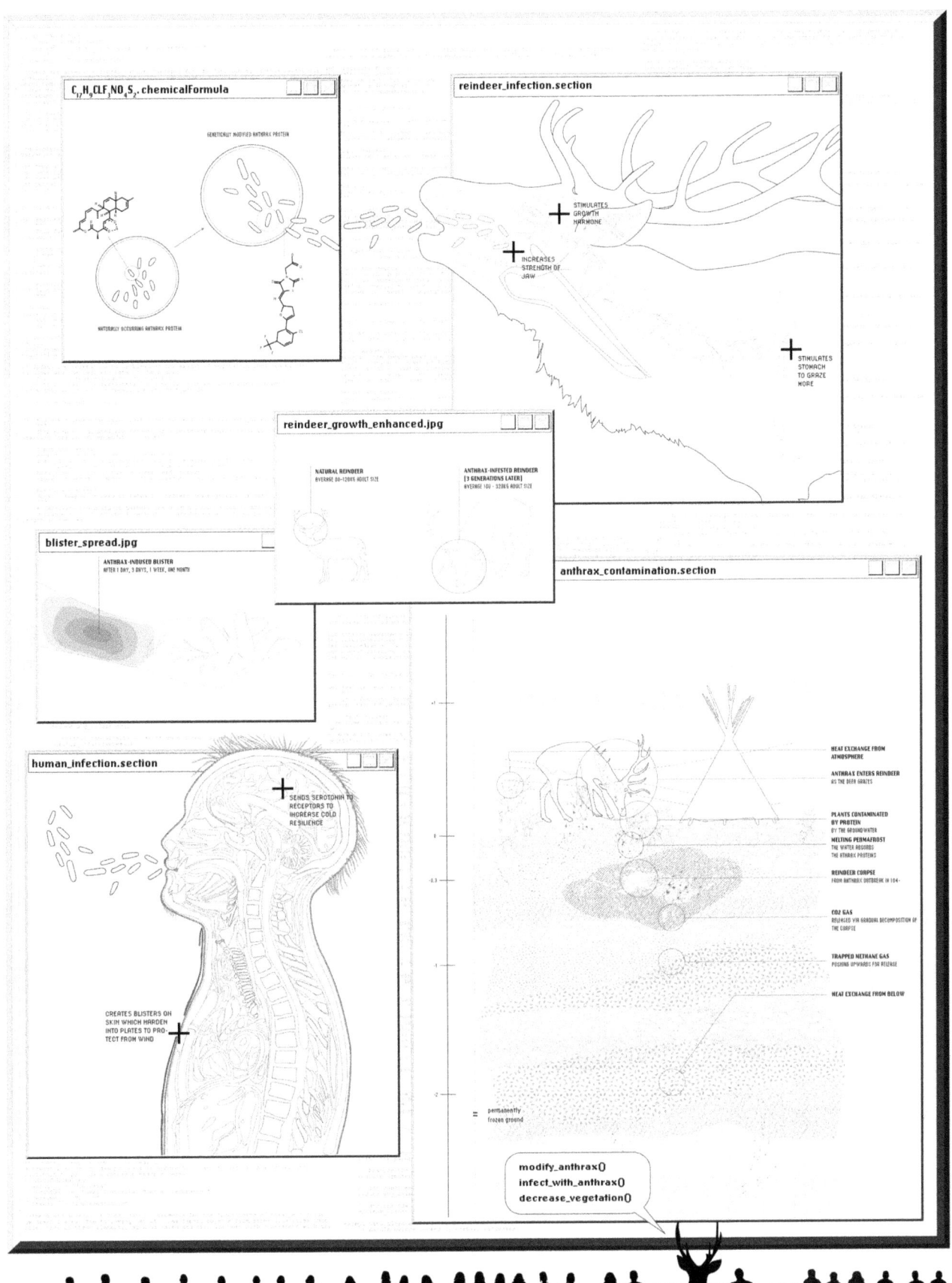

3   Influences of the new Anthrax strain on the reindeer and indigenous populations.

Nenets header: Artificially increasing reindeer numbers disrupts controlled markets (Stammler 2024). Reindeer periodically die from illness outbreaks like in 2016.

The 2016 Anthrax outbreak killed 1,200 reindeer and affected Nenets peoples, especially children (The Siberian Times reporter 2016). Livestock grazing in anthrax-contaminated fields can spread the illness to humans (Galante 2022). The 2016 outbreak resulted from thawing permafrost and carcasses of reindeer from a previous epidemic (Ezhova et al. 2021).

Scientist (CDC): We could use modified Anthrax spores as carriers to genetically modify the reindeer, increasing their size and grazing capacity.

Genetically modifying Anthrax spores can create strains that increase cattle size instead of killing them. Helicopter dispersal would spread the modified strain to enhance grazing and decrease vegetation (Figure 3).

CHAPTER 2: CH_4

Mediator: Today, the council discusses methane on the Yamal Peninsula and the dangers of gas emission craters.

The Yamal-Nenets Autonomous Region is a major gas producer, contributing 80 percent of Russia's natural gas and 15 percent of the world's total (Novatek 2013). The region's continuous permafrost contains large amounts of methane gas, making it attractive for extraction but also causing dangerous gas emission craters.

Leader (Nenets peoples): These craters are unpredictable and pose a threat to wildlife and people. We must stop their formation immediately.

The Yamal and Erkuta craters emerged in 2017, releasing methane gas bubbles from the permafrost due to melting soil (Chuvilin et al. 2020). These craters are not cryovolcanoes as initially believed (Gray 2020), but methane releases. Many similar craters have been discovered near oil extraction sites (Bogoyavlensky et al. 2021).

Leader (Nenets peoples): We've noticed these craters appear near dome-shaped hills called 'pingos' or 'bulgunnyakhs' that change in elevation seasonally (Gray 2020).

These craters, formed by warming permafrost and vegetation cover, release methane gas that further contributes to Arctic warming. Directly capturing methane gas from the soil can capture 82 percent of the gas (Davidson 2020) (Figure 4).

Extracting methane from the rising pingos before they explode is possible within the craters' 2–5-year life cycle (Gray 2020). The empty craters eventually fill with water and freeze, stabilizing the permafrost. Using rotating drill systems instead of traditional fracking constructions, gas can be extracted from methane bubbles and the equipment can move on. A separate facility is needed to convert methane into methanol for fuel and export to Asia (Figure 5).

CHAPTER 3: H_2O

Mediator: The council convenes to discuss the Northern Sea Route (NSR) and its development.

The NSR refers to the waters between Novaya Zemlya and the Bering Strait (Gribkovskaia, Kovalenko, and Morgunova 2018). The arctic and Yamal Peninsula have historically been challenging to navigate. The NSR played a vital role following the implementation of accident-free shipping conditions were established, leading to a boom in trade shipping over the next two centuries. Cargo passing through the NSR doubled every five years until the 2020s, with oil export from the Yamal Peninsula driving increased traffic (Berry 2008). In recent years, the NSR has been profitable for Russian gas and oil exports, particularly liquefied natural gas (LNG) and gas condensate (Humpert 2023).

President (Russian Federation): "The Arctic provides the shortest route between Europe and Asia-Pacific, reducing shipping costs significantly."

Although primarily facing west towards Europe, the NSR has increasingly turned towards Asian countries, notably China and India. The NSR reduces the distance from East Asia to Western Europe from 21,000km via the Suez Canal to 12,800km (Sharma 2021). Russia has become China's largest natural gas supplier, and China plans to expand its "Polar Silk Road" vision, connecting with Russia and Nordic Europe. India's involvement in the Arctic is also growing.

President (Russian Federation): "Developing modern infrastructure along the Northern Sea Route is a major objective... We plan to expand existing ports, including Sabetta on the Yamal Peninsula" (Putin 2011).

Sabetta, the port associated with the Yamal LNG extraction site, handles over half of the NSR's shipping traffic, primarily exporting oil ("Sabetta 2019 | Northern Sea Route Information Office" 2020). The port's location provides easy access to the West Siberian oil basin reserves and the center of the NSR, enabling transportation to the East and West ("Port of Sabetta, Yamal Peninsula" n.d.).

Governor (Yamalo-Nenets Autonomous Okrug): We should follow the successful example of Sabetta and expand our other port cities in the Ob Bay, such as Mys Kameny and Novy Port.

The ports are expanded, with additional access points along the Yamal Peninsula, including Bovanenkovo, Kharasavey, and Tamb (Figure 6).

REFERENCES

Barry, Roger G. 2008. "Remote Sensing of Sea Ice in the Northern Sea Route: Studies and Applications." Eos, Transactions American Geophysical Union 89, no. 27 (July 2008): 248–248. https://doi.org/10.1029/2008EO270011.

Bogoyavlensky, Vasily, Igor Bogoyavlensky, Roman Nikonov, Vladimir Yakushev, and Viacheslav Sevastyanov. 2021. "Permanent Gas Emission from the Seyakha Crater of Gas Blowout, Yamal Peninsula, Russian Arctic." Energies 14 (17): 5345. https://doi.org/10.3390/en14175345.

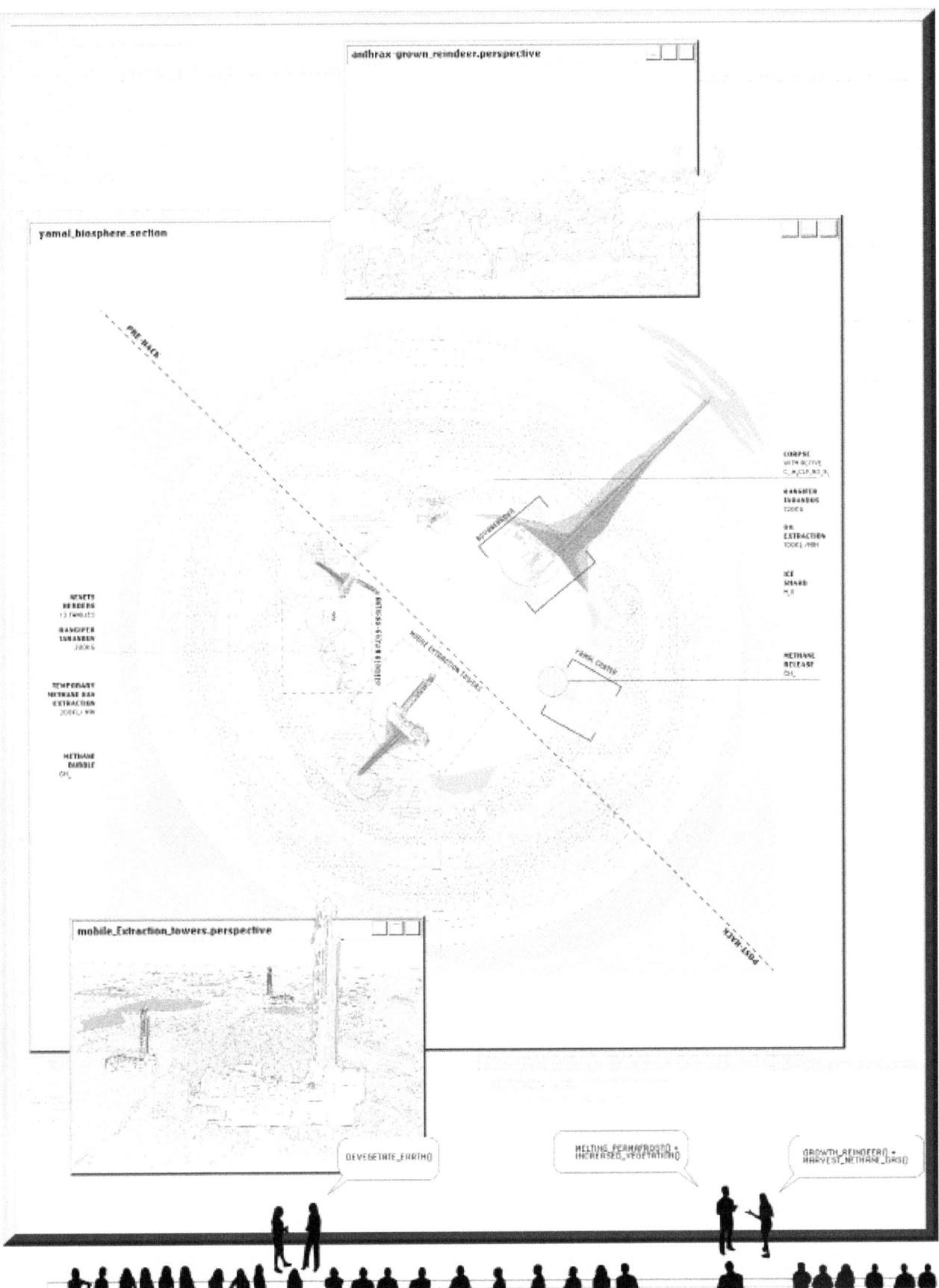

4 This biosphere compares existing land conditions with the consortium's proposal.

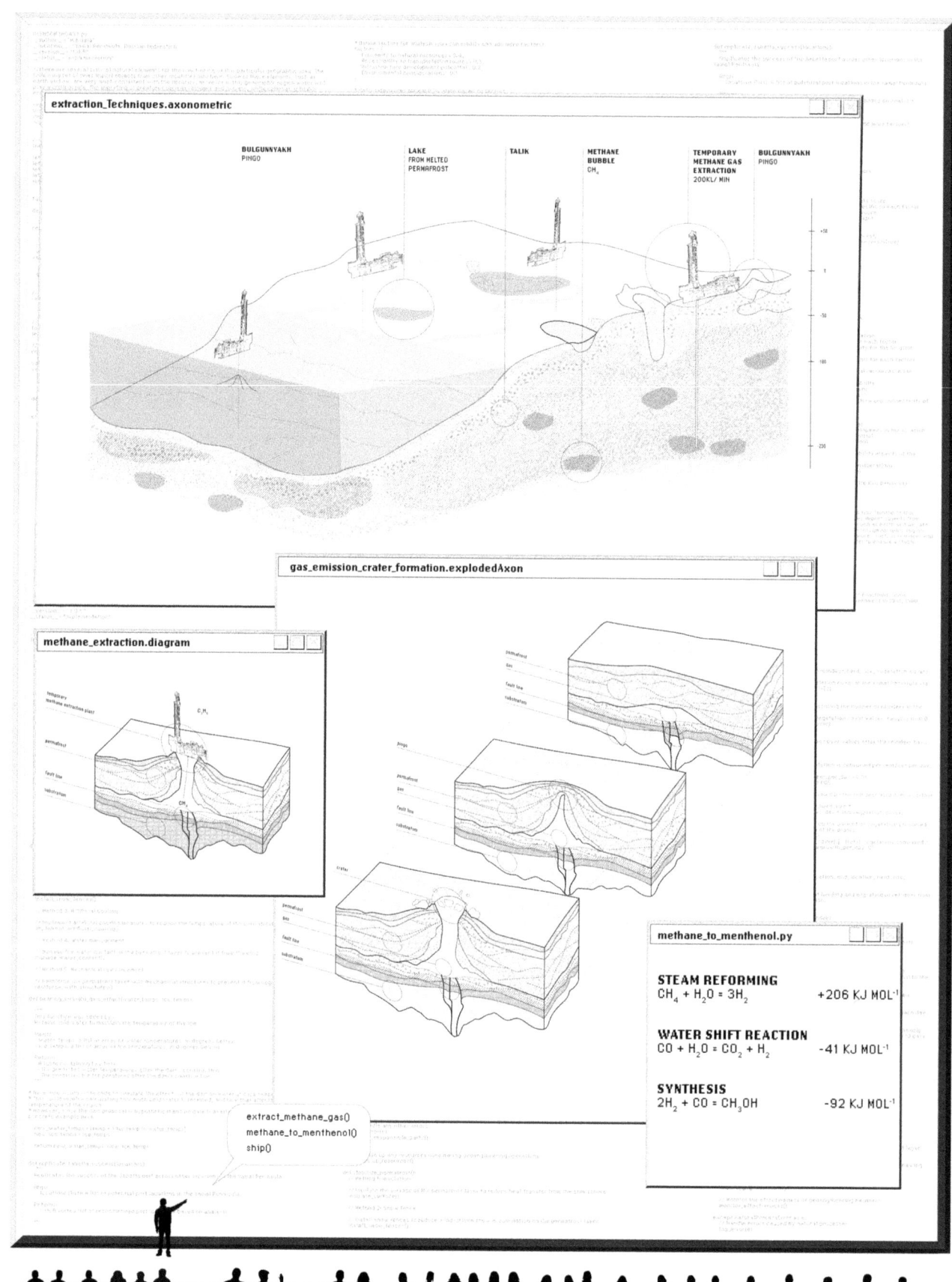

5 Gas emission craters and the extraction of gas from the pingos.

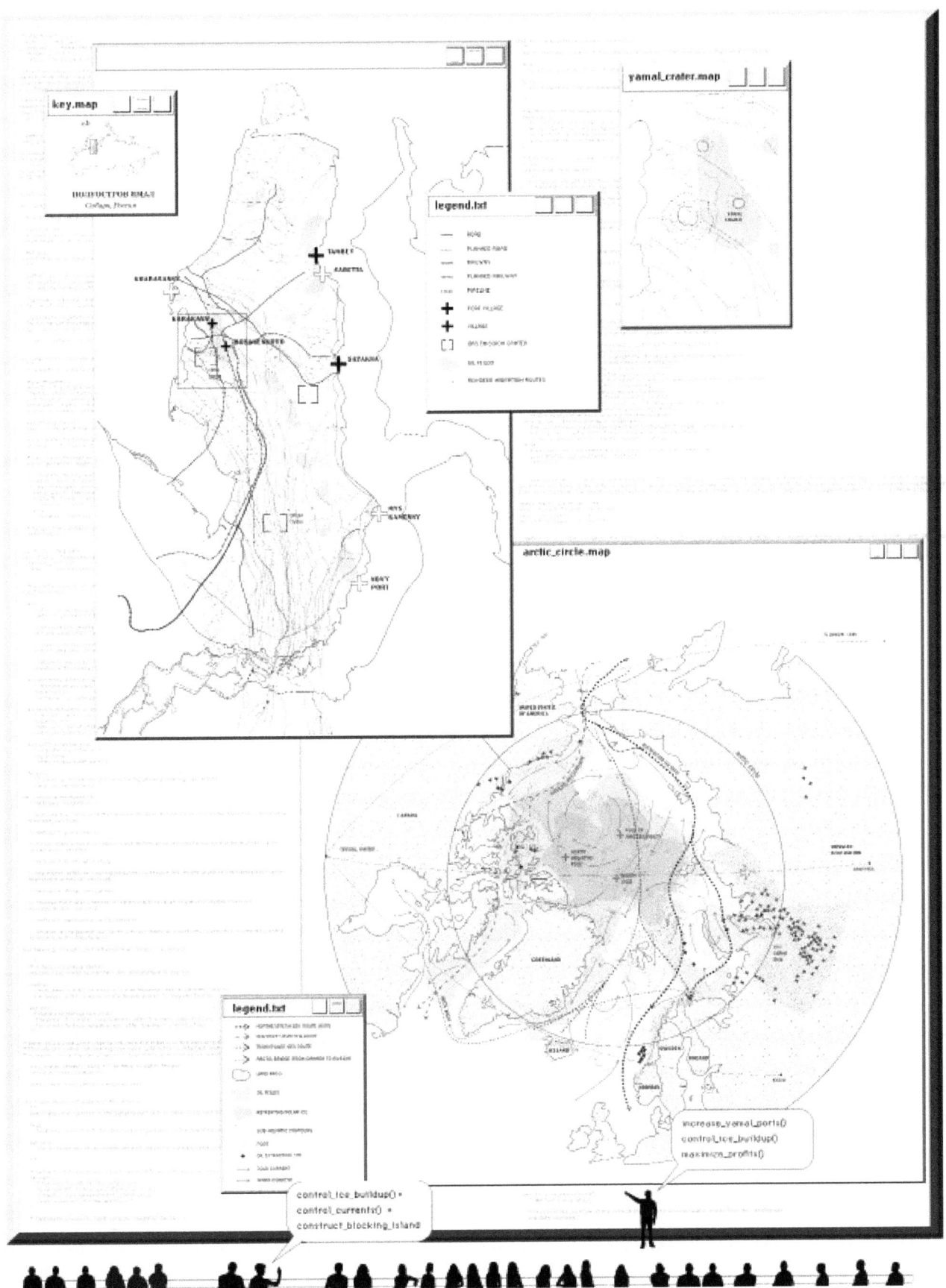

6   Current and proposed NSR, its reach, and the role the Yamal Peninsula in its development.

Chuvilin, Evgeny, Julia Stanilovskaya, Aleksey Titovsky, Anton Sinitsky, Natalia Sokolova, Boris Bukhanov, Mikhail Spasennykh, Alexey Cheremisin 1 , Sergey Grebenkin, Dinara Davletshina, and Christian Badetz. 2020. "A Gas-Emission Crater in the Erkuta River Valley, Yamal Peninsula: Characteristics and Potential Formation Model." Geosciences 10 (5): 170. https://doi.org/10.3390/geosciences10050170.

Davidson, Jordan. 2020. "Scientists Find a Cleaner Way to Extract Methane From Permafrost." EcoWatch (blog). January 3, 2020. https://www.ecowatch.com/methane-extraction-permafrost-2643757072.html.

Ezhova, Ekaterina, Dmitry Orlov, Elli Suhonen, Dmitry Kaverin, Alexander Mahura, Victor Gennadinik, Ilmo Kukkonen, Dmitry Drozdov, Hanna K. Lappalainen, Vladimir Melnikov, Tuukka Pet, Veli-Matti Kerminen, Sergey Zilitinkevich, Svetlana M. Malkhazova, Torben R. Christensen, and Markku Kulmala. 2021. "Climatic Factors Influencing the Anthrax Outbreak of 2016 in Siberia, Russia." Ecohealth 18 (2): 217–28. https://doi.org/10.1007/s10393-021-01549-5.

Galante, Domenico. 2022. "Anthrax in Animals - Generalized Conditions." Merck Veterinary Manual. 2022. https://www.merckvetmanual.com/generalized-conditions/anthrax/anthrax-in-animals.

Gray, Richard. 2020. "The Mystery of Siberia's Exploding Craters." BBC Future. 2020. https://www.bbc.com/future/article/20201130-climate-change-the-mystery-of-siberias-explosive-craters.

Gribkovskaia, Victoria, Alina Kovalenko, and Maria Morgunova . 2018. "Infrastructural Synergy of the Northern Sea Route in the International Context." https://www.researchgate.net/profile/Maria-Morgunova/publication/330648496_INFRASTRUCTURAL_SYNERGY_OF_THE_NORTHERN_SEA_ROUTE_IN_THE_INTERNATIONAL_CONTEXT/links/5dbffe06a6fdcc212800b4b1/INFRASTRUCTURAL-SYNERGY-OF-THE-NORTHERN-SEA-ROUTE-IN-THE-INTERNATIONAL-CONTEXT.pdf?origin=publication_detail.

Humpert, Malte. 2023. "Russia's Northern Sea Route Sees More Traffic Despite War and Sanctions." 2023. https://www.highnorthnews.com/en/russias-northern-sea-route-sees-more-traffic-despite-war-and-sanctions.

Molloy, Mark. 2016. "How Reindeer Help Protect the North Pole from Climate Change - Study," December 22, 2016. https://www.telegraph.co.uk/christmas/2016/12/22/reindeer-helping-protect-north-pole-climate-change/.

Northern Sea Route Information Office. 2019. "NSR Shipping Traffic – Activities in Sabetta in 2019." 2020. March 30, 2020. https://arctic-lio.com/nsr-shipping-traffic-activities-in-sabetta-in-2019/.

Novatek. 2013. "NOVATEK and the Silk Road Fund Conclude Framework Agreement on Acquisition of Stake in Yamal LNG." Novatek. 2013. https://www.novatek.ru/en/press/releases/index.php?id_4=984.

"Port of Sabetta, Yamal Peninsula." n.d. Accessed May 22, 2023. https://www.ship-technology.com/projects/port-sabetta-yamal-peninsula-russia/.

Putin, Vladimir. 2011. Prime Minister Vladimir Putin takes part in the second International Arctic Forum "The Arctic – Territory of Dialogue" in Arkhangelsk. http://archive.premier.gov.ru/eng/events/news/16536/print/.

Rubenstein, Dustin R., Daniel I. Rubenstein, Paul W. Sherman, and Thomas A. Gavin. 2006. "Pleistocene Park: Does Re-Wilding North America Represent Sound Conservation for the 21st Century?" Biological Conservation 132 (2): 232–38. https://doi.org/10.1016/j.biocon.2006.04.003.

Sharma, Anu. 2021. "China's Polar Silk Road: Implications for the Arctic Region." Journal of Indo-Pacific Affairs.

Stammler, Florian. 2004. "The Commoditisation of Reindeer Herding in Post Soviet Russia: Herders, Antlers and Traders in Yamal." Bernhard Streck (Hg.): Segmentation Und Komplementarität. Organisatorische, Ökonomische Und Kulturelle Aspekte Der Interaktion von Nomaden Und Sesshaften. Beiträge Der Kolloquia.

The Siberian Times Reporter. 2016. "40 Now Hospitalised after Anthrax Outbreak in Yamal, More than Half Are Children," 2016. https://siberiantimes.com/other/others/news/n0691-40-now-hospitalised-after-anthrax-outbreak-in-yamal-more-than-half-are-children/.

Yu, Qin, Howard Epstein, Donald Walker, Bruce Forbes. 2011. "Modeling Dynamics of Tundra Plant Communities on the Yamal Peninsula, Russia, in Response to Climate Change and Grazing

ACKNOWLEDGEMENTS

The author would like to thank Rania Ghosn of DesignEarth for leading the GeoDesign seminar in which this project took shape.

IMAGE CREDITS

Figure 1: © Dmitry Moiseenko
All other drawings and images by the author.

Tatiana Estrina Originally from Canada, Tatiana studied architecture at Toronto Metropolitan University in Toronto before journeying to Cambridge to work towards a Master of Architecture. Along the way Tatiana had the opportunity to work at multiple companies, including Tesla in the Bay Area, PARTISANS in Toronto, and hold assistant positions within research and teaching where she investigated possibilities of extended realities, digital fabrication, and videogame architecture. Tatiana continues to investigate my current interests in digital design, virtual spaces, computation, and futurology at Massachusetts Institute of Technology.

"Kepiting Bambu": Mixed-Reality-Aided Bamboo Construction

Kristof Crolla
The University of Hong Kong
Building Simplexity Lab
Laboratory for Explorative
Architecture & Design Ltd.
(LEAD)

Garvin Goepel
The University of Hong Kong
Building Simplexity Lab

1   Bamboo support structure of "Kepiting Bambu", Ubud, Bali (Jumpa Zoe, March 2023, © Bamboo U)

PRODUCTION NOTES

Client: Bamboo U
Status: In progress
Location: Bali, Indonesia
Date: March 2023

Introduction

"Kepiting Bambu", or "Bamboo Crab" in Balinese, referring to the projects' particular roof geometry, consists of two permanent dormitory structures that were built in Bali's jungle in 2023, as part of a bamboo construction workshop conducted at Bamboo U (see Figures 1 and 2). The workshop focused on the integration of augmented reality (AR) technology in bamboo craft and construction to expand its locally practically feasible solution space. The workshop aimed to expose participants to the possibilities this opens up for bamboo architecture design. The workshop's objective was to optimize and test the construction processes of the pre-designed geometries by providing easily understandable construction information to both expert bamboo craftspeople and participants with no prior experience in bamboo construction. This report summarizes the key aspects and findings from the workshop, and highlights the role of AR in achieving efficient communication and the enhancement of craft.

AR-driven Construction
Step 1: Siting

Both bamboo structures were sited in wild, natural, and highly irregular jungle terrain with no access to utilities other than electricity. Although a rough location had been pre-assigned during the design phase, their final precise location was determined onsite in collaboration with the stakeholders through holographic projections using several HoloLens devices. By placing fiducial markers, and manipulating them collaboratively, the exact location, orientation, and rotation of the pods were decided, considering site

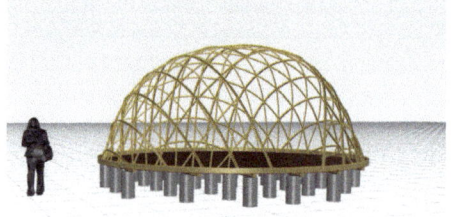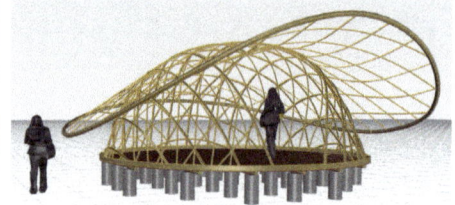

2   Project design and installation sequence, incorporating two equidistant bending-active bamboo grids made from bamboo splits.

3   AR display of design intent for in-situ decision-making of orientation and exact localization.

conditions, such as accessibility, view orientation, direct solar exposure, and more. This AR-enabled process significantly reduced the time required for configuration compared to conventional measurements, as those were incapable of fully capturing the complexities of the site's natural environment (see Figure 3).

Step 2: Foundations

Once the project location was finalized, skilled craftspeople used digital information that was holographically projected through HoloLens devices to position the center points of the concrete pile foundations (see Figure 4). Despite language barriers, digital instructions were quickly understood, allowing the marking to take place swiftly, followed by the subsequent concrete pouring and installation of the bamboo flooring.

Step 3: Ring beam installation

A ring beam, consisting of interconnected bamboo splits and fixed to the bamboo flooring, was installed, guided by AR, to serve as an anchor for the bending-active grid structure that defined the primary structure of the projects (see Figure 6). Identification points marking the intersection points of this grid structure and the ring beam were marked up following holographic guides to allow the accurate positioning of the grid during its in-situ bending in later steps.

Step 4: Equidistant, bending-active bamboo grid

The primary structure consists of a bent, equidistant bamboo grid made from splits. Following AR-guided marking of intersection points onto the splits, the flat grid

4   Labeling foundation position and installation of the floor.

5   Navigation through holographic interface (Jumpa Zoe, March 2023, © Bamboo U).

was assembled using wire connection on the pod floors under the guidance of AR instructors, who directed participants to allocate specific beam IDs to their respective locations (see Figure 7). Once assembled, participants lifted and centered the grids onto temporary support scaffolding, guided by AR instructions (see Figure 8). Augmented reality supervision facilitated identifying and correcting any deformations, ensuring the physical bamboo geometry matched the digital design as it was fixed to the base's ring beam. A secondary grid was laid on top to define the roof surface.

Step 5: "Lidi Bundle" roofline

The roof line was designed to be held up by a "Lidi Bundle", a flexible ring beam made from bundles of tied-together bamboo splits. Participants wearing HoloLens adjusted the prefabricated bundle's height and location in alignment with the digital twin representation. Bamboo poles were temporarily fixed to the ground and scaffoldings to finetune the bundle's position (see Figure 9). Support positions were marked by tape, allowing craftspeople to adjust bamboo supports without additional measurements.

Discussion

Training sessions were organized at the start of the workshop to familiarize certain participants with the extended reality (XR) operating devices, holographic instructions, and software required for independent use. These trained individuals then assisted their peers, thus contributing to a collaborative learning environment. This workflow worked well, which illustrates the ease of technology integration in labor-intensive construction workflows. Local bamboo craftspeople involved in the project rapidly adapted to their now AR-driven tasks, which could now be completed far more quickly than traditionally would have been possible.

It was necessary for the design team to create and maintain a nimble, procedural holographic drawing generator to make sure feedback from the site could instantly be processed to produce updated, most suitable, holographic content and notation styles. Participants initially exhibited a tendency to strive for hyper-precision in the marking and assembly processes – a quality with which current

6   AR labeling of ring beam.

7   AR labeling of the grids' bamboo splits.

technology still struggles, especially in irregular natural environments where "Simultaneous Localization and Mapping" (SLAM) technology struggles. Bamboo architecture, however, by its very nature, has a high tolerance towards material, craftworkership, or dimensional tolerances, as the variability of the natural materials doesn't lend itself to hyper-precision anyway. Hence, AR was found quite suitable to be integrated into this tectonic system.

While the project demonstrated that for certain highly repetitive tasks, AR might be redundant, for tasks involving non-standard geometries or irregular patterns, its guiding potential proved to be vital. This proves that AR can be a great tool to make non-standard design solution spaces, found on-screen, now practically possible in reality.

ACKNOWLEDGMENTS

WORKSHOP TEAM:
TUTORS | Dr Kristof Crolla, Dr Garvin Goepel
PROGRAMME DIRECTORS | Orin Hardy (Bamboo U)
ASSISTANTS | Cécile Durand, Rodrigo Novais Istchuk, I Putu Juliadi ("Pak Putu Abang", carpenter), Jeplin Kaban ("Pak Epin", carpenter), I Ketut Darmadi ("Pak Donal", carpenter)
PARTICIPANTS | Tualagi Nokise, Carly Althoff, Anke Fuerer, Rachel Ponder, Rohan More, Amar Gurung, Angelo Bayonito, Julia Frendo, Natalie Choo, Guilen Cannesson, Dipta Priyatna, Steven Verde, Corentin Haëner, George Bakardijev, Eleni Vournas Cedar and Tallis Robarts

IMAGE CREDITS

Figures 1, 5, and 8 (bottom): Jumpa Zoe, March 2023, © Bamboo U. All other images by the authors.

8   Assembly, bending, and popping up of the grid (bottom: Jumpa Zoe, March 2023, © Bamboo U).

9   Installing the "Lidi Bundle" roofline.

Dr. Kristof Crolla is an architect who combines his architectural practice, Laboratory for Explorative Architecture & Design Ltd. (LEAD), with his position as Associate Professor and Associate Dean (Special Projects) at the University of Hong Kong (HKU)'s Faculty of Architecture. He is based in Hong Kong, where his work has received numerous design, research, and teaching awards and accolades, including the RMIT Vice-Chancellor's Prize for Research Impact—Higher Degree by Research. He is best known for the projects "Golden Moon" and "ZCB Bamboo Pavilion," for which he received the World Architecture Festival Small Project of the Year award in 2016.

Dr. Garvin Goepel is a designer and researcher specialized in the field of combining Augmented-Reality (AR) with generative architecture. He pursued his PhD at the Chinese University of Hong Kong (CUHK) as an awardee of the Hong Kong PhD Fellowship Scheme (HKPFS), received his MArch degree, with distinction, from dieAngewandte, Vienna - Studio Greg Lynn, and gained professional experience working with several practices including Coop Himmelb(l)au in Vienna. He is currently holding a Lecturer and Postdoc position at the University of Hong Kong (HKU). His research advances studies in collaborative holographic-driven construction and expands opportunities for technology-infused craftsmanship.

Elevators, Hard Drives, and Teleportation

Chenoe Hart
Independent Scholar

The ability of computer code to arbitrarily link discrete self-contained spaces together within a virtual world can be interpreted as a continuation of the historical legacy of the development of physically isolated floors within buildings connected by elevators. Both modern touch-screen-enabled elevators and those using earlier push-buttons create conditions where their passengers navigate physical space through an electronic interface. As they place users at destinations designated by previously-established code, they exist in a comparable state of disrupted processional continuity to that of virtual worlds designed to make use of the computer's ability to process space through randomly-assigned indexes. An elevator passenger navigates via the inherently abstract act of pushing a button. The elevator control panel provides its users with a list of options for floors to travel to, labeled with specific whole numbers; as a quantized and finite set of information, that list might be conceptually understood to be specifically digital in its composition. It also doesn't necessarily correspond with the physical reality of the spaces it traverses; in Western culture that list commonly skips the thirteenth floor, or in many East Asian cultures the fourth floor.

That panel's ability to equalize the effort required to travel to different floors throughout a building renders the building's floors as though they were randomly accessible. The destination an elevator passenger reaches is also arbitrarily self-contained in relation to its surroundings, as exemplified by Rem Koolhaas's description of each floor in a multi-story building being capable of operating "as if the others did not exist" (Koolhaas 1997, 85).

Within virtual worlds, spatial access and continuity are modulated in some potentially comparable ways, as a result of the ability of digital information to connect virtual spaces via random addressing. A description exploring the capabilities of how information can mediate spatial connections within a virtual world can be found within Michael Nitsche's game design text *Video Game Spaces: Image, Play, and Structure in 3D Worlds*, in the author's description of the *Common Tales* project commissioned by Sony Computer Entertainment to "experiment with cinematic storytelling techniques in a game prototype" for which he served as a designer (Nitsche 2008, 85). The game's *Cube Club* level was constructed such that, in his words:

"... two opposing doors from one virtual room lead to similarly opposing doors in a different room. When an avatar leaves the first room through the northern door, he or she will enter the seemingly adjacent second room, also through the northern door—the same way the southern doors are connected. Both rooms occupy the same logical space—a physical impossibility." (Ibid.).

The character of that space is generated from its origins in loaded computer files, or in other words, the affordances of the computer to connect arbitrary and disparate pieces of information together. That condition means that locations within a game level can be "... arranged in a mathematically conditional way", with "no spatial connection" between their data files. That attribute consequently "... allows a designer to interlink them in any way." (Nitsche 2008, 119.)

Although the physically impossible travel path of the player in *Cube Club* exhibits obvious limits to its translatability to real-world spaces, the level illustrates one conceptual property of virtual worlds - their ability to achieve connections between spaces by means of what might be considered a form of teleportation - which parallels experiences observable along an elevator ride. One experiential attribute shared by both elevators and such game mechanisms might be the cinematic condition of montage, which Nitsche references in his analysis (Nitsche 2008, 117-118.).

Elevators have been criticized for introducing disruptive experiential conditions of potentially comparable similarity. In Philip Johnson's critique of the impacts of elevators in his 1965 *Perspecta* article "Whence & Whither: The Processional Element in Architecture," the architect placed their circulation method in opposition to design principles following conventional aesthetically-appealing rules of architectural procession under which a visitor to his Yale University Kline Biology Tower complex "... should be able to get *from* any door *to* any door *clearly*" (Johnson 1965, 170).

Where Johnson also described how within a building with elevators on both sides of its circulation path a visitor might have to take a different path each time they take an elevator trip (Johnson 1965, 168), the variations in spatial procession which those circulation methods generated would, like the "teleporter zones" connecting spaces in Nitsche's game world, be able to "reposition" a passenger or a game character "in a new area" (Nitsche 2008, 119-120). The shifting and moving spaces located behind an elevator door could share some aspects of unpredictability and arbitrariness with those modulated in games via teleportation to randomly-accessible locations stored in computer files. Like maps loaded within a game, the elevator connects spaces based on abstracted logical relationships instead of direct adjacencies. The potential similarities between building circulation systems and a computer's capabilities are significant enough that one early method of positioning a computer hard drive head, which happened to operate with a similar pattern of movement to an elevator serving all of its destinations in one travel direction at a time, the "SCAN algorithm", was also nicknamed the "'elevator' algorithm" (Worthington, Ganger and Patt 1994, 242.).

REFERENCES

Johnson, Philip. 1965. "Whence & Whither: The Processional Element in Architecture." *Perspecta* 9/10: 167–78.

Koolhaas, Rem. 1997. *Delirious New York: A Retroactive Manifesto for Manhattan*. New York: The Monacelli Press.

Nitsche, Michael. 2008. *Video Game Spaces: Image, Play, and Structure in 3D Worlds*. Cambridge: The MIT Press.

Worthington, Bruce L., Ganger, Gregory R., and Patt, Yale N. 1994. "Scheduling Algorithms for Modern Disk Drives." In *Proceedings of the 1994 ACM SIGMETRICS Conference on Measurement and Modeling of Computer Systems*, 241–51. SIGMETRICS '94. New York: Association for Computing Machinery.

IMAGE CREDITS

All drawings and images by the author.

Chenoe Hart is an architectural designer and researcher investigating how digital technologies can transform architecture's historical condition of being a passive and location-based form of media. She is located in New York.

Envisioning an Open Knowledge Network (OKN) for AEC Roboticists

Shahin Vassigh
Florida International University

Biayna Bogosian
Florida International University

1   Robotics Academy Virtual Reality Learning Environment.

Introduction

The construction industry faces numerous challenges related to productivity, sustainability, and meeting global demands (Hatoum and Nassereddine 2020; Carra et al. 2018; Barbosa, Woetzel, and Mischke 2017; Bock 2015; Linner 2013). In response, the automation of design and construction has emerged as a promising solution. In the past three decades, researchers and innovators in the Architecture, Engineering, and Construction (AEC) fields have made significant strides in automating various aspects of building construction, utilizing computational design and robotic fabrication processes (Dubor et al. 2019). However, synthesizing innovation in automation encounters several obstacles. First, there is a lack of an established venue for information sharing, making it difficult to build upon the knowledge of peers. First, the absence of a well-established platform for information sharing hinders the ability to effectively capitalize on the knowledge of peers. Consequently, much of the research remains isolated, impeding the rapid dissemination of knowledge within the field (Mahbub 2015). Second, the absence of a standardized and unified process for automating design and construction leads to the individual development of standards, workflows, and terminologies. This lack of standardization presents a significant obstacle to research and learning within the field. Lastly, insufficient training materials hinder the acquisition of skills necessary to effectively utilize automation. Traditional in-person robotics training is resource-intensive, expensive, and designed for specific platforms (Peterson et al. 2021; Thomas 2013). Furthermore, it fails to leverage the latest AI-driven learning technologies that offer personalized, adaptable, and inclusive experiences. These challenges underscore the necessity for an integrated approach that promotes collaboration, establishes industry standards, and provides comprehensive

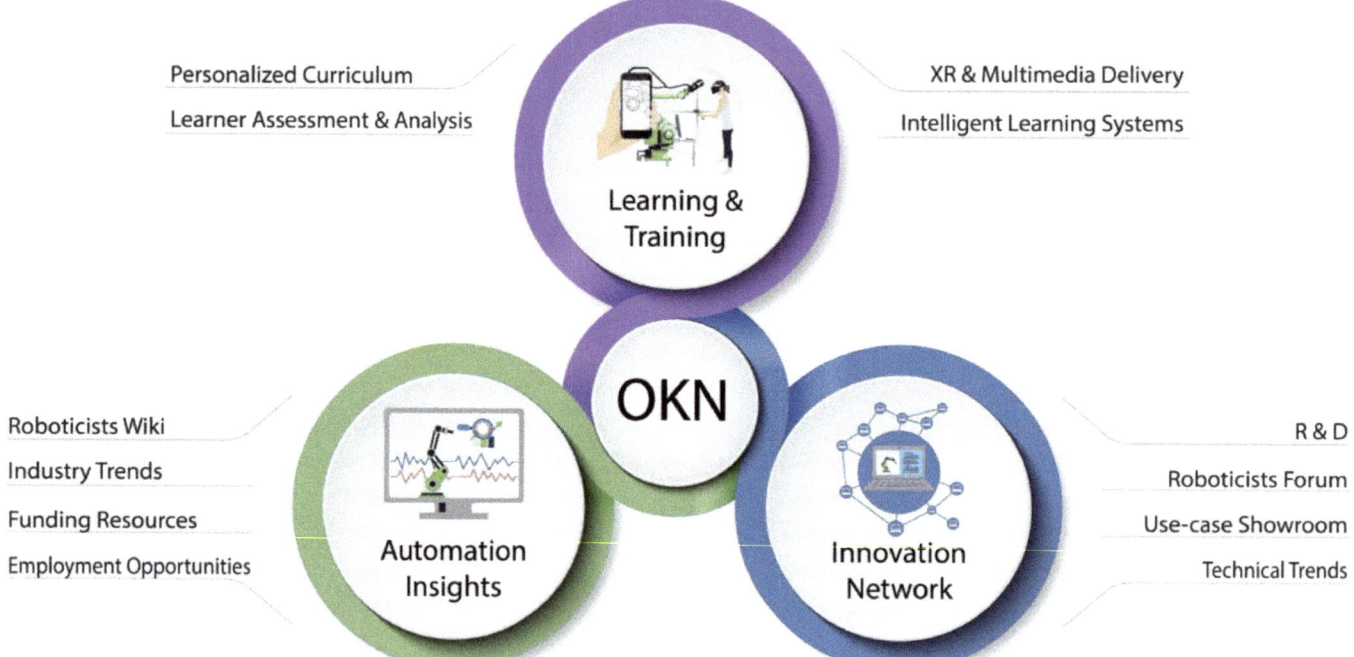

2 Diagram describing the main components of the envisioned Open Knowledge Network.

training resources. Such an approach is essential to unlock the full potential of automation in the construction industry.

Open Knowledge Network (OKN)
To address these challenges, we advocate for a collaborative approach involving AEC researchers, innovators, university programs, federal actors, and other stakeholders. Together, we can establish a shared platform for information exchange, standardized processes, and comprehensive training materials. In line with the definition of the Open Knowledge Network (OKN) (Baru et al. 2022; Sheth et al. 2019), we advocate for an online infrastructure that is open-source, AI-driven, and facilitates data exchange and knowledge sharing. This infrastructure will serve as a foundation for the accessible evolution of robotics technology in the AEC industry (see Figure 2). The components of the envisioned OKN could include the following:

Innovation Network: Facilitating knowledge sharing by creating a centralized hub where researchers, professionals, and students can share and access information related to robotics in AEC. This could incorporate the following:

• Research and Development Exchange Hub is a customizable library of information shared by users, including programming scripts, academic papers, instructional multimedia tutorials, and the latest research findings.

• Roboticists Forum provides technical troubleshooting assistance through a library of multimedia research and peer-to-peer discussions.

• A Use-Case Showroom is a virtual site for demonstrating the advances in robotics and automation technologies.

Automation Insights: Speeding the advancement and adoption of robotics in the AEC fields to encourage experimentation, ideation, peer feedback, and smooth transition of the workforce to high-tech jobs. This could incorporate the following:

• Roboticists' Wikipedia contains a library of terminologies, definitions, and descriptions of robotic processes designed to promote standardization of practice.

• Funding Sources, providing tools, and sharing funding opportunities for researchers, educators, and practitioners to collaborate on problem-solving, collectively.

Learning and Training: Allowing leading educators to offer accessible and innovative training materials and educational resources, thereby making it easier for new researchers and students to acquire necessary skills.

• Intelligent Learning Systems to leverage advances in AI and learning technologies for developing personalized learning environments.

3   Image showing a student engaging with the project's VR Interface.

4   Scenes from the VR learning prototype demonstrating the learner dashboard, including biometric analysis and further progress information.

• Increased Accessibility by promoting comprehensive online and virtual training models to democratize access to advanced knowledge and tools.

To establish an OKN, it is essential to work together across different fields, actively look for funding opportunities, and promote open discussions among all involved parties. This field note aims to spark a discussion with the goal of driving more in-depth conversations about the subject during upcoming ACADIA meetings of researchers and innovators..

A Work in Progress OKN: The Robotics Academy
Focusing on Learning and Training as an integral part of establishing an OKN for AEC roboticists, an interdisciplinary group of faculty and researchers have developed the Robotics Academy. This immersive online training program has received funding through consecutive grants from the National Science Foundation (NSF), including support from the Convergence Accelerator (C-Accel) program and the Research on Emerging Technologies for Teaching and Learning (RETTL) program. The project aims to build an AI-powered personalized learning platform that utilizes Extended Reality (XR) technology for curriculum delivery and student assessment (See Figures 3 and 4).

Robotics Academy leverages advanced big data analytics to gather and analyze performance and biometric data from learners for developing an Intelligent Learning System (ILS) (see Figure 5)

By employing data analytics, the ILS gains insights into each learner's abilities, learning styles, and past experiences, enabling personalized learning. In addition, algorithms and machine learning techniques identify patterns and correlations to adapt content delivery and pacing.

The team has completed a virtual reality (VR) prototype for training students with KUKA (KR10) and Universal Robots (UR10) to establish and test learner interactions. The Unity3D game engine has been used to develop the

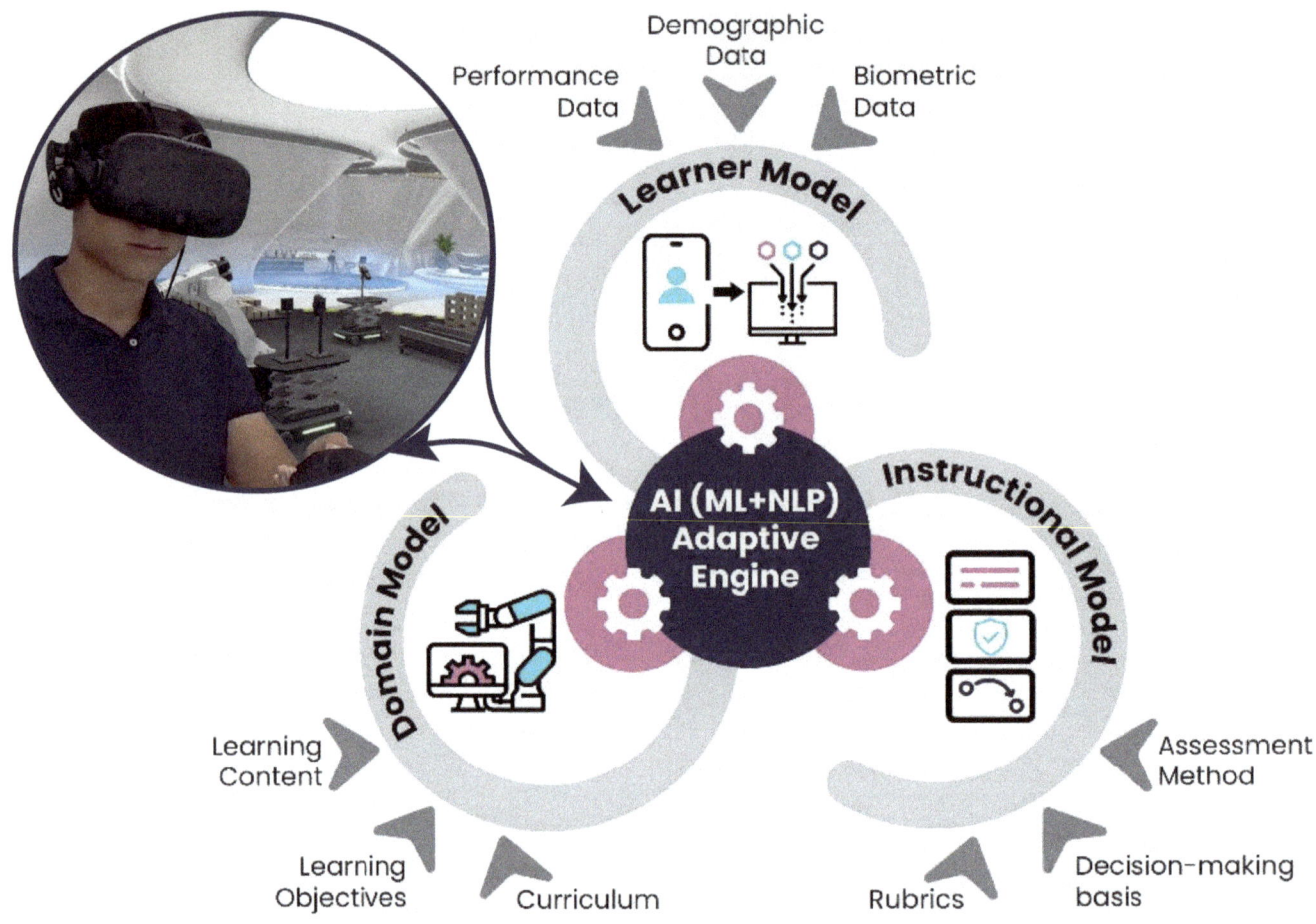

5   Robotics Academy's Adaptive Learning Systems Diagram for Personalizing Learning in VR Environment.

VR prototype for the HTC Vive Eye, head-mounted display. The steps involved defining learning objectives, adapting a robotics training curriculum content for VR (see Figures 6, 7, and 8), creating a Game Design Document (GDD), converting the GDD to an AGILE software development approach, and designing the architecture and assets of the VR training environment<.> The steps continued with developing primary features for user testing and data analysis using Machine Learning and Natural Language Processing, reworking features while conducting further user testing with an experimentation and control groups. The main VR features were designed and developed, incorporating vision, sound, and touch interactions. The integration of these steps resulted in the completion of the Robotics Academy VR prototype. This ongoing work includes creating a robotic brand-agnostic training curriculum, advancing game mechanics, building a procedurally generated robotic training space, improving biometric data collection, and advancing the implementation of the ILS in future prototypes.

Conclusion

The AEC industry is poised to bring transformational changes to how we approach design, construction, and impacts on the environment. Experts widely acknowledge that automation is vital in achieving sustainable, affordable, and efficient building construction. However, the current state of research and innovation on robotic automation in the industry must be more cohesive and accessible to overcome existing growth and innovation barriers. To tackle this challenge, this field note proposes the establishment of an OKN that provides a platform for sharing accessible research and innovation. The OKN is a model for fostering collaboration, knowledge sharing, and standardization within the AEC community. The development of the Robotics Academy, as a component of the OKN, highlights its importance and the potential for federal funding.

ACKNOWLEDGMENTS

The content presented here has been developed with the

6   This lesson challenges the students to match a "ghosted" robotic arm's position and orientation using Axis-specific and World-specific motion systems.

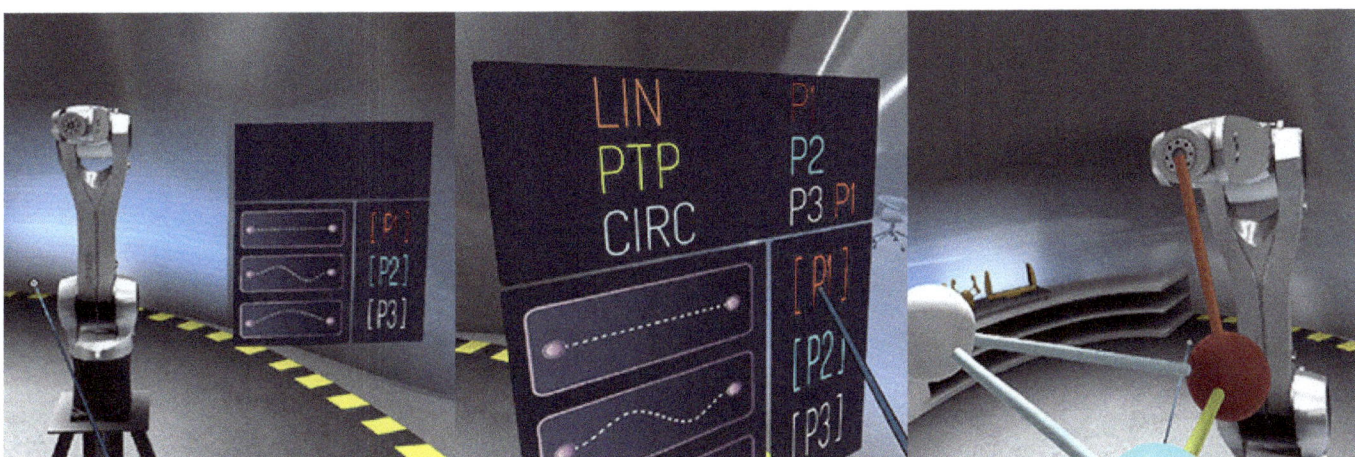

7   This lesson focuses on various movements.

backing of the National Science Foundation through the Award No. 2202610, under the purview of the Research on Emerging Technologies for Teaching and Learning initiative. The thoughts, results, and suggestions provided within this material represent the perspectives of the contributors, and should not be interpreted as an endorsement by the National Science Foundation.

REFERENCES

Barbosa, Filipe, Jonathan Woetzel, and Jan Mischke. 2017. Reinventing construction: A route of higher productivity. McKinsey Global Institute.

Baru, Chaitanya, Lara Campbell, Aurali Dade, Pradeep Fulay, Alex Loewi, Douglas Maughan, Ibrahim Mohedas et al. 2022. "The NSF Convergence Accelerator program." AI Magazine 43, no. 1: 6–16.

Bock, T.: The Future of Construction Automation: Technological Disruption and the Upcoming Ubiquity of Robotics. In: Automation in Construction, Vol. 59, pp. 113--121 (2015)

Carra, Guglielmo, Alfredo Argiolas, Alessandro Bellissima, Marta Niccolini, and Matteo Ragaglia. 2018. "Robotics in the construction industry: State of the art and future opportunities." In ISARC. Proceedings of the International Symposium on Automation and Robotics in Construction, vol. 35, pp. 1-8. IAARC Publications.

Dubor, Alexandre, Jean-Baptiste Izard, Edouard Cabay, Aldo Sollazzo, Areti Markopoulou, and Mariola Rodriguez. 2019. "On-site robotics for sustainable construction." In Robotic Fabrication in Architecture, Art and Design 2018: Foreword by Sigrid Brell-Çokcan and Johannes Braumann, Association for Robots in Architecture, pp. 390-401. Springer International Publishing.

Hatoum, Makram Bou, and Hala Nassereddine. 2020. "Developing a framework for the implementation of robotics in construction enterprises." In EG-ICE 2020 Workshop on Intelligent Computing in Engineering, Proceedings, pp. 453-462

Johnson-Glenberg, Mina C. 2018. "Immersive VR and education: Embodied design principles that include gesture and hand controls." In Frontiers in Robotics and AI: 81.

Linner, Thomas. 2013. "Automated and Robotic Construction: Integrated Automated Construction Sites."

Mahbub, Rohana. 2015. "Framework on the barriers to the implementation of automation and robotics in the construction industry." In International Journal of Innovation in Management 3, no. 1: 21–36.

8   A scene from the VR learning prototype demonstrating pick and place protocols.

Peterson, Eric, Biayna Bogosian, Jorge Tubella, and Shahin Vassigh. 2021. "Teaching Robotics with Virtual Reality: Developing Curriculum for the 21st Century Workforce." In Advances in Human Factors in Training, Education, and Learning Sciences. AHFE 2021. Lecture Notes in Networks and Systems, vol 269. Springer, Cham.

Sheth, Amit, Padhee, Swati and Gyrard, Amelie, 2019. Knowledge Graphs and Knowledge Networks: The Story in Brief. IEEE Internet Computing, 23 (4), 67–75.

Thomas, Ulrike, Gerd Hirzinger, Bernhard Rumpe, Christoph Schulze, and Andreas Wortmann. "A New Skill Based Robot Programming Language Using UML/P Statecharts." 2013 IEEE International Conference on Robotics and Automation, 2013. https://doi.org/10.1109/icra.2013.6630615.

IMAGE CREDITS

Figures 1 through 8: © All images by the authors.

Shahin Vassigh, Ph.D. is a professor of Architecture and the Director of Technology Research Development for the College of Communication, Architecture, and the Arts, and the Director of the Robotics and Digital Fabrication lab at Florida International University. Vassigh has a nationally recognized body of research centered on addressing climate change challenges, and teaching sustainable design and resilient built environments leveraging advanced technologies. Her research has been supported by multiple federal grants from the National Science Foundation and the US Department of Education..

Biayna Bogosian, Ph.D. is an interdisciplinary researcher developing spatial media and immersive learning approaches to enhance urban environmental innovation and civic engagement with data and design. She currently serves as an Assistant Professor of Architectural Technology at Florida International University (FIU) and has an additional role in FIU's Department of Electrical & Computer Engineering and Institute of Environment. She is the Associate Director of FIU Robotics and Digital Fabrication Lab. Since 2021, she has been a member of the ACADIA Board of Directors. Her research is supported by NSF and NASA grants.

Height-active Wood: Elasticity, Anisotropicity, and Hygroscopicity in Timber High-Rises

Nima Zahiri
NTNU: Norwegian University of Science and Technology
Department of Manufacturing and Civil Engineering Faculty of Engineering

INTRODUCTION

The term 'height-active' coined by Heino Engel refers to "structure systems, of which the main task is to collect loads from horizontal planes . . . and to vertically transmit them to the base . . . or high-rises accordingly." (Engel 2013, 14) The focus of this paper is on the characteristics of height-active wood structures due to their vertical extension and susceptibility to horizontal loading.

We shall argue that "more innovation can be expected from the advanced understanding of material characteristics, which can be integrated and taken advantage of in the design process, rather than homogenized, approximated or ignored." (Correa, Krieg and Meyboom 2019, 74) Conventional construction, insofar, has employed linear and planar wood elements in a hierarchical manner. There is an interest to take advantage of wood's flexibility to innovate free-form high-rise wood structures.

Digitized material application of wood has a wide range of technical and functional adaptation. This field notes essay highlights the importance of three main material characteristics of wood – elasticity, anisotropicity, hygroscopicity – for structural design typology of evolving high-rise endeavors.

ELASTICITY: INNOVATIONS IN FORM GENERATION

The use of elastic bending form-finding in long-spans is not common, but not impossible. "The Romans, for example, were notable for their use of wood in the construction of bridges that spanned rivers and in the multi-storey apartment blocks (insula) that housed a million residents in ancient Rome." (ARUP 2019, 10) Also, the planks of Viking age ships were cut along the natural grain of the wood with axes and wedges. This made them more flexible and easier to serve as bending-active plates.

The most pioneer modern architectural example, "the lattice shell of the Multihalle in Mannheim by Frei Otto" dates to 1975. In practice, the application of bending-active wood in high-rises is fundamentally understood to be dangerous due to uncontrollable large deflection under lateral loading conditions. Nevertheless, Helsinki Zoo tower lets the grid follow a vertical extension.

Rather than relying on complex steel joints or steel frame to build a framework for a timber skin or covering, the elastic natural bending of wood is strongly incorporated to the fluidity of form in design practice of building skins, compared to illogical linear timber elements to build a spatial framework.

ANISOTROPICITY: INNOVATIONS IN STRUCTURE

Anisotropic characteristic of wood, and consequently, variable stiffness in relation to grain orientation, enable elastic bending behavior in relation to the forces, through which a specific overall morphology can be form-found. Accessing the anisotropic property of wood for structural application requires a thorough understanding of each type of wood's material setup.

There are many examples of bending-active wood structure, but this approach has not been applied for relatively high-rise structures, in which we are usually dealing with greater forces, so "wood's varied dimensional range has been addressed through standardization, its heterogeneous fiber structure ground and reconstituted into homogeneous composites, and finally its complex aesthetic quality has even been caricaturized into a skin-deep plastic-wood veneer texture." (Correa, Krieg and Meyboom 2019, 61)

"In bending active structures residual stress caused by elastic deformation is used to act against external forces."
(Correa, Krieg and Meyboom 2019, 71) "The problem of high building design particularly concerns problems related to the limitation of horizontal displacements ... and resistance to dynamic wind action and seismic effects." (Szolomicki and Golasz-Szolomicka 2019, 2) The residual stress in bending-active components in a vertical setup could resist the lateral surface loading and its fluid form could cooperate in an aerodynamic condition.

There are only a few projects that seek to extend the scale of bending-active plates for a greater span or height. "A growing body of computational design scholars have engaged computation with local culture to enable new methods and expressions in architecture." For instance, this is possible to achieve desired curvature on wood plates by "reinventing traditional steam bending techniques ... and reviving bamboo [craftspeople]." (Noel 2022, 5)

The surface-active wood structures are not only connected with local forms (i.e., domes or half cylinders), but also are stronger than flat surfaces. They usually exhibit higher structural performance and present a solution for free-form timber structures.

HYGROSCOPICITY: INNOVATIONS IN MANUFACTURING

"Because of its differentiated internal capillary structure, wood is hygroscopic. It absorbs and releases moisture in exchange with the environment and these fluctuations cause differential dimensional changes." (Menges 2009, 66) The hygroscopic expansion or contraction of wood by the relative moisture change is coupled with the elastic behavior and anisotropic characteristic of wood, which allow bending of timber for being used in free form curved surfaces.

In practice, such complex geometries require a certain advanced level of prefabrication. Although the timber industry tends to limit or control this dimensional change, the idea is to use and augment the hygroscopicity to create high-performance building systems. Hygroscopic effect of timber could give form "for large-scale curved mass timber by using bi-layered wood structures capable of self-shaping by moisture content changes." (Grönquist, et al. 2019, 1) Integration of this expansion effect has been used in only a few experimental applications of shape changes for manufacturing of, for instance, "Urbach Tower, a surface-active structure made of single-curved CLT components". (Aldinger, et al. 2019, 421)

CONCLUSION

Wood is receptive to parametrically driven forms, not only those enabled by processed machining, but also those form-found by the elastic bending behavior, which is deployed in many archetypes. This reinterpretation of form generation requires not only a deep understanding of wood's material complexity, but also engaging a wider range of digital tools. This integration fosters a from-follow-material approach in architecture, exhibiting a great range of variation in form.

Understanding material culture of wood results in innovation in design, structure, and fabrication. Computational design and digital fabrication coexist with the leverage of material use in high-rise construction. By looking into these material setup innovations, we try to strengthen the argument that systematic wood innovations have the potential to create a large change in typology of high-rise timber buildings.

REFERENCES

Aldinger, Lotte, Simon Bechert, Dylan Wood, Jan Knippers, and Achim Menges. "Design and Structural Modelling of Surface-Active Timber Structures Made from Curved CLT - Urbach Tower, Remstal Gartenschau 2019." In Impact: Design With All Senses, 419–432. Berlin: Proceedings of the Design Modelling Symposium, 2019.

ARUP. Rethinking Timber Buildings: Seven perspectives on the use of timber in building design and construction. London: Arup, 2019.

Connolly, Benjamin. Digital Regionalism: Identity, Place, and the Ottawa Train Station. Ottawa, Ontario: Carleton University, 2015.

Correa, David, Oliver David Krieg, and AnnaLisa Meyboom. "Beyond Form Definition: Material Informed Digital Fabrication in Timber Construction." In Digital Wood Design: Innovative Techniques of Representation in Architectural Design, edited by Fabio Bianconi and Marco Filippucci, 61-92. Switzerland: Springer, 2019.

Engel, Heino. Structure Systems. 5. Ostfildern: Hatje Cantz Verlage, 2013.

Green, Michael, and Jim Taggart. Tall Wood Buildings: Design, Construction and Performance. Edited by Ria Stein. Basel: Birkhäuser Verlag GmbH, 2017.

Grönquist, Philippe, Dylan Wood, Mohammad M. Hassani, Falk K. Wittel, Achim Menges, and Markus Rüggeberg. "Analysis of Hygroscopic Self-shaping Wood at Large Scale for Curved Mass Timber Structures." Science Advances 5, no. 9 (2019).

Menges, Achim. "Performative Wood: Integral Computational Design for Timber Constructions." ACADIA 09: reForm( ) - Building a Better Tomorrow [Proceedings of the 29th Annual Conference of the Association for Computer Aided Design in Architecture (ACADIA), 2009: 66-74.

Noel, Vernelle AA. "Computational Regionalism: De-familiarization of Tectonics in the Wire-bending Craft." International Journal of Architectural Computing, 2022.

Szolomicki, Jerzy, and Hanna Golasz-Szolomicka. "Technological Advances and Trends in Modern High-Rise Buildings." MDPI Buildings 9, no. 9 (2019).

Nima Zahiri is a PhD researcher within the Computational Design and Production of Wood Construction program at the Norwegian University of Science and Technology (NTNU).

Kathy Velikov is Professor and Associate Dean for Research and Creative Practice at the University of Michigan Taubman College of Architecture and Urban Planning. She is a licensed Architect, founding partner of the research-based practice rvtr (www.rvtr.com), which serves as a platform for exploration and experimentation in the intertwinements between architecture, the environment, technology, and sociopolitics. Her work ranges from material prototypes that explore new possibilities for architectural envelopes that mediate matter, energy, information, space, and atmosphere between bodies and environments, to the investigation of urban infrastructures and territorial practices. She is a recipient of the Architectural League's Young Architects Award and the Canadian Professional Prix de Rome in Architecture. Kathy is co-editor of Ambiguous Territory: Architecture, Landscape, and the Postnatural (Actar, 2022) and co-author of Infra Eco Logi Urbanism (Park Books, 2015). Kathy served as ACADIA President from 2018-2020 and Vice President from 2021-2022.

Terry Knight is the William and Emma Rogers Professor of Design and Computation in the Department of Architecture at the Massachusetts Institute of Technology. She conducts research and teaches in the area of computational design, with an emphasis on the theory and application of shape grammars and making grammars. Her book, Transformations in Design, is a well-known introduction to the field of shape grammars. She has published on grammar-related topics in design research journals, and co-edited grammar and computation themed journal issues. Her current research explores what abstract, formal, and discrete computation can tell us about the active, sensory, and continuous temporal nature of making.

Knight serves on the editorial boards of the Journal of Mathematics and the Arts, Design Science, and Design Studies. She is a co-editor of the Routledge book series, Design, Technology and Society.

Joseph Choma is the Director of the School of Architecture and a Professor of Architecture at Florida Atlantic University. Previously, he taught at The Cooper Union, MIT, and Clemson University. He was also the 2019-20 NCCR Digital Fabrication Researcher in Residence at the ETH Zurich. He has received awards from the American Institute of Architects and the American Composites Manufacturers Association. His material explorations have been noted by CompositesWorld Magazine as "spearheading research into the use of foldable composites." He is the inventor of Foldable Composite Structures — U.S. Patent Number 10,994,468. Additionally, he is the author of three books, Morphing: A Guide to Mathematical Transformations for Architects and Designers (2015), Études for Architects (2018) and The Philosophy of Dumbness (2020). Joseph completed graduate studies in design and computation at MIT and completed his PhD in Architecture at the University of Cambridge, where he was a Cambridge International Scholar.

Odile Decq has seen her notoriety and the success of her firm founded in 1978 grow ever more. Her work encompasses a comprehensive universe where architecture, design, art, and urbanism converge, challenging and complementing one another. With a direct style and assertive personality, she combines bold geometries and innovative creations across various domains.

International recognition came very early, in 1990, when she undertook her first major commission, the Banque Populaire de l'Ouest in Britanny. This project, accompanied by numerous publications and 10 national and international awards, symbolized a new hope arising from the punk-inspired revolt against conventional norms.

Notable architectural achievements include the MACRO in Rome, GL Events headquarters, the FRAC Museum, Tangshan Geopark Museum, and lately, the "Antares" tower in Barcelona.

In 2014, Odile Decq established the "Confluence Institute for Innovation and Creative Strategies in Architecture" in Paris where implements an innovative pedagogy emphasizing student autonomy and self-directed learning.

NADAAA is an architecture and urban design firm led by principal designer **Nader Tehrani**, winner of the American Academy of Arts and Letter's 2020 Arnold W. Brunner Prize, member of the Cooper Hewitt, and newly elected member of the American Academy of Arts and Sciences. Tehrani is also professor and former Dean of The Cooper Union's Irwin S. Chanin School of Architecture.

NADAAA has evolved over three decades with a focus on the transformation of the building industry, innovative material applications, and the development of new means and methods of construction, especially through digital fabrication. Rather than focus on typology, NADAAA's portfolio is built on process, with examples of institutional, academic, housing, commercial, and civic projects.

NADAAA boasts an unprecedented nineteen Progressive Architecture Awards, numerous national and international awards, and consistently places among the top design firms in Architect's annual ranking, where it has been selected as the top national firm three years in a row.

AWARDS EVENT

Society Award for Leadership

Kathy Velikov
Professor and Associate Dean for Research and Creative Practice, University of Michigan Taubman College of Architecture and Urban Planning and Co-Founder RVTR

CULTIVATING A COMMUNITY OF PRACTICE

A community of practice can be defined as a group of individuals who "deepen their knowledge and expertise" around a shared topic of concern by "interacting on an ongoing basis." (Wenger et al., 2002, 10)

Because communities of practice are voluntary, what makes them successful over time is their ability to generate enough excitement, relevance, and value to attract and engage members. Although many factors…can inspire a community, nothing can substitute for this sense of aliveness. (Wenger et al., 2002, 46)

What produces this sense of aliveness as proposed by the authors of the book "Cultivating Communities of Practice" (Wenger et al., 2002, chap. 3), are design principles, which are intentional and strategic. These are activities and practices that have the underspecified goals to enable a community to develop, to maintain the fluidity of its boundaries, to enable differing levels of participation, to orchestrate group events and encourage interpersonal webs of relationships, to provide value to its members, to be simultaneously familiar and exciting, and to find the right rhythm of activities.

ACADIA is simultaneously a formalized organization, as well as a community of practice, that embodies that very sense of "aliveness." This has been produced not only because ACADIA has incorporated many of the principles that are characteristic of thriving groups, but primarily because of the people involved in producing, reproducing, and building anew that which we call ACADIA. The members of this community generously bring their curiosity, excitement, knowledge, and their willingness to share to each gathering and to ACADIA's activities. This, for me, is what I most deeply value about ACADIA—the colleagues, friends, collaborators, role models, and agitators—whose conversations, debates, and collaborations nourish and inspire my work, who challenge me to continually think about our work in new ways, and who help me think about work that we should produce together.

I first became aware of ACADIA in 2004, when the conference was hosted by Waterloo and Toronto. At the time, I was working professionally in Toronto, and teaching intermittently at both schools of architecture. I remember well the buzz, the exhibition, and the excitement of my colleagues that ACADIA had arrived in Ontario. A few years later in 2008, when I had begun to teach full time, and was in the process of spooling up our research-based

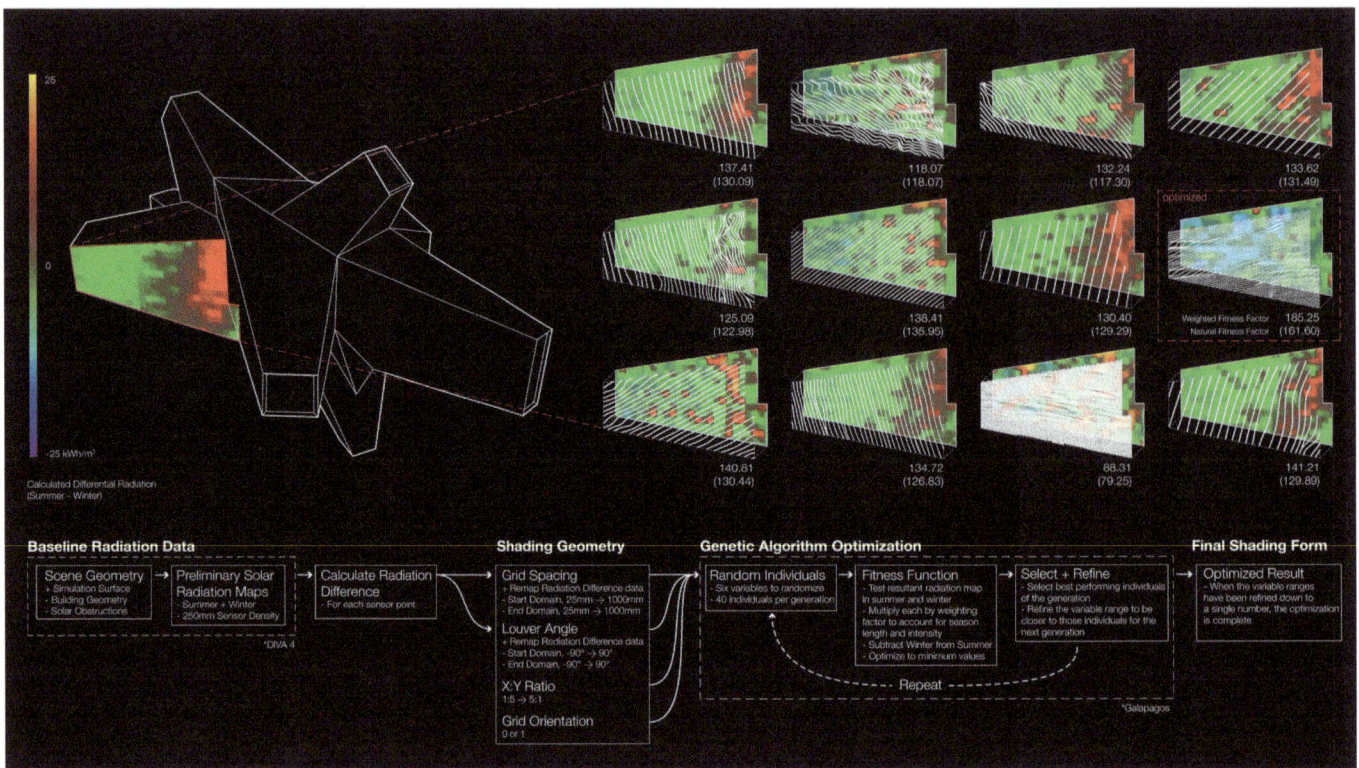

1   *Latitudo Borealis* computational design workflow using climate data and genetic algorithm optimization to produce the final shading configuration. Image by RVTR, 2017.

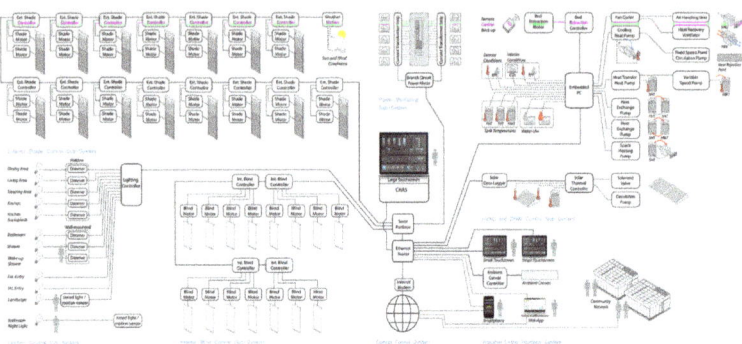

2   North House building prototype (above) total systems diagram of North House systems indicating addressable envelope components, HVAC equipment, smart-grid address, CHAS hierarchy and interface logics (below). For full credits see: https://www.rvtr.com/projects/north-house (©RVTR, 2009).

3   The Stratus Project installed prototype for an interior envelope as a thick, sensing dermis, reacting physically and in real time to humans and the air environment. For full credits see: https://www.rvtr.com/projects/stratus (©RVTR, 2011).

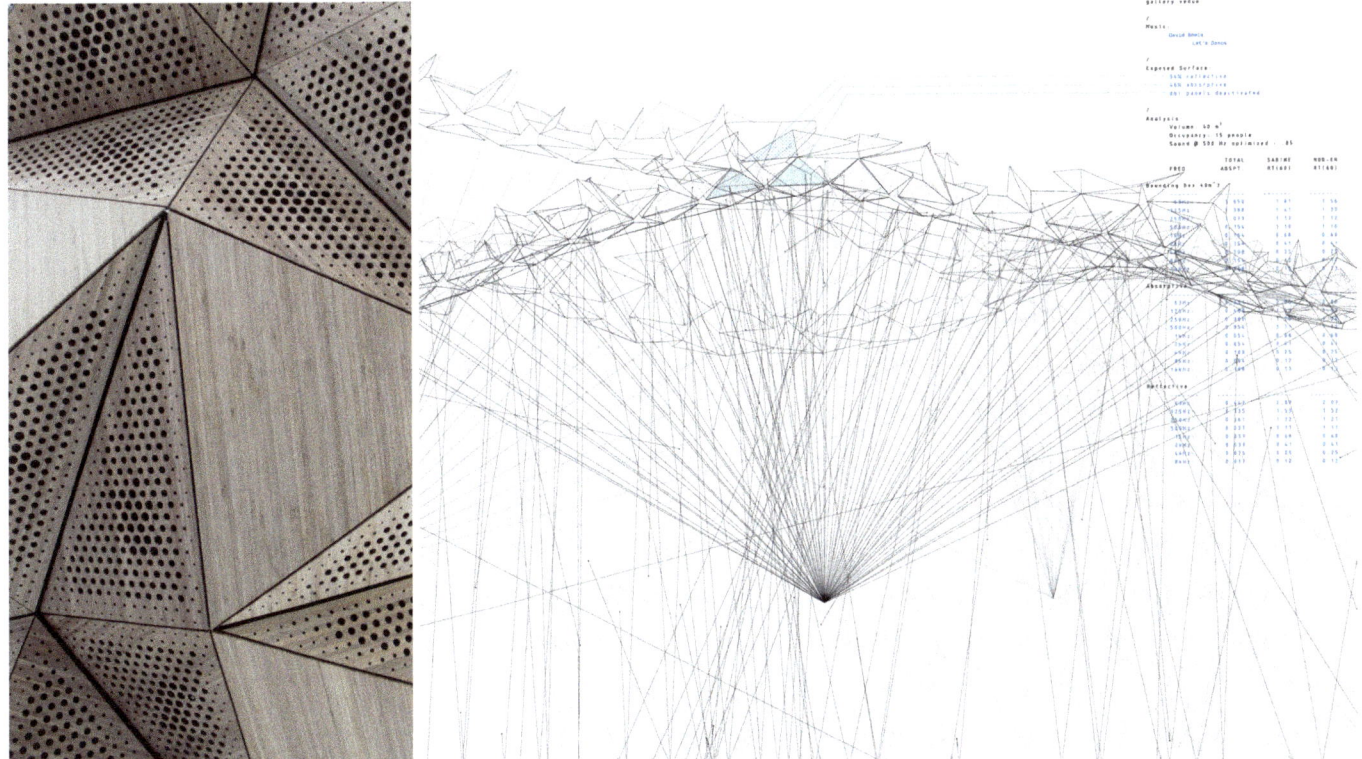

4   *Resonant Chamber* kinetic acoustic system prototype detail (left) and variable acoustic positioning and performance simulations (right). For full credits see: https://www.rvtr.com/projects/resonant-chamber (©RVTR, 2013).

practice RVTR, and collaborating with three universities on our North House project (Figure 2), the potentials for computational design and computational thinking to be a central ally in the work became apparent. It was thanks to our collaborators on that project, and particularly Phillip Beesley, that computational processes for design beyond the goals of form-making really opened up for me. I became deeply interested in behavioral paradigms for adaptive and interactive systems; how buildings could become sensing agents and constitute, in themselves, responsive systems that develop relations between humans and the environment.

After accepting positions at the University of Michigan in 2009, my partner Geoffrey Thün, and I initiated a series of projects that we refer to as responsive envelopes. These were speculative prototypes for novel building skins that combined performative geometries, aggregate assemblies, kinetics, and a sensing and control-based proto nervous system that simultaneously engaged dynamic environmental mediation, as well as questions of biopolitics and relational aesthetics. The ACADIA community of practice was then a ground in which to test these ideas and share our work.

The first ACADIA conference I attended was in 2011, where we presented The Stratus Project (Figure 3), a physical prototype and self-sensing environmentally responsive interior envelope system that constructs relations between breathers and the localized air environment. It was there that I realized what a remarkable community ACADIA was. I discovered a group that delighted in a sense of discovery, the open sharing of ideas, and the pushing of new boundaries, and it is this that I have continued to experience at every conference ever since. Geoffrey and I continued to work with architectural behavior(s) relative to a set of concerns—the matters of air, acoustics, thermal transfer—and how these might relate to architectural form, performance, and conception in subsequent experimental prototypes: Resonant Chamber, PneuSystems, Infundibuliforms (Figure 5), and Latitudo Borealis (Figure 1). More recent work has focused on multi-optimization solvers for environmental performance parameters, and with computational tools and environmental visualization at the territorial scale, as well as for urban access. We have collaborated on these with numerous colleagues, including those well known here—Wes McGee, Dan Tish, and Matias del Campo—and we have learned from many more.

Communities of Practice are voluntary ones; membership is not enforced by any institution or obligation. This

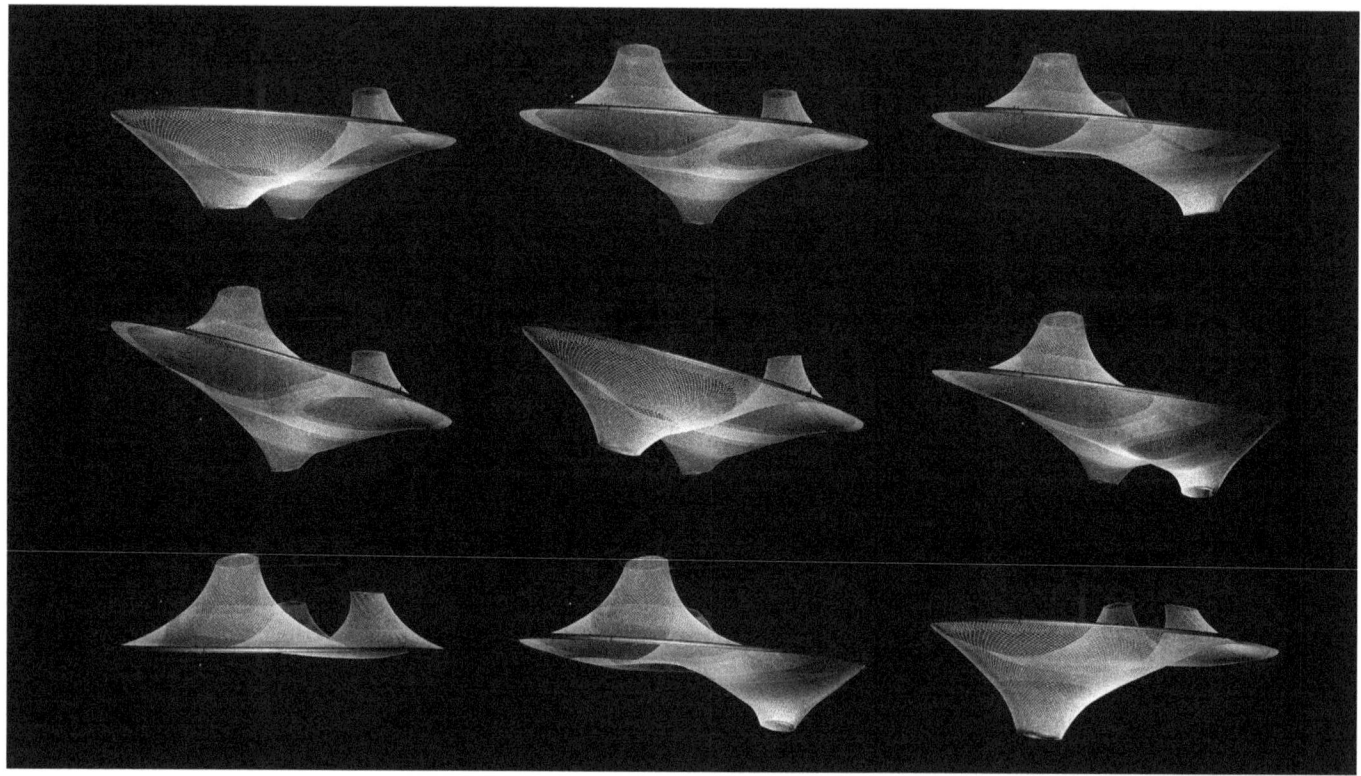

5   *Infundibuliforms* prototype for a kinetic cable-robot controlled surface in variable positions. For full credits see: https://www.rvtr.com/projects/infundibuliforms (©RVTR, 2016).

characteristic is what gives agency to the members to shape and reshape that community. It was not until I was elected to the Board of Directors, in 2015 and co-chaired the 2016 conference at the University of Michigan, that I began to appreciate the nature of this voluntary work: the combination of maintenance, stewardship, and leadership that is undertaken by the board, officers, and conference organizers. In this, I continued to learn from my colleagues, particularly former president Jason Kelly Johnson, and other colleagues. Serving as president starting in 2018, I also realized the ways that the "sense of aliveness"—of maintaining vitality, relevance, and value —can be cultivated through intentional actions that seed, stimulate, and nurture transformation, while they may also reshape and stabilize the core.

ACADIA has passed through many changes during the period I served on the board as president, and vice president. In 2015, the year I ran would be the last time (I hope) that there was only one female on the election docket. In 2021, all five of the newly appointed full board members were women. Starting in 2018, with the conference in Mexico City, ACADIA began to host conversations that introduced critical perspectives regarding the use of tools, access, equity, and alternative voices and approaches. ACADIA also expanded its community, particularly to underrepresented groups, by forging relationships with universities in Mexico, with National Organization of Minority Architects (NOMA), and since 2020, has been streaming conferences for free to students globally.

I am privileged to have been part of the incredibly dedicated and inspired group of ACADIA board members, officers, and conference chairs serving during this period, and doing what part I could in helping to maintain and amplify the goals and potential(s) of this organization -- one that is continuously vital, relevant, evolving, and that always knows how to throw a good party; because, after all, this is where we really meet and discuss how to shape collective futures of this amazing ACADIA community of practice.

REFERENCES

1. Wenger, Etienne, Richard McDermott, William Snyder. (2002) Cultivating Communities of Practice a Guide to Managing Knowledge. Harvard Business School Press, 10.
2. Ibid, 46.
3. Ibid, Chapter Three.

Teaching Award of Excellence

Terry Knight
Professor of Design and Computation
Massachusetts Institute of Technology

TEACHING STATEMENT

My work is research focused. Broadly speaking, I'm interested in the "How" of creative production, as opposed to the "What". I ask "How is this?" not "What is this?" I am interested in "How" designs and things are made or become, in the processes or paths to form, whether abstract or material. As a process carried out over time, computation offers a unique means for understanding and describing the "How" of design and making. I explore this potential with shape grammars and, most recently, with making grammars. The unique visual and spatial nature of the rules and computations of these grammars is aimed at unveiling the "How" in design.

My primary teaching responsibilities at MIT include a course on Visual Computing (grammars) for undergraduate and graduate students, and a graduate seminar, Inquiry into Computation and Design, which is grounded in the work of our computation faculty and in the history of computation. Figures 1-6 that follow illustrate work from my Visual Computing course.

Here are a few teaching principles I (try to) use across my courses.

Suspend Your Disbelief

This is one of the first things I tell students. They may be about to hear something they have never heard before and may sound far-fetched ("computation without computers?"). I ask students to temporarily put aside any incredulity to engage with the material introduced, and to accept that the value of a class may not be apparent to them until the end of the course or even much later (perhaps never). Often, it is those initial disbelievers who come up with the most imaginative ideas.

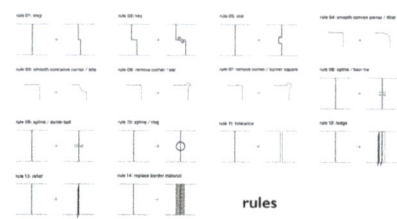
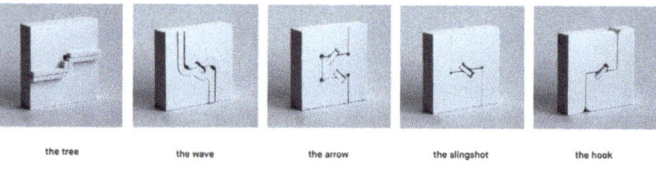
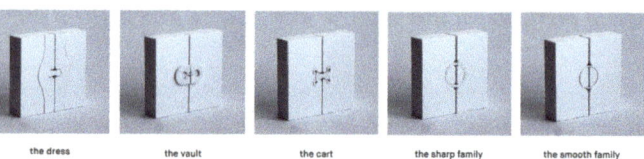

1   Over/Under: Timber - Bamboo Modular Dwelling (Wu Ji "Ryan", 2021)

2   Interlocking Detail Grammar (Ariza Inez, 2015).

So What?

This principle – a question, actually – is related to Suspend Your Disbelief. I think I am renowned in my Inquiry seminar for this question. It's a tough question that needs to be asked continually. When students present their own work or the work of others, I ask them "So What?" What is the problem being explored and why should anyone, apart from the author of the work, care about it? What will motivate someone to suspend their possible disbelief? I ask myself the "So What?" question over and over every time I start a new research project.

The Toolmaker's Paradigm

The Toolmaker's Paradigm is a radical model of communication introduced as a critique of a pervasive and corrosive misconception about communication called the Conduit Metaphor. The Conduit Metaphor, introduced by the linguist Michael Reddy, likens communication to putting our thoughts in a container (or words), sending the container through a physical conduit to a listener/reader who simply unpacks the container (words) to retrieve and understand the thoughts of the sender, with no effort. By contrast, the Toolmaker's Paradigm assumes that successful communication and understanding is highly effortful. We each inhabit our own cultural, social, and personal environment, with our own "tools" or ways of working and living. People from different environments, backgrounds, and experiences must work hard through numerous, back-and-forth exchanges to build mutual understanding, meaning, and trust. I assume the Toolmaker's Paradigm in teaching. To create an inclusive and equitable classroom, I work to understand and respond to the diverse perspectives of my students – to see their ideas, intentions, and work as they see them.

Have a Point of View

Perspective-taking is important, but it's equally important for an instructor to have, and express, their own point of view as a locus for a class. Curating the views of others is not enough for learning. Students look for, and learn, from the instructor's singular point of view, whether they agree with it or not.

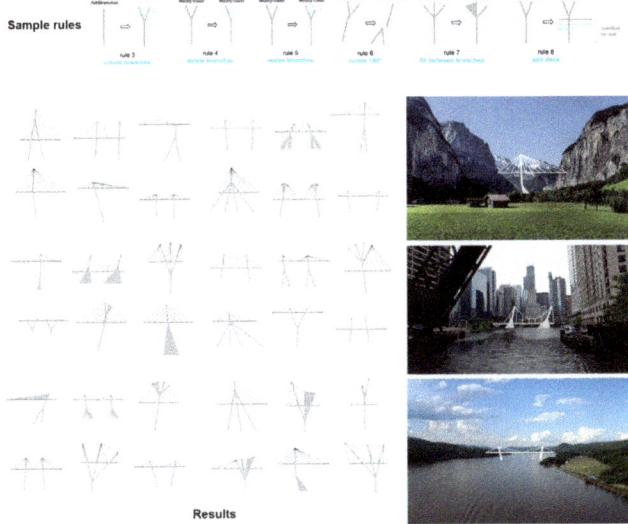

3   Trans-Typology Structural Grammar (Mueller Caitlin, 2011)

4   Prefab/Modular Apartments (Gealy Rachel, 2014)

Copying is Good

Copying is learning. Copying or reproducing another's ideas or work is a powerful way to understand the work and then build on it. For class projects, I encourage students to copy from each other, for example, to take a classmate's grammar they admire, develop it, and make it their own. There's no such thing as "starting from scratch". I don't have much success with students with this idea because our culture continues to celebrate and reward individual originality and achievement, but I persist in encouraging it.

Collaborate, Construct, and Slow Down

I promote collaborative, active, doing and making in my classes. Making tangible, public artifacts for reflection and conversation is key to learning. I also promote slowness. In my Visual Computing course, students practice unhurried, reflective, by-hand shape calculations in class to develop a rich understanding of the potentials of shape grammars and the "How" of design. Computers do not have a central role in this learning environment. Students are the computers – slow computers.

And to quote a colleague, most importantly... Have Fun

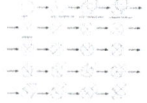

5   Building the Rock and the Hard Place (Luciano David, 2012)

6   Lygia Clark's Bichos (Eyzaguirre Jaya, 2017)

Figure 1: © Wu Ji "Ryan", 2021
Figure 2: © Ariza Inez, 2015
Figure 3: © Mueller Caitlin, 2011
Figure 4: © Gealy Rachel, 2014
Figure 5: © Luciano David, 2012
Figure 6: © Eyzaguirre Jaya, 2017

AWARDS EVENT

Innovative Research Award of Excellence

Joseph Choma
Professor of Architecture
Director of FAU School of
Architecture

Constraints as Opportunities

Transforming a single, flat sheet of material into a rigid, three-dimensional structure through folding seems simple and straightforward. However, it is precisely that self-explanatory nature of folding that is so attractive. When reflecting on my research in the area of foldable structures and materials, a series of conceptual ideas resonates with the work beyond the literal technical contributions (images 1 to 4).

There is nothing worse than seeing a student sitting at their desk, scratching their head, not knowing what to do. If you do not know what to do, do something. Sometimes within my research I do have a specific idea or problem which I am trying to solve. For example, designing an ultra-thin folded formwork for concrete casting. However, many times I just fold paper as a means to openly explore the unknown without any pragmatic agenda. In the end, both approaches (conceptually-driven and tool-driven) are equally valuable.

There is a quote by Rodney Brooks which I have memorized over the years. "The way in which a problem is decomposed imposes fundamental constraints on the way in which people attempt to solve that problem" (Brooks 1999). Depending on which tool or medium is utilized will influence the set of possible results. For example, folding a sheet of paper will yield a different set of choices than making a model with a series of sticks or by writing an algorithm. Each tool or medium has biases and constraints, which will lead to a different series of opportunities. That said, a tool is not just a tool, but an instrument-to-think-with (Choma 2018).

Instead of searching for an optimized solution, we can search for the most number of possible solutions, because choices are important (Foerster 2003). Just as Heinz Isler searched for more shell geometries (Isler 1961), my research continues to open up new possibilities for folding applications in architecture.

1 Above: Folded fiberglass arch spanning 16 feet; below: Four folded fiberglass structures.

2 Above: Folded fiberglass composed of twenty concentric circles; below: 8-foot-long folded fiberglass panel.

"Minimum means, maximum effect" (Albers 1969). A series of concentric circles on a piece of paper, may appear to be a trivial bullseye. However, after folding that pattern, alternating between mountain and valley folds, a three-dimensional saddle emerges (Wingler 1969). Sometimes the simplest two-dimensional crease patterns are the most powerful.

Within mathematics, there is the equation and the shape. The equation is the DNA or set of rules to describe the geometry. Similarly, within foldable structures there is the two-dimensional crease pattern, which is the instruction to describe the three-dimensional folded geometry. Whenever possible, it is valuable to explicitly and transparently describe geometries through a rule-based framework.

A physical model, purely used as a representational artifact, is drastically different from the way Frei Otto used physical models as a form of structural simulation (Otto and Rasch 1996). Similarly, a mock-up or full-scale prototype is drastically different from a model. When folding a paper model or folding a large-scale pop-up structure, you literally "feel" the structural forces through the geometry.

As a result, physical making should never be considered subservient to digital simulations.

There is an important distinction between technology and innovation. Oftentimes, the word technology is thought of as something "high-tech," such as robotic fabrication. Just because something is fabricated with a robotic arm does not make it innovative, and just because something is fabricated by hand does not make it obsolete.

We have an ethical obligation to not only design and build, but also to design the way in which something is built. Just because we can build it with our current means and methods does not mean we necessarily should.

It is important to understand the past as a means to move forward. We never design or conduct research in a vacuum. If a precedent is understood through a series of rules, it is possible for that analytical process to become generative. Before designing a "new" crease pattern, I almost always begin with an existing crease pattern and then transform it according to desired criteria.

3   Folding fiberglass along concentric curved creases..

4   Above: Detail of a concrete column which was cast in a folded paper formwork; below: Looking up at a folded fiberglass pop-up structure. The full-scale prototype spans 22 feet, stands 10 feet tall, and has a material thickness of 1/16 inch.

Lastly, it is important to remember to forget. Sometimes in order to see new opportunities, you need to forget how something has been done in the past. For example, when given fiberglass, the thought is you must use a mold. As soon as you intentionally "forget" how something is done (or how something is defined), you can "see" new possibilities (Choma 2020).

References

Albers, Joseph. 1969. Creative Education. In H. M. Wingler (Editor), The Bauhaus: Weimar, Dessau, Berlin, Chicago (pp. 142–43). Cambridge, MA: MIT Press.

Brooks, Rodney A. 1999. Cambrian Intelligence: The Early History of the New AI. Cambridge, MA: MIT Press.

Choma, Joseph. 2018. Études for Architects. New York: Routledge.

Choma, Joseph. 2020. The Philosophy of Dumbness. Novato, CA: ORO Editions.

Foerster, Heinz von. 2003. Understanding Understanding: Essays on Cybernetics and Cognition. New York: Springer.

Isler, H. 1961. New Shapes for Shells, Bulletin of the International Association for Shell Structures, 8, (pp. 123–130).

Otto, Frei and Rasch, Bodo. 1996. Finding Form: Towards an Architecture of the Minimal. Stuttgart: Axel Menges.

Wingler, Hans M. 1969. The Bauhaus: Weimar, Dessau, Berlin, Chicago. Cambridge, MA: The MIT Press.

AWARDS EVENT

Design Excellence Award

Odile Decq
Founder of Studio Odile Decq and Confluence Institute for Innovation and Creative Strategies in Architecture

STUDIO ODILE DECQ PHILOSOPHY

In a society where all productions tend to insidiously become uniform, ignoring any cultural particularism, historical or social, the philosophy of Studio Odile Decq (the Studio) has always been to be specific and particular. By questioning the command, the use, the matter, the body, the technique, and the taste, the invented architecture offers a paradoxical look, at the same time tender and severe, on our world. In a creative and positive work process, the obstacles are always transformed into advantages, all while developing a specific image for each project with the most advanced contemporary technologies.

On the occasion of the realization of numerous architectural projects, the Studio has also often developed the interior fittings and the furniture, in a continuity of thought and in relation with needs, each time different and specific. The Studio's work is a complete universe, in which architecture, design, art and urbanism come together, challenge each other, and respond to each other. The direct style of Odile Decq is matched by her architecture, with bold geometries and innovative creations. In the same continuity, the Studio interfaces with industrial companies, in fields as dåiverse as lighting, acoustics, glazing, and furniture design, responding each time to special technical requirements. The conceptual process, centered around experimentation, is closely followed by Odile Decq herself. Thus, the design includes, from the start all the parameters to succeed, in an initially iterative approach, to arrive at a perfectly integrated project.

Our global approach is more about hypotheses than doctrines. To develop a theory is to call on the imagination, creativity, and invention. It's imagining a mode of operation, a process, rules of the game, and relationships between elements that attempt to explain phenomena whose mechanisms we don't know. It means establishing provisional principles and then subjecting them to experimentation. Such a process leaves plenty of room for doubt and lack of certainty. Because it is part of a research process, a theory's interest lies in its creative potential. It is an attitude of permanent dissatisfaction, of doubt that leads to the constant need to shift and question. Faced with the inefficiency of some

1 Antares Tower, Barcelona, 2015. Image by Fernando Guerra.
2 Banque Populaire de l'Ouest, Rennes, 1990. Image by Stephane Couturier.

systems at our disposal, we try to respond to circumstances in a state of relative uncertainty.

Confrontation with complexity, successive experiments, analysis and criticism of results, without preconceived ideas, have led us to adopt an attitude of continuous adaptation and adjustment. To design is to confront circumstances, to accept hazards, to play with contradictions, to accept and amplify the possibilities of ambiguity... in other words, to be open to possibility. Always being on the edge of a precipice, on the brink of breaking and falling, is in essence a situation of total instability. Faced with this feeling of permanent swell, we have always thought that being in motion, moving and advancing, enabled us to keep our balance. To stand still is to fall! Since everything around us is moving and changing, the world creates a situation of instability and movement, which we use to our advantage. It is this search for balance in movement that guides our creation.

"To be imaginative is to take risks in the face of ready-made thinking", says astrophysicist Jean Pierre Luminet. To live is to take risks, to create is to take risks, to design is to take risks, and to take these risks, you need to have the courage to assert what you think, and to see our ideas through to fruition. The old French expression "l'aventure est au coin de la rue" ("Adventure stands at the street corner") meant that everyone had access to their share of exaltation. To discover is to take the risk of the unknown and of what is different. Creation, like scientific research, means accepting that our certainties are called into question, and to travel is to desire the strangeness of people and places.

"Travelling towards the horizon is both an adventure and a negotiation.
The horizon can never be reached.
The horizon is never unique, but constructed from multiple points of view.
The horizon line is a permanent temptation, exciting the desire for the beyond.
The absence of limits blurs perception and creates ambiguity, fusion and illusion.
Awareness of the elsewhere and perception of the space beyond generate a mutual attraction on either side of the horizon.
Crossing the horizon is like going through the looking glass, but unlike Alice's world, the other side is not upside down.
It's simply beyond.
Such is architecture."

- Odile Decq

3   Top: Experimental Glass House© Philippe Ruault.

4   Bottom: FRAC ©Odile Decq - Roland Halbe.

5 Top: MACRO (c) Roland Halbe

6 Bottom: Tangshan Museum (c) Roland Halbe

KEYNOTE EVENT

Digital Practice Award of Excellence

Nader Tehrani
Principal of NADAAA

PRINCIPLES: OF UNLEARNING
The terms research, practice, and pedagogy form a trinity that many architectural academics share as an ethic—that when left unchecked can easily lapse into cliché. In this sense, establishing a set of principles around the three terms is an important step to articulate their meanings, practices, and motivations. In this instance, I might supplant "play" for research, "resistance" for practice, and "learning" for teaching, if not to polemicize the terms, but simply to clarify how behind the declaration of titles there almost always lies other activities that characterize our work in a more productive way.

For all the weight that bears on research practices in both history and the sciences—and from which we borrow as architects—the process of design most resembles a form of play, a term frequently demoted for its lack of scholarly connotations. Still, it is in this very play that the designer solves riddles, uncovers patterns, and makes forensic discoveries. For all the conceptual questions posed by academics at large, the architect's agency revolves around their ability to translate them into formal, spatial, and material specifications, however speculatively. Consider the sheer pleasure of being able to produce new forms of knowledge through play, that in the establishment of principles, truths may be uncovered a posteriori through the interplay of accident, happenstance, and a bit of failure.

If research is meant to leave behind a trail of certainty, then the hope is that it translates into forms of practice that yield the highest level of professionalism. At the same time, the temporal cadence of institutional practices often tends to unravel at a slower pace than what research yields, almost always ensuring they are out of synch. With much of zoning ordinances, codes, and basic laws of architectural engagement constraining design processes, this means that the actual reach of young designers is often far more

1   Entrelac Detail. Image by Roland Halbe

limited in professional practice than in a more speculative environment. For this reason, as we view the calcification of construction practices, the legal mandates that limit the architect's control over means-and-methods, among a host of other things, it is primarily through resistance that we uncover possibilities of disciplinary evolution, architectural invention, and the advancement of the institution at large.

Considering this, the framing of pedagogical mandates revolving around the preparation of students for practice often seems misplaced: what does it mean to prepare young architects for practices that are on the verge of obsolescence? This is not a challenge to all professional practices, but more so to the ideological underpinnings that suggest that professors are able to 'teach' with unambiguous certainty--when arguably the academy is better positioned as an open environment from which all can 'learn', even professors. Developing pedagogical environments that frame spaces of intellectual exchange amongst disciplines will help to situate architecture within a larger social and political context, also allowing its professors to learn from different intellectual forces outside the autonomy of their own cohorts.

In play, resistance, and learning, there is also the shadow of unlearning: that is, not only the capacity to internalize new material, but indeed to overcome that which one has ingested over a lifespan, what becomes naturalized, conventional, and institutionally expected. The capacity to incorporate alternative methods of analysis, the utilization of unprecedented models of representation and simulation, the anamorphic view onto a well-known canon, the capacity to critique one's own position—these all contribute to a productive environment of unlearning, the ability to expand by shedding habits and the revelation of ideological veils.

Within this context, the assembly of our work oscillates between three poles of reference, research begetting play, practice prompting resistance, and pedagogy calling for alternative modes of learning. Research has been conducted through material explorations, challenges to the means and methods of fabrication, and the invocation of inventive aggregations. By way of small-scale installations, Entrelac and Compressive Catenary are two examples of how structural and material play open new trajectories of work: Entrelac through collaborations with local weavers, whose labor is translated beyond the exhibition towards refugee blankets in Syria, and Compressive

3 Villa Varoise. Image by John Horner

8 Melbourne School of Design Coffer Delivery. Photo by Latreille Delage

6 Melbourne School of Design Studio Hall, Photograph by John Horner

Catenary whose distributed structural units form a field of keystones that keep a suspended vault locked in compressive tension, imagining new and improbable structural modalities.

In practice, we confront the intersection of a stubborn building industry loathsome of risk while at the same time, we confront trades whose skills are beckoning space for transformation. To this, we bring a combination of resistance and critical collaboration, with Villa Varoise and Tanderrum Bridge deploying salient local practices towards new heights. For Villa Varoise, working with local concrete manufacturers, we were able to concoct a mixture of local earth to achieve the warmth of Mediterranean colors, while deploying boat builders for the formwork, whose ruled surfaces form the underbelly of an extraordinary threshold, what is at the same time normative to maritime structures. For the Tanderrum Bridge, the simple appropriation of rebar bending protocols establishes a mode of weaving the envelope of the bridge to include its structural body –manifesting the maximum moment, wrapping its railings, and extending the lighting, all from the same system.

Finally, in spaces of pedagogy, we are able to capture not only schools of thought, but didactic moments within its architecture, whose relative failures and successes become manifest in the very details of the buildings they articulate. In both the Melbourne School of Design and the Daniels Building, the roofs establish the buildings' paradigmatic moments, not only as structural feats, but the basis for daylighting, programmatic transformation, and hydrological control. These buildings don't so much teach as help students to unlearn what a classical education might have entailed, deploying speculations tested out at the scale of installations, instigating resistance to conventions of construction, and enabling forms of invention.

HABITS OF THE ANTHROPOCENE
KEYNOTE
PROLOGUE PANEL
HABITS OF THE
ANTHROPOCENE

This session focuses on the ever-evolving tapestry of biological design, urban informatics, and experimental fabrication research. These groundbreaking trajectories have emerged, challenging our perceptions of the built environment. The first delves deep into the confluence of architecture and biology, presenting a radical reimagination of design principles. Here, traditional architectural paradigms are recalibrated through the lens of bioinformatics, synthetic biology, and materials science. This line of inquiry introduces the concept of 'biodesign', where living organisms are not mere bystanders, but active participants and collaborators in the design process. Structures envisioned through this lens possess the ability to 'metabolically' adapt, akin to organisms responding to environmental stimuli. The implications are profound, suggesting a future where the built environment exhibits homeostasis, dynamically balancing and adjusting to external and internal changes. Such an approach holds the promise of dramatically reducing the embodied energy of materials, and crafting structures capable of adapting to climatic shifts and aberrations. The second trajectory centers on the synthesis of urban informatics and responsive fabrication. Here, the city is not viewed merely as a physical entity, but as a cyber-physical system, deeply embedded within networks of data and computation. Materials and fabrication practices come to the forefront of shaping cities in an age of scarcity. Drawing inspiration from computational design, embedded systems, and urban ecology, this research postulates cities that are both responsive and predictive, and that utilize contemporary waste streams. Through decentralized data networks, urban morphology becomes a dynamic entity, constantly evolving based on real-time data and feedback loops. This vision shifts fabrication paradigms away from static outcomes, embracing a fluidity that is data-driven, adaptive, and aligned with material availability and optimized site-specific morphologies.

Both these research avenues challenge entrenched academic dichotomies and offer fresh perspectives that can redefine the very foundations of architecture and established construction methods. As we delve deeper into these ideas today, let us be prepared to question, reimagine, and embrace the transformative potential they present. When we fuse these two trajectories, we unearth a vision of the future where buildings and cities operate in symbiosis. The structures, living and breathing through principles of biodesign, communicate and align with an urban fabric that's digitally attuned to its inhabitants and the environment. It's a harmonious feedback loop, where biology informs data, and data guides biology. This convergence of ideas signals new models for making, challenging us to reimagine architecture and cities, not as distinct entities, but as interconnected ecosystems pulsating with life and technology.

Assia Crawford

Site Chair

Martyn Dade-Robertson is a Professor of Emerging Technology at Newcastle University, where he specializes in Design Computation with a special interest in emerging technologies, particularly Synthetic Biology. Martyn's core research is in the emerging field of Bio Design – specializing in Synthetic Biology, a field that applies engineering design thinking, from fields such as electronic engineering and computing science to biological systems. In the UK, Synthetic Biology has been heralded as one of the "Eight Great Technologies", which includes, for example, robotics and advanced materials. Martyn has led multiple research groups, including the EPSRC Funded Projects Computational Colloids and Thinking Soils, both concerned with developing bacteria-based sensors capable of detecting mechanical changes in their environment and synthesizing strengthening materials. He is also the founder of the Hub for Biotechnology in the Built Environment (HBBE), a new research center integrating design, biology, and engineering to develop new 'living' buildings. The Hub consists of more than 30 researchers, and hosts 4 new research facilities, including an experimental house called the "OME".

Martyn Dade-Robertson holds degrees in Architectural Design, Architectural Computation, and Synthetic Biology. He studied Architectural Design as an undergraduate at Newcastle University, and later at Cambridge University for an MPhil and PhD funded by the Arts and Humanities Research Council. His focus throughout the early part of his career was on 'Information Architecture', specializing in information systems, drawing parallels between the topological organization of physical and digital information spaces. His PhD was supervised in the Schools of Architecture and of Computing at Cambridge, and was nominated for the Royal Institute of British Architects' research prize, and was published as a Routledge book entitled "The Architecture of Information". He is currently the editor for a Routledge book series on Bio Design, and has completed the first book of the series entitled "Living Construction in 2020".

Areti Markopoulou is a Greek PhD architect, researcher, and urban technologist working at the intersection between architecture and digital technologies. Her research and practice focus on redefining the architecture of cities through an ecological and technological spectrum combining design with biotechnologies, new materials, digital fabrication, and big data. She currently holds the position of Academic Director at IAAC in Barcelona, and she leads the Advanced Architecture Group, a multidisciplinary research group exploring how design and science can positively impact and transform the present and future of our built environment. She is co-editor at Urban Next, a global network focused on rethinking architecture through the contemporary urban milieu, and has been consulting and developing urban and research projects on topics including urban regeneration through data science (Leading Cities), guidelines for urban technologies in public space (Barcelona City Council), circular design and construction (Digital Matter), and multidisciplinary educational models in the digital age (IAAC, SISD, UNIGE).

Markopoulou is the editor and co-author of "Learning Cities" from Actar in 2022, "Edible" from TAB, 2022, " Black Ecologies" also by Actar, published in 2019, and "Disrupting through Circular Design" from IAAC 2019. She is the chair of Responsive Cities International Symposium that she co-founded in Barcelona in 2016, and she has served as Head Curator of international exhibitions such as Edible at TAB 2022; Future Arena & On Site Robotics for Building Barcelona Construmat 2017-19; Print Matter atIn3dustry 2016; HyperCity at the Shenzhen Bi-city Biennale, 2015; BB MAKE for Beijing Design Week, 2014; and, MyVeryOwnCity at World Bank, BR Barcelona, 2011. In 2022, she was appointed the Head Co-Curator for the Tallinn Architecture Biennale 2022 under the theme "Edible, Or, The Architecture of Metabolism".

Urban Mining: Material Resources for Circular Construction

Areti Markopoulou
IAAC, Institute for Advanced Architecture of Catalonia

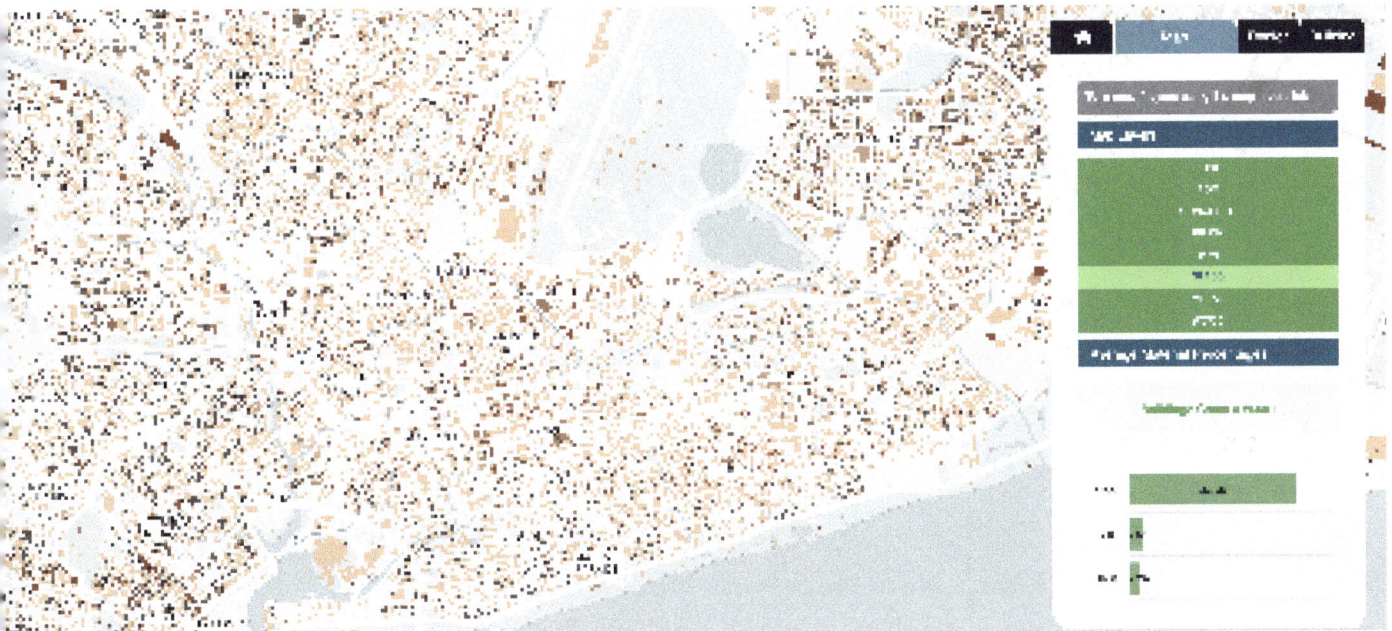

Towards a paradigm of resource abundance
The material balance of the Earth is being challenged. The year 2020 was marked as the year when the total weight of human-made materials globally surpassed the weight of all life on Earth, while it is estimated that in the years to come the growth rate of mass added to the anthroposphere will increase exponentially (Elhacham et al., 2020). In this context of hypergrowth coupled with the climate emergency, the growing rate of urbanization and the increasing social and political awareness on the matters of the Anthropocene, the topics of resource depletion or insufficiency are being reframed.

This keynote lecture at ACADIA 2023 highlights the importance of redefining resources and is introducing a new cultural, design and construction paradigm. Operating from an abundance mindset rather than from scarcity (Gausa et al., 2020) presents a new paradigm, particularly relevant in the design and production of the built environment. This approach expands the definition of resources, encompassing raw, non-raw, renewable, and recyclable materials. Shifting attention to the Anthroposphere as a source rather than just a destination for processed goods has the potential to disrupt linear design patterns and enhance circularity in cities and the built environment.

Within three scales of design and planning, the keynote lecture delivered at ACADIA 2023 presented current research – developed at the Institute for Advanced Architecture of Catalonia (IAAC) – that examines the applications of "waste to matter" processes driven computational technologies, digital manufacturing, robotics and life cycle assessment.

1   City library is an AI-driven digital interface developed to detect existing building material stock and enhance material reuse (© IAAC).

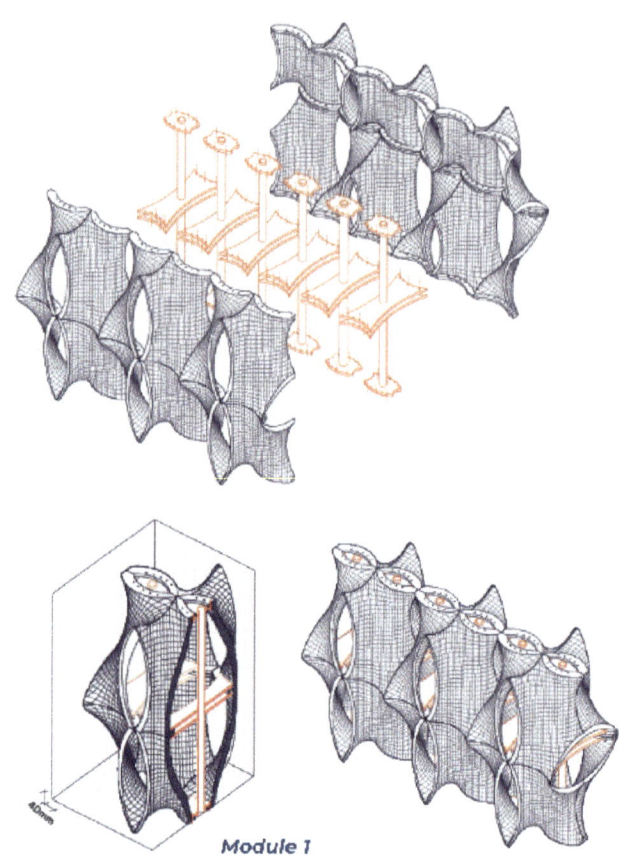

2   Geopolymer modular bricks free from any binding material and made from upcycling Construction and Demolition Waste (CDW), IAAC Digital Matter 2023

The goal of the research presented sets up protocols for enhancing processes of urban mining and material reuse in future circular construction. This is explored by developing methods for detecting, clustering and scoping material resources of existing building stock as well as urban and industrial waste streams while developing processes for material reuse.

In the material scale (i), selected projects from IAAC studio *Digital Matter* explores up-cycling waste for the creation of new engineered composites for construction. Starting from the material scale, we can observe that different types of urban or agricultural waste have the potential to become a new class of sustainable building composites through different processes that enhance their properties to match them with the building industry needs. From geopolymer derived from Construction and Demolition Waste, to upcycled cork, biochar or even polyester and the leftovers of a highly contaminating textile, these approaches explore the benefits and potentials of applying waste or 'pure' residue material in the Built Environment.

Additionally, 1:1 scale prototypes of 3d printed earth-based circular, 0km and affordable housing are presented as the outcome of the long term research of IAAC at the 3d printing Architecture program.

In the building scale (ii), diverse methods are presented to create digital twins applications that can contribute to the generation of Material Passports for buildings, documenting detailed information about the materials used, including their properties, lifespan, maintenance history, and end-of-life options. Additionally, the keynote presented research projects developed at IAAC *Robotics Lab* that use robotic or scanning technologies such as 3D Lidar combined with computer vision to scan on site and sort the materials from existing buildings intented for deconstruction or renovation, generating a database of elements that can be recycled and reused in circular construction (Batalle Garcia et al., 2021). Finally, in the urban scale (iii), the keynote showcased processes and tools developed by IAAC AI for Architecture & the Built Environment for combining image based segmentation with cadastral data

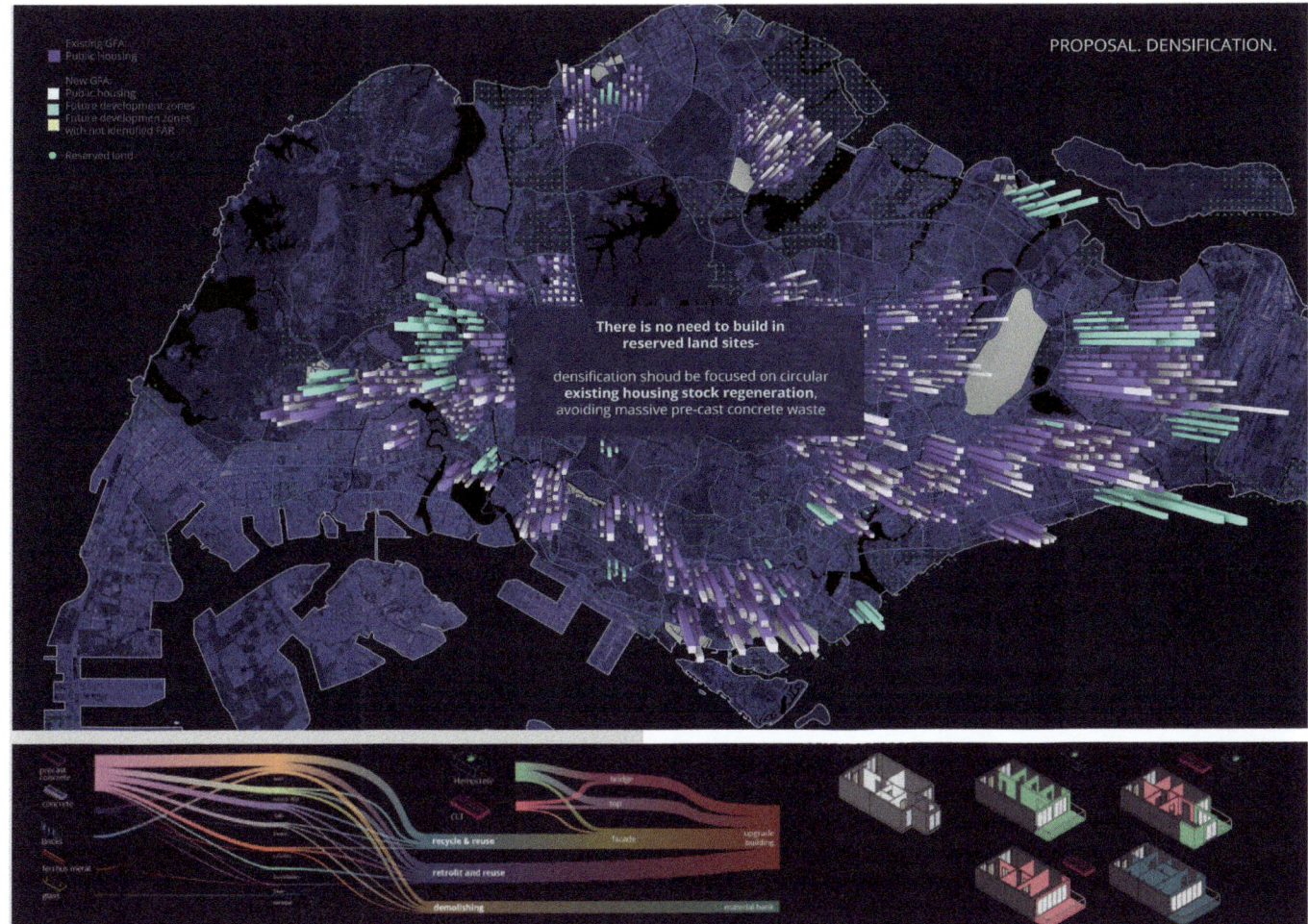

3   Densification proposal for the city of Singapore, reusing existing building material stock of pre-cast concrete for new constructions, IAAC MaCT 2023

in a GIS database and create open repositories to map the material availability in the existing building stock of a city. The goal of the research is to enhance building public datasets related to material stock in cities where data on the built environment is scarce. The developed methods propose alternative automated ways to physical inspections which makes them applicable to different cities that lack registers of building data. The data repository maps are developed in the format of an interface, so that it can be used by different stakeholders including decision makers for the formulation and planning of urban material reuse strategies and architects for implementing the data in early-stage design of circular buildings using existing building stock as new materials for construction.

The IAAC research on Urban Mining calls for agents involved in design, planning and construction to shift their focus to the anthroposphere as a source of, rather than just a destination for, processed goods. Reframing waste products generated in the urban environments, or through urban activity, as anthropogenic stock, helps to shift the perception of resource from a finite starting point in a linear use process to a cyclical state of material in a circular process. The concept of "urban mining", thus, is revisited to manage the material stock in urban systems and the use of anthropogenic resources in new production cycles.

Through a multi-scalar approach, the outcome challenges the foundation of our material practices, presenting the potential to disrupt linear patterns of design and making in the built environment.

ACKNOWLEDGMENTS

The research presented has been developed in the Master in Advanced Architecture (MAA), Master in Robotics for Advanced Construction (MRAC), Master in City & Technology (MaCT) and 3d printing Architecture postgraduate program (3dpA) at IAAC. Projects presented include contributions by faculty and researchers: Areti Markopoulou, Alexandre Dubor, Aldo Sollazzo, Oana Taut, Nikol Kirova and Hesham Shawqy and by students: Evangelia Sarantopoulou, Snehal Pare, Yuvraj Shirke, Anna Batallé, Irem Yagmur Cebeci, Matthew Gordon, Roberto Vargas and MaCT

4 3d printing earth-based architecture, IAAC 3dpA 2023

5 Cable robot adjusted for printing earth-based architecture, IAAC & Tecnalia, 2019

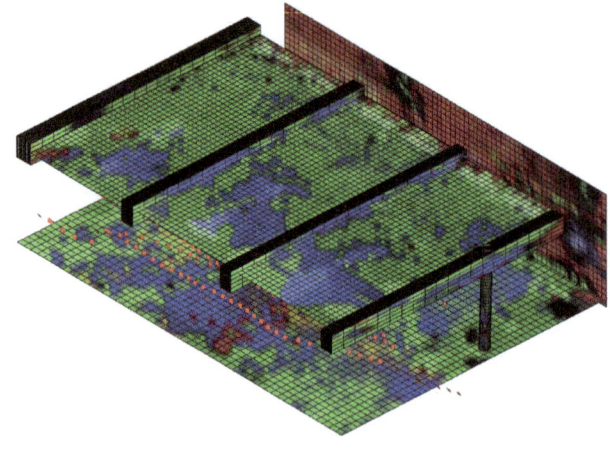

6 Material localization through computer vision on scanned industrial building, IAAC MRAC 2020

students from 2021-22 and 2022-23. The research has been partially supported and co-funded by the European Commision.

REFERENCES

Elhacham, Emily, Liad Ben-Uri, Jonathan Grozovski, Yinon M. Bar-On, and Ron Milo. 2020. "Global Human-Made Mass Exceeds All Living Biomass." *Nature* 588 (December): 442–44. https://doi.org/10.1038/s41586-020-3010-5.

Gausa, Manuel, Areti Markopoulou and, Jordi Vivaldi. 2019. *Black Ecologies*. Barcelona: Institute for Advanced Architecture of Catalonia, Actar Publishers.

Anna Batalle Garcia, Irem Yagmur Cebeci, Roberto Vargas Calvo, and Matthew Gordon. 2021. "Material (Data) Intelligence - towards a Circular Building Environment," January. https://doi.org/10.52842/conf.caadria.2021.1.361.

Areti Markopoulou, Oana Taut, and Hesham Shawqy. 2023. "Enhanced Databases on City's Building Material Stock. An Urban Mining Method Based on Machine Learning for Enabling Building's Materials Reuse Strategies." *Sustainable Development Goals Series*, November, 685–701. https://doi.org/10.1007/978-3-031-36554-6_44.

IMAGE CREDITS

Figure 1 © IAAC MaCT, Areti Markopoulou, Oana Taut, Hesham Shawqy.

Figure 2 © Evangelia Sarantopoulou, Snehal Pare, Yuvraj Shirke. Faculty: Areti Markopoulou, Nikol Kirova.

Figure 3 © Reda Petravičiūtė, Naohiro Miyaguchi, Roman Pomazan, Faculty: Areti Markopoulou, Oana Taut, Hesham Shawqy.

Figure 4, 5 © IAAC 3dpA, Faculty: Alexandre Dubor, Edouard Cabay

Figure 6: © Anna Batallé, Irem Yagmur Cebeci, Matthew Gordon, Roberto Vargas, Faculty: Alexandre Dubor, Aldo Sollazo

REFERENCES

Authors should refer to both the *Chicago Manual of Style*, and the examples below.

[Book] Fox, Michael and Miles Kemp. 2009. *Interactive Architecture*. New York: Princeton Architectural Press.

[Book Chapter] Hasdell, Peter. 2009. "Pneuma: An Indeterminate Architecture, or Toward a Soft and Weedy Architecture." In Design Ecologies: Sustainable Potentials in Architecture, edited by L. Tilder and B. Bolstein, 92–113. New York: Princeton Architectural Press.

Designing with Agential Matter

Martyn Dade-Robertson
The Hub for Biotechnology in the Built Environment,
Living Construction,
School of Architecture, Planning and Landscape,
Newcastle University, UK

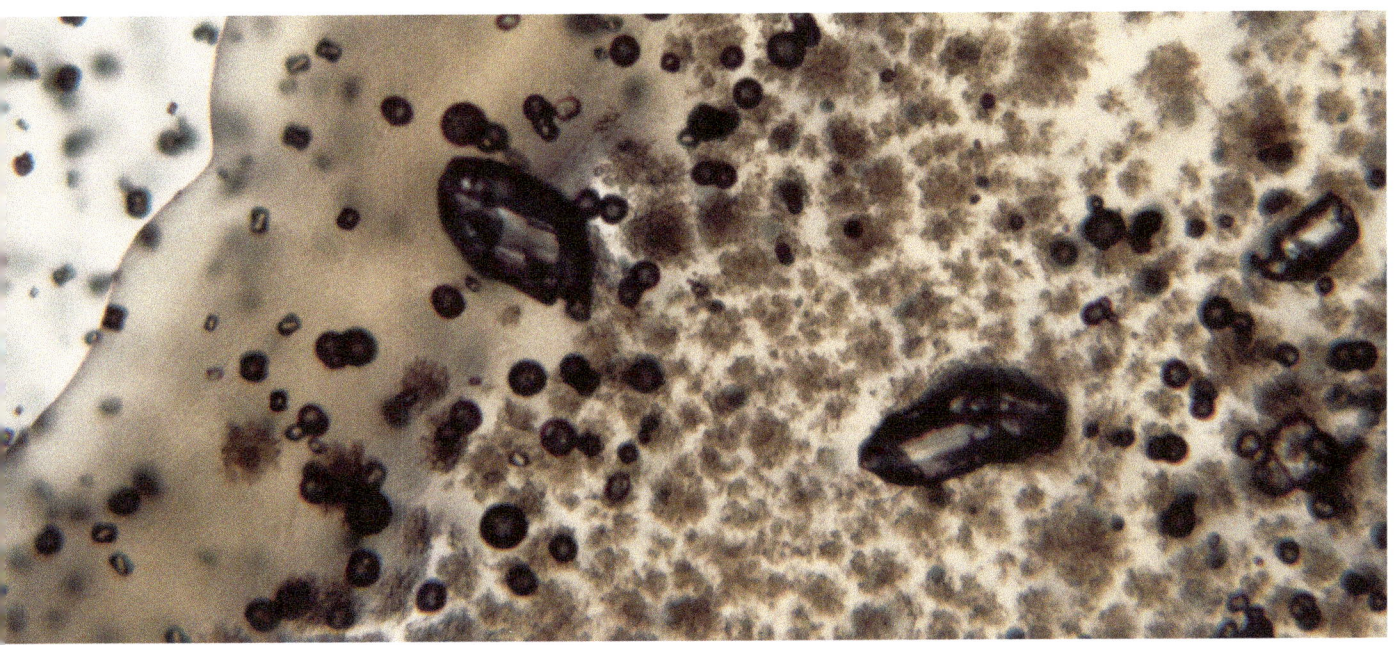

1   Crystals of calcium carbonate induced by microbes

There have been, very broadly, three eras in the understanding of matter in design. The first, associated with an Aristotelian view of matter as inert and as a receptacle of form, has dominated many of the formalisms in Architectural Design from the Renaissance through to Modernism. The second, sometimes described as "new materialism" (Menges 2012), considers matter as active through design processes which work with materials' inherent tendencies and capacities. This has led to now-familiar design methods, including Material Based Design Computation (Oxman 2009), and many experiments with active materials such as bilayer metals and hygromorphs. These materials can be programmed to respond to their environments and often take inspiration from biology. I want to suggest that we are entering a new era of understanding matter, which I refer to as the "agential era."

The term "agential matter" was coined by two developmental biologists, Davies and Levin (2022). In the process of developing methods for tissue engineering, they observed that living cells constantly confound expectations of their behaviour, exhibiting complex and emergent capabilities. In a significant experimental example, Levin and colleagues repurposed skin cells from a frog (Xenopus laevis) embryo, reassembling them into new cell clusters termed "xenobots." These xenobots exhibited motility (Blackiston et al. 2021) and collective swarm-like behaviors, as well as self-replication (Kriegman et al. 2021). The Xenobots project did not involve modifying the cells' genes but instead removed the cells from their typical developmental context. The new behaviors emerged spontaneously based on their response to being in a different environmental context, free from the influence of the frog's usual cellular environment. The team also demonstrated that by

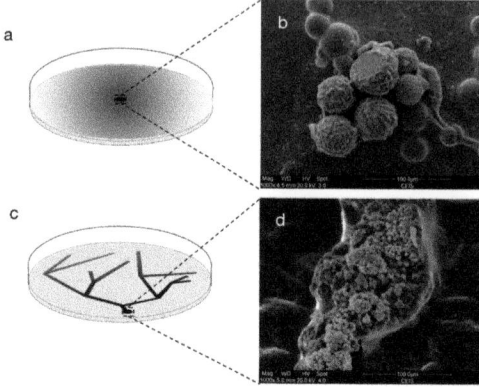

2   Image to show different morphology of microbial produced crystals.

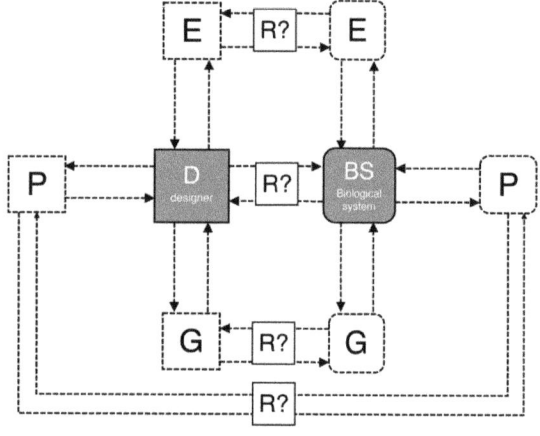

3   Diagram based on (Oxman 2006) to show the interactions between the designer, biological system in terms of (G) generation, (P) performance and (E) Evaluation

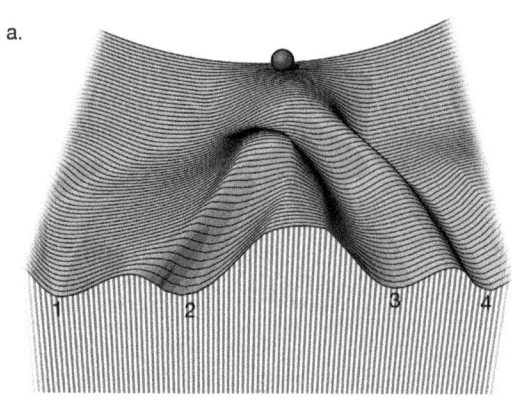

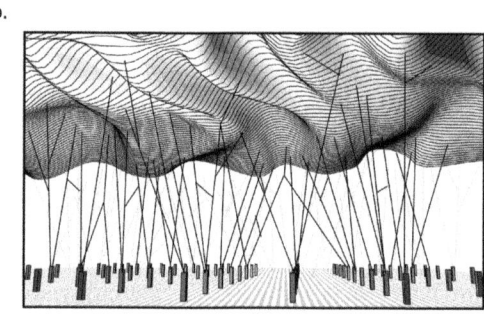

4   The 'epigenetic landscape' based on (Waddington 2014)

observing the cells' natural responses to this unfamiliar configuration, they could engineer cell assemblies to perform predictable behaviors. This insight suggested that when taken outside their developmental context, the cells exhibited a nascent form of cognition.

There has been a surge of interest in the development of biological materials for architectural applications, facilitated by the cultivation of, for example, mycelium, microbial cellulose, bioplastics, and biominerals. These materials can be synthesized through a type of controlled agriculture. As such, their properties can be cultivated rather than manufactured through post-production processes. However, our interactions with these materials remain bounded by more traditional research methods. The forms, such as mycelium bricks and cellulose panels, derive from traditional material practices of molding and casting.

In this keynote presentation, I will argue that we need alternative design models when working with agential materials. Starting with ideas familiar to the ACADIA audience from parametric design (notably the work of Oxman 2006) and moving to ideas from the early history of developmental biology, including the Creodic method (Waddington 2014) and modern theories such as TAME (Technological Approach to Mind Everywhere), the "continuum of agency," and the "axis of persuadability" (Levin 2022), I will integrate these theories with examples from our work in the Living Construction group. I will propose a new agenda for designing computational software and hardware in the context of emerging "wetware" technologies.

5   The Gardened Bridge design concept presented as part of the Venice Architecture Biennale.

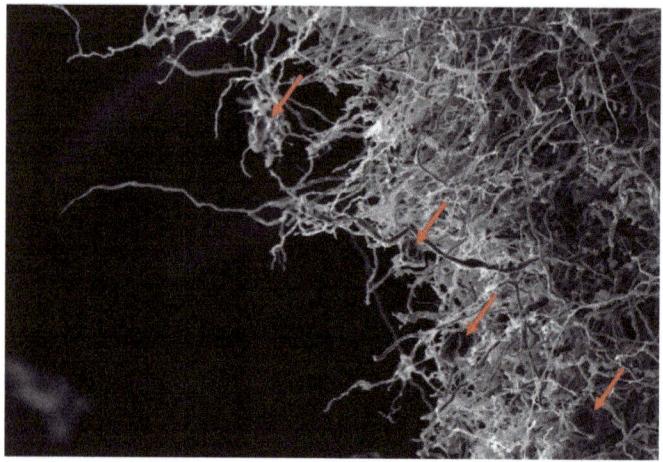

6   Electron microscope of spores embedded in a mycelium network.

7   3D scan of mushroom growth under different environmental conditions.

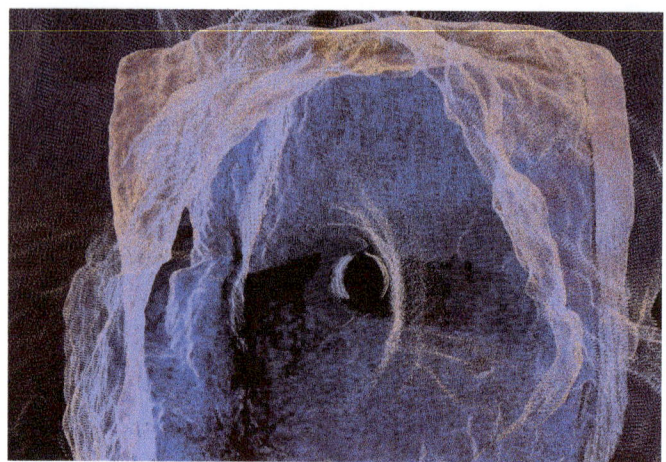

8   3D scan of casts of microbial cement.

9   Photograph of the Living Manufacture Engineered Living Fabricator

There have been, very broadly, three eras in the understanding of matter in design. The first, associated with an Aristotelian view of matter as inert and as a receptacle of form, has dominated many of the formalisms in Architectural Design from the Renaissance through to Modernism. The second, sometimes described as "new materialism" (Menges 2012), considers matter as active through design processes which work with materials' inherent tendencies and capacities. This has led to now-familiar design methods, including Material Based Design Computation (Oxman 2009), and many experiments with active materials such as bilayer metals and hygromorphs. These materials can be programmed to respond to their environments and often take inspiration from biology. I want to suggest that we are entering a new era of understanding matter, which I refer to as the "agential era."

The term "agential matter" was coined by two developmental biologists, Davies and Levin (2022). In the process of developing methods for tissue engineering, they observed that living cells constantly confound expectations of their behaviour, exhibiting complex and emergent capabilities. In a significant experimental example, Levin and colleagues repurposed skin cells from a frog (Xenopus laevis) embryo, reassembling them into new cell clusters termed "xenobots." These xenobots exhibited motility (Blackiston et al. 2021) and collective swarm-like behaviors, as well as self-replication (Kriegman et al. 2021). The Xenobots project did not involve modifying the cells' genes but instead removed the cells from their typical developmental context. The new behaviors emerged spontaneously based on their response to being in a different environmental context, free from the influence of the frog's usual cellular environment. The team also demonstrated that by observing the cells' natural responses to this unfamiliar configuration, they could engineer cell assemblies to perform predictable behaviors. This insight suggested that when taken outside their developmental context, the cells exhibited a nascent form of cognition.

There has been a surge of interest in the development of biological materials for architectural applications, facilitated by the cultivation of, for example, mycelium, microbial cellulose, bioplastics, and biominerals. These materials can

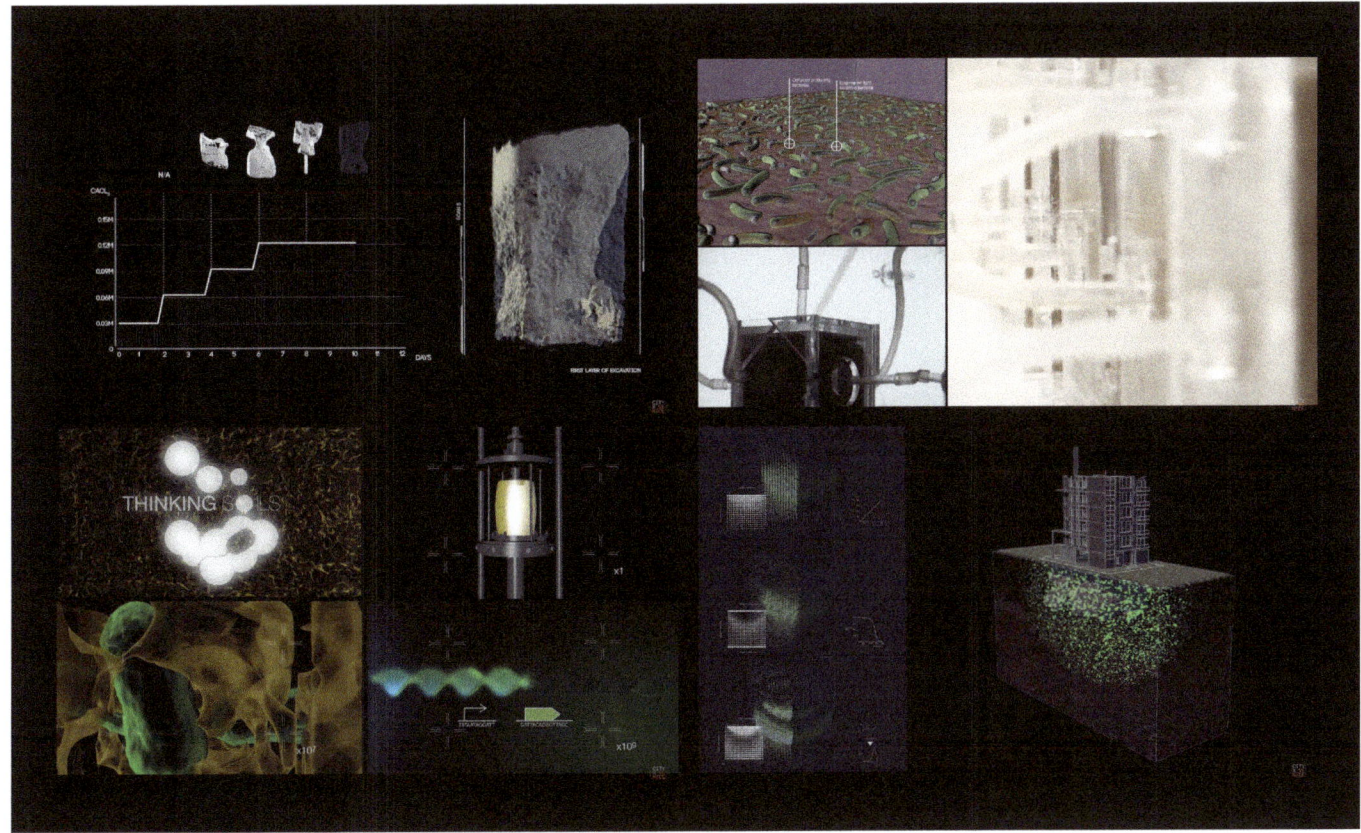

10 Screen shots from 'Can we Grow a City'. Video produced as part of the Venice Biennale 2019.

be synthesized through a type of controlled agriculture. As such, their properties can be cultivated rather than manufactured through post-production processes. However, our interactions with these materials remain bounded by more traditional research methods. The forms, such as mycelium bricks and cellulose panels, derive from traditional material practices of molding and casting.

In this keynote presentation, I will argue that we need alternative design models when working with agential materials. Starting with ideas familiar to the ACADIA audience from parametric design (notably the work of Oxman 2006) and moving to ideas from the early history of developmental biology, including the Creodic method (Waddington 2014) and modern theories such as TAME (Technological Approach to Mind Everywhere), the "continuum of agency," and the "axis of persuadability" (Levin 2022), I will integrate these theories with examples from our work in the Living Construction group. I will propose a new agenda for designing computational software and hardware in the context of emerging "wetware" technologies.

ACKNOWLEDGMENTS

The research presented has been funded by Research England (Examining Excellence in England Scheme) and the EPSRC Thinking Soils (EP/R003629/1) and Principles for a Microbial 3D Printer (EP/V050710/1). Projects presented are from members of the Hub for Biotechnology in the Built Environment including contributions from .

REFERENCES

Blackiston, Douglas, Emma Lederer, Sam Kriegman, Simon Garnier, Joshua Bongard, and Michael Levin. 2021. 'A Cellular Platform for the Development of Synthetic Living Machines'. Science Robotics 6 (52): eabf1571. https://doi.org/10.1126/scirobotics.abf1571.

Davies, J and Levin, M. 2022. 'Synthetic Mophology via Active and Agential Matter'. OSF Preprints [Epub Ahead of Print].

Kriegman, Sam, Douglas Blackiston, Michael Levin, and Josh Bongard. 2021. 'Kinematic Self-Replication in Reconfigurable Organisms'. Proceedings of the National Academy of Sciences 118 (49): e2112672118. https://doi.org/10.1073/pnas.2112672118.

Levin, Michael. 2022. 'Technological Approach to Mind Everywhere: An Experimentally-Grounded Framework for Understanding Diverse Bodies and Minds'. Frontiers in Systems Neuroscience 16 (March): 768201. https://doi.org/10.3389/fnsys.2022.768201

11 Screen shots from 'Can we Grow a City'. Video produced as part of the Venice Biennale 2019

Menges, A. 2012. 'Material Computation'. Architectural Design 82 (2): 14–21.

Oxman, Neri. 2009. 'Material-Based Design Computation : Tiling Behavior'. In ACADIA 09, 122–27.

Oxman, Rivka. 2006. 'Theory and Design in the First Digital Age'. Design Studies 27 (3): 229–65. https://doi.org/10.1016/j.destud.2005.11.002.

Waddington, C H. 2014. The Strategy of Genes: A Discussion of Some Aspects of Theoretical Biology. Abingdon: Routledge.

IMAGE CREDITS

Figures 1, 8-9: © Thora Arnardottir
Figure 7 © Dilan Ozkan
Figure 2-5: © Martyn Dade-Robertson
Figure 6: © Elise Elsacker
Figure 10-11: © Living Construction Group including work by Dilan Ozkan, Thora Arnardottir and Emily Birch

Martyn Dade-Robertson is Professor of Emerging Technology at Newcastle University and co-founded the Hub for Biotechnology in the Built Environment (HBBE) Martyn co-leads the Living Construction theme in the HBBE and is Editor in Chief for Cambridge University Press Journal: Biotechnology Design and the Routledge Book series Bio Design.

Keynote Prologue Panel: Panel Discussion

Martyn Dade-Robertson, Areti Markopoulou.
Moderated by Conference Site Chair Assia Crawford

I think you both raised incredibly pertinent points, and I suppose I would like to pick up where, Areti, you started off, in terms of the difficult context that we are currently facing, but also matters of equity and pedagogy. You have both entered various realms that perhaps strayed from what we have traditionally defined as architecture and architecture pedagogy, especially at a foundational level. But we are also entering this new era where some of the emerging tools may perhaps liberate us as practitioners to actually venture more into these realms. So I suppose my first question is: "How do you think this is going to affect the wider architectural framework of architectural pedagogy, but also in terms of equity, how accessible is this going to be internationally within various contexts?"

MARTYN DADE-ROBERTSON = (MDR):
MDR:
One thing I would say is that the thinking source projects and the HBBE, and the other stuff that you saw there, started off as a teaching initiative. It was a master studio that allowed us to do the experimental work. And I think a lot of us do that. It is somewhat unusual in architectural education, unlike in other academic fields, where you don't do your most experimental work in your teaching place. You leave that outside. And so a lot of the early concepts came from the designing studio. So that's the first thing, and actually one of the things I have really missed in the last couple of years. And I haven't had as much time to teach as I would have liked.

In terms of these enabling tools, one of the things that we found about bio-design is that there are two sides to it: there's this kind of very high-tech version of it, which is in labs and with incredibly expensive equipment that, you know, nobody can really afford -- not even we can really afford them. Then there is a whole community of people who are just doing this in their kitchens and their bathrooms. And we have dissertation students who make incredible mycelium things at home. And there's something quite liberating about that.

One of the things that we have been thinking about is liberating the biological techniques, as well, and so there's a great movement towards community. There's a release of all of these hardware/software methods. And we see lots of innovation in that community, and in the bio-design community, particularly set up in that way, actually, to try and democratize those things, I think. So we see a lot of promise there.

I think there is still an inequity of knowledge, to some extent. I think the collaborations that we do -- we find a lot of people coming to us because they don't necessarily understand some of the fundamentals. And they've not had the education of the fundamental aspects of biology that some require. So I think there's a need to do that. And we are thinking about programs that will do that. Yeah, that would be mine.

ARETI MARKOPOULOU = AM:
AM:
Maybe from my side, I think that there are two key words on that question. The first one is open source. Martyn mentioned that. There is an exceptional community out there that are sharing their knowledge. And there are platforms that also help them to share that knowledge. And one peer is learning from the other. And I think that we need to find ways to reinforce these communities, and also to equip these communities with skills and funds, you know, for them to further operate.

And the second word maybe I would say is distributed education. I think this is something very important. We took a lot of lessons during Covid. At IAAC, we have been running a distributed program since 2007. We did that, of course, in collaboration with the Center for Bits and Atoms at MIT, but it's the Fab Academy Program, which is a program that is distributed, and is connecting different Fab Labs around the world.

And based on that program, we are also now setting up other distributed design and distributed educational programs that have different levels of accessibility, from free accessibility to, you know, the possibility of getting into different nodes and different places in the world and sharing all of the knowledge. And I think that this kind of new example of distributed education could also expand and be allowed to reach more people and allow new technological models that have, in their core, inclusivity and equity.

AC:
In terms of collaboration, you both had a very extensive list of collaborators, both human and non-human, alike. How do you envision the future of the architect? What is going to be our role in the emerging contexts that we are seeing, in terms of resources? In terms of ecology, political contexts, et cetera? We have seen a lot of shifts in the last few decades.

AM:
First of all, I think that the idea of the architect dies. The architect, I believe, is going to be the last one. I really admire him. He is a good friend. But he's going to be the last one, I believe. That idea dies, and I think that's fantastic because we really need to start establishing more collaborative ways of working.
The architect is not going to be about a decision or a wish of a form and trying to materialize that form. It's not anymore about imposing form into matter, no? We are going to move towards a discipline of architecture that includes a lot of different areas of expertise. We already start to see that offices have biologists, computer scientists, economists, and ecologists, so architects will become the mediator of these different disciplines. And this is why we also need to be able to know bits of everything so that we are able, not necessarily to code ourselves -- I don't code, but I do understand what code can do -- and what the different kinds of software can do. And I think that this is something very, very important for the architect, but also for the discipline of design, in general.

MDR:
I couldn't' have said it better, really. That would be my sense, as well, that losing the ego is when you are sitting in here as a keynote and you are losing an ego. I think there's a lot of that. I would say from a research perspective, we've done very well in being seen as being a serious, fundable, research institution, in part by pretending not to be architects, because to me -- what is very strange to me is that I pretend to be a synthetic biologist or a microbiologist with my technology, so whatever it is, the reason we are successful in the projects that we do is partly because we are governed by an architectural way of thinking, which we don't well articulate. And this can be applied in lots of things to do with the built environment, and sometimes outside of it, as well.
But we never really describe those as mathologically, such that the scientific research community will take that seriously and then invest in it in that way. What we do is we pretend to do other things. When I started my synthetic biology course, to try and make this shift, I was clearly very nervous, for lots of reasons. I was well out of my depth, and I was really helped by the fact that I opened the first page of a cell biology textbook, and the first reference there was to Buckminster Fuller and to the tensegrity structure. Bucky Fuller came up with the tensegrity structure as a design before it was discovered that it was the way in which cell structures hold form. And that said something about that way of thinking, which I think we need to actually celebrate.
So in a research context, we think in architectural ways. And that gives us a kind of -- and I still don't know how to articulate it -- it's a spatial structural material knowledge. There's something about process in there, as well. We don't articulate it very well. And what we are trying to do in research is actually make that thinking come alive, to do things that are not necessarily designing for the built environment, that might end up in all kinds of other things. And so I feel there is something of a turn there. I hope that there are a number of people who are demonstrating that in our community, actually. And that's my hope, anyway.

AC:
Thank you. I would like to open the discussion to our audience at this point. Because I realize we are a little bit behind schedule and I am sure they have a lot of pertinent questions, as well. So we are just going to circulate the microphone. I think we have somebody over there.

Audience Participant:
Thank you both. Really amazing presentations. My question is more for Martyn. There was a question earlier today that I'm sorry I couldn't' steal, which was about killing the living system, particularly mycelium. But there was also a kind of question about

maintenance. And I'm wondering -- when I saw your presentation, you were talking about persuasion. And I kept thinking about bonsai trees and how they require a certain constant persuasion to be a certain way. But in a way, you can kind of liken that to maintenance, right? Is that something that's part of what you are thinking about with these living systems? And, if so, in what way?

MDR:
Yeah, interestingly in my -- and I sound like I am promoting my book again -- I'm going to say, in my book, I use the bonsai tree as an example of this -- actually, no. I don't use it as persuasion, at that point, but it is that kind of cultivation -- very close cultivation. So, yes, we do. There's a field of engineered living materials, which is, I think, that's a central question of that, which is to say that what we would really like is for our materials to retain life and to continue because, functionally, they can do all kinds of interesting things by staying alive. They can self-heal, they can change, and they can adapt, and so on. I would say the other thing that I have learned in biology is that the boundary between living and dead is not so clear, either. A work that we did in our group, led by one of our post-doctoral researchers, looked at the self-healing of mycelium after it has been treated. The mycelial bio-composite she produced and then was able to put holes in it, that it was effectively dead, for all intents and purposes. She put holes in it and then renutrified the holes, and the material rehealed. And it was because of that particular type of mycelium spareolites, they are spores or seeds, so it retains that capacity for regeneration and life.

One of the areas we are thinking of is that middle ground where we get these materials that we need to be dormant and static. With a mycelium leather jacket, you don't want mushrooms growing out when it starts to rain, but you also want to retain those lifelike qualities, and so there are these gradients in this. And it's true, actually, of many of the structures you saw -- the living room, the biologically knitted structure -- that was effectively dead, but it carried on living. There were mold and all kinds of things growing on it. It provided a new habitat for new things. And we kind of want to celebrate that, as well. So there is that. It is part of our thinking that an old fabrication method might just be to kill the material, but what can we do that retains that aliveness, to actually do something useful for us, and maybe for the environment, as well?

AM:
I like the idea of care, rather than maintenance, especially when we are talking about living systems, because we have a forest in our forest compound. In order to maintain the health of the forest we need to cut trees down. That's part of the forest management, or the health of the forest. Of course, I don't know how exactly it is in your case, but I guess, like removing moss and trying to maintain, quote-to-quote, "something alive" is more like taking care, rather than maintaining.

HABITS OF THE ANTHROPOCENE
SPECIAL TOPIC KEYNOTE PANEL
MULTISPECIES MENTALITIES AND ECOLOGICAL MATERIALITY

Phil Ayres is an architect, researcher and educator. He holds the Chair for Biohybrid Architecture within CITA, which he joined in 2009 after a decade of teaching and research at the Bartlett, UCL. His research primarily focuses on the design and production of novel bio-hybrid architectural systems that couple technical & living complexes, together with the development of complimentary design environments. This research has been pursued in the context of the EU projects flora robotica, Fungal Architectures and the recently awarded EIC Pathfinder project, Fungateria. which is exploring the development of mycelium-based materials within an Engineered Living Materials context.

Joyce Hwang is associate professor and director of graduate studies with the Department of Architecture at UB. She is also founder of Ants of the Prairie, an office of architectural practice and research that focuses on confronting contemporary ecological conditions through creative means. For over a decade, Hwang has been developing a series of projects that incorporate wildlife habitats into constructed environments. She is a recipient of the Exhibit Columbus University Research Design Fellowship (2020-21), the Architectural League Emerging Voices Award (2014), the New York Foundation for the Arts (NYFA) Fellowship (2013), the New York State Council on the Arts (NYSCA) Independent Project Grant (2013, 2008), and the MacDowell Fellowship (2016, 2011). Her work has been exhibited at Matadero Madrid, the Venice Architecture Biennale, and the Rotterdam International Architecture Biennale, among other venues. Hwang's projects and writing have been featured in publications including Curbed, Good, Praxis, Azure Magazine, Architect Magazine, Architectural Review, AV Proyectos, Bracket, MONU, Biophilic Cities Journal, Volume Magazine, and Next Nature. She is a co-organizer of the Hive City Habitat Design Competition and a co-editor of Beyond Patronage: Reconsidering Models of Practice, published by Actar. Hwang is on the Steering Committee for US Architects Declare, and serves as a Core Organizer for Dark Matter University Hwang is a registered architect in New York State, and has practiced professionally with offices in New York, Philadelphia, San Francisco, and Barcelona. She received a post-professional Master of Architecture degree from Princeton University and a Bachelor of Architecture degree from Cornell University, where she was awarded the Charles Goodwin Sands Memorial Bronze Medal.

Orkan Telhan is the Chief Information and Data Officer at Ecovative. He serves as the president of the Biodesign Challenge. He was Associate Professor of Fine Arts - Emerging Design Practices at University of Pennsylvania, Stuart Weitzman School of Design. Telhan investigates critical issues in cultural, environmental and social responsibility. Telhan's individual and collaborative work has been exhibited internationally in venues including the Istanbul Biennial (2013, 2022), Istanbul Design Biennial (2012, 2016, 2021), Milano Design Week, London Design Week, Vienna Design Week, the Armory Show 2015 Special Projects, Ars Electronica (2007, 2017), ISEA, LABoral, Archilab, Matadero Madrid, Architectural Association, the Architectural League of New York, MIT Museum, Museum of Contemporary Art Detroit, the New Museum of Contemporary Art, New York, the Philadelphia Museum of Art, the Walker Art Center, the Design Museum, London, and Museo Reina Sofia.Telhan holds a PhD in Design and Computation from MIT's Department of Architecture. He was part of the Sociable Media Group at the MIT Media Laboratory and a researcher at the MIT Design Laboratory. He studied Media Arts at the State University of New York at Buffalo and theories of media and representation, visual studies and Graphic Design at Bilkent University, Ankara. Telhan was a co-founder of Biorealize.

Sensitive Scaffolds - Towards Dialogues with Living Complexes

Phil Ayres
Chair for Biohybrid Architecture, Institute of Architecture and Technology, Royal Danish Academy

1   Detail of the triaxially woven Shimoni Cave, exhibiting complex morphology through the application of systematic topological rules within a continous materially interlaced structural lattice.

The increasing research momentum within the field of Living Architectures offers promising avenues of architectural development for articulating couplings with the living world, rather than the conventional architectural tendency of obscuring them. It also offers novel pathways towards a more sustainable building practice that could contribute in the effort to address the complex and entangled challenges facing the built environment sector, including well quantified detrimental environmental impact, raw material scarcity and burgeoning demand due to population growth. Within the field of Living Architecture, biological targets as diverse as bacteria, fungi, plants and social insects are being leveraged as materials, components, co-fabricators and contributory partners for architectural synthesis. The current diversity of biological targets being studied represents an enrichment of a fringe architectural practice in the applied use of living complexes that extends, at least, to the beginning of the eighteenth century. This is evidence by Friedrich Küffner's scholarship on tree-shaping towards architectural configurations (Küffner, 1716). In this work, Küffner documents strategies of pleaching and inosculation drawn from horticulture, but articulated towards architectural objectives and integrated living structures.

Working with living complexes as construction material challenges many of the orthodox foundations that we take for granted in the design and production of conventional architectures. For example, the use of representation to develop a complete-determination-in-advance, construction as a discrete phase of activity and the convenient false notion of completion, all require revision. In addition, and more practically, there is the issue that living complexes generally take time to acquire or produce the requisite material properties and manifest architectural scale. By extension this leads to two issues – supporting plants during growth pahses where they lack self-support and the design problem of how to communicate anticipated design targets to an audience over a potentially extended timeframe. Interestingly, horticulture provides a long-standing strategy for dealing with both the practicality of support, and the issue of spatially projecting design intent, through the device of the trellis. Indeed, across the 16th – 18th centuries the design and making of trellises became an artform in its own right, radially transcending the functional requirement of plant support and drawing upon architectural reference, both stylistic and organisational (Nonaka, 2017). Elaborate constructions combining porticoes, gates and covered galleries structured outdoor spaces, with the full intention of them become colonised by living matter.

In the speculative design work briefly presented here, our aim is to build directly upon the tradition of Treillage with the explicit intention of expanding the spatial vocabularies, functionalities and sensitivities of architectural scaffolds for promoting living architectures. The work presented, draws upon research projects conducted over the last 10 years, although they are not presented in chronological order. Rather, they are arranged to build a narrative of increasingly enhanced and expanded scaffold properties that operate through abiotic to biotic systems and varying material logics of filament interlacing, both structured (weaves and braids) and unstructured (non-woven). Through the articulation of these properties, the objective is to foster increasingly sensitive dialogues with the biological complexes being coupled. This progression across the work is manifested in systems that initially seek conformity of the biological entity to a pre-determined design target, to systems that foster reciprocal dialogues and invite design indeterminacy by embodying tactical abilities and agency through sensing and response mechanisms. In the first instance this is explored in the coupling of an abiotic scaffold with a biological complex, and finally, we investigate the scaffold itself being a biological complex.

Our explorations into developing expanding forms of sensitivity begin by enhancing the space of morphology possibility. We approach this by employing technical weave system that provides a systematic and rationalised method for achieving near-net approximations of any rational fixed geometric target. The weave method employed is based on a tri-hexagonal lattice and embodies systematic principles for inducing double curvature. This is achieved by introducing a polygon into the regular lattice with

2 Detail of near-net-approximation of cave features within the triaxially woven Shimoni Cave.

a greater number of edges to induce negative gaussian curvature, or a lesser number of edges to introduce positive gaussian curvature. Through the diligent placement of these 'singularities', complex geometries can be approximated as we have demonstrated in a full-scale weave produced in collaboration with Cave_bureau and Louisiana Museum of Art, Denmark (Figures 1, 2). This 300m2 weave comprises micro, meso and macro scale features that approximate the geometry of the Shimono Cave in Kenya. The multi-scalar character of these features results from the scale of embedding of singularities within the lattice – in this case c. 5000 singularities located within a lattice of c.60000 woven cells, the placement of which being computationally determined using a mesh relaxation method (Ayres et al.,2024).

Opening the space of morphological possibility allows for greater sensitivity in exploiting and/or creating specific environmental conditions conducive for biological colonization. In the Fungal Architectures project, we utilise this strategy by making triaxially woven structural gridshells combined with secondary woven surfaces (Figure 3). These weaves act as stay-in-place moulds and reinforcements that can be filled with mycelium inoculated substrates. Being woven from ligno-cellulosic materials allows

3 Full-scale fragment study of the dual scale weave and mycelium surface for the Fungal Architectures project.

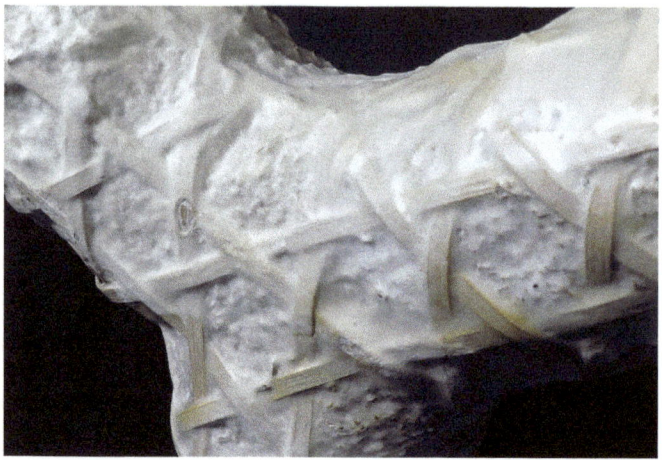

4 Detail of a mycelium composite branching component study. The Kagome weave provides acts as a stay-in-place mould and reinforcement.

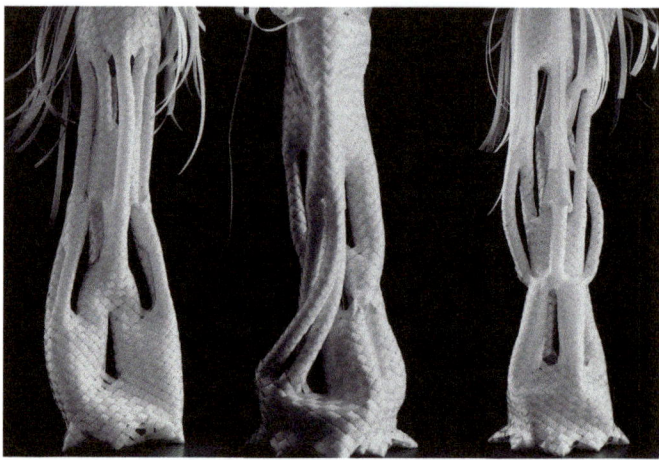

6 Full-scale physical studies of braid different topologies and their effect on morphology in the Flora Robotica project.

5 Fungal architecture design speculation. The spatial and tectonic language is poised in an indeterminate zone between building and landscape.

7 Kinetic briads operated by an evolved controller in the Flora Robotica project with the aim of responding to natural growth of the plant.

them to become colonized and integrated by the mycelium through a process of fermentation (Figure 4). Given the novelty of the fabrication process and the resultant materials, we speculate on what a Fungal Architecture could be. Here, we develop a spatial and tectonic language that is poised between building and landscape, openness and enclosure, the fixed and the indeterminate, underpinned by a fabrication process that involves a complex relationship between growth and decay (Figure 5).

In the preceding two examples, the principle underlying the tradition of Treillage - as a provider of pre-determined design intent – is fully preserved. In the Flora Robotica project, this principle of pre-determination is questioned by giving the scaffold the ability to alter shape. In the first case, this is conceived by exploiting the potential of continuity inherent in interlaced material systems. The proposition that extends from this is that braided structures can be topologically extended in response to, or in anticipation of, plant growth (Vestartas et al., 2018). This artificial growth introduces the possibility for a sensitive and reciprocal agency (Figures 6 & 8). In the second case, the braided structures are topologically fixed but are fitted with evolving controllers that activate the braid kinetically (Figure 7). An evolving controller is necessary

to retain performance fitness in a context of exogenous, such as plant colonization, or endogenous factors such as material fatigue (Stoy et al., 2021). In these explorations, the tradition of Treillage is extended by giving the scaffold properties of controlled movement and topological extension. These extended properties offer a spectrum of design opportunities for sensitively nuancing the relationship between the pre-determined and the indeterminate, articulating spatial responses and mapping these in the temporal domain.

In the final example, which is work-in-progress, we are actively exploring a strategy in which the scaffold itself is a living complex (Figure 9). This is being explored within the Fungateria project which focuses on bringing mycelium-based materials into an 'Engineered Living Material' (ELM) context. ELMs are a novel class of materials that either fully, or partially, comprise living cells that remain biologically active in use-cases. Maintaining the viability of the cells offers radically new and tailored functionalities over conventional non-living materials, irrespective of their biotic or abiotic provenance. With living materials, properties of self-regeneration and repair (Figure 10), adaptation to environmental cues and self-organisation across hierarchies of scale and structure

8   Climbing plant integrated within the sensing braid. The Flora Robotica sought to give agency to scaffold through dialogue with the plants inhabiting it.

are fore-fronted. The field of ELMs is strongly anchored within the discipline of synthetic biology, which provides the tools and methodologies for the tailoring of functionalities at the genetic level. In this project, we are targeting three primary objectives: 1) to develop a portfolio of ELMs using a co-cultivation process employing mycelium and bacteria; 2) to develop a modular and generic ELM manufacturing platform; 3) to probe the emerging ethical, social and environmental issues for ELM technologies. Whilst the project aims to develop materials within a targeted built-environment use-case of bioremediation, the three objectives defined above are purposefully use-case agnostic, setting out goals that contribute to building the scientific, technical, social and ethical foundations for the ELM field.

The brief descriptions of our enquiries above focus on the material systems and their extended properties in relation to the tradition of Treillage. It is important to note that these material investigations, and the effective leveraging of these extended properties and attributes across spatial, temporal and functional domains, requires expanded models for representation and design. Guiding concepts in the development of these models include the need to consider construction as a continuum and the ability to represent and assess a landscape of divergent growth careers driven by differences in anticipated growth conditions – effectively, the model needs to describe the phase space of the system. It is also essential to note that as we extend our design space and architectural investigations into increasingly novel properties governed by novel materials and living complexes, we require effective cross-disciplinary collaboration and the interfacing of new knowledge domains and practices. Through an expanded professional domain, new scales of operation and intervention across space, time, matter and energy will open up, through which we can manifest increasingly sensitive dialogues with the living world.

ACKNOWLEDGMENTS

The Shimoni Cave was the result of a collaboration between Cave_bureau, Louisiana Museum of Modern Art and CITA, https://louisiana.dk/en/exhibition/cave_bureau/.

The FloraRobotica project received funding from the European Union's HORIZON 2020 Research and Innovation programme under grant agreement No. 640959

The Fungal Architectures project received funding under the European Union's Horizon 2020 Research and Innovation

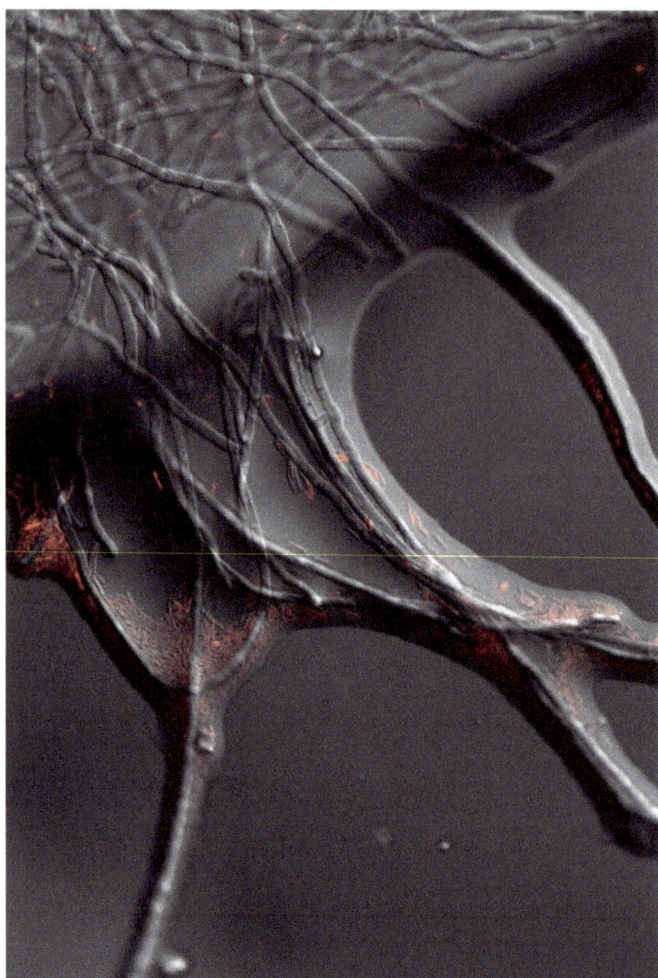

9 Confocal microscopy image used to study the co-cultivation dynamics between a living fungal scaffold and bacteria.

10 Examples of self-healing fungal leather produced by resaerchers Elise Elsacker and Simon Vandelook, exhibited at the Venice Biennale 2023.

programme FET OPEN under grant agreement No.858132. The FUNGATERIA project received funding from the European Union's HORIZON-EIC-2021-PATHFINDER CHALLENGES programme under grant agreement No. 101071145. It is co-funded by the UKRI

REFERENCES

Küffner, Friedrich. Architectura viv-arboreo-neo-synemphyteutica pomonea, horologica, floralis…., hydraulica, sylvestris, fortificatoria, henotica et hypomnematica: oder neu-erfundene Bau-Kunst zu lebendigen Baum-Gebäuden… Vol. 1. 1716.

Nonaka, Natsumi. Renaissance porticoes and painted pergolas: Nature and culture in early modern Italy. Routledge, 2017.

Ayres, Phil, Jack Young, Kjeld Kjeldsen, Mette Marie Kallehauge, Brian Lottenburger, Kabage Karanja and Stella Mutegi. "Weaving the Shimoni Cave - amplifying craft practice through computation." In FABRICATE: Creating Resourceful Futures, pp. 284-291. UCL Press, 2024..

Vestartas, Petras, Mary Katherine Heinrich, Mateusz Zwierzycki, David Andres Leon, Ashkan Cheheltan, Riccardo La Magna, and Phil Ayres. "Design tools and workflows for braided structures." In Humanizing Digital Reality: Design Modelling Symposium Paris 2017, pp. 671-681. Springer Singapore, 2018.

Stoy, Kasper, Karen Walker, Stig Anton Nielsen, Phil Ayres, Mary Katherine Heinrich, David Andres Leon, and Ashkan Cheheltan. "A large-scale, light-weight, and soft braided robot manipulator with rapid expansion capabilities." In 2021 IEEE 4th International Conference on Soft Robotics (RoboSoft), pp. 495-500. IEEE, 2021.

IMAGE CREDITS

Figures 1-2: © Phil Ayres
Figures 3-4: © Fungal Architectures/Phil Ayres
Figure 5: © Fungal Architectures/Phil Ayres & Claudia Colmo
Figures 6-8: © FloraRobotica/Phil Ayres
Figure 9: © VIB BioImaging Core, Ghent & the Metabolic Engineering Group (MEMO), Ghent University/FUNGATERIA
Figure 10: © Marjan De Mey/FUNGATERIA

Phil Ayres is Chair Professor of Biohybrid Architecture at the Royal Danish Academy – the first chair of its kind within the Danish research context. The design research within this chair focuses on the coupling of technical and living complexes to create novel materials and architectural systems. This research has been pursued in the context of the EU funded projects flora robotica and

In Consideration of Neighbors

Joyce Hwang
University at Buffalo SUNY
School of Architecture and Planning,
Department of Architecture
-
Ants of the Prairie

1   Pest Wall (image by: Joyce Hwang/Ants of the Prairie).

JOYCE HWANG, SPEAKER

RICHARD BECKETT (Introduction):

Thank you so much, Phil. Our last speaker is Joyce Hwang. She is an Associate Professor and Director of Graduate Studies of Architecture at the University of Buffalo, State University of New York. She received a Post-Professional Master of Architecture degree from Princeton, and a Bachelor of Architecture degree from Cornell, where she was awarded the Charles Goodwin Sands Memorial Bronze Medal.

She is also a registered architect in New York State and founder of Ants of the Prairie, an office of architectural practice and research that focuses on confronting contemporary ecological conditions through creative means. In addition, she is co-organizer of the Hive City Habitat Design Competition and a co-editor of "Beyond Patronage Reconsidering Models of Practice" published by Actar.

JOYCE HWANG:

Thank you so much for the invitation to speak here. It's just been so inspiring to see the work yesterday and today, and I'm really looking forward to the presentations tomorrow. So just to jump into my presentation - I'm going to first reflect on the title of my talk. I'd like to start by asking, "Who do we think of as our neighbors?" and "Are they only other humans?"

2   Habitat Wall (photo by Joyce Hwang, 2015).

3   Bat Cloud (photo by Sharon Li-Bain, 2012).

4   Bat Tower (photo by Albert Chao, 2010).

As architects, we often think of clients and users as our stakeholders. But outside of that, there are others who are affected by what we design and build. In my work, over the last almost 20 years, I've been really interested in these questions. And also, in particular, in the conflicted perceptions that we as humans have towards animals and living with them.

So in the artifacts that we design, we see this conflict playing out. So we like seeing birds in the park and in our backyard, but at the same time, we want to keep them away from our buildings. And under-maintained sites, such as these, are typically great for habitat, but oftentimes things like this are perceived as places without care -- with a lack of care.

And so in my view, this conflicted perception is a problem, especially, biodiversity loss is an urgent global issue that needs to be addressed. And so many years ago, I was thinking about ways to reconsider buildings to include habitats through some speculative projects and sketches, such as these, and simultaneously, around that time, I started developing a number of small-scale installations to test out some of these design ideas.

For example, my first installation, which is bat towers (the project in the lower right-hand side), I was interested in developing a functional bat habitat, but at the same time to kind of draw from the tendency that bats have to live in tight spaces, but also to make a project that, you know, where there's a kind of spatial idea about layering thin spaces and crevices together. The overall project was a kind of large, conspicuous tower that's both a sculpture in a sculpture park, but also a habitat that was consistently covered with bat poop or guano.

So around that time, two years later, I did a small project called "Bat Cloud", and after doing this project -- it was probably my scrappiest project -- I started getting a bunch of questions from people in Buffalo like, "How do I get bats out of my house?" or "Could I sell them some of these pods?" I got questions from Boy Scouts asking if I could help them with their Eagle Scout project. And so, while these are small installations, I started to realize that they

5 To Middle Species, With Love - created for Exhibit Columbus 2021 (photo by Joyce Hwang, 2021).

6   Bower, at Artpark WNY (photo by Joyce Hwang, 2016).

7   Life Support, rendering (image by Joyce Hwang, 2017).

8   Toad at To Middle Species, With Love (photo by Joyce Hwang, 2021)

9   Hidden in Plain Sight, catepillar's eye rendering (Double Happiness, 2019)

have the capacity to instigate curiosity in a broader way and for a public audience.

And this, in my mind, could start to combat the kind of negative stereotype as rabid vampires, which I think is kind of really important, especially in thinking about conditions -- ecological crises -- such as white nose syndrome, which is a condition that has been killing off bats in great numbers for nearly 20 years, but something that people are hardly thinking about.

So I began at that point, also, to think about the impact of small-scale projects and how they can become sort of activists' works, as well, like how might they be perceived in a kind of broader context? And thinking more pointedly, you know, about bird-glass collision which, as many of you know, is one of the major leading causes of bird deaths in urban areas, since birds can't see transparent or reflective glass.

There are already a number of organizations that are taking on these issues, but I've been interested in exploring these ideas in a more visceral way. This is a project called "No Crash Zone." It's a temporary renovation of a glass window to make visible the logics of bird-strike prevention through this graphic interference pattern on the glass. Here's another photo of it.

And in 2016, I became more actively involved in advocating for the environment through the arts, which included working with an arts organization founded by the renowned land artist, Mary Miss, called "Cities Living Lab". These are some pictures from some walks where I was leading workshops on bird-glass collision. And through this relationship with Mary Miss, I was commissioned to develop an environmental advocacy installation working with a visual artist, Ellen Driscoll, who was creating a number of paintings about the environment. And so we incorporated these paintings into the project. The project is essentially -- it's called "Bower". It's essentially a series of fragments that are scattered across the landscape at Art

10   For Our Neighbors, at Brooklyn Botanic Garden (photo by Joyce Hwang, 2022).

Park in Western New York.

There are a number of bird habitats, bird nesting boxes up top, and the project incorporates these kinds of custom glass windows, or custom glass pieces, with drawings by Ellen that show local birds and vegetation, and also incorporate anti-bird strike patterning.

In addition to working with arts organizations, these small projects have also instigated a number of collaborations with the colleges and scientists, and maybe, I think the project that best exemplifies this type of collaboration is this project in Australia, which is called "Life Support". It's a vertical habitat structure that I designed working with an ecologist in Canberra named Darren Le Roux, and a digital visualization designer at Australian National University named Mitchell Whitelaw.

The project really began with Darren's research into the ecological value of very large, old trees in enhancing urban biodiversity. When large trees are cut down, they are typically made into firewood or mulch, but here, armed with Darren's research, we decided to make use of this tree and worked to basically get this tree removed in as few pieces as possible. After it was taken down, it was transported to an ecological offset zone called Barrer Hill. And this is the tree being moved. Barrer Hill is a site in Canberra that's undergoing a process of landscape regeneration.

As you can see, this whole land has been deforested. All these pink stubs are trees that were planted recently. While they are waiting for new trees to grow, they are trying to basically install artificial vertical habitats, which is where I came into the picture. The project was, essentially, to find a way to use an existing tree that was removed and to use its parts to create a vertical -- a tall habitat structure -- this is about 45 feet tall -- and also using the kind of offcuts of the project to make bird and bat nesting boxes.

We used photogrammetry to model these parts. It actually became very useful even to work with structural engineers to figure out, you know, how this was really going to work. Here's the project under construction. And it was completed in 2019.

11 Multispecies Lounge at the Bentway (photo by Joyce Hwang, 2023).

12 Multispecies Lounge at the Bentway (photo by Joyce Hwang, 2023).

Another exciting part of this project is that we mounted cameras on the structure to detect and document animal occupation, which feeds into a database. For the first six months, there were actually 1,500 bird observations captured from 24 bird species, which was significantly higher than what was recorded previously. We were really just amazed with our kind of collaboration, as well, so we even made a diagram about it and wrote a paper about it. But one of the things I reflect on here is how -- you probably remember this from professional practice class -- but how we can rethink the seemingly clean logics of the architect's triangle and reveal, instead, more messy relationships between collaborators to describe the nature of shared authorship, and also, how these kinds of relationships complicate and intensify one another. But in terms of now thinking about going back to this idea of animals as neighbors, I want to shift gears slightly and talk not only about design projects as collaborations for environmental activism and, you know, working in interdisciplinary ways, but thinking more explicitly about the agency of animals themselves, so going beyond ecosystem services.

This is a project called "To Middle Species, With Love". It was developed as an installation for Exhibit Columbus in 2021, in response to the theme of New Middles. I started thinking about, you know, the idea of middle species in contrast to flagship species. We typically think of certain animals when we think of conservation, but what about the animals around us? And the animals that are part of our neighborhoods that are community members. Who are the animals that are there that we are overlooking?

And to start with this project, I made a trip to Columbus, walked around with a lot of bat detection equipment, which you see here, looking for sites, but also looking for bats. And also thinking about elevational strata, so who's occupying spaces above in the air? Who is below? The project was made essentially for bats in the area above and the kind of hibernacula for smaller terrestrial animals, and amphibians and reptiles below.

The project was located in Mill Race Park. It's essentially a series of nine towers that are arranged in a way where the towers are acknowledging each other, as well as the existing tower in the background, which is a building by Stanley Saitowitz. The park is by Michael Van Valkenburgh. The project was sited at the confluence of two rivers at the edge of this park, aligned with some of the nearby trees.

Because it was in this kind of flood zone, there were a lot of amphibians in the area. And so this idea of stacking stones, dry-stacked stones, was actually really important for habitat in this project. Since it is located in this kind of flooding area, these stone bases were actually used, even as we were installing the project. As we were installing the project, toads were trying to hop into the project.

One of the things we noticed is that the toads were actually smacking themselves against the steel, so the base was actually a little too high. We actually had to modify it slightly and then stack the stones a little bit differently to allow them to enter. And so here is the project overall, so kind of amplifying habitat in the area. It's a place for people to walk around, a place for people to sit. And I think one of the interesting things about the project, as well, is that I had the opportunity to collaborate with the Indiana Department of Natural Resources and with the biologists who loaned us a lot of bat-detection equipment. In case you're not familiar, bats -- we can't hear them with the human ear -- they communicate at a frequency that's too high for us. So their voices are translated in this way (Joyce played a video with audio of what a bat's language sounds like here). This is what a bat sounds like.

And another fun aspect of this is that in working with two musicians, Shawn Chiki and Onokio, we start to think about how the voices of bats can be digitally mixed to create soundscapes and music. Here's a sample. Okay, so this bat music and the idea of creating, you know, a kind of sense of non-human charisma, was really important to me in moving beyond the notion of ecosystem services. In other words, how do you move it beyond this idea of the environment serving us as humans and, instead, thinking about the environment as our community?

Along these lines, I'm going to show a couple of projects that attempt to bring us closer to understanding, and maybe even empathizing with our non-human neighbors. In 2019, I worked together with Nerea Feliz, who is a faculty member at UT Austin. We worked together on "Double Happiness". We worked on a project to promote species awareness at Matadero, Madrid, which is a former slaughterhouse that is now an arts institution.

And this project, which is called "Hidden in Plain Sight", is part of a larger project called "Cyber Garden", which Orkan was also a part of. We were in this project interested in insects, in particular, and vegetation, and specifically thinking about the kind of -- what we were told to kind of think about -- were the nature-based solutions for addressing urban heat island effect in Matadero's public plazas. So, of course, we were interested in these kinds of topics, but also in the idea of vision and perception of insects and how we can begin to bring this experience to human audiences.

Here are some drawings showing, you know, the point of view of insects. The proposal was essentially a series of pavilion-like structures that serve as planters for pollinator gardens, seeding, and other amenities. And here's the exhibition at Matadero. We developed a number of prototypes. There were planters for trees, pollinator gardens, and places to sit. A refuge for caterpillars. There was a project that we called "Arthropod Cinema", which would be a place where you could see a nightly show of insects.

This is one called "Human Cocoon", which is a spot where humans could sort of gather in an intimate sort of semi-enclosed space and look through apertures at the world as if you were an insect. And you might see something like this. This was our drawing of what insect vision might look like. We worked with a filmmaker named Don Swaynos, who produced a video for the exhibition that would approximate insect vision. Insects see certain colors, so this is what a field of flowers might look like to a butterfly flying through this. This is called "Butterfly Vision". There are certain colors they can see. There are certain colors they can't see. So we were interested in just trying to understand what the point of view of an insect might be.

The last project I am going to show is our more recent project, which I also developed with Nerea. And this is called "Multi-Species Lounge". It's a commission from the Bentway Conservancy in Toronto to develop a public installation to bring attention to the ecologies in the neighborhoods around the Gardiner Expressway, which is a massive highway in Toronto. Overall, the project is basically public seating in a square -- in a park. And at the top, there are three different types of bird house prototypes. There are a number of insect habitats for solitary bees at the kind of mid-level. And at the ground level, there is hibernacula for small terrestrial animals.

These are basically gabion cages filled with concrete rubble from a nearby demolition site, and so here's a video -- it was conceived of as a lounge -- so a public space. And another aspect of the project was a kind of beauty

-- reflective patterning -- that we put on the habitat boxes that you see here. And this was our way of attempting to approximate a way for humans to see how animals might see. Insects and birds see UV reflective light, which is why some kind of bird-safe glass has UV-reflective patterning on it.

Another feature is this web-based component that we've called "Lounge Voices". And this is basically a series of narrations told from the first-person perspective of local animals. You can scan a QR code and listen to these stories of their lives while you're lounging in the space. For example, here's a groundhog. This is a groundhog that literally lived by the Bentway Terrace, our site.

THE GROUNDHOG: (Narrative of a groundhog talking from the video being presented)

"I am a groundhog. But some folks call me a woodchuck. My ancestors are from North America. We are a family of builders and take pride in the way that we create our burrows underground. We've owned some clever methods of construction over the generations. For example, we dig our inground entrances in a way that protects our homes from flooding. In creating any new tunnel, the first step is to dig for a few feet down, then dig uphill for a few feet, and then . . ."

JOYCE HWANG:

There are a lot these. There are like 14 of them. But we imagined that, you know, if you were there with your friends and you were scanning in codes, listening to animals, you might hear a mix of voices, like this – with multiple animals speaking simultaneously.

THE BARN SWALLOW: (Narrative of a barn swallow talking from the video being presented)

"I am a barn swallow. You could say that my family is quite cosmopolitan. My relatives live all over the world. My ancestors live in crystal caves, but now . . ."

THE SWEAT BEE: (Narrative of a sweat bee talking from the video being presented)

"I am a sweat bee. You can find my family in southern Canada and in the United States and Mexico. We are small, but we are easy to find because of our bright metallic green or blue color . . ."

THE DEKAY'S BROWN SNAKE: (Narrative of a snake talking from the video being presented)

"I am a Dekay's brown snake. My family is from Southern Ontario and the eastern part . . ."

JOYCE HWANG:

And so, in conclusion, I have talked about multi-species design in terms of enhancing biodiversity, ecosystem services, advocating for the environment, empathy building, and so on, but if we zoom out to where we are as a human species right now, why are we still doing stuff like this? This is actually something that a community decided to do to a tree, where they put anti-bird spikes in the trees. And in our current culture of building and living, we are far more used to basically keeping animals out by patching and fixing things, but instead, I would like you to kind of reconsider how we design with our neighbors in mind.

This is a project called "For Our Neighbors", where we were basically looking at a kind of roof structure that could be amplified to house different types of birds. This was at Brooklyn Botanical Gardens. And the idea of designing for birds is not new. We've seen a lot of projects that welcome birds in different ways, such as pigeon towers in Iran from the 16th and 17th Centuries, but there's a lot of these.

Why are we designing against animals, anyway, when they are already outsmarting us? So many of you probably saw this news recently where a researcher, a Ph.D. student from the Netherlands, discovered these undocumented birds' nests that were made out of these bird-prevention spikes. So they are outsmarting us already anyway, so why are we even worrying about this?

We are at a moment now when animals such as dolphins, whales, chimpanzees, elephants, and others are being considered as non-human persons, as well as bodies of water. There are rivers that are also given personhood status. Even Sophia, the robot, who obviously is nonhuman, has been given citizenship to Saudi Arabia, so what does that mean?

In the global context of recognizing nonhumans as persons, what does this mean for us as architects and designers, and how can we begin to think about the environment in a more radically inclusive way? That's a question that I would like to leave you with. Thank you.

RICHARD BECKETT:

Amazing stuff! Thank you, Joyce. Thank you, once again, to our speakers. I think, unfortunately, we've run completely out of time for the Q & A, so I think I am going to hand you over at this point to Marc. Thank you so much.

MARC SWACKHAMER:

Those were very incredible lectures. Thank you, all three of you, very much.

ACKNOWLEDGMENTS

Thank you to the ACADIA Conference organizers for generously inviting me to participate as a speaker.
I would also like to thank my collaborators and sponsors on the projects represented:
Bat Tower: made possible with a grant by New York State Counctil on the Arts (NYSCA);
Bat Cloud: created by invitiation to participate in the Fluid Culture Event Series, by UB Humanities Institute, second iteration made possible by grant from Awesome without Borders;
Habitat Wall: commissioned by School of the Art Institute of Chicago for the "Outside Design Exhibition," curated by Jonathan Solomon. Design made possible by the MacDowell Fellowship;
Bower: commissioned by City as Living Laboratory and Artpark WNY, developed in partnership wtih Ellen Driscoll, in collaobraiton with Matthew Hume;
Life Support: developed in collaboration with Darren LeRoux and Mitchell Whitelaw, with support from the Australian National University School of Art and Design, and ACT Parks and Conservation;
Hidden in Plain Sight: commissioned by Matadero Madrid, curated by elii architecture office, created in partnership with Nerea Feliz;
To Middle Species, With Love: commissioned for Exhibit Columbus, curated by Mimi Zeiger and Iker Gil, commissioned by the Landmark Columbus Foundation, with support from the UB School of Architecture and Planning;
Multispecies Lounge: commissioned by the Bentway Conservancy, created in partnership with Nerea Feliz;
For Our Neighbors: commissioned by the Brooklyn Botanic Garden.

IMAGE CREDITS

Figure 4: © Albert Chao, 2010
Figure 9: © Double Happiness, 2019l
All other drawings and images by the author.

Joyce Hwang is an architect and educator. For nearly two decades, she has been developing projects that incorporate wildlife habitats into constructed environments. Hwang is a recipient of the Exhibit Columbus University Research Design Fellowship, the Architectural League Emerging Voices Award, the New York Foundation for the Arts (NYFA) Fellowship, and the MacDowell Fellowship. Her work has been featured by MoMA, and exhibited at Brooklyn Botanic Garden, Matadero Madrid, and other venues. She is an Associate Professor at the University at Buffalo SUNY, School of Architecture and Planning, Director of Ants of the Prairie, and Core Organizer for Dark Matter U.

Growing Towards Mycelium

Orkan Telhan
Associate Professor of Fine Arts (Emerging Design Practices),
Weitzman School of Design, University of Pennsylvania

My name is Orkan Telhan. I am currently the Chief Information and Data Officer at Ecovative. And I would like to give you a little insight towards my journey on how, as someone with design and computation and a little bit of architecture background, ended up being a Chief Information Officer for a company that manufactures mycelium-based products. It's an odd proposition, but I think architects can do a lot these days. So hopefully this talk will give us some insight towards what else we can do to make this world a better place.

The title of my talk is called "Growing Towards Mycelium". You have seen many talks about mycelium, you know, these past two days. Somebody in the audience who I was chatting with said, "Orkan, are you going to really talk about mycelium projects?" I said, "Maybe, maybe not after seeing all of this." But my goal is really to change the perspective a little bit. I don't want you to think about how do you bring mycelium into architecture -- your architectural projects? I want you to really think about as an architect, what can you do for mycelium? And how can you make mycelium-based products when you embrace a very mycelium-centric thinking?

I come from a background in design -- interdisciplinary design. I studied product design and architecture. Terry Knight was my PhD adviser, just to put a little plug here. I did come from a very particular way of thinking about computation and technology. But my path changed because I started teaching a contemporary art program at the University of Pennsylvania. I didn't go through the traditional route of being an architect. But I started making art installations, product design, and different kinds of critical provocations using biology.

I met with biology over 15 years ago, and I kind of call myself a biodesigner. And I try to really contribute into the space of art and design, equally. But now I am at Ecovative, and I have a different role, which I will talk about in a second.

My introduction to biology was not directly about growing biomaterials. I didn't really know much about materials. I don't come from this very traditional way of really thinking. Materials, whether it's soft or hard or, you know, in a context of fashion or architecture, but I come from a perspective from how do you build environments so that you can grow microorganisms to learn from them, to explore them, or to study them, so that you can build different relationships with them?

In the technical world, we call them incubators -- bioreactors. Some organisms grow in liquid some organisms grow in solid state. I built climate-controlled environments, also known as buildings, for microorganisms and, of course, they have different conditions -- you control the heat; you cool, you know, shake them; and you build software that monitors them over time for different applications.

Some of these projects were mostly about really bringing these tools to people who don't really have ways to access them, right? Coming from a product design architecture background, you don't necessarily think about, "Oh, how do I work with microorganisms to do anything, whether it's biomaterials or food?" I started teaching at Penn, and the first biodesign class probably around 2011 to '12. Penn is a very resourceful university, so you can go to the biology department and say, "I really need some space to teach synthetic biology. Can you give me some?" "Here is the lab. Here is the classroom. Just go for it."

But that's not the case for a lot of places in the world. And even if you want to teach biodesign, you don't want to go to the biology department to really bring all your messy design tools to really work with biology. I wanted to bring biology back to the design studio so that you can grow your organisms next to your [...], your laser cutter, or other fabrication tools.

What you are seeing in the image is a bioreactor -- we used to call them B-reactors, and we gave one to a fashion designer and let them grow organisms in these little syringes, and then dye their threads with different micro-buildings, micro-built dyes, and then stitched them on a canvas to jeans, and then sell them on Etsy. So no biology lab, no biology mold, but just growing microorganisms in safe and sound ways, and really exploring how to work with biology.

So accessibility -- which is a theme that came up a couple of times in the past two days -- is important when we design tools. I would also like to show both the tools and the prototypes of what we do with the tools in the same space. Here, the important thing is that I mostly prefer to work with living materials, so when we say "living materials", I don't also call them metaphors, like literally, these living things have living organisms inside them. You are looking at some prototypes which we developed for Puma for an exhibition where the material already had organisms in it, so that as you wear the shoes, the sneakers, they will biodegrade over time.

So safe shoes, safe organisms, GMO, non-GMO -- how do you keep them under control and how do you really design a product? These are all open questions, but then again, my interest was not really to think about a new biomaterial, but rather how do you design with a living organism and really have a relationship with it, which really affects the life cycle or the performance of your sneakers.

Another experiment, this time you have live organisms inside the inflatable packaging. You program the lifecycle of this packaging by designing the attraction between these two species. When one species enters into the territory of the other one, they trigger a chemical reaction and you deflate the package. So that when the package is one day old, three months old, 24 months old, you can control, predictably, when it needs to deflate and disappear.

All prototypes, all interesting questions, but none of them really realized and commercialized. I underline this because it's very important to show you what is developed in the studio, and what leaves the studio and becomes a product outside. One more example from the old work -- these are from a 2018 collaboration between MIT Design Lab and my lab at Penn. This time, not the tool itself is important, but growing the organisms with the tool. In this case, you are looking at algae. How do you build enclosures, also known as other kinds of architectures, for algae -- so that they can sense the carbon dioxide in the environment and respond to it? As you run in a more polluted environment, higher carbon dioxide triggers more color change, and then the patches that you put on your body tell you to stop running and go back home. This was also exhibited in 2018 in the Atlanta Design Show.

These days, I work at Ecovative, and the paradigm that we work there is called The Foundry -- Mycelium Foundry. The previous examples that I showed you, building tools and building products, were called microbial. And they were in the microbial domain, so I would call them s microbial studio, but there is a little bit of a scale shift. And I will use the word "scale" a couple of times today. There's a little bit of a scale shift to where you start growing things, not in your studio, not in your desktop, but literally in a farm environment, in a big manufacturing environment. You grow real products that have standards that have certain certifications that they need to meet. Otherwise, they cannot be sold in the market.

I also brought one of these packages with me so that you can see that. We saw a lot of pictures today, so I wanted to show you real mycelium in a real package. I saw this same picture in four presentations already. And I wanted to really show you one more time because I really wanted to ask you, "What do we really see when we look at his image?" Think about it. You see, you know -- a drawing, a figure -- and then I put a photograph next to it so that it gives you a little bit more information. But when we look at this drawing, the problem is the "seeing" part. You see -- you really think that you are seeing mycelium, but there is really no mycelium in that drawing. Because mycelium is really the relationship between that species and its environment.

There are lots of other species around. You don't see the pH in the environment. You don't see the RH in the environment. You don't see the bacteria in the environment. The photograph gives us a little bit more clue, but only the microbial scale. These drawings are misleading. You really have no idea what is going on there.

I wanted to show you this because sometimes it's also important technology -- the limits of representation -- when you start seeing mycelium in a particular way with these networks of fibers that are going inside the substrate. It just limits the way you think about mycelium. Or you imagine mycelium in different contexts.

We will come back to this, but I just wanted to show you

this today because I want you to distinguish the traditional way of thinking about mycelium, which is the mycelium that grows in the substrate. And I put a little note here. Let's treat mycelium as an organism and not a material for these next couple of slides. I want to show you a different version of that in a second. You have seen these slides, as well.

So I work at Ecovative. I have seen many versions of these things. But when you think about mycelium as this white fibrous thing that goes around in a substrate and binds this different substrate inside a mold, you think about architecture in a particular way. You make bricks. We have seen wonderful presentations about how we can imagine bricks in a different way, but mycelium with its substrate inside a mold makes a very particular type of brick. It literally actually limits the way you think about the "brickness" of a brick when it comes to mycelium.

The same thing with packaging. If you grow mycelium into a mold, you can make amazing packaging. But is it really what you should be doing with mycelium? Let's look at a couple of different options. This is another drawing. We haven't seen this in this presentation or in this conference. I might have missed it, if we did. I wanted to show you this because there is also a different way of thinking about mycelium that is above the ground.

Mycelium can depart its substrate. Mycelium is a three-dimensional organism. It shoots its network of fibers anywhere. Again, if you think about mycelium only as a network of fibers, but because of its relationship to its environment, it departs. It grows towards something else. But what it grows towards is actually not an easy phenomenon. Because mycelium doesn't really know what it grows towards. In a given condition, it may figure out to reach out to a certain place for reaching out for food; in other cases it has other preferences. So only by studying the mycelium in a particular way, you learn what you can do with it.

So this is Forager. This is Ecovative's sister company that commercializes aerial mycelium-based products. These are things that are flexible. You can imagine them as textiles, foam, or leather alternatives. I also have some examples with me, if you want to touch them. But it is made of aerial mycelium. And here you don't see the organism mycelium, you see the products themselves, because this is after ten years of experimentation -- that particular phenomenon of growing aerial mycelium. Now there are other opportunities to imagine the organism in a different way. You can also make bricks. But aerial mycelium allows you to think about many different directions. You start to think together with mycelium, in this case.

I will give you a little bit of what I do to be able to really contribute to this adventure. When I was hired, when I was invited to really join Ecovative, I was making these liquid incubators that you have seen in the first slides, and I was an academic at my position at the University of Pennsylvania. And I was invited to build a research platform to do [...] screening of these different kinds of behaviors that mycelium and aerial mycelium might exhibit in different environments.

Now you can think about many different architectures, many different incubators running in parallel, where you can run hundreds or sometimes thousands of experiments, so you can really explore what else mycelium can do. This is a step in the research project that allows you to think about how you can identify the behaviors, identify the recipes, identify the right modalities, so that you can start manufacturing with mycelium.

But that's not the only way to think about mycelium. Mycelium that's grown in a petri dish, in a tube, or grown in a big chamber behave very differently. So you need to experiment at multiple scales at the same time. So while you are doing [...], you can also think about how you can grow mycelium in a higher volume, so you make more of it, but while you are making more of it, you also ask different kinds of research questions that you cannot ask in a smaller scale.

You grow on a cellular scale in a petri dish. You have seen lots of good pictures of it. You grow them in bigger, you know, distributed incubators, lots of them at the same time, and then you start using software and algorithms. That's where the competition comes in, which finds you the right patterns, which finds you the right recipes, that allow you to really scale things up or scale things out. Because one of the goals of Ecovative is really not to grow everything in their own farms -- we call them 'farms' -- but really to distribute manufacturing in a different way. This is one of the habits I think we should be questioning of the anthropocene. How do we manufacture things; how we used to manufacture things; and how we can manufacture things differently in the next decade.

In this case, I am contrasting the word manufacturing with farming, because there is a lot of knowledge, a lot of craft. It is not coming necessarily from computation, software, and building incubators, but also the big accumulation of knowledge that comes from traditional mushroom farming. If you merge farming and manufacturing skills together, you really arrive at a place where different kinds of knowledge are shaping the behavior.

I will also add one more scale to the small scale/big scale, the creative and the critical scale. Remember, I said that I am an artist. I think about mycelium also from an artistic land, as well. This is also an important responsibility to remind ourselves that as architects or people who go through architecture education, we are not necessarily only builders or programmers or form-finders. We are also critical members of the society where we probe, where we speculate, where we really like to ask tough questions. I also think that this is important to mention in a conference because many of you are already doing this in your own work. So this is my way of doing.

Changing some gears, you are looking at the design installation which was done in 2019 at the Philadelphia Museum of Art. The installation is called "Breakfast Before Extinction." It's a collaboration between Andrew Pelling, a very renowned tissue engineer, Grace Knight, the product designer at Ecovative, and you are looking at -- I will show you what you are looking at in a second -- you are looking at a number of different, you know, these little pucks that have grown human cells on them, which is served as a meal on a dinner table which is part of a bigger installation called "Breakfast Before Extinction."

The piece is a critique of tissue engineering in the field of cellular agriculture. This is basically the field that says we should stop growing animals, whether the animals are chicken, fish, or bovine, and grow detector cells, and grow them in petri dishes, and really make, you know, victims' meat. You know, you take the cells, you grow in the dishes. It's very similar to mycelium, but this is animal cells. You feed mice with them in different ways, but this time you need to feed them with something called the fetal bovine serum, which is something pretty expensive. This morning, I looked at it and it was $446 dollars a bottle. If you imagine, instead of killing a cow, you are buying the unborn cow's blood for $446 dollars per bottle and feeding them to yourselves to make a burger. And it's a long and expensive process. My work, and my collaborative work, was to really problematize this whole process -- this tissue engineering -- the ability to take cells from different animals and really grow them in a petri dish to offer as a solution for a very overcrowded planet, so that instead of killing them, you just grow them in your dishes. We decided to really ask the question a different way. Instead of being solutionists, and instead of saying that, you know, "Will this ever work?" We said, "Let's look at waste products, right?" As architects and designers, we really like to look at waste products and try to really find a system to bypass this whole fetal bovine serum situation.

We found out that there is a lot of expired blood -- human blood -- in hospitals that you can actually use for growing cells. And we also looked at tissue engineering as a fabrication method. If you take cells, human cells, and if you feed them with expired human blood, and if you put them on mycelium scaffolds, this is where the aerial mycelium comes into place. As you see there, they are nicely patterned as snakes eating their own tail. After you grow them for about three months, they turn into these blobs of meat. I kind of call this tissue engineering a manufacturing method, but it's not very different from cancer itself. These are cells that are growing outside the human body. Now, they are seated on a mycelium scaffold. It has a very tectonic relationship with mycelium itself, because mycelium spreads the cells onto the surface. It becomes a support structure and, you know, lots of architecture terms that I use in one sentence, and eventually you make these blobs of meat.

Let me pause here. I just described to you that this is a project about growing human cells on human expired blood to make these blobs of meat. Obviously, you know, if you look at these close things, it is a pretty speculative idea. And it's also, again, a good way to think about how does this actually work? If somebody shows you a picture of this, and you look at this stuff and you're like, "Okay, is this really going to work? Is this going to happen?" If you do this three months to yourself -- that was the big idea about the project -- it's not about eating somebody else's human cells, human blood, on these mycelium scaffolds. If you do this on your own for three months and built these little scaffolds, would you actually eat that tissue that is cultivated from yourself?

Underneath this weird blobby thing is mycelium, but you are looking at your own cells. These are cells that are not from me or from collaborators. We obtained them from a cell bank because of some ethical reasons. You know, it's really difficult to work with human cells with consent. And I just put that little word here "consensual consumption" because, ultimately, where you source your microorganism, where you source your mycelium, where you source your living things, has to be with consent, right?

I don't know how many of you ask yourself that question of consent when you think about biomaterials. It took me a while to think about this. And consent, in this case, is really probably the most consensual relationship you can have in this world, is with yourself. If you eat a part of yourself, it shouldn't' be a big problem. Of course, this is a fairly controversial topic. Lots of news and media outlets made a big deal out of this. We were called cannibalists, but actually, technically, if you are not eating somebody else, this is not cannibalism. Is it auto-cannibalism or not? It's a big deal. But remember, underneath all of this are these amazing mycelium scaffolds.

The "New York Times" made it on its cover in the arts section. They were not worried about mycelium or tissue engineering. They were really worried about -- or they were wondering -- why people reacted so much to the idea of growing your own cells for human consumption. It's an art piece. It's speculative design. In fabrication terms, you can probably expand this whole logic and really grow other kinds of body parts. You know, tissue engineering is a very legitimate field. And people make lots of implants, and so on.

But our goal was to really leave it behind and really think about what else you can do with mycelium. So I showed you this bacon slice before. This was my transition from really thinking very critically about this whole idea of feeding lots of people with animal products. You might be a vegetarian or a vegan. It doesn't really matter. There is a huge appetite for eating and feeding billions of people by the year 2050. And it's an alternative protein source. I was fortunate enough to really join Ecovative to really understand how you do this with mycelium cells. It's with your own cells.

I'll play you a video because I also don't want to portray you – I'll show you a very critical speculative project. I also don't want to portray you a very peaceful story because when we work, what you're looking at is a farm bed that is growing these amazing, beautiful, lush mycelium which then gets cut and sliced and served into bacon.

But when I am looking at this, I see a battlefield. I see an ecosystem that I think every ecosystem is a kind of battlefield. I see struggle. I see mycelium trying to grow when it's competing with all kinds of organisms in the environment. It's clean. It's hygienic. But, you know, nothing is purely hygienic. Mycelium really needs to outcompete and really needs to grow in a certain period of time so that it can have access to all of its nutrients.

When we think about biomaterials, you have seen a lot of pictures of mycelium-based building components and all kinds of structures around. You have seen that they all have like these weird things on them, right? It's sometimes mold. It's sometimes other mycelium, not your favorite mycelium growing on it, so it is not very easy to grow this pure thing. It is a constant struggle to really think about scalability, especially if you need to really grow this in very high volumes. The farm structure that Ecovative possesses has about two to three million pounds per year of mycelium production capacity. So you need to grow these things so pure, so clean, so hygienic. And you have to consume so many ingredients. They have to be resourced, you know, ethically, with the right dollar amount so that it can be profitable. So there is a lot of, you know, economics involved in making this beautiful material.

My job from designing these incubators, these research environments, shifted towards thinking about the economics or the actual materialization of these projects, beyond just prototypes, because things at scale, things at these big numbers, really matter a lot. And I think a lot of these things really need architects and architectural thinking to really think true, and to solve some of these problems so that they become profitable.

I also want to show you this image because it's an important summary of what kind of challenges that we see in the biomaterials world. These are not building components. This is particle biomaterial that can be used equally in the same way for food or textile production. It's not the same organism, so I don't want you to look at this and say, "Orkan showed us this bed of fluffy material and we will make leather shoes out of this". It's a different organism. It looks pretty similar, but it is a different organism – a different species.

But when you think about this commercial scale, when you think about these giant, massive, you know, production beds, you have to think, "Is this really still generative? Or is this really becoming extractive? Where are the materials coming from? Whose labor is involved? Is it the mycelium labor? Is it the human labor? What happened to the question of killing, you know, like lots of people ask about the question of killing."

If you really want to hear my perspective, I can share with you at the end with the questions, but it's really important to think about accountability as a general framework, not only just the ethics of working with living systems. I have a very clear conscience. I can eat this mycelium bacon a hundred times more when it's compared to an animal product. It's not that different from eating, you know, tomatoes or other vegetables. But it is very important to literally be able to ask, "What is the accountability associated with that?"

And all of this is, you know, my day job, basically, once it requires me to think about this, not just human labor, microbial labor or algorithmic labor. It's a big system. You know, architects are really big systems' thinkers. These are big environments. These are big input-output relationships. And, ultimately, if you really want to produce millions of pounds of mycelium from factories, you have to really put them together.

I work a lot with AI and algorithms to optimize these processes. A good summary slide, you know, I wanted to show this so that we can look a little bit beyond the horizon of mycelium. You know, you may not be interested in making human cells on your mycelium scaffolds. You may not be interested in textiles. You may not be interested in building components. But there's a lot more that you think about mycelium if you really fine-tune them to their needs.

I have listed a bunch of things that are possible with aerial mycelium. The most important thing -- I will not go through all the details -- you can take a picture of this slide. But it's really important to think about the mycelium in a field of structural biology or structural material. And architects -- do they know tectonics and structures really well? How you view the fibers of mycelium, micron by micron, to make different kinds of structures is totally up to us. It requires a different way of thinking about space; it requires a different way of seeing things. It is very hard to make drawings of it. It is really very hard to use our visual thinking skills on this. But there is a lot of possibility to imagine what mycelium can become.

And the most important thing here to mention is that mycelium doesn't become aerial mycelium in nature. Mycelium only becomes aerial mycelium in this big fluffy form in an environment that is artificially constructed by humans. Mycelium -- aerial mycelium -- is almost like a relationship that we domesticated, but it also domesticated us, because it can grow into these forms only in the presence of us.

It is a weird interspecies relationship, and we can problematize that. I don't want to pick and decide because I think I want to tell you a little bit about these little fellows. I talked about farming. I talked about gardening. I talked about building things. I'm showing you videos of leafcutter ants. You may have heard their stories. They live mostly in the southern part of the continent of the Americas. And they cultivate mycelium in their rooms, in their little houses, to feed their offspring. And this is a symbiotic relationship that has evolved over probably millions of years. And you can look at this white stuff that you see around. It's basically mycelium that is carefully gardened by these leafcutter ants. These videos show a little colony of mycelium cutting the leaves, going to their houses, and there's a special bacteria in the guts of the ants that are

actually used for digesting the mycelium. There is actually a third component that's not visible. But I am showing you this because we are not the only species that has been gardening mycelium.

To wrap up, I wanted to say a couple of things. Remember I said that that bed is actually a very -- it's a battlefield, you know. When we work with mycelium, when we think about ecosystems as large, I feel like we need to be a little more careful not to romanticize things. As humans, we really believe in our exceptionalism. We really think that we are at the center of the world. And every design practice is an agonistic practice. We really assert our own interests into the environment. We really kill things that we want to kill. And we save things we want to save. There's really no such thing as a clean, clear, ethical, accountable design practice. We have to be really careful when we say "designers working with biomaterials".

I think the word 'agonistic' is really important, meaning that we are never going to resolve the peaceful relationship with nature, but we can work harder and really make it a bit more equitable towards future generations. The other thing that I want to tell you, as a most important thing for me, is to learn how to be humble in this relationship. Every day, I learn a lot more about mycelium and I really understand more and more the desire that you can really learn from studying and investigating these organisms more and more by actually spending time with them.

In the beginning, I was trying to look at them as food, materials, sensors, and structures, but actually, as organisms, they are very, very valuable teachers. I think I'm going to finish here. I'm a little bit out of time, but my last thing is that in the introduction it is mentioned that I'm the Board President of the Biodesign Challenge. The Biodesign Challenge in 30 seconds -- it's a different community of designers. And some of you might [...] in this, you know, familiar faces. It's not a design and computation community. It is designers working with biology in their own ways to address ethical, critical, social, and cultural questions. And please, you know, look at BDC -- the Biodesign Challenge -- and if you have questions, please find me. And I look forward to hearing your questions at the end. Thank you.

HABITS OF THE ANTHROPOCENE
KEYNOTE
EPILOGUE PANEL
OPERATIONAL
TRANSITIONS

Simone C Niquille is a designer and researcher based in Amsterdam. Her practice »Technoflesh« investigates the representation of identity and the digitization of biomass in the networked space of appearance. She holds a BFA in Graphic Design from Rhode Island School of Design and an MA in Visual Strategies from the Sandberg Instituut Amsterdam. She teaches Design Research at ArtEZ University of the Arts Arnhem and is Chief Information Officer at Design Academy Eindhoven. She is a 2016 Fellow of Het Nieuwe Instituut Rotterdam and is recipient of the talent development grant by The Creative Industries Netherlands 2016/2017. Niquille is commissioned contributor to the Dutch Pavilion at the 2018 Venice Architecture Biennale. Currently she is researching the use of digital capture technology for evidence production with the long-term project »Parametric Truth«.

Chris Cornelius is a citizen of the Oneida Nation of Wisconsin and Professor and Chair of the Department of Architecture at the University of New Mexico. He is the founding principal of studio:indigenous, a design practice serving Indigenous clients. He served as a cultural consultant and design collaborator with Antoine Predock on the Indian Community School of Milwaukee (ICS). ICS won the AIA Design Excellence award from the Committee on Architecture for Education. Cornelius holds a Master of Architecture degree from the University of Virginia and a Bachelor of Science in Architectural Studies from the University of Wisconsin-Milwaukee. Cornelius was the Spring 2021, Louis I. Kahn Visiting Assistant Professor at Yale University. He has previously taught at the University of Wisconsin-Milwaukee and the University of Virginia.

Chris is the recipient of numerous awards and honors. Including the inaugural Miller Prize from Exhibit Columbus, a 2018 and 2022 Architect's Newspaper Best of Design Award, and an Artist residency from the National Museum of the American Indian. Chris has been exhibited widely including the 2018 Venice Architecture Biennale. Studio:indigenous received a 2021 Architect's Newspaper Best Of Practice Award – Best Small Practice, Midwest. Chris lives and works on the ancestral lands of the Pueblo, Tiwa and Piro people.

AM Kanngieser is an award-winning geographer and sound artist, working through listening and attunement to approach the relations between people, place and ecologies. Over the past decade they have focused on experimenting with sonic methods and practices (including field recordings, radio building and training, sonic ethnographies, oral testimonies, songs, sonifications, composition, sound walks) for environmental-geographical research. These methods and their application have been developed through sound events with The Natural History Museum London, Live Art Development Agency, Sound and Music and 2 Degrees Festival/Arts Admin and been variously outlined in papers for interdisciplinary journals including South Atlantic Quarterly, WIRES Climate Change, Progress in Human Geography and Environment and Planning D amongst many others.

Since 2015, AM has been collaborating with Pacific women, queer and transgender artists, organisers and scholars through Climates of Listening, an ongoing project that amplifies movements for self-determination in relation to continuing colonisation through resource extraction, environmental racism and ecological disaster. This research emphasises the nuanced and variegated ways that communities and people understand, produce knowledge about, and collectively attend to their lived experiences of ecocide. This has included running podcast production workshops with groups in Fiji and the Marshall

Islands for which an Introduction to Podcasting manual was complied with the Fijian audio producers Mere Nailatikau and Krystelle Lavaki-Danford from The Two Fishes show.

Alongside academic publications AM has concentrated on producing collaborative audio compositions and prose works for radio and installation to disseminate material more accessibly to national and international audiences. This has required them to place importance on making their work more broadly resonant, including for festivals such as Sonic Acts, Unsound, Transmediale, With For About 2020 and Liquid Architecture. This work has been featured on, and commissioned by, Documenta 14 Radio, BBC 3, ABC Radio National, Arts Centre Melbourne, Radio del Museo Reina Sofía, Savvy Gallery Berlin, Warsaw Museum of Contemporary Art, Deutschland Radio, and QAGOMA, and will be unfolded through a forthcoming monograph Between Sounds and Silence: Listening for Environmental Relations. Interviews on this work can be found in Wire Magazine: Adventures in Sound and Music, Mediapart and Radio Web MACBA.

AM is a Marie Curie International Research Fellow in Geography at Royal Holloway University of London. Prior to their current role, they were a Senior Research Fellow with Seedbox Environmental Humanities Laboratory, University of Sydney, and held a Vice Chancellors Research Fellowship in the School of Geography and Sustainable Communities, University of Wollongong. They have also held a continuing lectureship at Goldsmiths College (Sociology) and a Postdoctoral Fellowship at Royal Holloway (Geography), University of London. AM has received funding from the European Commission, the Economic and Social Research Council UK, the British Academy/Leverhulme Trust, the Australian Research Council and the Australia Council for the Arts.

Model Home

Simone C Niquille
technoflesh Studio

Well, hello. Thanks for having me. Hopefully, not everyone is too exhausted. But we'll get through it.

So, you know, in some ways I feel like a guest, an intruder -- there's different words -- to a conference such as this. I am trained as a graphic designer and a photographer. But somehow, you know, I find myself between disciplines. And one of them is architecture.

What we will talk about today is a project that started around 2018 called "Model Home", which is sort of the larger chapter. Most of the work I do is either in writing essays, as well as film. There's not enough time to show the film today, but if you are interested, just come and ask me after.

What I want to talk about is a lot of the background, research, and information that goes into making these 3D animated movies. They deal with computational seeing, so computer vision, and what I am interested in is a direct departure from work I was doing on face recognition. And with face recognition, I realized that I kept on -- you know, one of the main questions to me was from a career perspective. How is computer vision used as a way of being read, right? Like you're a coded body. How do you want to be read? Is this actually the way you want to be perceived? And, of course, tons of super privacy questions that are embedded in surveillance in wanting to represent a certain way, but there is also being this idea of control and, also, accuracy, as we've just heard in being able to really identify you as you versus someone else. Some of that is common sense, and I think this is something that we will see in the presentations that have come back.

Face recognition work has made me make a decision to look at architecture, specifically the domestic space, for several reasons. One was wanting to understand, not just comment on the technology, but understand how it actually works, and from a human perspective, and less from a technical perspective. And that led me to looking at training data sets.

One of the reasons is that domestic spaces, how do you access them? I mean, how do you access them, right? How do you gather enough images and visual material of what a domestic space is like to train a computer vision model to sort of say, "Well, this is how people live." I think that is one central question of this research. And the other was that there was no human body, right? There was no representation of the human figure; it was only supplied either on the furniture or in the spaces. And that was very freeing.

I didn't have to reproduce my own critique, as in why do we keep on distributing peoples' faces? We don't know why our Facebook databases, profiles scraped for research purposes which, in some way, just talk about that. I was doing the same thing. And so I think the domestic space became a really important site for this research.

Computer vision, essentially, is pattern recognition. This paper from 1955, I think, has this really beautiful way of talking about this where as a human being, as someone who speaks English, you read this as "The Cat". Even though the agents are a similar figure, you complete them in your minds through common sense and through the knowledge that you possess in a way that you can just read it as a cat.

For a computer vision model, that is not such a thing. An image like this, again, I think is interpreted in a certain way. We find it funny. It's a shark. Is it a cow? Is it to milk a cow that's purple? Running it through different computer vision models also means that it is seen in a different way. So on the one hand, there's a model called ResNet 101, and it sees different kinds of fish. And then there's BagNet and it sees Sorrel as a type of grass. So it predominantly looks at the grass. And the others are types of brown furred animals, so either dogs or a gazelle or an ox. And what it turns out to be is that on the one hand, you look at shape, and on the other, a texture. And that's the way a model is trained. It defines what it sees. I mean, we are using these human words to talk about technology. That doesn't really make sense, but we somehow have to communicate and, you know, try and figure out how these I-models function.

Again, I think there's always a certain absurdity and humor in my work to make it accessible, but at the same time, it becomes quite drastic quite quickly. So sure, there's a shark. What does it mean within a domestic space? You have a couch that looks like a cow. It could also still be funny. It becomes less humorous pretty quickly when, again, there are people involved. And there are always people involved in a domestic space.

This article from 2015, which has a really sensational headline, as this robot is suddenly eating this woman's hair. It certainly doesn't' have any agency. It's a Roomba -- a self-cleaning robot. In 2015, the Roombas didn't have computer vision. They worked on infrared sensors, so they were just looking at distances. But I think there's certain parameters built into how to or what operates that are assumptions by whomever has created this thing, right?

At what point of day does it clean? Which is based on like a 9:00 to 5:00 schedule. Now, you can define this yourself in the app, but we're talking a bunch of years ago. At the same time, there was a bed, right? Sleeping on the floor or sleeping on a futon is not the way you sleep. Obviously, a bed is like a raised sort of western piece of furniture. So there's all of these sort of ideas of not just common sense but also, again, what do the design spaces look like and who is defining them to these automated systems?

And I mean, again, sort of domestic spaces. I think some of this is speculative. Some of these products already exist. Some might be in your own houses. Some, you know, might never exist. Boston Dynamics really wanted to have this SpotMini in 2018, at least, as something that would sort of cohabitate with you. Now, we have seen it become a completely different animal, which is to surveil public spaces. But what they all have in common is that they do have a camera. The thing I want to talk about is the camera, less the object. I think the object always kind of sensationalizes computer vision. It puts it in sort of science fiction space of like a robot. We need the robot so the camera can move through the space, but at the end of the day, the robot also needs the camera to navigate. And that relationship is the important one.

So one, sort of, thing we can talk about today is, at least for, me this idea that computation is the new object, so that Kodak sort of wanted to have in the fifties and the sixties where there's not so much a point of capture anymore. There's, I think for iPhone, there's one trillion processes that happen once you actually take a photo before the image appears. So computational photography is in Smart Phones, but it is a different idea of capture. So optics, at this idea of a camera seeing, has dramatically changed technology and the ways of seeing.

"So machine learning is a clean, mathematical apparatus that gives the status quo the aura of logical inevitability. The numbers don't lie." This is a quote from an article that was looking at the way face recognition and computer vision technologies were used in the hiring process, so that you would prescreen candidates before you would have human-to-human interviews to figure out if they would be a right fit. And for me, at least, this quote would directly attack with the research I am doing, like is this actually a logical inevitability? Perhaps, but to what ends? And what is actually the question you want to direct computer vision to?

And so this directly leads me to synthetic data. Synthetic data is the type of data that used to train computer vision in at least a domestic sense. I think one reason being that there simply aren't enough[...]. There aren't enough photos of domestic spaces. And who I am talking about are computer engineers that have probably most often not spoken to any designer or a philosopher that similarly have addressed these questions, right? All of this research happens in sort of a vacuum of solving a computer scientist's question, which is creating an algorithm or creating a computer vision model that can recognize certain objects. But what those objects are aren't necessarily questioned. And I think, as we've seen over these three days, they definitely are. They're just happening in a different discipline than the ones here. And there's a lack of connection oftentimes between these different research endeavors.

Synthetic data is gathered to generate and, what I mean is there are 3D floor plans and there are furniture, accessories, et cetera, and they're automatically generating architectural spaces having cameras on precalculated trajectories or like paths for these 3D spaces. And the videos that they generate, then, become the training data. Ultimately, it's still about a 2D image, but its frame is extracted from rendered videos.

And here we are looking specifically at one of these data sets, which is produced by the Dyson Robotics Lab at

Imperial College in London -- Dyson from the Dyson vacuum cleaners. And this one is called CNET RGBD. And what I was interested in is, okay, but then what is this architectural space, right? How do you define it? And you, again, being computer engineers, they were really specific in having categories of rooms, one being bedrooms, offices, kitchens, living rooms, and bathrooms.

Again, I think there's a huge assumption that everyone lives like that. There are definitely very different living arrangements. I don't have an office. And at the same time, there are also very strict lists of the categories of objects that will be placed in these different kinds of room types. I have just highlighted a few here that stand out. Some we can agree on, something like a chair and a lamp. Seems pretty straightforward, rather mundane. But then, Media Player iPod, like why is the iPod not a media player?

On the other hand, there's a gun and sword and a toy. Are we talking about weapons? Are we talking about a toy? Again, I think there are all kinds of questions that basically become -- they are being treated logically as a category. And the deeper meaning behind them is completely lost. There is no context to any of these categories.

For example, taking -- this is still out of one of the movies -- taking this object of the gun, rendering it as a depth image, which we have seen in some of the other presentations, depth images would -- it's a representation of the distance from a virtual camera to, well, whatever is in the background receding. The black here is the darkest and furthest away from the virtual camera. And the light is the closest. You're not really seeing a gun; you're just seeing distances since the distance reveals the object.

But then rendering it in a different way of seeing, you know, you can reveal the different kind of textures. In this case, it is a plastic gun but, of course, this could be completely different. And so, again, looking at what information is contained within an image, what sort of context is missing or can be added? And also, what are the implications of such?

One more look at the CNET RGBD data sets, I was particularly intrigued by the image that is circled in yellow. What we are looking at is different kinds of office scenes. The top right image also has this thing called a projection space. It would have media, places, like TVs, and these spaces automatically get textured. And I was particularly struck by this one. Looking in the folders, because a data set is a set of folders that you can open in your finder, there are two images in projection spaces, the two textures that you can use to apply to these media surfaces. And both of them are from FOX News which, you know, normally speaking in Europe, I had to be introduced about what FOX News is here.

I don't. But, you know, there's again, there's this sort of question of "Is that an assumption? Is that an intention?" Probably it's just, you know, happenstance, like "I have to" -- I being, again, someone doing this job. I have to find textures, images, that represent media, TV, well, maybe I have my Facebook open. I put it in there.

I don't think there are so many deep reflections, probably, in how these data sets are assembled, but one of my main questions is there isn't so much annotation. And this happens. Why, actually, are there two FOX News images in there? There's no documentation of the process.

Similarly, here, we are speaking to one of the scientists from CNET RGBT, which is one of the things I tried to do, you know, getting a sort of contact which normally kind of confused like, "Why do you want to talk to me?" And I think for me that's really important because, obviously, there are always people involved in making things. And speaking to them about their work reveals a lot about their intentions, about the way they've made things, maybe what they want the thing to end up with, the context, and the applications.

This specific case was interesting because they were very frustrated as to how there were mailboxes in all of these rooms. You know, they were mailboxes that were supposed to be outside of the house; they shouldn't be inside. And it just happened in the way that the mailbox was categorized. It was a box. A box is like a mundane object. It could be in any room. But it ended up just being that they were mailboxes. I mean, it wasn't like a technical mistake, right? It was just the way that these files were sorted in the folders.

So again, a still from the video. Tons of mailboxes inside. Again, I mean, now we are in an architectural context. But similarly, linguistics has tackled or at least tried to address some of these difficulties, one being this idea of fuzzy borders, right? So that an object always needs a context. And the context defines the way it's named -- the way it's seen. Something like where does a vase begin or where does the bowl end? Like where do these objects kind of meet? And there's always a spectrum.

Computer vision training sets, at least for now, they can't -- you know, there's no context to the data itself. What happens -- well, first this one. William Labov, who is a linguist, in 1975 was, you know, he had a specific data set. And he asked people with these objects, "Hey, if it's in a full context. If it's in a neutral context. Is it now a cup? Is it a vase? If you put flowers in it, is your cup still a vase? If it has a handle, et cetera." Really sort of questioning what these, you know, industrial products mean to you as the user. And so he sort of decided, "Well, there is a calculation I can make, like there's a statistic." But the point is this statistic only applies to the exact data set that he has, right? It's not generalized; whereas, the computer vision researchers I've been talking to, their aim, really, is to make something that is universal, right? Something that you can create in an incubator and then scale on a global level.

And one more example for this data set is in the group "Chair" which, again, feels like something you can kind of, you know, decide upon what a chair is. It isn't so straightforward. There are also these four objects among other ones that are more or less disturbing. And on the one hand, you know there's armchair, armchair, armchair. Straight chair. None of them are actually that.

Again, I think there's humor, but there are also very grave situations that are completely neglected and put without any context at all in a space that they are not supposed to be in.

Putting [...] Hahn, who is a fantastic researcher, computational engineer, who has written a paper called, "The Impossibility of Automating Ambiguity" through the practice of clustering, sorting, and predicting human behaviour and action. These systems impose order, equilibrium, and stability to the active, fluid, messy, and unpredictable nature of human behaviour and the social world at large. What I'm interested in is what she is saying. And what she is saying is again, this I think on the one hand scale, like you might create something for a very specific use, okay, but at the moment that you scale it, there's a certain absurdity or a certain violence that can appear. But at the same time, life is much messier than the logic that machine learning may or may not want to impose on it. And I think that doesn't mean that it should be scraped, right, but it's more like there should be an awareness -- there should be an annotation or documentation in how these tools are being put together, by whom.

Some of these things I am trying to tackle in a new research lab at Design Academy Eindhoven titled, "Parametric Truth", which is that term that sort of, you know, carried on through my practice, which is simply trying to look at the sort of the very, you know, softwares, that have become so standardized and normal in our practices talking about, like, as designers, for example, the Adobe Suite.

And just trying to, you know, sit with it. Why does the button look a certain way? What do I expect the interface to do if I don't know, if I use this one slide or why does it behave a certain way? And not so much from a coding standpoint, but really just as someone using it, and not just taking it as a given. And so really starting a dialogue again, not so much also saying "No" to things, but trying to find a position where you can make decisions again and not just sort of just take tools for granted.

What it means, specifically, for the model home research is for me at least making a documentation of the training data sets that I found and trying to figure out how they correlate. There might be a new paper in 2021 with new data, but the data might actually be siphoned from a paper from 2017 or 2019.

Simply, there isn't so much -- of course there's references. But most of this I figured out by downloading the data sets and literally just going through it. Because they might be named newly, right? They're repackaged, where there isn't necessarily suddenly new 3D data. A lot of this comes from game asset stores, like Unreal. Most of it is from the [...] Warehouse. There's only a certain amount of data that is added to this. So again, I think a documentation strategy is important here.

And another way I've been interested in, you know, how do you interact as someone that makes -- it's an implicit position, like I like to make things. But that also means that I am using the tools I'm critiquing. And one thing I have been interested in, as well, is how do you, through the act of making, have a research position? Can you test boundaries? Can you figure out how far a tool works or isn't supposed to work, if such a thing exists? And what I am trying here is a new tool from Luma AI, which is texture 3D, so you would insert a prompt and you get a 3D image back which, of course, is just a sort of ultimate idea for computer vision training that you could prompt data sets.

The thing here is that they have everything that people have prompted online. What you are looking at -- I just packaged them in these sort of fake action figure packages -- but I have downloaded the figures. And so what you are looking at is the woman of my dreams and the man of my dreams. That's someone's prompt. And what they get back are these two very wonderful sort of Netflixy personas.

And at the same time, also the very simple character design of the normal man is a very specific typology of what a man is supposed to look like, right? So why is a man that and not all of the other possibilities of the spectrum?

And I think some of that is very important seeing how, you know, practices are becoming much more digital, but also the players are, to some extent, a little bit undefined. I think in video it's really important in how they are setting up a platform called Omniverse, which some of you may or may not be familiar with. And they are really interested in sort of rebuilding -- well, making everything accessible as a 3D model for the purpose, of course, to be able to model. But there are similar limitations in terms of what's available is actually what you are going to be building with. If you scale it up, that also means is everything going to start looking the same?

You know, scale is unlike variety. I think to repeat some of the questions and thoughts, but I think there is, you know, sort of an impossibility at creating very general AI applications. At the same time, I don't think scale is a way to solve diversity. I think at least in the research that I've been doing, you see that a lot where to create something that addresses more or different kinds. Data sets are scaled up, but I mean all of that has to come from somewhere. And if something is not documented, then it's still not going to be in there.

And with that, of course, also comes the question of "Do you even want to be included?" And you could be a person. But of course, you could also be your environment. Could be things you do. And so, you know, the questions are much more complex. I think on the one hand, one of these things is that they probably should be addressed in a much more interdisciplinary way and at least from the perspective that a lot of the research happens in pockets. But they share research questions.

There isn't so much of it dialogue, often times. And, you know, some of these questions might have been addressed by disciplines in different ways. But it isn't necessarily integrated into a larger practice. Thank you.

Relatives

Chris Cornelius
Professor and Chair
University of New Mexico

So I said in Oneida that I extend my greetings, love, and thankfulness to all of you. I am Chris Cornelius of the Wolf Clan, and People of the Standing Stone is the earth that I come from. I am very happy to be here and thank you for the invitation to share my work.

I've entitled my talk "Relatives". It is a concept in Indigenous culture that all living things are related. And we speak of all of these things as our relatives, including stones. Stones are our grandfathers. They are just living in a much longer timeline than we are as humans.

I think about both humans and non-humans and how we interact with one another and being good relatives with each other. I started my practice in 2003, when I was asked to be a culture consultant and collaborative designer with Antoine Predock on the Indian Community School of Milwaukee. It is a K through 8 private school. Students only have to prove Native ancestry to attend the school. There are about 350 students that attend the school.

The school purchased nearly 200 acres just southwest of Milwaukee, in Franklin, Wisconsin, and students come from the metropolitan Milwaukee area to this place. But it's a place of community, as well as a school. It was started by three mothers in the late sixties who were unhappy with how their children were being taught history, the history of this country.

One of the things that we did on the project, and that really served my primary role, was to layer our culture into the architecture, and translate the culture of the 11 tribes of Wisconsin that are attending the school. One of the things we did was to strip all of the institutional names from things in the school. For instance, they have never called the place that they eat "the cafeteria." It is called "Feast." This is the student entrance. It's called "Migration." And the school opened in 2007, and they still call those things the same names today.

So largely, my role was embedding the culture into the architecture. These tree columns were harvested from the Menominee Nation in Wisconsin. Many of them are over 300 years old and they hold stories that are pre-European contact. And they are inside the school to begin to tell those stories.

One of the images that I have created early in the project was this vertical graphic of everything from the site, all the way up to the moon, really understanding that when we are creating architecture in a place, we are intervening in a system of reciprocities. And how does the work interact in those reciprocities? And then what lessons can we learn from our non-human inhabitants? What lessons can we learn from animals that burrow into the earth? There's a depth of frost in that area of Wisconsin that's four feet, where the animals, birds, butterflies, bees, everything that is migrating across the air. Where are the seasonal winds? Where does airline traffic happen? Where does space travel happen? Where are satellites? All the way up to the moon, understanding, again, that those are a series of reciprocities, and that intervening into that system, we have a responsibility as designers to understand that and to begin to think about that relationship.

This is an image that I did that we translated many cultural values into these graphics. And so one of the Indigenous concepts I wanted to share with you that is really important in my work, and in the way that I see myself as a designer, is this idea of relationality. In Indigenous culture, we talk about things as if we are related to them. That's why we call the Earth our mother. The moon is our grandmother. The sky is our father. Stones are our grandfathers. We almost mean that literally in a very familial way and how those things are related. So, again, our non-human relatives are also our relatives. And we think of them in that manner.

In many Indigenous cultures, not all, we have talked about plants as our oldest relatives, meaning that some are food; some are medicine. They have seen good growing seasons, bad growing seasons, and droughts. I do believe that we should be talking about buildings as our youngest relatives, thinking about them as if we were related to them. It changes the responsibilities that we have as designers when we are putting them into the world.

If we think about it, they are very much like children, right? They produce waste. They consume a lot of resources. They breathe. They sweat. We need to think about those things in the way that we are putting things into the world. And so, for me, this is how I began to think about architecture as if we are related to it.

Early on in my career, shortly after the Indian Community School, I started to make these models and drawings. And I was trying to escape this idea of design, especially for Indigenous people, as everything is a metaphor for something else. But really thinking about things, for instance, what if we weren't clear about who or what made this thing or designed it? Was it a human? Was it a non-human? Was it some other sort of phenomena? Was it things that understood nature, weather, in ways that we couldn't'? I made them in these found boxes. I thought of the boxes as being similar to the architectural site. It has a history. It is confined. We can't make it bigger. We can't make it smaller. It has all these other contingencies.

And instead of making humans as the scale figures, I started to put animals in them. And in this, I'm not really answering the question of whether this deer is admiring this thing; has just happened upon this thing; has designed this thing. All of those things are in the realm of possibility. And so some of these are like 3-dimensional sketches. I was sort of building them as I was designing them. I cast these plaster landscapes for them and really started to think about what if I didn't try to make a thing as a metaphor for another thing?

Some of them started as drawings. Some of them really quick sketches, like this one on the far left. I was thinking about what if cladding was like feathers? If it interacted in that way in the middle? What if I started to play with the moray pattern of this mesh, and what if I had put a thing in a box that was intended to open and close, but it could never close again, and was really just a seat to see the moon and begin to think about that?

I started to see this as a kind of almost athletic conditioning, meaning that it was preparing me for the race. It was preparing me for the competition, expanding my ideas about architecture. And when I was teaching, I talked to students about that, that we should be using all cognitive parts of our brain, even the ones that are our subjectivity. And it's one of the things I think we don't normally teach our students to do very well, but it is something that I think about.

I then did this series of drawings that I call the Moon Domiciles. They are all based on my tribe's moon calendar. There are 13 moons. Many Indigenous cultures have these calendars. They are based on the new moon. And usually, they are named after something that is happening in the environment. And so, again, I was using non-humans as the kind of scale figures.

And this one is called the Thunder Moon. It would need an apparatus on the top of it. What if the first clap of thunder actually happened while it was sleeping? And I needed to be awoken by that. And the apparatus itself was like a deer's ear because a deer is largely prey. It has to hear its predators. And so that's why I put it into this drawing.

When I'm drawing these things, I started to do this in 2003 when I was the Artist in Residence when I was drawing things. I was trying to draw my tribe's creation story. I stopped erasing things in my sketch book. I stopped erasing anything. I didn't start over. I didn't turn the page. I just kept drawing over these things. And that's how I came at this sort of layered approach to drawing.

And each one of these are -- I'm just looking at different things the ways that you get into the structure. What if the structure itself was different? What if it didn't have columns? In this case, what if it was just a bundle of sticks? What if humans weren't involved in this at all? The bear is pulling out this sort of irrigation device that irrigates its landscape, and the top catches rainwater.

And then I started to render differently. I was making these Rhino models when I was doing the drawings. I originally just did it so that I was casting shadows correctly when I water-colored them. But then I started to think, "What if I started to render differently? What if I changed the camera view from being that sort of standard human eye level? What if it was at the eye level of a wolf? What if the structure of this thing was like organic and structural hair? Like a porcupine's quills. What if there was just so much of it that it actually held this thing up? And what if the wolf could see things in the sky that I can't see as a human? We know that birds can see things that we can't see, right? We know that birds can see magnetism, so they fly towards it, and they fly away from it. But what if the wolf can see things in the sky that I can't see? I was thinking about rendering these possibilities as rendering these things visible in the work.

In 2018, I did this installation, and was part of a residency at the Bookworm Gardens, the children's literature garden in Sheboygan, Wisconsin, just north of Milwaukee. I wanted to explore this idea of the trickster in Indigenous storytelling. And the trickster is usually an animal. Sometimes it's some other sort of phenomena, but the animal does things to teach us about our own humanity. It teaches us things about greed, vanity, gluttony, those kinds of things. It might eat too much. It might hunt things that it's not supposed to hunt. It might think that it's things that it's not. It might think that it's a fox.

And so the structure itself doesn't really follow any sort of form. It doesn't have a program. Because it's in this children's literature garden, I wanted children to see it and then start to tell their own stories about it. I happened on a young woman while I was making the thing. She didn't know I was the person that was making it. I asked her what she thought of it, and she said, "Well, it looks like it's from a movie that I don't know about yet. Or it's something that animals made and then people came later." And I was like, "That's exactly right. That's exactly what you should be doing with this thing."

And so I made it from trees that were harvested from the garden. I used the same exact copper mesh on the piece that I was using on the smaller models earlier. And it's really some sort of impromptu structure. And I'm really just thinking about simple structural principles here, similar to how Indigenous people in the Great Plains had made tee pees, where you loosely tie together three trees, and then you walk those trees up. And then you start to tie them together.

I also started to think about this idea that why can't architecture have regalia, too? And thinking about the role of regalia in Indigenous culture. It's not just aesthetic. And it's not just ornamental. It actually tells us things about who you are, where you came from, what you may have accomplished, and so on. On the right is a headdress of a Mohawk male. I know that it's Mohawk because it has three feathers up. The Mohawk are part of the Haudenosaunee Confederacy. My people, the Oneida, are also part of that Confederacy. If it had two feathers up and one feather down, then I would know it's Oneida.

It has antlers, so I know that it's a chief. The chiefs are elected. It is sort of a democratic republic that we had. You can look this up. The U.S. Constitution is largely plagiarized from the Haudenosaunee Confederacy. It is the longest running democracy in the world, ever, still running today.

I started to think about what if architecture could have similar regalias? When I was making these models, I would put these things on it, and so when I made the trickster -- the full-scale one -- I did a similar thing. The one that I made is loosely made on this model. I also started to think about the role of drawings, models, buildings and/or structures in architecture, and how we are taught about that as being a kind of linear process, right? We think of the thing. And then we represent the thing through drawings. Those drawings are typically handed off to someone else who might make a model. There is also a scale or a sort of representation of the thing. And then the building is supposed to be the same thing.

But what if there was a real dialogue between those things? And I didn't do a set of drawings for the trickster? And I didn't make a model of it before I made it? I just made it. And so I was really thinking about the dialogue between all of those things -- the drawings, models, and structures -- when I made that trickster.

In 2021, I was asked to do a permanent land acknowledgement for Lawrence University, a small liberal arts college in Wisconsin. They wanted to acknowledge the fact that their campus is on Menomonee land. The Menomonee are Indigenous to the State of Wisconsin. It is called Otaeciah or crane, which in the Menomonee language, it means crane. And the crane is part of their clan structure. The crane is in charge of architecture and art. It's one of the few sort of instances that I know of where a clan is in charge of art and architecture. And that is their responsibility.

This is the original land base of the Menomonee in the state. You can see it's a very large portion of the state. It's kind of hard to see. If you look at a satellite photo of Wisconsin, you'll see this sort of rectangle. It looks like a photoshop or a glitch. That is the boundary of the Menomonee reservation. They have always sustainably harvested that land. Over the past 100 years, they have increased the yield of that land from 125 to 140 percent. They only take trees down when they're too old or they're shading. They have a very strict sort of forestry plan. And Lawrence University is located kind of right in the middle of that. So they wanted to acknowledge the fact that their campus is on that land.

The thing that was also important to me is that I engaged the Indigenous students at the university. These are students that are not just from Wisconsin; they're from all over the country. Lawrence University has a program called College Horizons, where they bring Indigenous students to the campus. And they basically talk about what it means to go to college as an Indigenous person. And one of the things that really struck me about their presence and how they thought about themselves, and the university, was that they don't see anything that is Indigenous. They don't see anything that represents them. They don't have places to go that they can begin to identify with.

So this piece is something that you can get into. It's in a sort of major thoroughfare of the university, right next to the library, and students use it, and have used it, as a place of gathering, a place of protest. It is a thing that now they can identify with. All Indigenous students that come there are intended to sort of engage with the piece. It has a geometric pattern that is from the Menomonee, similar to their artwork and the custom perforation of the piece. And, like I said, you can get inside it. And it is a thing to begin to reflect on that landscape.

I was asked, as one of five designers, to contribute to this exhibition at the Crystal Bridges Museum in Bentonville, Arkansas. The exhibition is called Architecture at Home. And each one of us were funded to build a full-scale prototype of housing. I wanted to address Indigenous housing in general. This is the HUD house that I grew up in on my reservation. I can identify myself to anyone that's from my reservation. They'll know what I mean when I say I grew up in Site 1, which is how we identify ourselves.

If you grew up in Site 2, we kind of know where that is, as well. But this is the Google street view -- the current Google street view. It's a little bit of an improved sort of home than what I grew up in. I went to high school nine miles away, and what I saw in my non-Indigenous friends' neighborhoods, I saw that their houses were close together. They had sidewalks. They had trees. They had garages. We didn't have a garage. We didn't have a porch. We didn't have a sidewalk. There were no trees on the outside of that, so there was this sort of way of seeing the world that I think started to shape me as a designer and an architect that I saw that there was a sort of fundamental lack of care with these things, meaning the house and how they work.

And this is an image that one of my students from Yale produced in the studio that I taught that semester in Spring '21. We are working in the top right image and that community, the Opaswayak Cree Nation in Manitoba. I was explaining to the students that this house, the exact same house that I grew up in, is deployed all over the U.S. in the Southwest, in the Great Plains, and in Canada. It doesn't reflect the people. It doesn't reflect the environment. It doesn't reflect the landscape. And when I say it's the same house, the floorplan is almost exactly the same. So the one that I grew up in in Wisconsin looked like this. This is a floor plan from a house in South Dakota, and I'll tell you it's almost exactly the same floor plan of the house that I grew up in. I would say that this one is a bit of a fancier version because it has a Master bath and a regular bath. We only had one bath in our three-bedroom home.

My response to this was that I wanted to make a thing that was not my HUD house -- is not this thing. My HUD house didn't have a porch. My HUD house didn't have a place for a fire. It didn't have a view to the sky. It didn't have a place for my non-human relatives. It didn't have a place for me to do my homework. It had a living room, a bedroom, and a kitchen.

In thinking about Indigenous space, I was thinking about how if we didn't have these kinds of spaces, right? Like a bedroom, a living room, and kitchen. What if we had open spaces, spaces of production, culture, ritual, diplomacy? That's what Indigenous dwellings actually were. And what if our non-human relatives could also be housed in these things? What if I was making habitats for them, as well?

I created these renderings that show a bear and a wolf coming up to the house, and this is the prototype that was built, and we installed it in August of '21. I think it's going to be de-installed sometime next month, but I was thinking about this as a modular thing, as well. The housing didn't reflect how we lived on our reservations. In many cases, you might have multiple generations living in a home. You might have adult children who have children. For a period of time, my grandmother lived with us. I slept on the couch. She slept in my bedroom. Families can expand. They can contract. And what if we built these in modules where we could add a bedroom? Or we could take a bedroom off? Or we could have basically what is an accessory dwelling unit where my grandmother could live?

On reservations, we don't need property lines because the connection of land ownership is in the collective. The people own the land, and so when you own a home on the reservation, you only own the structure, and you are leasing the land. But what would that do to the shapes of these homes? And what would it do to the ways that we begin to live?

So this one, I didn't have the budget to build a sort of big masonry hearth, so I built this big steel frame to stand in the place of that hearth. But the idea that that is the place of fire, and that fire is the place of council, there might be a place of cooking, it might be a place of ceremony. And all of that happens within the home.

And so this house has the regalia of my culture on it. My HUD house did not have those things. And beginning to think about how that actually works. These are jingles that are on Indigenous womens' dresses, so it's kind of a [...] Indian culture at this point. But it is intended to begin to signal you're dancing and walking, so they are usually sewn onto a dress, closely packed together and they make a noise when women are dancing.

On the inside, I am trying to bring in light in different places. My HUD house didn't have any light on the inside. And it didn't have a view to the sky. And this one does. So I am bringing light in high and low. This idea of the view fo the sky is usually coupled with fire or with the place of ceremony. And I'm just trying to tap into those things within Indigenous architecture.

These are historical images of architecture all over the country. My people are in the lower right. There is a Haudenosaunee Longhhouse, and it has a hole in it for where the smoke comes out. This is a term that I wish I had invented, but it is "indigenuity" -- this idea that Indigenous people were really highly sophisticated builders, but they had spaces that you could have a fire and let smoke out of, so my house has that, as well.

In thinking about my non-human relatives, we did this rendering early before the project was built. We put this deer on the porch. And then there's a snow owl in the hearth looking for its prey. But one morning when I came to the site during the installation, I saw these deer tracks that were walking right up to and then disappear. So that means that the deer either went into the house; they definitely went onto the porch. But it wasn't afraid of the thing. Someone else sent me an Instagram video of deer walking up to the thing. And that way, for me, it confirms that I'm trying to be a good relative to this thing, right? The sort of little ledges on the openings were there for birds to think about nesting in.

The last piece I want to show you is ukwe-tase which means stranger in Oneida. This will be opening at the Chicago Architecture Biennale on Wednesday. It is currently being installed as we speak. But I wanted to approach the idea of land acknowledgements slightly differently because I've been asked to do these things in other communities. And in Chicago, I didn't want to say something very specific about the Indigenous land there. I wanted to say something about the fact that I'm Indigenous and I'm a stranger in that land, too. I'm a visitor.

I don't have some sort of secret knowledge about Indigeneity. So that's one aspect of it. That's why it's called "The Stranger." The other part of it is this idea within Indigenous knowledge, epistemology, ontology, that we have things in our culture: visions, dreams, stories, that are regarded as truth that is part of our knowledge system. They are not fantasy. They're not fables. They are truth. And one of these truths is demonstrated in this image from the show Reservation Dogs, if you've seen it on Hulu. In the first season, they introduce a story -- the Deer Woman. It happened to be a few weeks before this actually aired, I happened to have a discussion with Edgar Heap of Birds who is an Indigenous artist. I said, "Do you have stories within your community that you don't normally share with other people? You might share with other Indigenous people? And he said, "Yes." There is the Deer Woman.

The Deer Woman appears as a very attractive woman. And she attracts bad men. And once she attracts these bad men, they are never seen again, right? So it's implied that this is the consequence of being a bad man. In the show, we see the attractive woman, but when she gets in the car, that's when we see the feet of the deer. And so in Indigenous knowledge, I believe that to be absolutely true.

I have a story about this in my community. I won't share it, but I believe it to be true. I never saw it. I just believe that it was there. And so this piece is intended to do some of that. The feet of a deer can be on a woman. And that is true, right? And this piece is not only a structure, but it is an animal. What if it was more like an animal? So I cut it into these three pieces. The haunch, the tail, and the carapace. It will have cladding of deer hides on one portion of it. It will have more jingles than my HUD house had. And then the carapace of it will have a different pink finish on the inside that's intended to be like the turtle shell.

Also, on the inside, this chimney in which I can literally have a view to the sky. It's going to be one of those sort of big gallery spaces and exhibition spaces in the Chicago Cultural Center, but it will have a screen that has recordings of the sky in New Mexico. It's one of the things where I live that is just so striking and amazing. The sky there is amazing! It's one of the things that's my way of bringing the view to the sky. It's broken, like I said, into these three pieces: a part that has fur; a part that has these jingles; and a part of this is the shell. And so just like a thing can be a deer and a woman, it can be an animal and a building.

It is scaled so that it is not quite to full scale. It's bigger than a model. It's smaller than a building. People can get into it, but maybe not so much comfortably. You can see here the chimney, which has the screen that we can see the sky. For me, I'm trying to think about architecture and seeing it as one of my relatives and beginning to think about how we really sort of mean that.

Can architecture have this sort of state of being that ties into Indigenous knowledge? And architecture for Indigenous people?

Ethics and Ecocidal Listening: Oceanic Refractions as an Artistic Case Study

AM Kanngieser

Transversal Geographies, Marie Curie International Research Fellow in Geography, Royal Holloway University of London

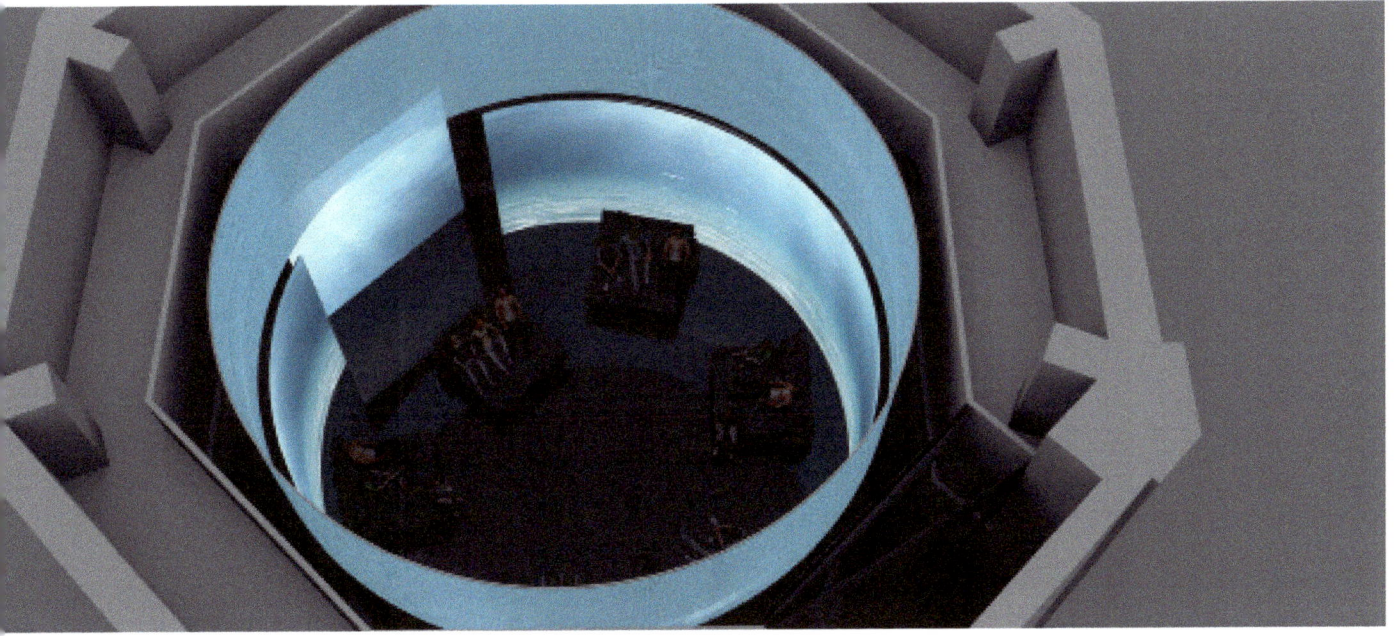

1   Oceanic Refractions Kuppelhalle Berlin

In 2018 I was invited to visit the archipelago of Kiribati, located in the Pacific Ocean around 1000 miles from Hawaii. A big ocean state, Kiribati holds a land mass of around 315 sq. miles and an oceanic economic zone of 1,328,890 sq. mi. Tarawa, the most inhabited of the islands peaks at around 3 m above sea level. I went to Kiribati in part to meet with Dr Teweiariki Teaero, a renowned scholar, poet and educator who had directed the Oceania Center at the University of the South Pacific in Fiji for many years before returning to his homeland where at the time he had been planning on running for government. Teweiariki spoke with me at length about the status of Kiribati as one of the already most critically affected frontline nations. I asked him what was a lesson for non-Pacific Islanders to learn about understanding everyday life there. He said to me "Two ears, one mouth, don't talk too much. Learn to listen more. Not only to hear, but to be able to develop another thing and that is to be able to interpret. These things are different, they occur at different levels. The hearing and the interpretation of the sound...it's very much part of our world" (Teaero 2018).

I start with this invitation from Teweiariki, who has now passed, to listen because it is widely emerging as a methodological concern in approaches to understanding our continuing planetary existence. In her book Undrowned, Black Feminist Lessons from Marine Mammals, Alexis Pauline Gumbs asks "how can we listen across species, across extinction, across harm?" (2020, 15). The question posed by Gumbs is one that many of us are actively grappling with. The catastrophes of climate crisis, expressions of the colonial-capitalist violences of white supremacy, are multiplying rapidly and the urgency to do something sits in tension with a lack of knowing what to do and how. While disciplines invested in tech are trying to forge ahead through ostensibly sustainable and green solutions, the arts are trying to communicate what is oftentimes barely comprehensible, let alone easily distilled. It is apparent that more interdependent orientations are needed, which foreground how people and communities relate to the earth as a part of the earth.

In my work as an interdisciplinary sound artist, geographer and writer I develop practices of listening and attunement to approach the relations between people, places and ecologies (Image 1). My training as a geographer informs how I come to the sonic field because I am interested in deconstructing what it means to listen to, make sense of, and translate the sounds of environmental and human entanglements through the assumption of an Anglo-European onto-epistemological lens. A crucial aspect of what I do is situating what how I listen as a white European-Australian, and how I inhabit place as a settler-coloniser. My work is grounded in a commitment to finding ways to be in what Metis Professor Zoe Todd calls "good relations" (Kanngieser & Todd 2020) with where I am, and most crucially, knowing the boundaries around this and what that means for how I comport myself in the communities I collaborate with.

For the past several years I have been speaking with communities about the impacts of the climate crisis in the Pacific and examining how European colonisation through resource capitalism and environmental racism exacerbates these. My orientation in this is toward the everyday ways that communities determine their own practices of liberation and care within and despite ecocide. In my work with communities on climatic crisis and survival, I prioritise listening to contested and difficult environments with sensitivity and pause. This listening doesn't just mean the physiological and psychological process of hearing. It's listening also to silences and cacophonies of expression by people and environments, and attempting to understand how to interpret these appropriately across local and global contexts. For the largest part, what this listening tells me are the many ways that my own assumptions, directions and interpretations are wrong. In this brief paper I want to emphasise how over the years my collaborators and I have slowly and carefully implemented what we have been told, particularly in the space of artistic production.

I am going to focus on our upcoming large scale audio-visual installation, Oceanic Refractions, co-produced with Fijian artist Mere Nailatikau and Fijian Australian artist Eliki Reade. This piece is launching in January 2024 in Berlin across two long-standing European art and media festivals, Transmediale and CTM. Oceanic Refractions emerges from years of consultation, preparation and consideration of what it means to ethically share frontline stories to audiences with different ways of knowing and being. Oceanic Refractions has its foundations in a longer-term project Climates of Listening, which began in 2015 working with predominantly Pacific women, queer and transgender artists, organisers and scholars to amplify movements for self-determination and liberation in the face of resource extraction, environmental racism and ecological disaster. The Pacific region is susceptible to a number of devastating changes including sea level rise, erosion, intensifying drought, floods, earthquakes, cyclones and tsunamis. Along with intersecting challenges such as economic development, health epidemics, and under and unemployment, nations of the Pacific, like other small island developing states, are held up as case studies for vulnerability. Through this lens of vulnerability, the sea of islands that Pacific poet and educator Epeli Hau'ofa spoke about becomes reduced to the limited perspective of "islands in a far sea" (1994, 152), which emphasizes remoteness and marginality over self-determination and autonomy. To counter the narrow definitions of resilience and vulnerability that the region tends to get pushed into through government, policy and NGO discourses, the project seeks to showcase the nuanced and variegated ways that people understand, produce knowledge about, and collectively attend to their lived experiences of ecocide.

Prior to Oceanic Refractions were a number of audio and audio-visual commissions including this year's Listening Across Faultlines: a long form three-part radio series for Deutschland Radio, and Crenulations Pacific Drift: an installation created in partnership with audio company Bang and Olufsen for the Struer Tracks Biennale in Denmark. Both of these works curated over thirty quotes from extensive ethnographic interviews with community Elders and advisors, fisher people, scholars, cultural ministers and chiefs. They focused on the testimonies of Professor Unaisi Nabobo-Baba, Dr. Teweiariki Teaero, Philip Tacom, Lydia Jacob and Simione Sevudredre from Kiribati, Papua New Guinea and Fiji on the themes of sound, silence and environmental relations. The thematic of listening and silence was substantially influenced by a book written by Professor Nabobo-Baba in which she outlines a typology of silence in Indigenous Fijian (iTaukei) knowledge systems, which allow for a "pedagogy of deep engagement" (2006, 94). Ideas and practices of listening as an Anglo-European construct are not adequate to encompass the vast meanings of listening as held by Pacific cultures. Simione Sevudredre notes:

I remember seeing in some print, the Indigenous way of listening is similar to how a psychologist listens. The listening is not only for the vocabulary and the intent, the subjects, the tone, the intensity, all these are taken into account and analysed, so we not only listen, we hear. What do we hear? We hear the said and the unsaid. So this is how relationships are very important in Indigenous iTaukei society. When the living people are in harmony, the land and the sea will reflect that, because they are an extension of us, we are an extension of them (Sevudredre 2022).

Rather than reconstruct conventional frontline narratives, it was important for us to orientate away from what Unangax̂ scholar Eve Tuck calls damage centred research – research that submerges the contexts of colonization and racism to locate "deficits" within minoritized communities rather than in the processes those communities are forced to endure. By emphasising Pacific cultural approaches that prioritise intergenerational knowledge of land and environments, we acted on the interviewees guidance to turn toward relations and care.

Throughout our process we consulted with our advisory board of Pacific Elders and community members who underscored that sensory engagement is endemic to Pacific storytelling; that it is heard, felt and seen. In a paper for WIRES climate change (2017) Harriet Hawkins and myself identified the need for sensorially attuned audio-visual work to address audiences on embodied and experiential registers. Rather than seeking to invoke empathy, Oceanic Refractions moves towards immersion and resonance – an attempt pay respect to the expression of the ocean as a "corporal and psychic relational vehicle" (2008, 111) as Banaban, I-Kiribati and African-American anthropologist Katerina Teaiwa describes it.

The project does this through a number of artistic technologies and techniques. In its largest site-specific iteration, Oceanic Refractions will be installed to fit the 17m high and 202m sq. Silent Green Kuppelhalle in Berlin (Image 2). We have worked with fabrication and projection specialists, Sara Murphy and Frank Prendergast at Space Forms and Olan Clarke at Algorithm, to create 5D immersivity. The installation features two ground level curved screens and the vertical space is hung with two flying screens and a flying string curtain onto which underwater videography produced by Fijian filmmakers, Dave Lavaki and Meli Tuquota, will be mapped. The projections feature a spacious array of underwater scenes predominantly taken from a diving depth of 2-3m below surface level, with a focus on light diffractions to emulate floating underwater looking upward toward the sky. We are working with olfactory artists Smell Art to create the oceanic scents choreographed with the audio-visual storyline. The audience are situated on custom built seating that mimics the ebb and flow of currents and drift; a movement intensified through the use of transducers that reverberate with the sound composition.

I want to stay for a moment with the sound as my area of expertise. The surround sound multichannel audio, composed by myself and musician Joseph Kamaru, comprises excerpts from the testimonies of Unaisi Nabobo-Baba, Teweiariki Teaero, Philip Tacom, Lydia Jacob and Simione Sevudredre, considering the cultural significance of water, marine subsistence, sea level rise and practices of listening to the ocean. The field recordings featured in this composition come predominantly from the places where the Elders we are hearing from reside, and there is an ethical and spiritual importance in keeping the integrity of these sounds, and voices, in emplaced relation. This is explained by Teweiariki:

If you look at the environment, it's part of the land and everything that surrounds that. In fact, in Kiribati, if you look at the language very closely, the word of our people and the word for land is the same. We call it te aba. ABA. You can talk to te aba and you mean land. You can talk about te aba and you mean people. So, there's a very close connection between land and people (Teaero 2018).

The sound recordings and the voices cannot be separated because peoples, lands and oceans cannot be separated. This onto-epistemology is almost impossible to reconcile with European ways of approaching environmental relations, which always inevitably centre the human even when attempting to dissolve this division. Because of this irreconcilability we are actively working with, rather than against, the tension and inexperience with unbiased listening. Xwélméxw (Stó:lō) philosopher Dylan Robinson writes that settler coloniser listening "is hungry for the felt confirmations of square pegs in square holes, for the satisfactory fit as sound knowledge slides into its appropriate place" (2020, 51). Such settler coloniser listening positions constitute, as Robinson puts it, "particular assemblages of unmarked structures of certainty that guide normative perception and may enact epistemic violence" (2020, 10). By dislocating the hierarchy of voice over environment and playing with non-didactic storytelling, Oceanic Refractions invites audiences into a comportment that may be more suited to approaching Pacific ways of interdependence.

By attending to these different sensorial registers, Oceanic Refractions seeks to create portals for intentional listening. Across the team's extensive experience in community advocacy, environmental and arts research and regional Pacific governance we are acutely aware of the challenges in asking audiences to not only listen, but also change behaviour. A number of existing Pacific centred climate projects, such as Our Home Our People and Sea of Island, even Tuvalu's own metaverse project, are deploying VR and other technologies to preserve memory and compel empathy. There are enormous impediments to systemic change over individual, national and international scales, and it is critical that projects offer audiences pathways toward education. Projects that work closely with communities are best equipped for clarifying community needs. Fundamentally, for Oceanic Refractions to complete its cycle the request has been made that it is returned to its homes in the Pacific. There is a stated desire that the work is accessible to use as a teaching resource for school curricula. There have also been requests to store interviews, recordings and transcriptions in local and national archives that are accessible to community members. As part of the listening work of the project we have drawn together a collective philosophy influenced by Pacific Research protocols, which explicitly lays out the importance of relationships to the longevity of the work – this extends from how the material is gathered and disseminated, to who is cited and how, to how money is distributed and circulated, to cultures of communication and respect for differing needs.

As I have outlined here, the larger project of Oceanic Refractions is founded on ethics of care and interdependence that incorporate humans and ecosystems beyond Anglo-European worldviews. This is a material shift that is relevant to projects and disciplines intent on cultivating respectful relations for anti-colonial social and environmental liberation. The commitment of relationality, writes Trawlwulwuy geographer Lauren Tynan, is "not a new metaphor to be reaped for academic gain, but a practice bound with responsibilities with kin and Country" (2021, 598). By pausing on listening and silence, with Oceanic Refractions we hope to contribute to the much larger and ongoing commitments to overturning and repairing the violence caused by Anglo-European colonisation and white supremacist, capitalist systems and their beneficiaries.

REFERENCES

Gumbs, Alexis Pauline. 2020. Undrowned, Black feminist lessons from marine mammals. California: AK Press. https://doi.org/10.3898/SOUN.78.01.2021

Hau'ofa, Epeli. 1994. "Our Sea of Islands". The Contemporary Pacific 6, no. 1: 148–61.

Hawkins, Harriet & Kanngieser, AM. 2017. "Artful Climate Change Communication: Overcoming Abstractions, Sensibilities and Distances". WIRES: Climate Change 8, no. 3: 1-12

Kanngieser, AM & Todd, Zoe. 2020. From environmental case study to environmental kin study. History and Theory: Studies in the Philosophy of History 59, no. 3: 385–393. https://doi.org/10.1111/hith.12166

Nabobo-Baba, Unaisi. 2006. Knowing and Learning: An Indigenous Fijian Approach. Suva: University of the South Pacific, Institute of Pacific Studies.

Robinson, Dylan. 2020. Hungry listening: Resonant theory for Indigenous sound studies. Minnesota: University of Minnesota Press.

Sevudredre, Simione. 2022. Personal interview with Mere Nailatikau. Suva, Fiji.

Teaero, Teweiariki. 2018. Personal interview with AM Kanngieser. 3 March. Tawara, Kiribati.

Teaiwa, Katerina Martina. 2008. "Saltwater Feet: The Flow of Dance in Oceania." In Deep Blue: Critical Reflections on Nature, Religion and Water, edited by Sylvie Shaw and Andrew Francis, 107-126. London: Equinox.

Tynan, Lauren. 2021. "What is relationality? Indigenous knowledges, practices and responsibilities with kin". Cultural Geographies 28, no. 4: 597-610. https://doi.org/10.1177/14744740211029287

IMAGE CREDITS

Figures 1 © Sara Murphy

Operational Transitions: Panel Discussion

Simone C Niquille, Chris Cornelius, Amer Kanngieser.
Moderated by Shelby Doyle.

AUDIENCE PARTICIPANT:
Hi. I have three questions for Simone. They are kind of built on top of each other. I will try to be as brief as I can. The first is about language. You talked about how object recognition algorithms have these kinds of different categories, such as the difference between iPod and media player. So how much of the kind of errors we are seeing in the case of the chairs are contributed by the limits of the language? And the second question is kind of built on top of that. It's like the matter of context. When those chairs, as shown without background, they are kind of floating objects. So how would multi-modal inputs, such as image to image, or video to 3D, will contribute or improve the algorithm's understanding of the context? And the third one is something that you haven't talked about as much as the matter of user agency. I was thinking about the diagram between the cup and the bowl. And something similar, such as a glass used for drinking water when it's tall enough. At some point, it can be used as a vase. What kind of situation would enable users to make different decisions about what the object is used for?

SIMONE NIQUILLE:
Thank you for these questions. I think the first one on language, I mean it's also important to point out that at least the specific data set that I showed, but also otherwise, the ones that I have access to are in English. That doesn't mean that there's no others. It's also my own limitation, as in my mother tongue will be Swiss-German. There's definitely none because it's not a written language. German, there's none that I'm aware of. So think, first of all, it's sort of my level of accessibility, in terms of just being able to type stuff and like find things. But I think a similar situation is reflected in at least the data sets that I see, where the research community is often also are multi-lingual, right? But English becomes a little bit of a default in terms of how these objects are labeled.

And, yeah, that is a very limited source of knowledge to that effect. I mean, we have seen in the other presentations -- I mean, there's many different ways of interacting, calling, you know, naming the world. And so I think one of the really obvious questions I'm sort of obsessed with this object of the chair. And, you know, I'm curious there. Are we talking about something to sit on? But then, why isn't the carpet also part of that data set and, you know, I think to some extent it's negotiations that we have on a human level that's deeply part of language and communication that, to a large extent, is removed in technological systems.

And I think some of it, to answer your other questions, the image of the shark? It's not always so much about improving the system, perhaps. It's also about being aware of its limits. I think, you know, yes, the Roomba can be fed with more and different kinds of languages with different typologies of a bed. But will it ever encapsulate sort of the vastness of a lived experience? The vastness of different cultures? DIY? Do we? I guess there's only this sort of very general "we", but it's not even sort of a solution that is something to strive forwards.

I personally would think, no. It's much more interesting to have tools that are incredibly specific, of being aware of their limitations and being able to use them to their abilities in whatever space necessary, rather than trying to solve them all. And at least, as a designer, I think that's always a little bit of a strange position because it will now make it better, right? You've identified the design problem. And now go and make the solution. And I think, at least my own position is so much more always as in, well, I just have tons of questions and I don't know how this works. I mean, let's start there. And then sort of through realizing and annotating and sort of understanding how something might have become what it is, being able to figure out its application. Again, thank you.

AUDIENCE PARTICIPANT:
My question is always coming as the mic goes closer. Such beautiful presentations. I can't thank each of you enough. Absolutely powerful. And what I am thinking about in all your presentations is how, through your work, you are showing us the intelligence of humans in that you all are able to bring together histories, fables and folklores, sound, in ways that technology -- the truth of technology is distilling, abstracting, and separating these things to understand them, but in all your works you are showing how we, as humans, understand these things deeply in ways that technology cannot. How we think about discretizing things in technology. And so with that in my mind, and your very grounded ways of acknowledging humanity, the environment, and its knowledges, what are your approaches, positions -- no, positions, that's a strong word -- approaches or thinking when it comes to, you know, a field of computational design, technology. What are your approaches to how you think through, think with, and use technology in your projects?

CHRIS CORNELIUS:
At least for me, I think that one of the things that, at least from my understanding, my own cultural understanding, that I tried to share is that we never saw humans at the top of the pyramid, let's say, right? That humans did not have dominion over nature as explained in the Book of Genesis. That's not how we saw these things.

But we saw this as in relation to one another. I just personally believe that technology is within that, right? Like it's about responsibility as being a good relative and how can I technologically be a good relative, as well? I know that there are people, Indigenous people, working in the gaming industry now, right? Like this is a way of how do we explain these cultural aspects of what we do?

When I taught the studio at Yale, too, I had one student who was really interested in gaming engines and gaming technology. I just asked him, because we were working in this community, the studio was in Spring '21, so it was virtual. We couldn't' actually go to this community. We had to engage them through this sort of digital interface. But I said, you know, knowing and seeing virtually the terrain through Goggle Earth and the place and understanding and that, can you show me how a wolf will see this landscape? How a deer will see this landscape? And how a muskrat will see this landscape? And he did it.

He did it with a gaming engine, because then he could begin to understand from that point of view how those things actually work. And I think it's really just about, for Indigenous people, it's really about understanding that Western knowledge had tried to almost dismiss everything else and say, "This is the way of thinking. These are the valuable sets of knowledge, and this is how we see the world."

For me, as someone trained as an architect and educated as an architect, I was always drawing these parallels between what I was learning and what my culture was. Because I never saw anything Indigenous. Those things weren't presented to me. I certainly am trying to change that. At the University of New Mexico, we do that. And they have always done that. And that's kind of why I went there.

But it's really about understanding that sort of relationship. But I do think that we should be thinking about the responsibilities we have in being good relatives. And are we using technology to separate people, which is what colonization is fueled by? It's creating this sort of radical otherness. Or are we trying to be inclusive, right, in understanding the limits of technology? And understanding where we can actually leverage it to begin to think about other things?

And for me, it's thinking about domesticity, even like how I grew up was like it's similar to the technology in a way that it's like making these containers. I'm supposed to sleep in this place. I'm supposed to eat in this place. And I'm supposed to relax in this place. And I can't do the other things anywhere else, right? Like I can't do these other things. Where I grew up, everyone is hacking their house, right? Everyone is hacking their home. How am I going to do my homework? Where am I supposed to do that? You know, if there's no space to do that?

Someone told me this story of Indigenous housing that they had engaged in in the Great Plains. They saw this house and it had this huge hole in it that went into the bathroom. And they were like, "How are you living like this? Why is that hole there?" And the guy said, "Well, how else is my horse supposed to drink?" The horse walks up to the house, puts its head through the hole, and it can drink out of the bathtub. That's how things were working. People were adjusting, right? People were adjusting to the landscape.

And what I am advocating for is for us to begin to think about how we can make better-suited environments for fostering culture and connection. But I do also think that certainly I have colleagues that are working in the realm of technology, and I have an artist friend who does a lot of AR work in parts and in engaging, so that thinking about Indigenous stories seen through the lens of technology is not a foreign thing, right? It's not something that is displacing that activity and way of knowing and understanding. It's actually just helping really augment it.

SHELBY DOYLE:
AM, do you want to take that question, too?

AM KANNGIESER:
Yes. Thanks for such a wonderful, generous question. I can't see you but thank you very much. I think it's a really interesting question, you know, especially thinking about, again, like I said at the beginning, I come at this as a geographer and as a social scientist. I am not an architect. The kinds of questions that concern me are about the material histories of technologies, as well. Obviously, I'm thinking, as well, of what is currently happening in the world and the way that different technologies come out of military R&D. You know, a lot of sound technologies that I am using have a very brutal and violent history, particularly in engagement with Indigenous communities, like sound and recording technologies, come out of military R&D, and have been used in ethnography, in anthropology, in disciplines to create particular kinds of knowledge and to, I suppose, render particular kinds of knowledge knowable and authentic in particular kinds of ways.

When I am using technologies in my work, I am always thinking about what are the histories of the technologies that I am using? And what do they carry with them, you know? What do they communicate with them? Obviously, if you are working with sound technologies and recording technologies, there are very big differences between using technologies with peoples' permission and with consent. And also, things like eavesdropping and surveillance and things like that. Those are concerns that always sit with me when I think about the technologies that I am using within this work.

Another thing that I really do need to comment on, as well, particularly in working across the Pacific, is what is the access to technology of the people that I'm working with. In a lot of the places that I work, there is very limited Internet access. Internet is hard to come by, and it's extraordinarily expensive. Even when thinking about making things like websites or putting audio online, and things like that, who is actually going to be able to access it? How is it going to speak to the audiences that I am speaking to and I'm working with? How is it actually going to be engaged with by the communities that I'm working with?

And I think one of the things I've been thinking a lot about recently, and it's probably something that not many people are aware of, is like I mentioned in my talk, the situation of the island nation of Tuvalu making a version of itself in the metaverse. And if you think about what that actually means, Tuvalu is one of the lowest-lying island nations in the Pacific, and along with Kiribati is probably the most at risk and under threat island in the Pacific due to rising sea levels.

Tuvalu has decided that because the land is very likely very soon to no longer exist, that they will make an iteration of themselves in the metaverse to be able to keep tradition and culture alive in that kind of aspect. And I think something like that, that's far too big for me to be able to speak on. Like the tragedy -- the absolute tragedy and the absolute violence of a situation like that -- coming to pass imminently is something where we do have to think about, like there is absolutely, fundamentally, a role for technology there, and a fantastic role, as well, but at the same time, practices like deep seabed mining are necessary. And different kinds of different forms of terrestrial mining, which are necessary in order to create and get the material resources and parts to create, the technologies that we often take for granted. You know, also contributing to the environmental and ecological destruction that are then causing places like Tuvalu to make iterations of themselves in the metaverse to be able to continue into the future. I think for me, personally, the questions of technologies and the kinds of technologies that we use, are really complicated ones.

HABITS OF THE ANTHROPOCENE
WORKSHOPS

This year's workshops showcased a range of groundbreaking topics that redefine architectural design and technology boundaries. In essence, these workshops presented a compelling blend of innovation and tradition, where emerging technologies are being harnessed to enhance, augment, and redefine architectural practices. They reflected a broader trend in the field of architecture towards embracing digital transformation, while still valuing the tactile and intuitive aspects of traditional design and making.

'Exploring Building Topology Through Graph Machine Learning' utilized graph theory and machine learning to dissect architectural networks. Participants used spatial modeling with artificial intelligence (AI), transforming 3D models into insightful graphs, and advancing architectural analysis and design. 'Today Once More: Filmmaking with Photogrammetry and Neural Radiance Fields' followed revolutionizing architectural representation with volumetric capture techniques. It emphasized precise point cloud manipulation and spatial collage using neural radiance fields (NeRF), culminating in distinctive cityscape interpretations, and showcasing technology's role in architectural visualization. The technology focus extends to 'Task and Motion Planning for Robotic Assembly,' delving into robotic applications in architecture. Attendees gain practical insights into robotic kinematics and computational models, bridging theory with practice in architectural robotics.

Shifting to virtual reality, the 'Immersive Realities Workshop' explored the capabilities of Grasshopper VR to integrate extended reality into architectural design. This session offered a real-time, immersive experience, redefining architectural interaction and presentation.

Concluding the workshop section, 'Hybrid Making: Physical Explorations with Computational Matter' merged the digital and physical realms. Participants engaged in an innovative design approach using digital components and micro-sensor-embedded physical artefacts, exploring tactile and intuitive design aspects, and challenging traditional architectural practices.

Thora Arnadottir

Workshops Chair

Exploring Building Topology Through Graph Machine Learning

Wassim Jabi
Cardiff University

David Andres Leon
Institute for Advanced Architecture of Catalonia

Abdulrahman Alymani
Alfaisal University

Selda Pourali Behzad
Cardiff University

Michelle Salamoun
Cardiff University

1. Graph Machine Learning (GML) Dataset samples on building ground relationship typology, Alymani, A and Jabi, W, 2022.

Abstract

Graph theory offers a powerful method for analyzing complex networks and relationships. When combined with machine learning, graph theory can provide valuable insights into the data generated by 3D models. This workshop integrated advanced spatial modeling and analysis with artificial intelligence, highlighting the importance of technological advancements in shaping the future of architecture and design. It introduced participants to novel workflows that link parametric 3D modeling with concepts of topology, graph theory, and graph machine learning. We used Topologicpy, an advanced spatial modeling and analysis software library designed for Architecture, Engineering, and Construction, paired with DGL, a powerful machine learning library that provides tools for implementing and optimizing graph neural networks (Figure 1). In essence, this process blends cutting-edge technologies and architectural principles that will shape the future of design. Participants learned how to use these workflows to convert 3D models into graphs, analyze their properties, and perform classification and regression tasks. Participants also explored how to create synthetic datasets based on generative and parametric workflows, and build and optimize graph neural networks for specific tasks.

Introduction

Graph theory, a branch of mathematics focused on nodes and the edges that connect them, has emerged as an indispensable tool in various scientific and engineering domains. By facilitating the understanding of intricate relationships within networks, it has powered many modern applications. When combined with the capabilities of machine learning, especially the potential of deep learning, graph theory becomes vital in understanding the multidimensional data that 3D models generate (Jabi and Alymani 2020).

This workshop aims to connect the future of architecture with the latest technology by blending advanced 3D design, analysis, and artificial intelligence. The workshop introduced participants to innovative workflows, combining the power of 3D modeling with important concepts like topology, graph theory, and the burgeoning field of graph machine learning (Figure 2).

The main toolkit of the workshop is Topologic (Aish et al. 2018; Jabi et al. 2018) and a new python-based Aplication Programming Interface (API) called Topologicpy developed by Professor Wassim Jabi. Topologicpy is an AI-powered spatial modeling and analysis software library, crafted especially for the spheres of Architecture, Engineering, and Construction. To ensure that participants are equipped with the power of machine learning, the workshop also utilized DGL (Deep Graph Library), which is integrated into Topologicpy. Deep Graph Library stands out as an adept machine learning library, for using and improving graph neural networks.

As participants engaged with this experience, they obtained a hands-on understanding of transforming 3D models into structured graphs. This transition allowed them to delve deeply into analyzing the inherent properties of these graphs, and further, to embark on tasks such as classification and regression (Alymani, Jabi, and Corcoran 2022a).

Additionally, this workshop provided participants with a set of skills, from creating synthetic datasets rooted in generative and parametric workflows to building and refining graph neural networks for various tasks. By the end, participants were well-equipped with the knowledge and skills to use graph theory and machine learning together, ensuring they remained at the forefront of architectural and design innovation.

Workshop Description

The ACADIA 2023 Workshop, from the 21st to the 23rd of October, delved into building topology using Graph Machine Learning. Over three days, the attendees' journeyd through a structured curriculum, as follows:

Day One, 'Introduction', began with a participant and team introduction, followed by lectures on topologic theory and applications and the synergy of Graph and Machine Learning. The day concluded with focused dissertation lectures (Figure 3), a Q&A session, and an optional installation/testing session.

Day Two, titled 'Generating Graph Dataset', offered insights into data generation in automation and hands-on experience with generative parametric models using Rhino/Hops installations (Figure 4). Participants learned about converting Rhino and Grasshopper geometry to topological models, extracting graphs, and generating datasets. The day ended with a lecture on Jupyter Notebook dataset structures.

The final day, 'Applications', immersed attendees in Graph Neural Networks (GNN) hyperparameter optimization, followed by model training, validation, and testing (Figure 5). A hands-on session on parametric generative building prediction, using a specialized model, was a highlight, followed by participant-driven experiments. The workshop concluded with future insights and an open Q&A session.

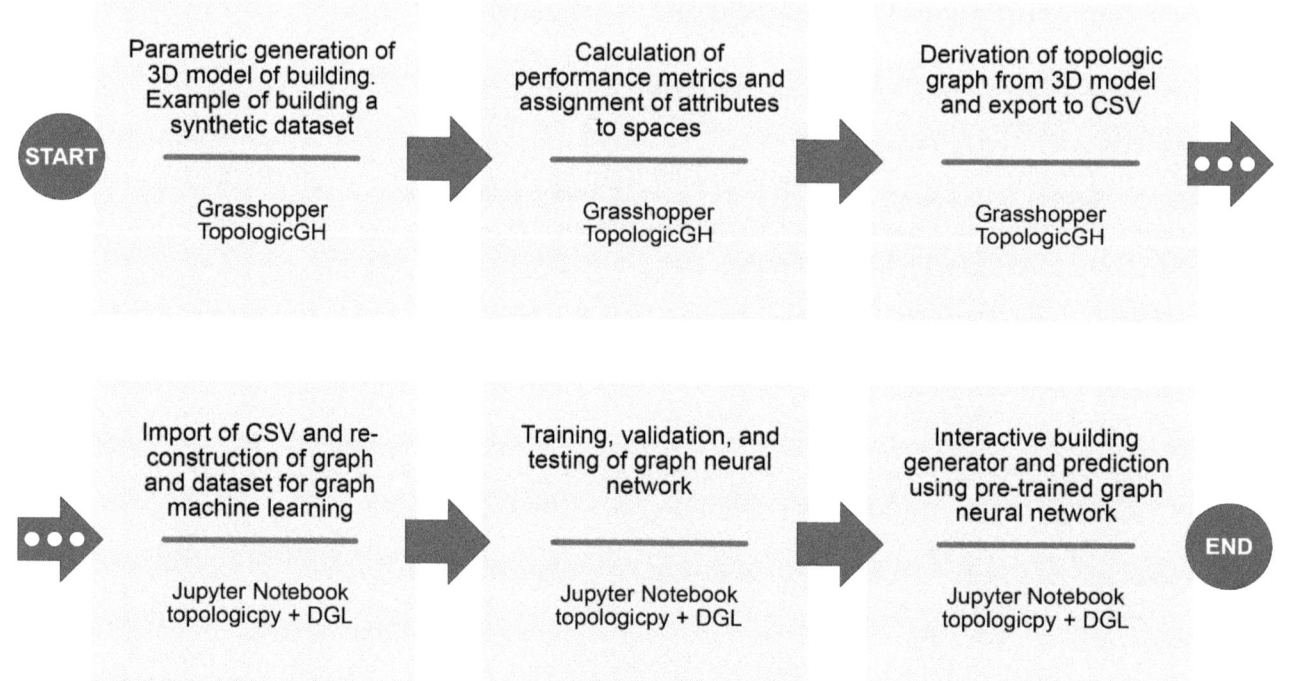

2. Workshop Workflow Diagram, Authors, 2023.

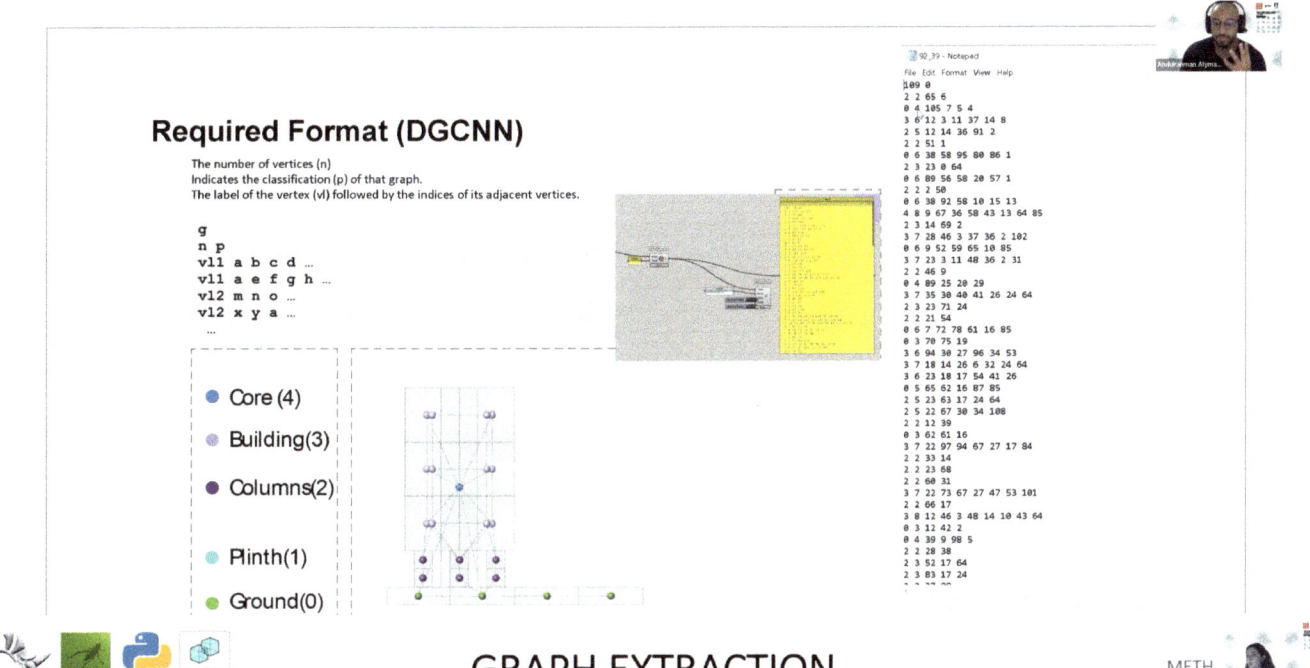

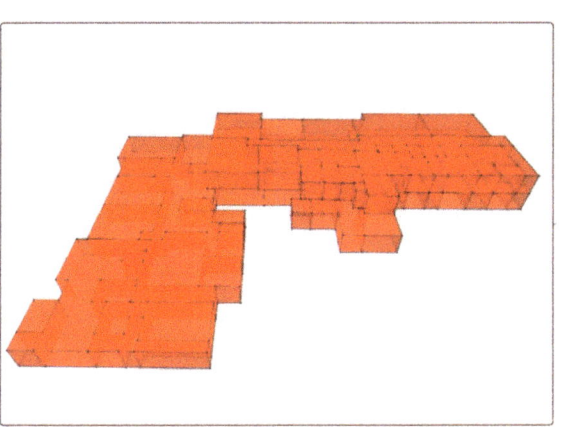

3. Presentations by Abdulrahman Alymani, Selda Pourali, and Michelle Salamoun, day one, 2023.

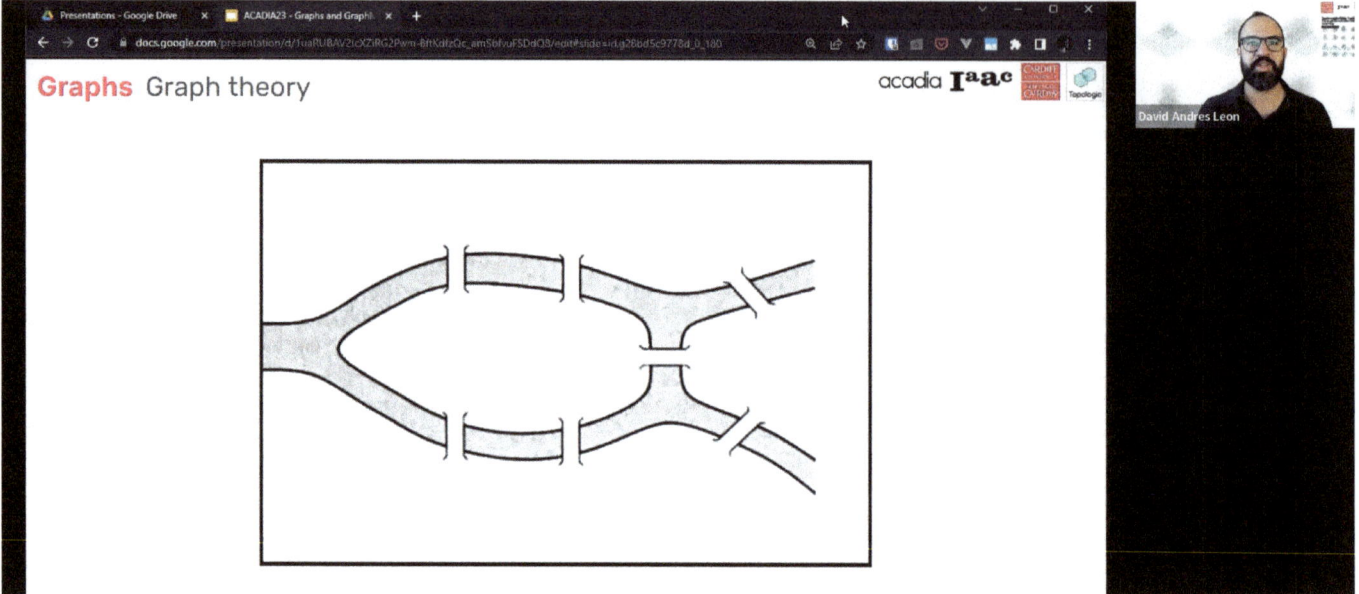

4. Presentation by David Andres Leon, day two, 2023.

Workshop Outcome

The workshop outcome was divided into two distinct parts, which the participants followed. The first part involved generating 3D topological datasets. In the second part, participants utilized the building and ground relationship (BGR) dataset to demonstrate how to train a machine learning model. After training, the model was tested for validation purposes (Alymani, Jabi, and Corcoran 2022b).

In the final stage, participants developed a 3D design with a simple topology and then converted it into its dual 3D topological graph. Applications such as Jupyter Notebook and Grasshopper were utilized to design and produce the graph. Subsequently, the graph was exported to an Excel CSV file to predict the participants' 3D design using the pre-trained machine learning model (Figure 6). By following this methodology, participants were able to demonstrate the effectiveness and accuracy of the machine learning model in predicting building and ground relationships in three-dimensional space.

Acknowledgment

The workshop instructors want to sincerely thank the ACADIA 2023 Workshop team for their support in conducting this workshop.

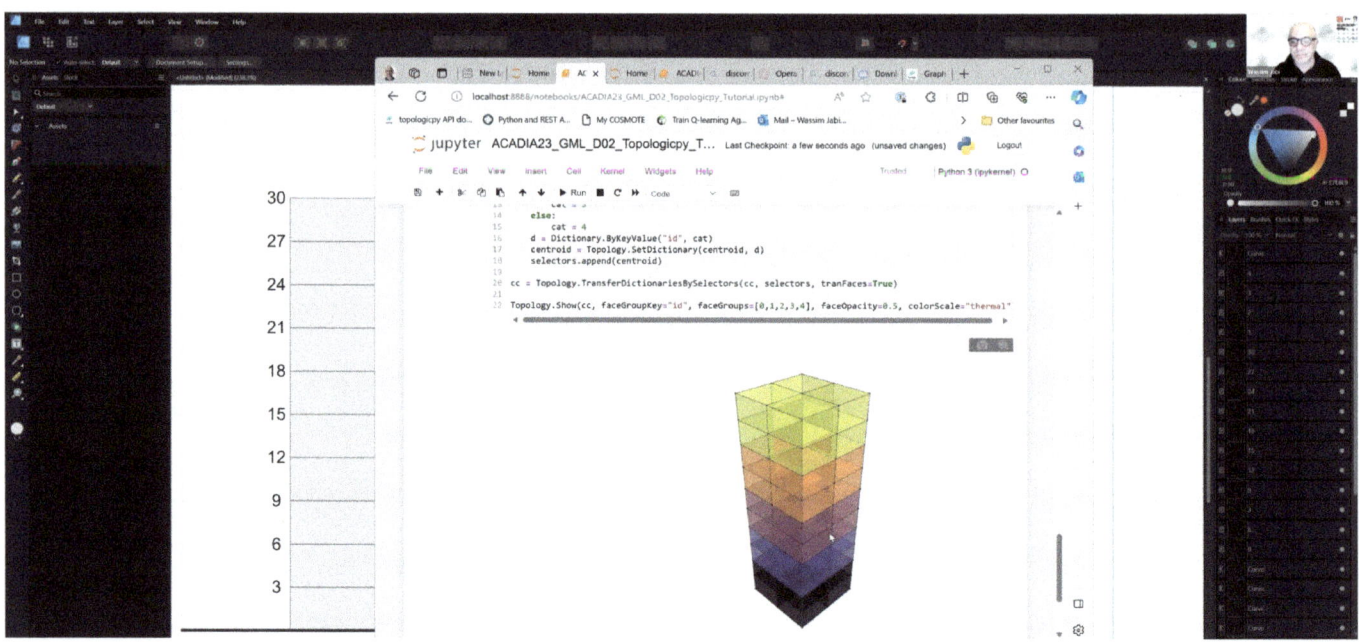

5. Presentation by Wassim Jabi, day three, 2023.

References

Aish, Robert, Wassim Jabi, Simon Lannon, Nicholas Wardhana, and Aikaterini Chatzivasileiadi. 2018. "Topologic: Tools to Explore Architectural Topology." AAG 2018: Advances in Architectural Geometry 2018, no. September: 316–41.

Alymani, Abdulrahman, Wassim Jabi, and Padraig Corcoran. 2023. "Graph machine learning classification using architectural 3D topological models." Simulation 99, no. 11: 1117-1131.

Alymani, Abdulrahman, Wassim Jabi, and Padraig Corcoran. 2023. "Modelling the relationships between ground and buildings using 3D architectural topological models utilising graph machine learning." In International Symposium on Formal Methods in Architecture, pp. 287-305. Singapore: Springer Nature Singapore.

Jabi, Wassim, Robert Aish, Simon Lannon, Aikaterini Chatzivasileiadi, and Nicholas Mario Wardhana. 2018. "Topologic A Toolkit for Spatial and Topological Modelling." In SHAPE, FORM & GEOMETRY. http://papers.cumincad.org/

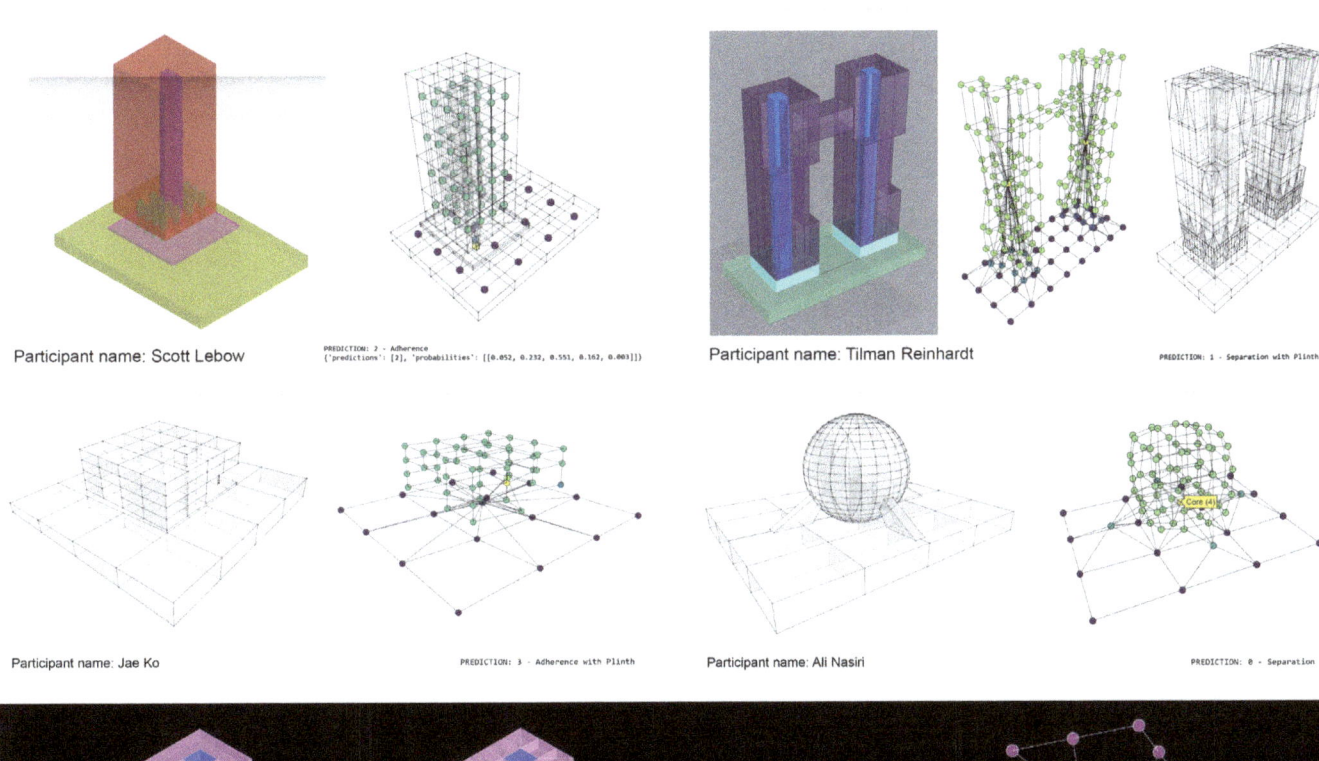

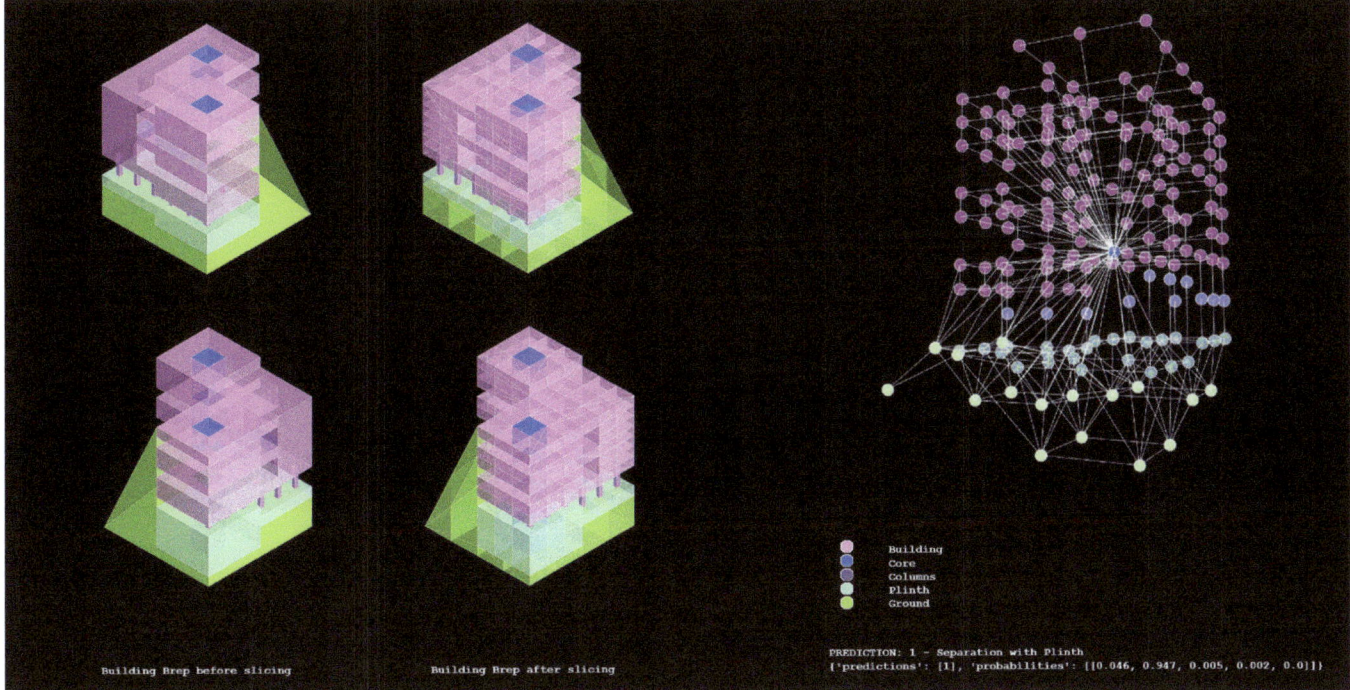

6. Sample of the workshop results by the workshop participants, 2023.

data/works/att/ecaade2018_310.pdf.

Alymani, Abdulrahman, Wassim Jabi, and Padraig Corcoran. 2023. "Graph machine learning classification using architectural 3D topological models." Simulation 99, no. 11: 1117-1131.

Image Credits

Figure 1: © Alymani, A and Jabi, W, 2022.

Figure 6: © Lebow, S., Reinhardt, T., Ko, J., Nasiri, a., Gao, J., 2023.

All other drawings and images by the authors.

About Instructors

Wassim Jabi. Professor Wassim Jabi is the course director of the MSc Computational Methods in Architecture program at the Welsh School of Architecture, Cardiff University, in Wales, the United Kingdom. He earned his M.Arch. and Ph.D. from the University of Michigan and taught at various universities in the U.S. before moving to the UK in 2008. While teaching in the U.S., he secured a National Science Foundation (NSF) grant as Primary Investigator. Professor Jabi has published widely on topics ranging from parametric and generative design to the role of light in architecture and building performance simulation. He has authored a book titled "Parametric Design for Architecture" (Laurence King Publishing, London). In 2013, Professor Jabi won funding from the university's internal competitive funding scheme to purchase a large, 6-axis high-accuracy industrial robot to investigate innovative digital fabrication processes. His current research is at the intersection of parametric design, the representation of space, building performance simulation, machine learning, and robotic fabrication in architecture. In 2019, Professor Jabi concluded a grant from the Leverhulme Trust as Primary Investigator to study spatial topology in building information modeling (BIM). This resulted in the on-going development of a software library called Topologic (http://topologic.app).

David Andres Leon. David Andres Leon is an architect with the focus on the research and development of computational tools for AEC. He is a private consultant for digital technologies and directs the Master in Advanced Computation for Advanced Architecture MACAD in the Institute for Advanced Architecture of Catalonia IAAC. David also teaches programming for architecture in various programs such as the MPDA Masters program of the UPC, and is the author of various publications in the field of architectural research and computation.

Abdulrahman Alymani. Dr. Abdulrahman Alymani is an esteemed Assistant Professor at Alfaisal University and founder of CM-iTAD Research Lab. With a PhD from Cardiff University, UK, his research leverages innovative Machine Learning techniques to explore building-environment interactions. He's a former Assistant Teacher at Cardiff University and holds a master's degree from the Southern California Institute of Architecture SCI-Arc, USA.

Dr. Alymani specializes in computational methods in architecture, with a keen interest in AI and ML applications. His expertise covers parametric, digital, and generative design. Known for his interdisciplinary collaborations, he works with experts in computer science, landscape architecture, and urban planning. A visionary educator and researcher, Dr. Alymani is dedicated to advancing architectural knowledge through innovation and interdisciplinary approaches.

Selda Pourali Behzad. Selda Pourali is a computational designer and researcher at Cardiff University, UK. With a background in architectural engineering, she pursued her post-graduation in computational methods in architecture at the same university. Her main focus is on exploring innovative workflows that optimize design processes using Machine Learning and Deep Learning. She is applying these workflows to develop an innovative platform with the "Topologic" team at Cardiff University. Selda firmly believes that computational and data-driven design methodologies can effectively develop adaptive solutions from design concepts to fabrication. Throughout her career, she has consistently prioritized integrating technologies into design methodologies. Currently, as a researcher in the "Ardaena Academy", she applies this mindset to design challenges, emphasizing performative and functional design aspects.

Michelle Salamoun. Michelle Salamoun is an architect and a recent MSc graduate in Computational Methods in Architecture. She has worked in several architectural fields, including concept development, design, site work, construction, interior and product design. She participated in humanitarian architectural projects, focusing on refugee camp infrastructure in Lebanon and post-2020 Beirut blast reconstruction. Inspired by her experiences, she is now focusing on creating digital tools for architecture, exploring deep learning for automated object detection, and graph machine learning applications in 3D model generation.

Today Once More: Filmmaking with Photogrammetry and NeRF

Haotian Zhang
The University of Hong Kong

Introduction

Photogrammetry and Neural Radiance Fields (NeRF) are volumetric capture methods that enable high-fidelity documentation of spatial and chromatic details of existing environments. These methods, alternative to canonical architectural drawing as characterized by the abundance of textural data, offer a new realm of representation that could potentially shift our perception of the city. This workshop searched for their medium specificities, particularly addressing the gap between faithful reference to the real world and speculation in the digital realm, while harnessing the tension in between.

This workshop introduced the two techniques and relevant tools in the context of filmmaking, providing tutorials on NVidia Instant-ngp (NeRF), COLMAP, RealityCapture (photogrammetry), and Blender (point cloud manipulation). It unpacked the tools to understand their mechanisms and capabilities, ultimately working toward collective films about Hong Kong.

In our exploration, we analyzed the mediums to use them critically. This analysis examined the unique qualities of each medium in two ways – by assessing its capacity and identifying its constraints. The capacities and constraints set it apart from other mediums or reality, the gap between which manifests the inherent characteristic yet to be aestheticized.

Precise Manipulation of Point Cloud

Instead of considering point cloud as painterly and promiscuous, we explored precise manipulation of points using Blender geometry node, a visual scripting tool that allows for

1 Visualizing the echolocation of a bat.

WORKSHOP INFORMATION

ACADIA/CAADRIA joint workshop.

Hybrid mode, taught at the University of Hong Kong

Additionally supported by the Special Projects Fund from the Department of Architecture, HKU

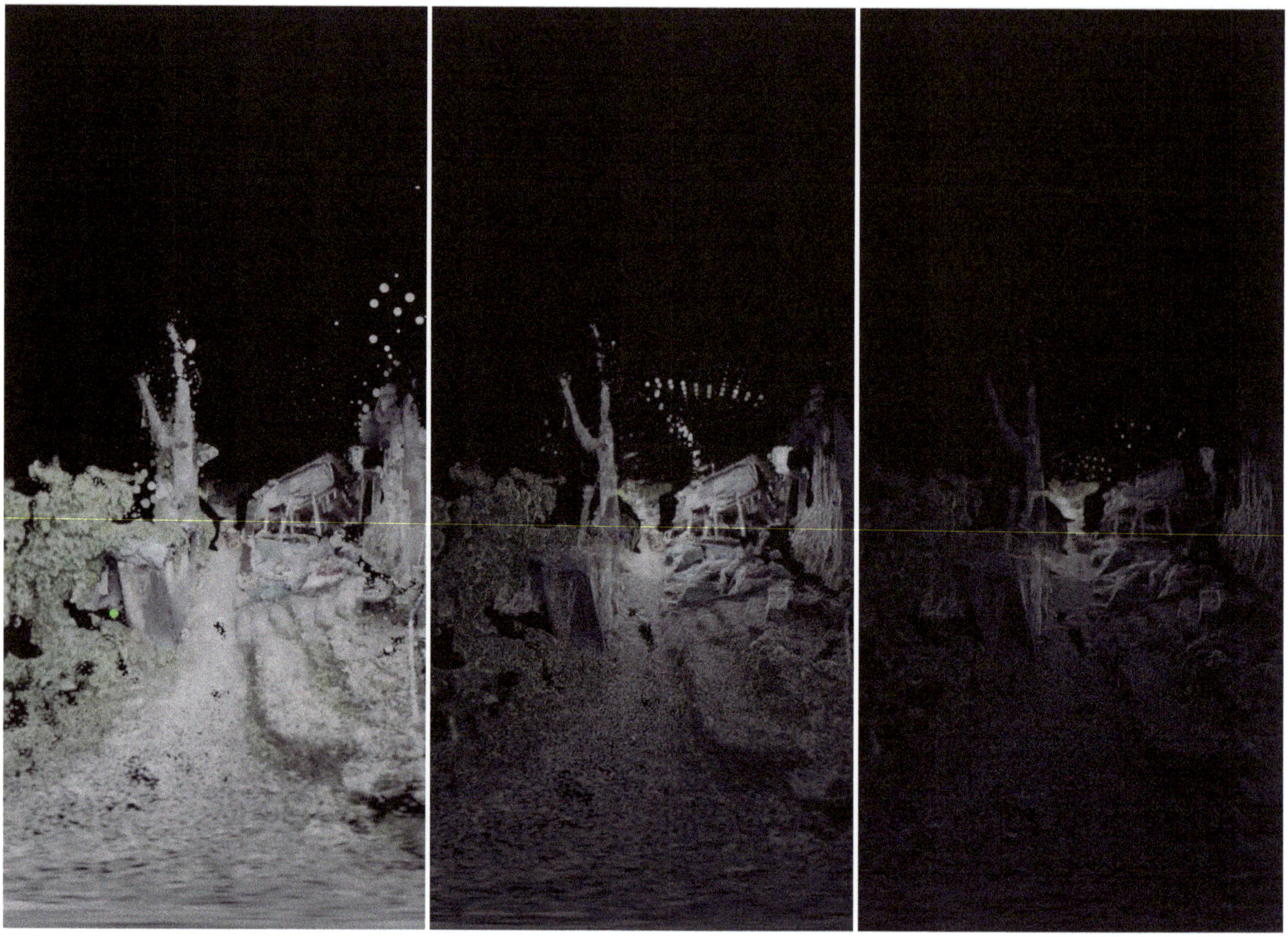

2 Still shots from the point cloud film.

3 Still shot from the NeRF film.

WORKSHOPS   HABITS OF THE ANTHROPOCENE   186

Model 1

Model 2

Mask

Video
collage
+
Camera
locations

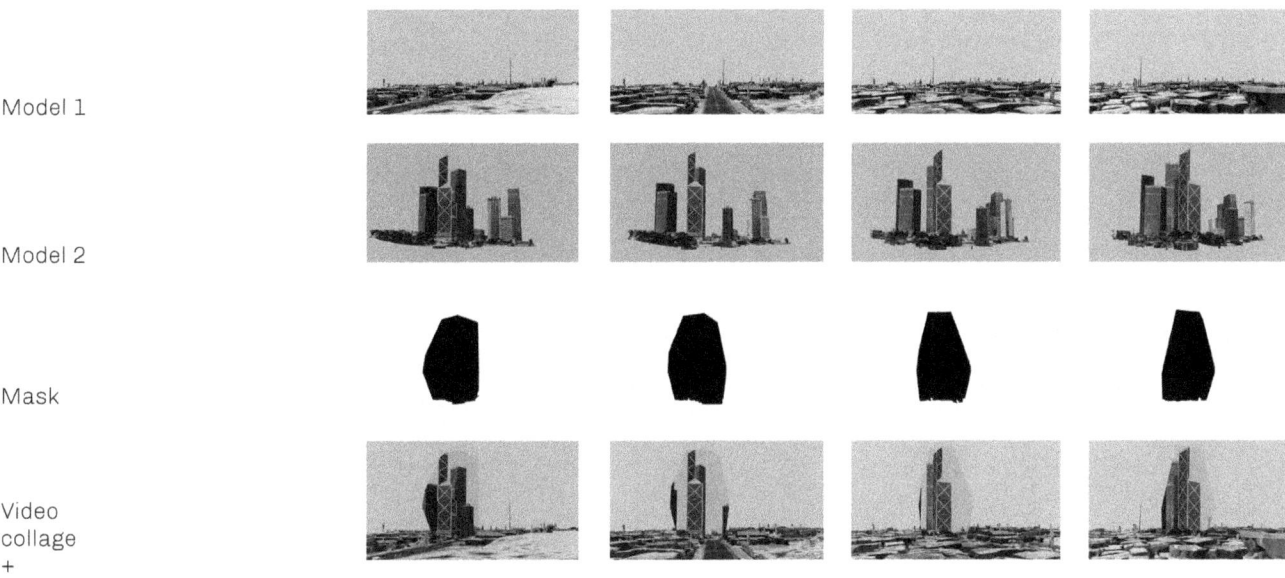

NeRF
result

4   The generation of NeRF collages.

the transformation of spatial coordinates. Participants learned to orchestrate the points through rule-bound operations as rigorously as in architectural drawings.

The skills were exercised in the visualization of how a bat sees the city. To represent the echolocation, participants manipulated the points of 3D scanned cityscapes with regard to the camera position, and choreographed the camera to imitate the journey of the bat (Figures 1 and 2). The clips contribute to a film under production titled Homecoming, which renders Hong Kong through the eyes of an insect, a bat, a boar, and a whale.

Spatial Collage with NeRF
As an emerging technique and digital format, NeRF's mechanism is constantly evolving, and its full potential is yet to be discovered. The workshop instead examined a fundamental difference from other 3D formats, such as mesh or voxel, as NeRF is not composed of "solid" substances, but units that emit rays at varying angles (Figure 3). A single point in space can display different colors and opacities when viewed from different directions. Such an attribute consequently facilitates the representation of reflection and refraction, which have been unattainable in photogrammetry or Lidar scanning.

We utilize NeRF as a 5D model (x, y, z, angle a, angle b) to intentionally construct spaces and objects that cannot be achieved in other 3D environments. In our methods, we synthesize images that do not belong to one 3D model into one object in NeRF, whose shape and texture transform as the vantage point moves. To achieve this, we first rendered multiple clips with the same camera path, but different digital scenes, which were then composited to create video collages. Both the video collage and the camera path were input into Instant-ngp to demand the NeRF reconstruction using images with discrepancies. Since the collages did not belong to one coherent 3D space, the final result in NeRF exhibited special qualities, for example, geometries appearing and disappearing with the changing view direction (Figure 4). In the exercise, participants combined fragments of Hong Kong and other cities to generate critical juxtapositions, revealing the contrast or consistency between them.

The workshop was led with teaching assistants Nomy Jianing Yu (BASc Design+ '23) and Jason Chun Hei Chan (BAAS '23). The research and teaching were additionally supported by the Special Projects Fund from HKU Department of Architecture.

IMAGE CREDITS

Figure 1: ©Zebin Zheng
Figure 2: ©Yuhang Chen
Figure 3: © Seren Siyuan Zhang.
All other drawings and images by the authors.

Haotian Zhang is a Lecturer at the Department of Architecture, the University of Hong Kong. He holds a master's degree from the Cooper Union, and master's and bachelor's degrees from Tsinghua University. His work focuses on realist digital media, investigating their representational potential and politics. He is the recipient of the Young Talent Award of the 9th Bi-City Biennale of Urbanism/Architecture. He co-founded FrankanLisa, a multidisciplinary design studio based in Hong Kong.

Task and Motion Planning for Robotic Assembly

Pok Yin Victor Leung
Gramazio Kohler Research
ETH Zürich

Yijiang Huang
Computational Robotics Lab
ETH Zürich

1   Robotic Motion trajectory created for timber aseembly process (Pok Yin Victor Leung, 2021, © Gramazio Kohler Research).

Task and Motion Planning

When programming robotic assembly processes, it is often necessary to create a sequential list of actions. Some actions are robotic motions (requiring motion trajectory), and some are for controlling external equipment, such as grippers and fastening tools. The act of planning these actions and motion trajectories is called Task Planning and Motion Planning.

Existing literature in robotics explored many different planning algorithms for planning a single trajectory to planning a complete sequence of tasks where continuity is maintained [Garrett et al, 2021]. Many application literature focused on the TAMP for service robots, medical robots, and self-driving cars, while there are few examples for architectural applications. For digital fabrication and automated construction, the planning method has to be adapted to the needs of architectural assemblies and the scale of construction [Leung et al, 2021]. Some of the unique challenges are the highly bespoke workpiece and assembly geometry, the large workpiece (e.g., long beams), and a dense collision environment. This three-day hybrid workshop addressed the needs of the architectural robotics community to use industrial robotic arms to assemble highly bespoke objects. The objects do not have any repetitive parts or assembly targets. The workshop leaders shared their experiences using industrial robots to construct large-scale timber structures. One of the most useful techniques is the recently published "Flowchart Planning Method," where task sequence is planned using a flowchart, and motion trajectories are planned in a second pass [Huang et al, 2021].

2   Robotic Process that is pre-planned can be executed with minimal human supervision and surprise error such as singularity and collisions.

3   The offline planning approach is compatible with manual operations

4   One major robotic assembly challenge is accurate alignment

The workshop began with a deep understanding of robot kinematics, tool space, joint space, and how computational models are used to describe various robotic systems. Examples of 6R, 6R1P, 6R2P and 6R3P robots are shown, including the famous 34 joints gantry robot in the Robotic Fabrication Laboratory (RFL) in ETH Zurich. Discussion included how robotic kinematics related to the assembly properties and how to make quick assessment regarding reachability.

Students learn the theory (mathematic background) and the practical knowledge (software libraries) to solve forward kinematics, inverse kinematics, collision checking, and motion planning for Cartesian linear and free motion. Students use compas, an open-source framework, for design modeling, geometrical computation and to access the software libraries for planning. One of the most convenient planning libraries is compas_fab [Rust et al, 2018], a plug-in for the compas framework that provides access to state-of-the-art motion planning libraries. The software workflow allows students to design a bespoke assembly in Rhino (with the help of Grasshopper) and to design the robotic process that assembles the object from its constituent parts. The trajectories for the robotic process are planned sequentially using scripts written in Python using compas and compas_fab. The resulting trajectories can be simulated in a virtual environment such as PyBullet or Rhino. Students who participated in person could also execute the planned trajectory with a 6R ABB GoFa robot to validate that the trajectories are collision-free.

Other topics such, assembly sequence, geometrical blocking, sweep (continuous) collision checking, neighbor detection, allowed collision matrix, and trajectory smoothing are also discussed. Students can identify the planning technique and planner features required for their future applications.

Finally, the instructors shared their experience in setting up a workflow for creating large scale experiments. This include hardware preperations such as preparing the

5   Planned trajectory visualized in Rhino. The image depicts a robotic arm in the RFL manipulating a piece of timber (cyan) in the middle of an assemble process. The robot, its gripper and the attached timber workpiece can be seen nevigating around a dense collision scene to reach its destination.

ground connections, scaffolding, robot calibration, gripper and tool design; Software preperation include modeling custom robot and tools features and tuning the parameters of the motion planner to balance planning speed, accuracy and optimality of the trajectory.

ACKNOWLEDGMENTS

The theoretical and technical bases of this workshop is developed during the doctoral research of the instructors [Huang, 2023] [Leung, 2023]. The continued development of this work is supported by the currently affiliated instutites of the instructors. Many thanks to all the researchers for sharing the algorithms we used for task and motion planning, openly and freely.

REFERENCES

Garrett, Caelan Reed, Rohan Chitnis, Rachel Holladay, Beomjoon Kim, Tom Silver, Leslie Pack Kaelbling, and Tomás Lozano-Pérez. 2021. "Integrated Task and Motion Planning." Annual Review of Control, Robotics, and Autonomous Systems 4 (1): 265–93. https://doi.org/10.1146/annurev-control-091420-084139.

Huang, Yijiang, Victor Pok Yin Leung, Caelan Garrett, Fabio Gramazio, Matthias Kohler, and Caitlin Mueller. 2021. "The New Analog: A Protocol for Linking Design and Construction Intent with Algorithmic Planning for Robotic Assembly of Complex Structures. In Symposium on Computational Fabrication. SCF '21. Association for Computing Machinery. https://doi.org/10.1145/3485114.3485122.

Huang, Yijiang. "Algorithmic Planning for Robotic Assembly of Building Structures." Doctorial Thesis, Massachusetts Institute of Technology, 2023.

Leung, Pok Yin, Aleksandra Anna Apolinarska, Davide Tanadini, Fabio Gramazio, and Matthias Kohler. "Automatic assembly of jointed timber structure using distributed robotic clamps." In PROJECTIONS–Proceedings of the 26th International Conference of the Association for Computer-Aided Architectural Design, vol. 1, pp. 583-592. Association for Computer Aided Architectural Design Research in Asia, 2021.

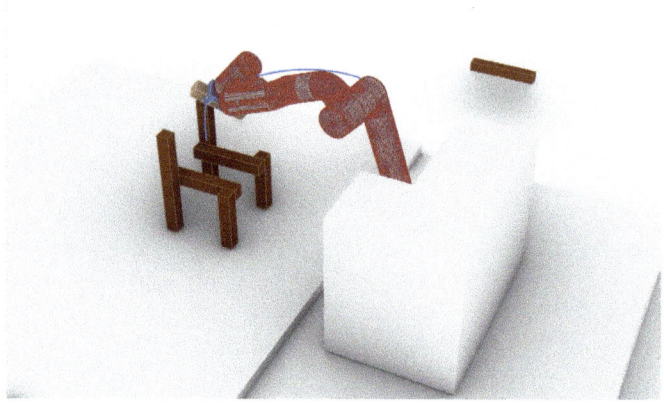

6 Student work by Jeremy Chen.

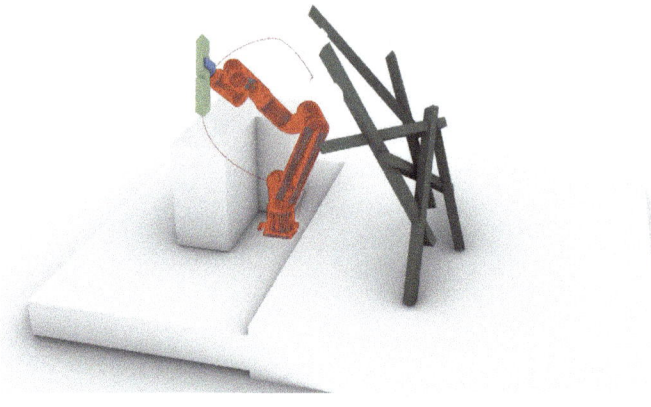

7 Student work by Lee Su Huang

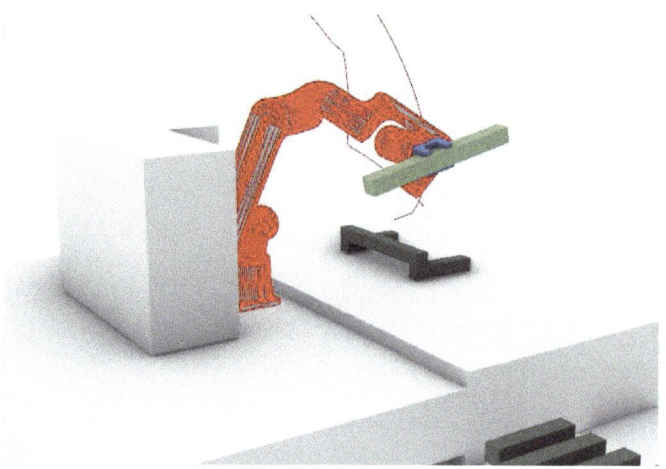

8 Student work by Chenxiao Li

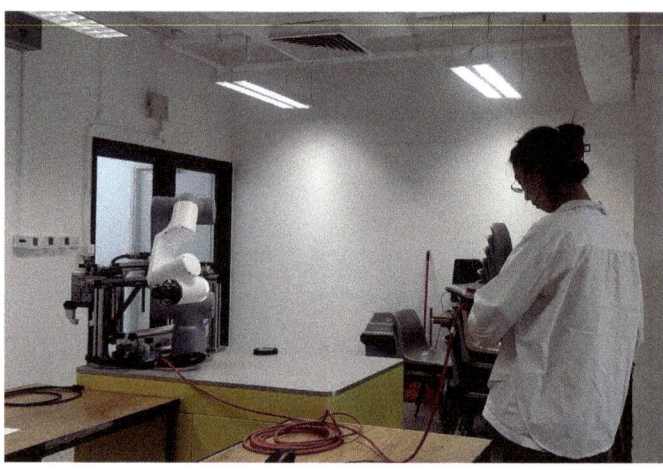

9 Students executing planned actions (Chenxiao Li and Namjoo Kim).

Leung, Pok Yin Victor. "DiRT: Distributed Robotic Tools for Spatial Timber Assembly with Integral Timber Joints." Doctorial Thesis, ETH Zurich, 2023.

Rust, R., G. Casas, S. Parascho, D. Jenny, K. Dörfler, M. Helmreich, A. Gandia, et al. 'COMPAS FAB: Robotic Fabrication Package for the COMPAS Framework', 2018. https://doi.org/10.5281/zenodo.3469478.

Ziqi Wang and Peng Song and Mark Pauly, 2021. State of the Art on Computational Design of Assemblies with Rigid Parts, in Computer Graphics Forum (Eurographics 2021)

Pok Yin Victor Leung is a researcher in the ETH Zurich investigating the use of Distributed Robotic Tools for assembling timber structures. He is obsessed with designing and making custom robots, machines and end effectors for digital fabrication. Victor has many years of experience in timber related topics, related to the digitization of the design-to-assembly workflow. This includes timber joint design, structural design, software development, mechatronics, robot control and motion planning. Victor also works as a consultant for digital artist and architects in the realization of kinetic installation, digital artwork, 3D printed structures, and various mechatronics project.

Yijiang Huang is a Postdoctoral Researcher in the Department of Computer Science at ETH Zurich. He researches at the intersection between Architecture, Computing, and Robotics to make design and construction more connected. Yijiang completed his Ph.D. in the Building Technology Program at MIT's Department of Architecture. Before MIT, he studied applied math and did research in computer graphics at the University of Science and Technology of China, where he received his Bachelor of Science.

Immersive Realities

Kristof Crolla
The University of Hong Kong
Building Simplexity Lab

Abdullah Tahir Sheikh
The University of Hong Kong
Building Simplexity Lab

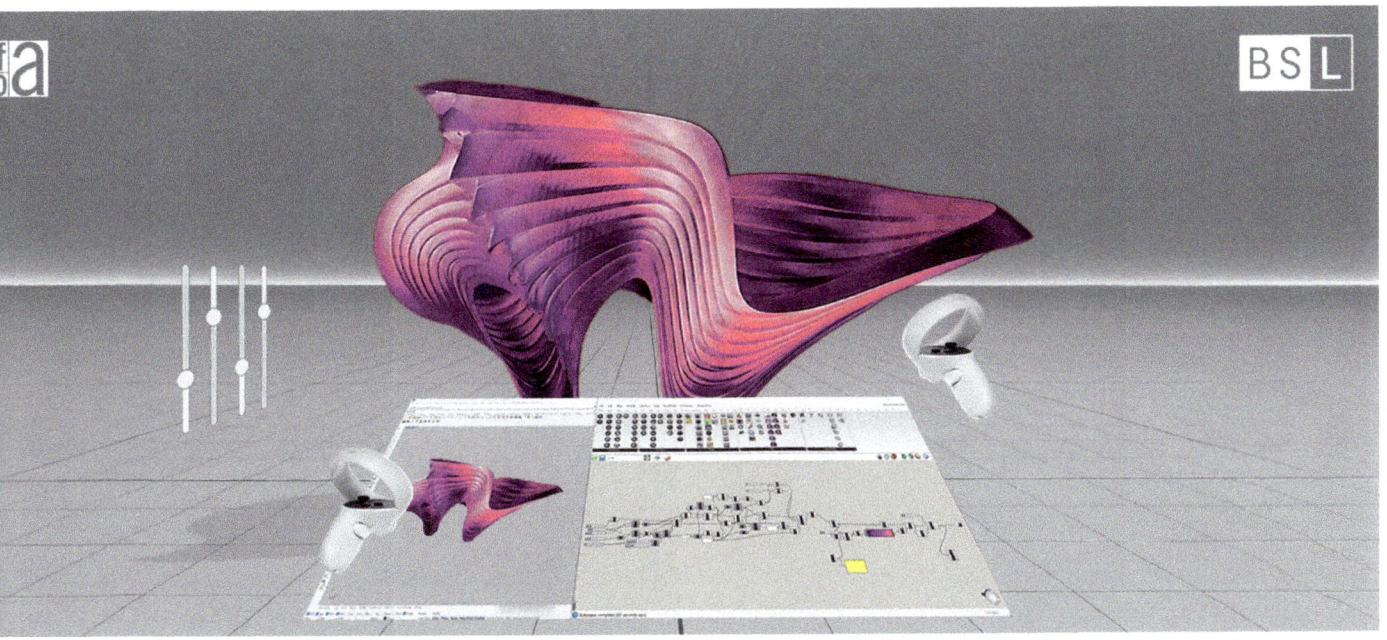

1   Workshop poster image.

WORKSHOP INFORMATION

ACADIA/CAADRIA joint workshop.

Mode: In-person.

Location: College of Architecture and Planning, University of Colorado, Denver, USA.

Date: 21-23 Oct 2023.

Workshop Setup

Workshop "IMMERSIVE REALITIES: Transforming Architectural Design Workspaces for the age of Extended Reality (XR)" (see Figure 1) was set up in response to observations that the potential of Virtual Reality (VR) for architecture design is relatively underused and under-implemented in architectural education and practice (Sheikh and Crolla 2023). The workshop introduced participants to the potential of a newly developed XR tool, named "Grasshopper VR 1.0 (Beta)" (GHVR) (see Figure 2), that allows architects and designers to work in VR in their usual Rhino + Grasshopper environment, while being immersed in their designs at full-scale in real time. This immersive virtual workspace instantly provides users with valuable insights into their parametric designs and allows them to explore the spatial relationships, scale, and overall experience of their creations. The workshop explained the tool's development, demonstrated its functionality, and guided attendees through its basic usage and potential applications..

Outcome

Attendees explored the potential of integrating XR extended workflows into their own projects, allowing them to visualize projects in real-time, navigate designs and mock-ups as if they were fully constructed, and adjust parameters and details effortlessly (see Figures 3 through 5). Feedback confirmed GHVR to be a promising tool with great potential for application in architecture design, education, fabrication, and practice. Suggestions for future application development centered on the desire to focus and expand on its intuitive usage and further provide everything a typical Rhino-Grasshopper workspace has in VR. Rather

2 Grasshopper VR Logo.

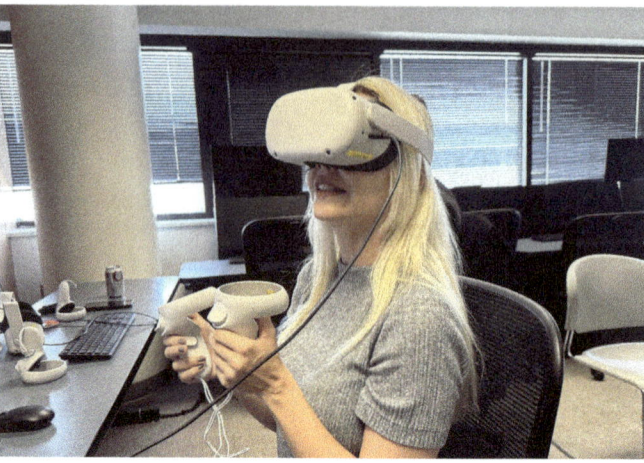

4 Workshop participants exploring tool applications.

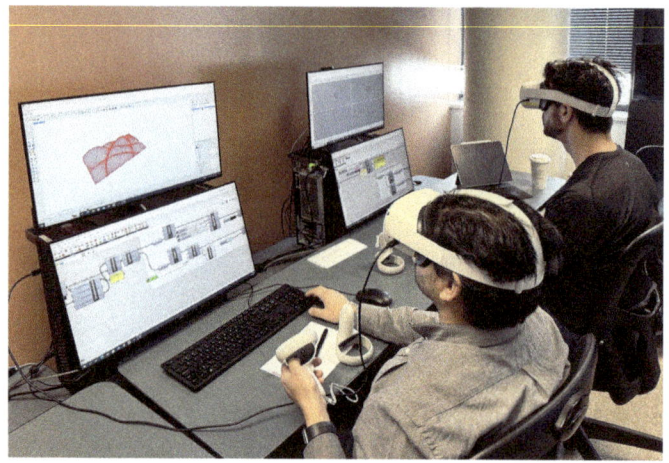

3 Workshop participants exploring tool applications.

5 Grasshopper VR presentation to the ACADIA community.

than competing with other VR visualization applications, focussing on photorealism, the primary goal should remain for GHVR to be a design tool.

ACKNOWLEDGMENTS

This research was supported by the University of Hong Kong's Teaching and Learning Quality Committee (TLQC) as part of the Teaching Development Grant (TDG) project titled: "Development of a Database of E-Learning Tutorials for Flipped-Classroom Teaching of Augmented/Virtual Reality Tools and Techniques for Architecture Design and Production" (Project No. 879).

REFERENCES

Sheikh, Abdullah and Kristof Crolla. 2023. 'Architectural Education with virtual reality', in Dokonal, W, Hirschberg, U and Wurzer, G (eds.), Digital Design Reconsidered – Proceedings of the 41st Conference on Education and Research in Computer Aided Architectural Design in Europe (eCAADe 2023) – Volume 1, Graz, 20-22 September 2023, pp. 159–168.

IMAGE CREDITS

All drawings and images by the authors.

Dr. Kristof Crolla is an architect who combines his architectural practice Laboratory for Explorative Architecture & Design Ltd. (LEAD) with an Associate Professorship and Associate Deanship at the University of Hong Kong (HKU)'s Faculty of Architecture, where he directs the Building Simplexity Lab (BSL). His work has received numerous design, research, and teaching awards, and he is best known for the "ZCB Bamboo Pavilion," for which he received the 2016 World Architecture Festival Small Project of the Year award.

Abdullah Tahir Sheikh is a BSL Senior Research Assistant specialising in Extended Reality (XR) interaction. He completed a Master of Robotics and Advanced Construction at the Institute for Advanced Architecture of Catalonia (IAAC) in 2021, where his thesis project focused on human-machine collaboration and the integration of robotic fabrication and extended reality in architectural material systems.

Hybrid Making: Physical Explorations with Computational Matter

Dr. Augusto Gandia (*)
MIT

Dr. Aileen Iverson-Radtke (*)
air-architecture

Andy Payne
Mc Neel &Associates

Richa Gupta
MIT

*These two authors contributed equally to this work

1 Vase design exploration through hybrid modeling and VR.

Introduction

This publication introduces hybrid making as the subject of a workshop conducted at the ACADIA Conference 2023 (See Fig. 1). We contextualize hybrid making in today's design digitalization marked by the opening of Artificial Intelligence (AI), wherein AI is seen as an accelerant in the ongoing digital evolution. In design-related practice and research, digital design is increasingly dominant (See Fig. 2); as shown in a quick survey of ACADIA 2022 wherein 10 out of 14 workshops focused on topics related to digitalization. Given this context, the subject of our workshop, hybrid making, highlights that which is excluded in purely digital processes, namely a richness of designing associated with the qualities of materials and fabrication (See Fig. 3). Hybrid making seeks to influence digital evolution with aspects of analogue processes such as the integration of constraints related to actual physical materials and their context. The task of hybrid making, therefore, is to introduce actual constraints into digital ones (See Fig. 4).

Thus, the hybrid making workshop introduces a methodology for including material and fabrication constraints, as well as human embodied intelligence in digitally produced artifacts, while retaining the full exploration of digital capabilities. The hybrid architectural modeling methodology consists of constructing digital components (parametric scripts and the digital objects they engender), as well as analogue components (physical

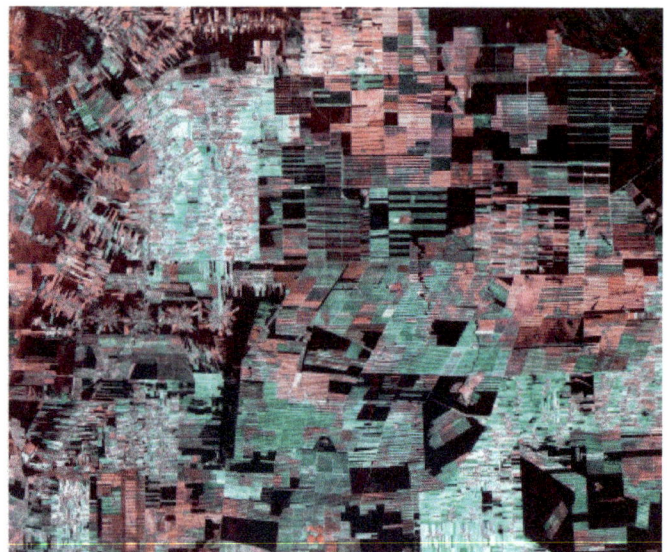

2   Manufactured Landscapes (Koert Van Mensvoort, 2013).

3   Pottery making (Tortus, 2023).

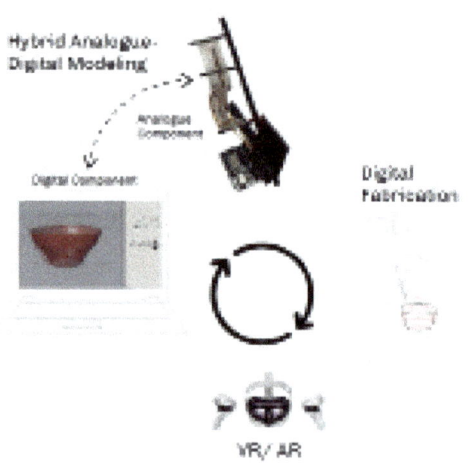

4   Hybrid Modeling Workflow.

scaled artifacts embedded with microsensors). The use of microsensors enables linking these analogue and digital components. Furthermore, to create a uniform "hybrid" modeling interface, digital material behaviors must be aligned (parametrically) to match physical material behaviors. By focusing on aligning across behaviors of analogue-digital media, hybrid making uncovers a novel approach to digital making: digital modeling based on the properties of actual materials and fabrication processes.

Meanwhile, the method allows a manual manipulation of digital objects through the analogue component interface. This manual access activates our sensory and intuitive intelligence with regard to our comprehension of the design object. Additionally, the manual design of digital models with (digital) material properties, includes characteristics related to the nature of such materials as they respond and react to their site conditions. This approach, digital design based on internal properties of materials and fabrication reacting to context, is in sharp contrast to the majority of current computation design based on image and geometry.

Workshop Content

Over the course of the three days, nine participants: Amanda Gioia, Fernando Lima, Kathleen Zimmerman, Daniel Merupu, Diego Camargo, Elena Maj, Ikyaz Sarimehmetoglu, Andy Van Mater and Romy Kaiser explore the introduced methodology through a fundamental design exercise: a rubber vase (See Fig. 5-8). The first day, the workshop focuses on developing the physical component, consisting of a rubber strip with integrated flex sensors that was supported by a 3D printed scaled stand (See Fig. 5). This set up allows the material behavior to capture the influence of gravity and manual forming. The rubber strip represents a cross-section of the vase. The second day concentrated on developing the digital component, which included translating sensor data using Firefly (Payne 2010) into the design environment Rhinoceros (Mc Neel 1990), defining the design parameters of the rubber vase within the parametric design environment Grasshopper (Rutten 2007) and sending a visual representation of the design object to the virtual reality environment Unity (Francis et al. 2002). Finally, the last day focused on individual projects for developing a concept to design vases through different methodologies within this hybrid making framework. This means the concepts had to take into consideration environmental factors (sound, wind, light levels, etc.) that could be collected by the microsensors and act as an influence on the vase design. The design concept also included how

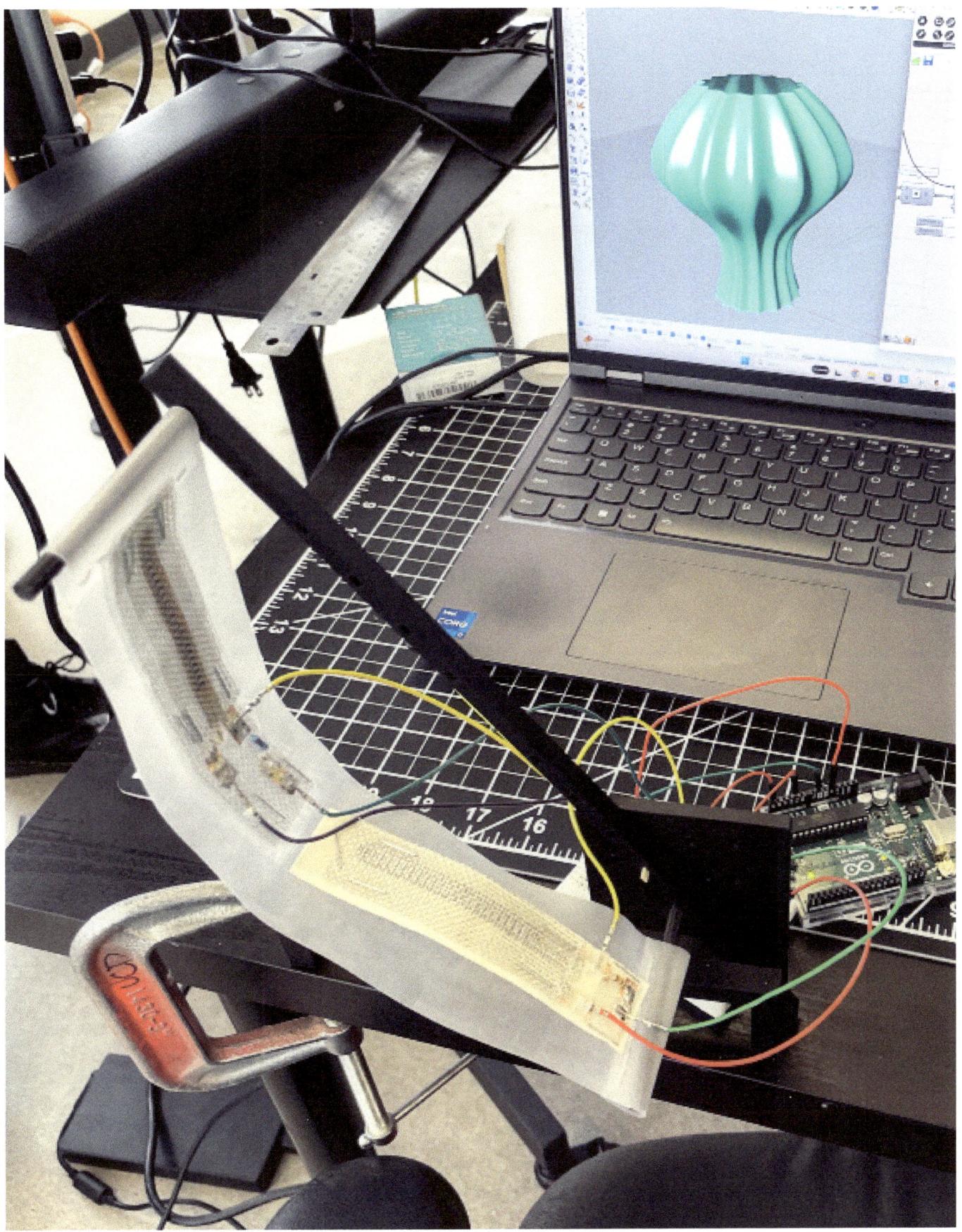

5   In person Hybrid Making workshop at the University of Colorado. Project: Extended Toolkit.

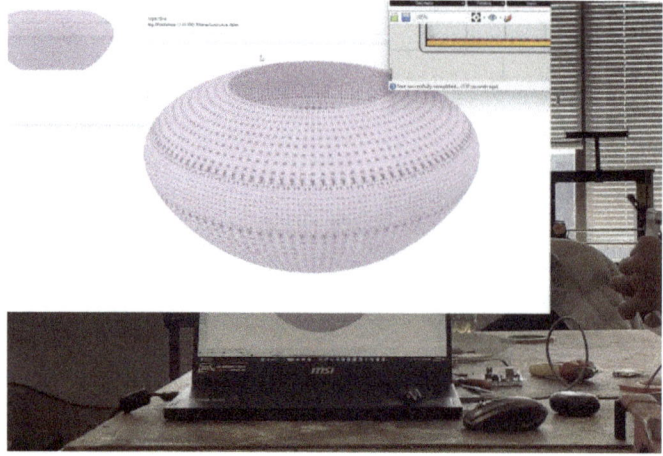
6 Project: Whistling Designs.

7 Project: Exploration through Gestures.

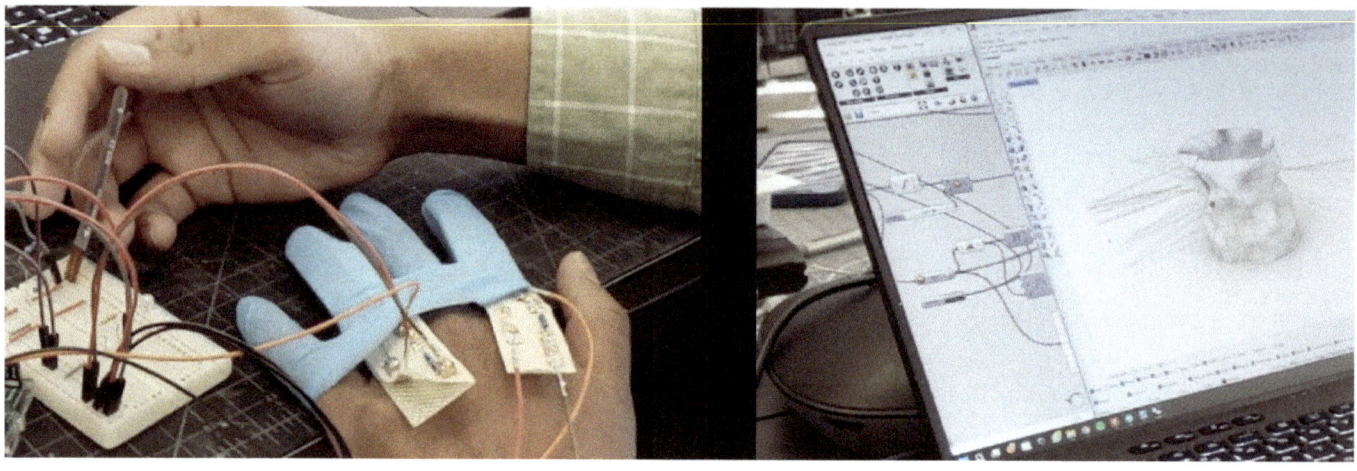
8 Project: Assymetric Sculpting.

manual shaping and gravitational pull informed the cross section of the vase. As such, the workshop conducted an introduction to basic electronics and circuit design using the Fritzing software (Interaction, 2012), to the Arduino (Banzi 2005) integrated development environment (IDE), to the parametric design environment Grasshopper, and to the data exchange library Firefly. In addition to these various platforms, participants were encouraged to engage with materials and analog tools, which served to re-connect with the processes of making.

The outcome of the workshop was nine innovative concepts that demonstrated the advantages and particularities of hybrid modeling in comparison to pure digital design computation approaches. From these, four projects are here selected that represent the wider range of contributions to the topic, as well as showcase the concepts through a clear key image.

First, the project "Extended Toolkit" (See Fig. 5) carefully combines sensors and parametric code to align the analogue material, gravitational force, and digital material.

This first step demonstrates the versatility of the hybrid modeling methodology to integrate analogue into digital and therfore, fully explore the implications of designing a "rubber" vase.

Second, the project "Whistling Designs" (See Fig. 6) extends the alignment of physical and digital materials by embedding information captured with a microphone. This enabled the exploration of vases by locating patterns on the vase through, for example, the sound of bird song, thereby attaching the digital object with its context. Third, the project "Explorations through Gestures" (See Fig. 7) integrated light sensors that captured hand movements acting on the physical component. This allowed shaping the vase and its parametrically described texture according to different movements. In turn, the project not only aligned material to its digital counterpart but linked design object to human haptic abilities.

Finally, the project "Asymmetric Sculpting" (See Fig. 8) allowed for designing the vase in a similar manner to traditional clay pottery (See Fig. 3); however, in this case,

9   Final Workshop Presentation.

the designer could quickly influence specific areas of the design. As such, the design is not restricted to revolution shapes, but results in asymmetric sculpted shapes.

Conclusion

In conclusion, the workshop introduced hybrid modeling, a novel design methodology for addressing the current separation between digital design and the intrinsic characteristics of materialized designs. In contrast to pure imagery or geometry-based design methods, the proposed approach exploits the potential of "digital materials" by aligning them with their physical component, which then not only bridges the analogue-digital gap, but relates them to their context.

This is explored and demonstrated by the group of nine participants, who learned and experienced the method by doing throughout the course of three days (See Fig. 9). The projects not only proved the potential of hybrid modeling to link design objects to their material nature and spatial context, to human haptic abilities and intelligence.

Workshops such as this one, are intended to develop the technique of hybrid modeling through multiple iterations, while also introducing the technique to the architectural community of practitioners, researchers, and academics. A future research stream arises that develops from the idea of analogue-based digital modeling and further develops the practice of integrating microsensors into analogue modeling materials as the interface to digital modeling. The workshop described here is an example of this option.

Then, hybrid making calls for an engagement with *spatiomateriality*—digital or physical materials that are connected rather than isolated from their physical and spatial context (Iverson-Radtke 2022). This ensures that the design media (analogue and digital) is 'live' and has reactions to their context, therefore has agency to influence, test, and critique design intent. In so doing hybrid analogue-digital modeling potentiates an entirely novel future for digital design in architecture, one based on the non-neutrality of digital materials and thereby, the digital design object.

ACKNOWLEDGMENTS

We want to thank the organizers of ACADIA, Assia Crawford, Thora H. Arnardottir, the assistance of Sarah Miller and Cynthia Fishman. Also the University of Colorado Denver Architectural Department, Department Chair Marc Swackhamer, Richard Beckett, Jamie Vanucchi, Leyuan Li, Nancy Diniz, Andrew Adamatzky, Joern

Langhorst and the entire staff for hosting this wonderful event. The workshop could have been not possible without the commitment and enthusiasm of the participants Keqin Cao, Amanda Gioia, Fernando Lima, Kathleen Zimmerman, Daniel Merupu, Diego Camargo, Elena Maj, Ikyaz Sarimehmetoglu. Special thanks goes to Andy Van Mater for his spontaneous support as unofficial workshop tutor. We also want to express gratitude to Dr. Axel Kilian, who provided suggestions regarding the workshop structure and its presentation. Finally, we want to mention that without the support of Richa Gupta, Dexter Callender, Dr. Ralf Meyer, Talis Reks (immersion lab) and STOA (MIT), we could have not achieve linking our physical and digital components through VR.

REFERENCES

Banzi, Massimo. Arduino url: https://www.arduino.cc/ (Accessed 01.7.24)

Francis, Nicholas, Joachim Ante and David Helgason. Unity (2002). url: https://unity.com/ (Accessed 01.7.24)

Iverson-Radtke, Aileen. "Rabbithole to Hybrid: Finding Digital Spatiomateriality Through Hybrid Modeling." Doctoral Dissertation, TU Berlin, Germany 2022. DOI: 10.14279/depositonce-15983

Interaction Design Lab, University of Applied Sciences Potsdam. Fritzing (2012) https://fritzing.org/ (Accessed 10.22.23)

Mc Neel & Associates TLM, Inc. Rhinoceros 3D (1990). url: https://www.rhino3d.com/ (Accessed 11.11.23)

Payne, Andrew, and Jason Kelly Johnson. Firefly (2010). url: http://fireflyexperiments.com (Accessed 11.11.23)

Rutten, David. Grasshopper 3D [5] (2007). url: https://www.grasshopper3d.com/ (Accessed 11.11.23)

IMAGE CREDITS

Figure 2: © Manufactured Landscapes, Koert Van Mensvoort, 2013
Figure 3: © Pottery making, Tortus, 2023

Augusto Gandia: is an architect and researcher with interests in design computation of fabrication-aware architecture. He completed his studies at the Mendoza University and Bauhaus University Weimar, as well as his doctoral studies at ETH Zurich's within the frame of the NCCR Digital Fabrication and Gramazio Kohler Research. He has worked at pioneering firms such as Designtoproduction. He is currently a postdoctoral associate at the Massachusetts Institute of Technology (MIT).

Aileen Iverson-Radtke: is a licensed architect with over 23 years of professional experience, and views architectural practice as spatial exploration through form-making. She sees practice as a nonverbal dialogue with media, generating unique understandings. In 2020, Aileen founded air-architecture, a theory-based practice pursuing making as a unique form of theorizing through objects, i.e., making-as-analysis. Aileen studied at the University of Florida and trained in esteemed firms in NYC and Berlin. Aileen earned her doctoral degree from TU Berlin, and her research underpins this workshop.

Andrew Payne: is an architect and computational specialist who founded LIFT Architects in 2007. Andrew received his doctoral degree at Harvard, held an Adjunct Assistant Professorship at Columbia University, and currently works for Robert McNeel & Associates. Andrew's work explores embedded computation and parametric design. In 2010, Andrew and Jason Kelly Johnson published Firefly - a comprehensive software plug-in bridging the gap between Grasshopper and Arduino microcontroller, allowing data transmission between the digital and physical worlds.

Richa Gupta: hailing from India, is graduate student at MIT and co-founder of ArchiDAO, a DAO aimed at the architecture, engineering, and construction (AEC) industry. Her vision is to democratize experience and decentralize the AEC Industry through emerging technologies, digital products, and global collaboration. As an architect and design technologist, she works in Extended Realities (XR) and adopts a cross-disciplinary method to architectural design.

Towards a Low Carbon Additive Manufacturing

DART
XTreeE
SIKA

In this workshop, the DART laboratory, Sika, and XtreeE collaborated to showcase the potential of 3D printing in reimagining the design-to-fabrication process, with a strong emphasis on rethinking concrete elements and enhancing their performance. More than a decade of digitization of concrete through 3D printing has primarily focused on labor reduction and process automation, often overlooking ways to enhance the quality of the output. The goal of this workshop was to raise awareness on the untapped potential of 3D concrete printing in advancing architectural possibilities and elevating the overall construction landscape.

Sika is a Swiss multinational specialty chemical company that supplies to the building sector and motor vehicle industry, headquartered in Baar, Switzerland. As a technology leader in its industry, Sika focuses its R&D activities on the development of more sustainable, user-friendly, and at the same time better-performing product solutions. With its concrete admixtures, Sika enables to incorporate calcined clay in concrete, and reduces the carbon footprint.

Digital Architecture Research and Technologies (DART) is a research laboratory at Taubman School of Architecture and Urban Planning, University of Michigan, founded in 2019 by Prof. Dr. Mania Aghaei Meibodi. DART research streams focus on developing novel computational design, robotics, and 3D printing technologies to enable creation of the next generation buildings and infrastructures with extraordinary structural performance, unseen architecture, and sustainable waste-free construction.

INSTRUCTORS
Gary Boon, Sika
Haripriya Nekkanti, Sika
Mania Aghaei Meibodi, DART Lab
Dominique Corvez, XtreeE
Alban Mallet, XtreeE
Romain Duballet, XtreeE
Ali Seyedahmadian
Ester Lo
Abdullah Kamhawi, DART Lab

XtreeE, the large-scale 3D company designs and manufactures large-scale 3D printers for construction. The company's mission is to shape a low-carbon living environment while increasing construction productivity. XtreeE is a technology platform that allows project owners, architects, engineers, product designers, construction, and precast firms to design & manufacture optimized building and infrastructure elements thanks to advanced large-scale 3D printing.

Throughout the workshop, participants had the opportunity to learn from leading voices in academia and industry. The online session covered topics such as cementitious materials, low-carbon construction, and robotic additive manufacturing. The in-person session, hosted at Sika's New Jersey headquarters, allowed participants to collaborate, leveraging their knowledge of low-carbon additive manufacturing to develop their designs. By the end of the workshop, participants successfully created their own design geometries, texture ornamentation, and gained a deep understanding of the physical differences between computational design and physical printing.

PARTICIPANTS

Oliver Perry

Christopher Prinz

Yao Lin

Mauro Rodriguez

Valery Kate Perez

Luis Pacheco

Biyang Yan

Timothy Sutherland

IMAGE CREDITS

ACADIA 2023 Towards a Low Carbon Additive Manufacturing workshop participants

Workshop

Habitat Formation

Dr Nic Bao
RMIT University
Dr Xin Yan
Tsinghua University

Since the introduction of computational-aided design technology in the late 20th century, form-finding based on structural performance has gained momentum in architecture. This evolution is intertwined with the development of structural morphology, from ancient Greece and Rome's barrel arches and domes to the Byzantine and Gothic periods' pendentives and flying buttresses. Architectural design has evolved from the physical models employed by visionaries like Antonio Gaudi and Frey Otto to the utilization of the topological optimization method proposed by Mark Burry and Mike Xie, reinforcing the relationship between architectural morphology and structural optimization.

This workshop introduces a novel approach to generative architectural design for human habitats. Participants will enhance their skills by applying topological optimization algorithms. The workshop emphasizes structural performance and draws inspiration from Gaudi's Sagrada Familia. It explores building element form-finding, optimization, and ornamental design.

Participants will tackle progressively challenging tasks, working on small and large-scale projects. They will design and optimize buildings or specific segments. The workshop concludes with a collaborative construction of a virtual exhibition space on an online platform. Its aim is to bridge the gap between architectural design and structural optimization, empowering participants to explore new frontiers in generative design and push the boundaries of traditional approaches.

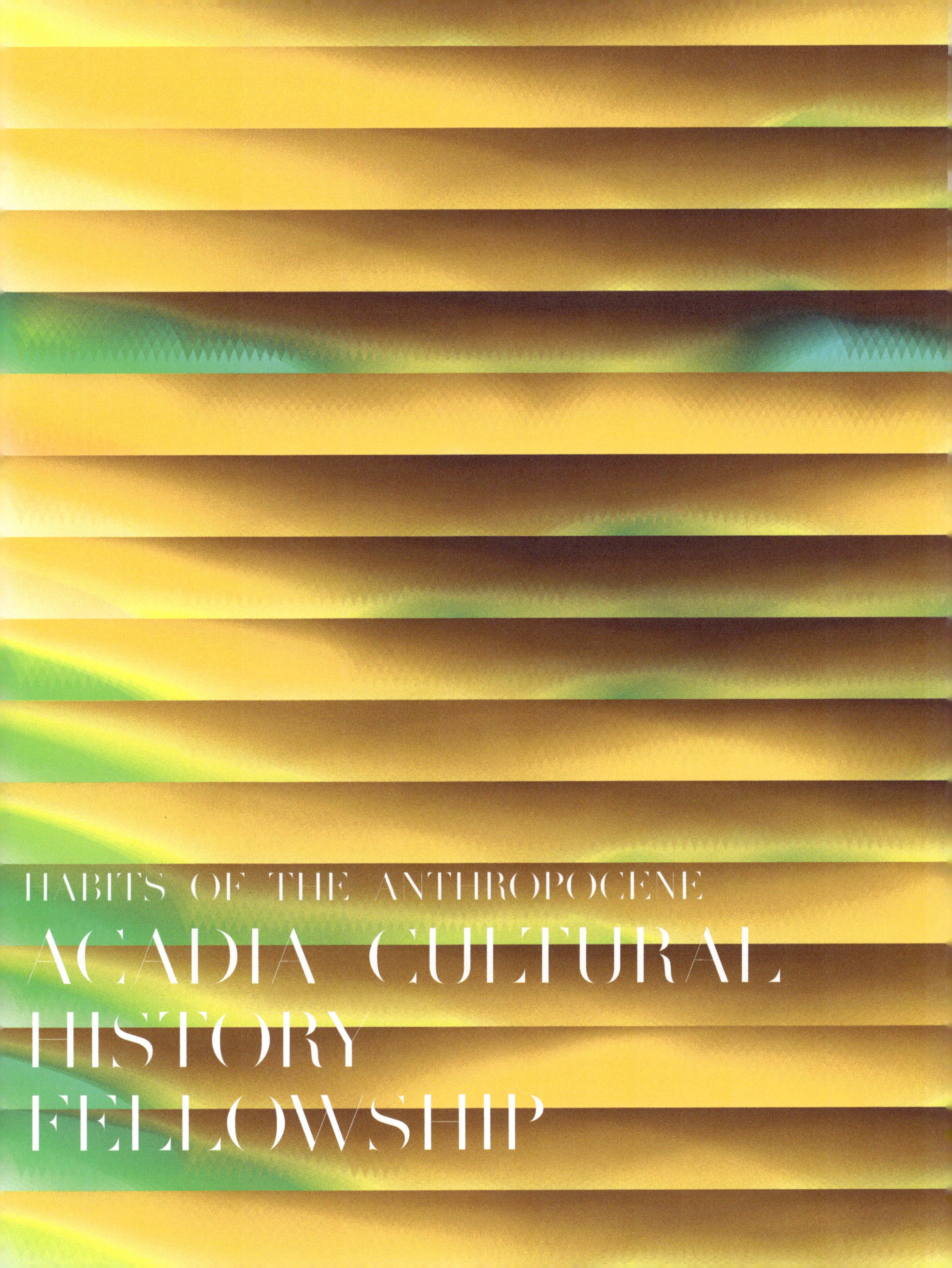

HABITS OF THE ANTHROPOCENE
ACADIA CULTURAL
HISTORY
FELLOWSHIP

ACADIA Cultural History Project and Fellowship

Shelby Doyle
Iowa State University

Biayna Bogosian
Florida International University

Melissa Goldman
University of Virginia

1   Detail of the 2023 ACADIA Cultural History Project Exhibition.

The Association for Computer Aided Design in Architecture (ACADIA) launched the Cultural History Project in 2021 to mark the 40th anniversary of the organization and the 41st anniversary of the conference. This initiative has provided an opportunity to reflect upon the legacy and trends of the organization as a method for considering its future. The Cultural History Project began with an open-access digital archive of the organization's Proceedings and Quarterlies and evolved into a larger discourse about how the ACADIA community values and promotes forms of computational knowledge. A summary essay included in the 2021 Proceedings (Image 2) reflects on what the archive reveals about ACADIA and its "habits". Habits are settled tendencies or practices, especially ones that are difficult to relinquish. The term implies repetition, perhaps unconscious, that becomes normalized through its reiteration. The 2023 ACADIA Conference, "Habits of the Anthropocene," marks the 43rd anniversary of the conference and the 42nd anniversary of ACADIA as an organization. What are the computational habits we need to identify, recall, question, break, and replace with new (or perhaps old) ways of thinking and working?

An exploration of the archival content revealed patterns and habits of the organization. One such habit was gender disparities in conference keynotes and awardees. Another pattern was the geographic distribution of ACADIA conferences across North America to highlight the concentration of resources and knowledge production. These habits and patterns were visualized as maps, graphs, and QR coded links, and then printed on textiles: a table cloth, placemats, and napkins. During the ACADIA 2022 conference, this spatiotemporal archival information was presented on a round table, a restful, yet curious space for conference attendees to engage with the content and in conversation with each other. The textiles were designed to be cumulative - to be mended and patched when new

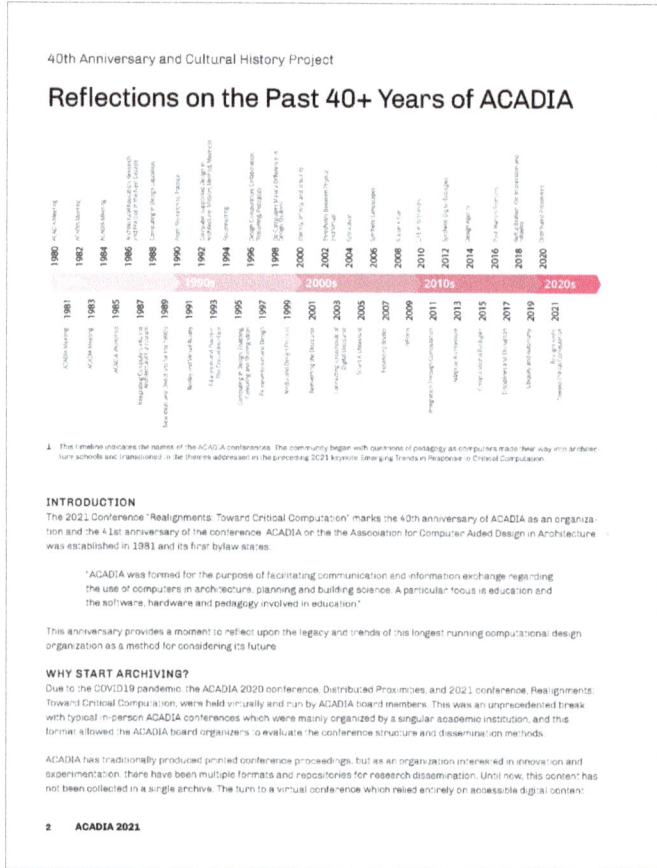

2 Reflections on the Past 40+ Years of ACADIA. Shelby Doyle, Melissa Goldman, and Biayna Bogosian in ACADIA 2021: Realignments Toward Critical Computation. Proceedings of the 41st Annual Conference of the Association of Computer Aided Design in Architecture. Edited by K. Dörfler, S. Parascho, J. Scott, B. Bogosian, B. Farahi, J. del Castillo y López, J. Grant, V. Noel. Online and Global. 3-6 November 2021. (pp. 650-657).

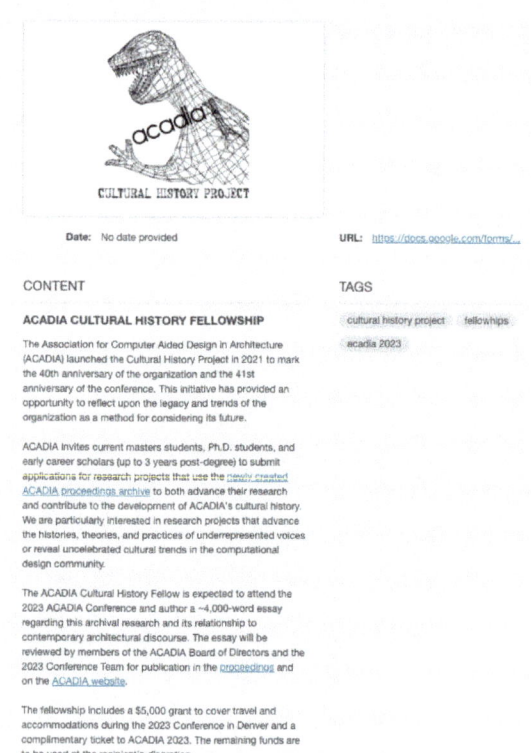

3 2023 ACADIA Cultural History Project Fellowship Call
Source: acadia.org/news/QWMTMG

information becomes available each year (Image 1). This year, the added 2022 conference graphics are printed as napkins, and the geographic location- Philadelphia- sewn onto the placemat maps.

In 2020 and 2021, when the COVID pandemic necessitated online board-run conferences, there was an opportunity to operate directly upon the habits identified by the experiences and habits of the community. The pandemic era conferences were noteworthy for female-majority keynotes and gender parity in conference attendance. This was not an accident - by recognizing the importance of facilitating knowledge access to a broader audience, the co-chairs prioritized sponsorship initiatives that facilitate free student live-streaming in order to increase global student access and welcome the next generations of the ACADIA community.
Since the intertwined crises of 2020, ACADIA has fostered a dual focus of examining the past as a method to continuously refine our community's visions, habits, and norms toward a more equitable future. In 2023, the ACADIA Board of Directors launched the inaugural ACADIA Cultural History Fellowship to encourage early-career research projects that used the ACADIA archive to advance the histories, theories, and practices of underrepresented voices or reveal uncelebrated cultural trends in the computational design community (Image 3). The call had an overwhelmingly positive response and the Board funded one fellow, as well as two honorable mention projects.
The inaugural 2023 ACADIA Cultural History Fellow was Hanan Kataw, a Ph.D. Candidate at Harvard University, with a proposal titled Expanding the Narrative of Diversity and Inclusion in Computational Design (Image 5). Through a historical exploration of ACADIA proceedings, this project seeks to highlight the diverse narratives, geographies, and institutions that intersected and met at ACADIA since the 1980s, offering a critical examination of the "conference" with its unique open call as a central institutional typology in the history of computational design.
Honorable Mentions for ACADIA Cultural History Fellows were Hayri Dortdivanlioglu, Ph.D. Candidate at Georgia Institute of Technology and Constantinos Miltiadis, Ph.D. Candidate at Aalto University (Image 5). Hayri analyzed evolving themes in ACADIA projects since 2010, tracking terminologies and diagramming the ebbs and changes in the community's research focii. The

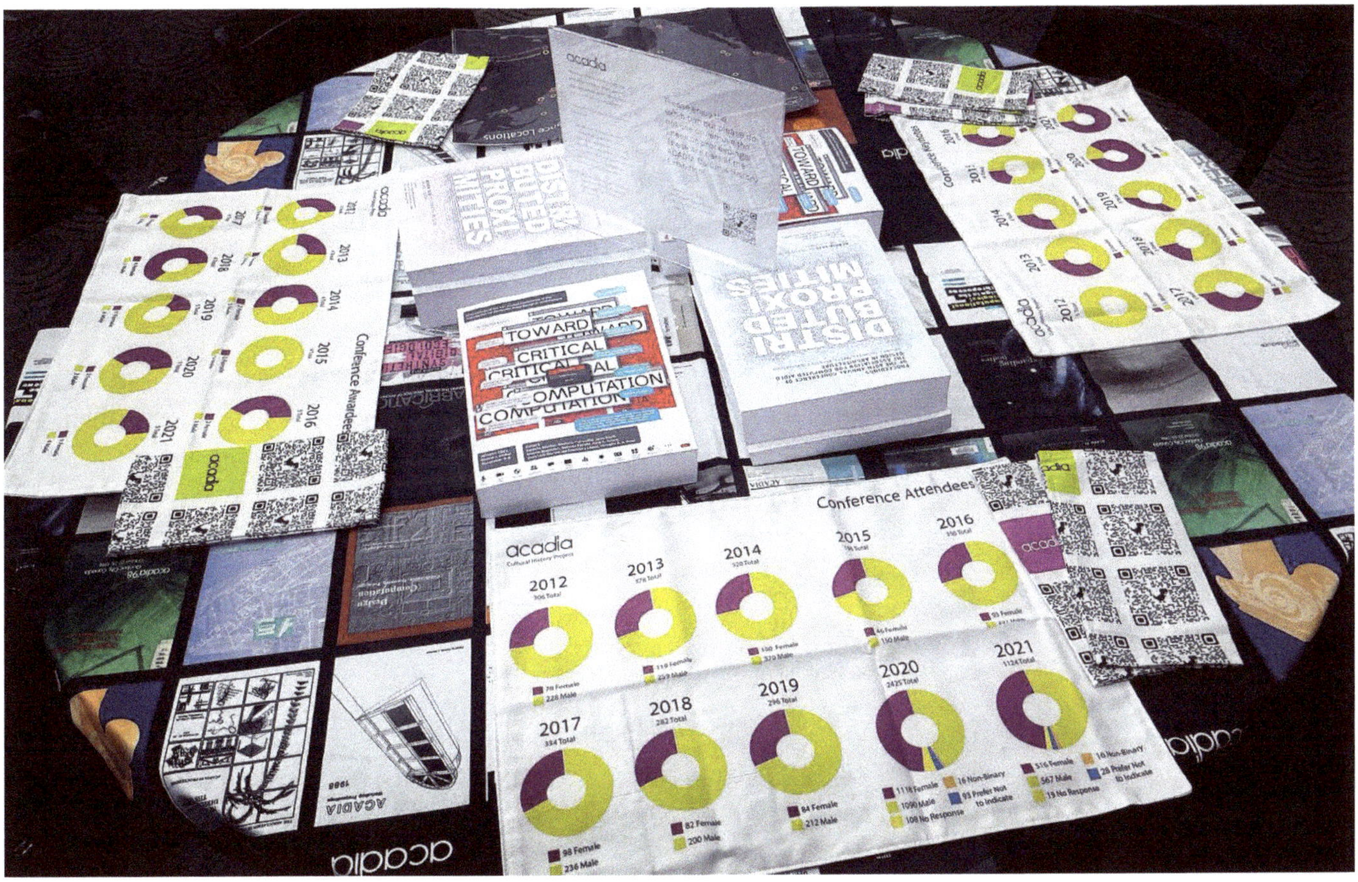

4 ACADIA Cultural History Project Exhibition Table. Top 2022. Photo by Authors. Bottom 2023. Photo by Hanan Kataw.

5   2023 ACADIA Cultural History Fellowship Recipients.

work illuminates the rising interests in the last twelve years of topics such as digital fabrication, computational technologies, and human relationships to ecologies and matter. Constantinos designed a web-based archive of ACADIA's published proceedings using an open access infrastructure to create new ways of seeing, accessing, and organizing the archive. This can be used by future researchers as a foundational tool to navigate themes and trends, tools and theories across ACADIA's history.

The three projects were displayed at this year's conference as prints and on screen as another layer of the Cultural History Project table (Image 1 and 4). In the following pages of these proceedings, each fellow has further documented their work on the ACADIA archive. We hope that by opening and highlighting our history, new knowledge and patterns can emerge to push the future of our community and its research.

IMAGE CREDITS

Figure 4: 2023 Table by Hanan Kataw.
Figure 5: Headshots from Fellows.
All other images provided by authors.

Shelby Elizabeth Doyle, AIA is an Associate Professor of Architecture and Stan G. Thurston Professor of Design-Build at the Iowa State University College of Design, co-founder of the ISU Computation & Construction Lab (CCL) and director of the ISU Architectural Robotics Lab (ARL). Doyle received a Fulbright Fellowship to Cambodia, a Master of Architecture from the Harvard Graduate School of Design, and a Bachelor of Science in architecture from the University of Virginia.

Biayna Bogosian, Ph.D. is an Assistant Professor of Architectural Technology at Florida International University, with secondary appointments in FIU Electrical and Computer Engineering and the Institute of Environment. An interdisciplinary researcher, she develops spatial media and immersive learning for urban environmental innovation and civic data engagement. She is the Co-Director of FIU's Robotics and Digital Fabrication Lab and has been a member of the ACADIA Board of Directors since 2021. Her research is funded by NSF, NASA, EPA, and Leonardo grants.

Melissa Goldman is the Fabrication Lab Manager at the University of Virginia School of Architecture, serves as the Communications Officer on the ACADIA Board of Directors, and is an active member of the Student Shop Managers Consortium. Melissa earned her Master of Architecture from Columbia's Graduate School of Architecture, Planning and Preservation and her BA in English from Harvard.

ACADIA's Open Call

Expanding the Narrative of Diversity and Inclusion in Computational Design

Hanan Kataw
Harvard University

1 "Apertures" pamphlets with an abridged version of this essay, which were displayed at the 2023 ACADIA Cultural History Project Exhibition.

WRITING ACADIA'S HISTORY

The Association for Computer Aided Design in Architecture (ACADIA) was founded on October 17, 1981. The first meeting was held at Carnegie-Mellon University and attended by 24 founding members. When the history of ACADIA is discussed, out of these two dozen founders, three are frequently noted: William Mitchell, Charles Eastman, and Chris Yessios. Mitchell was a pioneer in computer-aided design and smart cities research and is, as Wassim Jabi, ACADIA's 21st president put it, "one of ACADIA's most famous founding members."[1] Eastman was not only ACADIA's first president, but also one of the leading figures in the history of Building Information Modeling (BIM) and is often referred to as "the father of BIM." Yessios is widely known for his work at Ohio State University and his role in developing Form.Z.

If it is only a history of great men that we are looking for, we need to look no further. Such a history, to borrow the English essayist Walter Bagehot's turn of phrase, "is like the art of Rembrandt; it casts a vivid light on certain selected causes, on those which were best and greatest; it leaves all the rest in shadow and unseen."[2] The works of these three figures and their contributions to ACADIA, expansive and not yet properly studied, are more than enough to fill multiple volumes. Such a history, however, can only produce blinkered views, limited by its author's conception of "greatness" and overlooking those left in the shadow, who often play as important a role in shaping history as those brilliantly illuminated.

The remaining 21 founding members of ACADIA are: Harold J. Borkin, Peter Burgess, Kevin Cavanaugh, Donald Collins, William Cooper, Ulrich Flemming, Jay Garrott, Greg Glass, Jeff Hamer, Yehuda E. Kalay, R. I. MacDonald, John F. McIntosh, Rabindra Mukerjea, Richard W. Quadrel, Gary Stonebreaker, Luis H. Summers, John O. Tector, Robert Thornton, John W. Wade, Warren K. Wake, and Paul Winsberg.

Some of these men, including Borkin,[3] Flemming,[4] Kalay,[5] and McIntosh,[6] played leading roles in ACADIA's history and in developing computational design tools and education, while others pursued other paths. Expanding the history of ACADIA, computational design and architecture does not mean equalizing all actors. Instead, it involves a deliberate reevaluation of the narratives and an intentional shift in where the light is cast, moving beyond singular narratives to capture more comprehensive views. In the history of architecture, however, the light has often been cast only on the figure of the star architect, privileging the narrative of the sole male designer and the creative genius.

THE STAR SYSTEM

In her famous essay "Room at the Top? Sexism and the Star System in Architecture," Denise Scott Brown recalls an incident when the head of an architecture school, unable to reach her husband, Robert Venturi, called her instead and explained: 'Denise, I'm embarrassed to be speaking to you because we're giving a party for QP [a well-known local architect] and we're asking Bob but not you. You see, you are a friend of QP and you are an architect, but you're also a wife, and we're not asking wives."[7] Although published in 1989, Scott Brown originally wrote her essay in 1975—Things have since changed, one might think, or at least hope, whenever hearing such stories that many professional women of Scott Brown's generation can recount. Indeed, things have changed; not only do women appear more often on invitation lists, but many today lead architectural schools and decide whose name is on the list. Nevertheless, the star system and its embedded biases—sexism, among others—persisted well into the 21st century and have largely shaped the historiography of digital and computational design in architecture.

For example, in 2003, The "Architecture Non-Standard" exhibition opened at the Centre Pompidou in Paris with the aim to bring together "the most innovative research in architecture and design" advanced by the use of digital technologies.[8] Seven out of the 21 architects and designers represented at the exhibition were women. However, only one was included as a solo designer.[9] This could be read as a productive move away from the star system and toward a

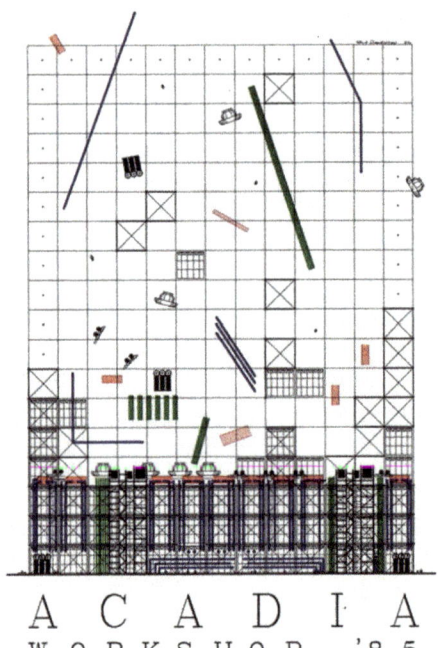

2   ACADIA's Charter (Acadia Newsletter, no. 5, 1984).

3   Cover of ACADIA 1985 Proceedings.

more collaborative framework. However, almost half of the offices included in the exhibition were led and represented by solo designers; all but one were men. The tendency to include women only alongside male partners was not unique to the "Architecture Non-Standard" exhibition. A decade later, in 2013, in *The Digital Turn in Architecture*, edited by Mario Carpo, while most of the book's essays were single-authored, women appear only as co-authors and only in four out of the 26 texts.[10] Around the same time, a list of 26 projects that were seen to have "marked the surge of digital practice within the discipline" was put together as part of the proposal for the Archeology of the Digital project at the Canadian Centre for Architecture, which included archiving born-digital design records and a series of exhibitions and publications.[11] Zaha Hadid was the only woman listed as a solo designer, while 13 solo male architects were included.

Discussing the inclusion of women, as opposed to non-western, people of color, and other underrepresented voices in the history of digital and computational design, does not mean that women are the only group systematically underrepresented within the architectural star system, a system that often favors the already privileged. However, despite methodological limitations regarding the classification of gender, the reliance on visual or name-based methods to quantify the representation of ethnic and racial minorities in the absence of data provided by the individuals remains more difficult. Yet, anyone familiar with the historiography of digital and computational design in architecture can attest to its predominantly white scene.

By centering the sole author figure of the architect, the star system also leaves in the shadow many non-architect collaborators. It "sees the firm as a pyramid with a Designer on top," as Scott Brown points out, and "has little to do with today's complex relations in architecture and construction."[12] In the historiography of digital design in architecture, that often meant the marginalization of various experts—software developers, technologies, and computer engineers in addition to the more traditional set of actors—whose contributions have been integral to architecture, yet the names of whom, with a few exceptions, are often left out of exhibition walls and architectural publications.

Another central category of non-architect collaborators whose contributions have had the greatest impact on the development of digital and computational design are the tech industry players, and the software and hardware developers behind the architect's digital tool kit. Those actors, although sometimes collaborators of architects, are creative designers in their own right and players in a market that, while largely distinct from the architectural one, have had a direct and tangible influence on the history and development of digital and computational design. Yet, the histories of computational design in architecture often address the work of these non-architect actors only from the viewpoint of architects and in relation to the impact of their tools on the creative processes of the architect, but rarely as separate, creative, economic and political actors whose work has had a larger impact on architecture design practice than many star architects.

Moreover, during the late 20th century, a conception of digital architecture as "computationally based processes of form origination and transformations" emerged, distinguishing it—as computers were becoming more and more ubiquitous—from the rest of computer-aided design.[13] According to this definition, it was not enough for computers to be used in the design process for the architecture to be considered digital; digital architecture needed to be one that "could not have been designed and built without digital tools."[14] And an architecture that could not have been designed without digital tools had to look the part. This conception of digital design influenced the mainstream discourse in architecture for years, largely reducing it to formal experimental and overlooking various other less visibly recognizable applications of computers in architecture.

Since Scott Brown wrote her essay, things have changed, and they keep on changing. In the past few years, many scholars have begun challenging the star-system-focused digital historiography and exploring more diverse voices, broadening the focus geographically, categorically, and thematically. However, many of the biases embedded in the star system persist, and more work that builds on the efforts of these scholars is still needed.

ACADIA'S ARCHIVES
Similar to many of the institutions of its time, ACADIA reflected some of the larger structural biases of the discipline, and its conferences were not immune to the prejudices that many conferences are prone to.[15] For example, between 2012 and 2019, only about 30% of ACADIA conference's attendees were women, and in 2021, only 28% of ACADIA's proceedings editors had been females. As Shelby Doyle, Melissa Goldman, and Biayna Bogosian concluded after discussing these figures, "there remains work to be done in representational equity but also in the types of content celebrated by the ACADIA community."[16]

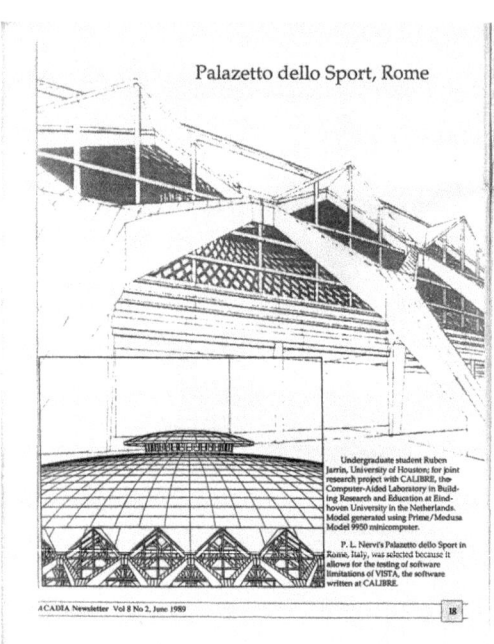

4 Pages from Acadia Newsletter 6, no.8 (1989) showing student work at the University of Houston using Prime's Medusa.

However, despite these limitations, unlike many other architectural cultural institutions that shaped the dominant narratives about the history of computation in architecture, ACADIA utilized open calls and was less reliant on professional networks compared to exhibitions, publications, and closed symposia where the star system was more prominent and curators, editors, and organizers relied heavily on their knowledge and professional network in deciding participation. Instead of having one person sitting down and writing a list, the open call, while still part of a review process, did not rely on fame and recognition alone, and in that, offered a slightly broader space for a diverse set of voices to join the conversation. This, in addition to ACADIA's focus on education and its openness towards works-in-progress instead of privileging only finished projects and flashy, eye-catching images, created the possibility for a more inclusive representation of the computer-aided design community.

This is, however, not an attempt to celebrate ACADIA's archive as an unbiased, inclusive representation of the history of computational design. Instead, it is an attempt to explore these possibilities that have been created by the unique structure of the conference as an institution. The ACADIA proceedings are filled with possible threads and openings that could offer a glimpse into a more expansive history and the possibility of a better representation of previously overlooked voices. Studying these openings is not necessarily a celebratory investigation, nor is it a quest to find new stars or heroes. It is, however, an attempt to arrive at a better understanding of both the history of computation in architecture, the various actors that played a role in its development, and the conditions of exclusion and inclusion that shaped its dominant narratives.

Following Ann Laura Stoler in her approach to reading along, and not only against, the archival grain, and in search not for "dramatic 'reversal,' 'usurpation,' and successful 'appropriation'" but "moments that disrupt (if only provisionally) a field of force, that challenge (if only slightly) what can be said and done, that question (if only quietly) 'epistemic warrant,' that realign the certainties of the probable more than they mark wholesale reversals of direction,"[17] I turned to the ACADIA archives in search of such moments, is search of openings.

An aperture is a small opening that allows light in. In a camera, this opening controls the depth of field and the level of clarity of the objects in the background. As part of ACADIA's Cultural History project, my search for apertures was an attempt to highlight some of the blurred figures in the background and the underrepresented voices that have met at ACADIA since the 1980s. It is a proposal to search for openings and ways in which the archive of ACADIA's proceedings can be a source for writing an expansive history, one that goes beyond celebrating a few famous figures and explores the diverse set of actors that has shaped ACADIA's history and the history of computational design in architecture.

APERTURES
Women at ACADIA

The brochure for the organizing workshop, ACADIA's first meeting in 1981, listed five aims for the association:

1. Gain financial support for CAD development in architecture.
2. Coordinate and share in software development.
3. Share materials for teaching and curriculum development.
4. Provide regular communication, e.g., a newsletter.
5. Organize symposia/ conferences.[18]

20 years later, in 2001, ACADIA had already made substantial progress on those aims. In her "Position Paper for ACADIA 2001", the Association's sixth president, Elizabeth Bollinger, underscored these achievements:

> Software developers have recognized ACADIA as a moving force in the field, and many members of ACADIA have provided valuable assistance and feedback in the technological development of CAD and related software. The ACADIA Quarterly, the annual conferences, and their resulting published proceedings all provide substantive exchange of ideas and information.[19]

Concluding her essay, Bollinger added, "I believe the organization has served the profession admirably. Congratulations to the founding fathers, and also to the many faithful members who have contributed to the continuity of the organization and the principles on which it was founded." Bollinger was right in emphasizing the role that ACADIA, with its growing network of members and far-reaching activities, had played in the development of computational design and its tools in North America. Its proceedings archives are a living record of these collaborations and achievements. She was also correct in referring to those who met at the first ACADIA meeting as the "founding fathers"—they were all men. By 2001, ACADIA had come a long way from its early days, yet it was still largely led by men. Only four of its first 20 presidents were women. When ACADIA celebrated its 40th anniversary 20 years later, the ratio had not changed.

That is not to say that women's contributions were not integral to ACADIA's success. A quick visit to ACADIA's archives reveals the names of numerous women who, as editors, organizers, committee members, and presenters, shaped ACADIA, and had a significant impact on the history of CAD. Their contributions, partly recorded in ACADIA's archives, still await further research and documentation. For example, should you choose to embark on a chronological exploration of the ACADIA proceedings archive, the first name you will encounter, on the cover of the 1985 workshop proceedings, is Patricia G. McIntosh. She is a pioneer researcher in the field of computer-aided design, the seventh president of ACADIA, the second woman to hold that position after Elizabeth Bollinger, and the first woman to join the faculty of the Arizona State University School of Architecture.[20] However, if, upon encountering her name a few times in the proceedings, you decide to conduct quick research about McIntosh and her work, your investigation will likely yield little satisfaction. Little is written about her, and that little is mostly woven into the biographies of her collaborators.

Before joining ACADIA, and during the 1970s, while pursuing her PhD in Architecture at the University of Michigan, McIntosh collaborated with James A. Turner, John Macintosh, and Harold Borkin on developing ARCH:MODEL, an innovative application of BIM that utilized a relational database system for architectural modeling.[21] ARCH:MODEL would go on to be taught at the University's "computer-aided studio" throughout the 1980s, introducing a generation of students to CAD, BIM, and computer architectural representations.[22] In 1982, she finished her dissertation titled "The Geometric Set Operations in Computer-Aided Building Design," and the following year, in 1983, she accepted a faculty position as an assistant professor at Arizona State University to teach computer-aided design.[23] While her dissertation and work at Michigan University focused on developing information-based computer modeling, later in her career, during the 1980s and 1990s, McIntosh worked on developing different approaches to computational design education in which the computer was envisioned as a tutor and a source for generating and exploring different design solutions.[24] The ACADIA proceedings archives provide a few openings onto her work and publications. However, the extent of her contribution to computational design is yet to be thoroughly documented and acknowledged.

Industry Players

The computers in computational design are not generic, nameless machines. They are the products of specific developers and companies, affected and shaped by market trends and fluctuations. The same goes for the entirety of the architect's digital tool kit, including its various software packages and digital fabrication equipment. An expansive understanding of the history of computational design can only be achieved if the usually overlooked markets and industry players behind these tools are centered and examined.

These players helped fund many of the early computer-focused university experiments and design studios around the U.S., and made many appearances in the acknowledgments and footnotes of ACADIA proceedings and newsletters. For instance, in a 1987 ACADIA newsletter, one can read about the grant that the University of Oregon received from Apple Inc. to establish an experimental design studio using Macintosh computers.[25] Another newsletter mentions that IBM funded a major research project, "Applications in Design School Education," at Harvard University and gave a grant to the University of Illinois Urbana-Champaign to experiment with the introduction of the computer to the architecture curriculum.[26] Around the same time, IBM also funded the incorporation of computers into architecture courses at the University of Florida.[27] Many other grants and funding are documented in ACADIA's archives.

These funds were not acts of philanthropy. As one dean explained, "Our [industry] partners have an investment, and they expect a return on their investment."[28] For the industry, these schools were testing grounds for their products, advertisement and PR centers, and training facilities for their future clients. The timing and requirements of these grants and funds also mirrored changes in product lines, marketing strategies, and market dynamics.

In 1984, Prime Computer, Inc. offered a grant to the University of Houston under the conditions that Professor Elizabeth Bollinger teach two CAD courses a semester and engage "in research toward architectural enhancement and development of the Medusa package," Prime's newly acquired CAD software.[29] The funding given to Houston came at a time when Prime, in an attempt to overcome financial troubles, had bought the Medusa software package and begun to put more emphasis on its CAD/CAM business line and its marketing. Funding university research was part of Prime's marketing strategy to appeal to architects and designers, and strengthen the user base of their CAD products. Numerous other companies followed similar approaches.[30]

In 1991, ACADIA received funding from a number of corporations, including Alias Research, Inc. and Wavefront Technologies Inc., two of the leading animation software developers in the 1990s.[31] At that time, the software packages offered by these companies were beyond the purchasing power of most architectural firms and departments, and most of the tools they provided were catering to their main client base in the lucrative entertainment industry and were of limited use to architects.[32] Yet the use of animation in the entertainment industry was not developing fast enough to sustain steady growth for these companies. They needed to find new markets for their animation products—architecture was one of these potential markets.[33] Not only did Alias and Wavefront make various appearances in the ACADIA proceedings after 1991, but the animation industry's interest in architecture, various fundings for architectural conferences, and the millions of dollars' worth of software and hardware donated to different architectural schools, led to the rise of the popularity of animation as a design approach in architecture in the 1990s. Exploring the traces left by the tech industry and its market dynamics within the pages of ACADIA's proceedings provides an opportunity to enrich the historiography of computational design, leading to a more comprehensive understanding of the overarching conditions and historical factors that extend beyond architecture yet significantly shape its development.

Non-Architect Actors

The work that architects do has changed throughout history, and that change has been accelerated in the last couple of decades with the introduction of computational tools. Many of the tasks and expertise that are today considered part of the architect's repertoire were the domain of computer engineers, software developers, and other technologists who used to write code, build digital models, transfer hand sketches into computer drawings, prepare animations and walk-throughs, and run environmental and structural simulations. Today, many architects do all of the above, and their work is valued as part of the creative and professional architectural labor. That has not always been the case. For decades, those tasks—considered complementary to, but not part of, the design process—were not centered and those who performed them have largely been left out of the history of computational design. However, in the ACADIA proceedings, the line between what is considered architectural labor and what is not is challenged, opening the possibility of a broader understanding of computational design in architecture.

In 1986, ACADIA's then president, Yehuda Kalay, defined ACADIA as "a forum to facilitate communication between educators (and perhaps professionals) who care about computer-aided design education in architecture."[34] Since its founding, this broad conception of ACADIA's community has made it a meeting place for many professionals and educators who work on computer-aided design, whether architects or non-architects. In the proceedings, we come across architects working outside the traditional realm of architecture—modeling dinosaurs for museum exhibitions,[35] visualizing medical data,[36] and working with aerospace engineering students to design space habitats.[37] We also find many non-architect actors working within architecture. This includes software developers—the creative minds behind a wealth of software applications such as CoDraw Grid Manager[38] and Electronic Cocktail Napkin[39]—as well as computer, civil, and electric engineers, whose work is often marginalized in architectural history despite being an integral part in the development of computational design processes and education, including incorporating energy analysis and simulation into CAD packages[40] and jointly leading various architectural computational design studios and teaching experiments.[41]

BEYOND SUCCESS AND FAME

Many of the experiments and research presented at ACADIA did not produce earth-shattering results. Their efforts were incremental, slowly nudging computational design in one direction or another. Only a few produced commercial software and applications that went on to have commercial success, and even fewer names rose to fame and wide recognition. Yet the projects that failed to gain traction tell us about the history of ACADIA, computational design, and the social and economic context in which they evolved, as much as, if not more, than the success stories. As Olga Touloumi and Theodora Vardouli remark in *Computer Architectures: Constructing the Common Ground*, "We need more histories of banality and failure. And we need to come to terms with delivering dry histories that do not climax or break ground, but rather shape ground."[42] Why did virtual architecture, once a popular topic of discussion, lose momentum? Why were the efforts to build voice-operated CAD tools intended for the use of individuals with a physical disability never widely adopted? Why did certain software applications gain more popularity than others? The pages of ACADIA Digital Archives might not provide full answers to these questions, but they are apertures through which we can glean insights into potential answers.

CONCLUSION

Although ACADIA has largely been operating within the same power structures and disciplinary norms that have long privileged certain White, Western, and male-dominated narratives, its conference—with its open call— presents an alternative to the institutional model of traditional architectural publications and exhibitions, which have relied heavily on privileged professional and social networks. The open nature of the conference defies that paradigm, and its past proceedings are an openings through which we can shed light on many overlooked actors in the history of ACADIA and computational design. The apertures offered here are not necessarily celebratory spotlights. Not all those who have been overlooked in history are heroes. Nor do these apertures provide full stories. These small openings, however, are possible beginnings for future research and invitations for further investigation.

ACKNOWLEDGMENTS

The research was conducted as part of ACADIA Cultural History Fellowship 2023. I am grateful to Shelby Doyle, Biayna Bogosian, and Melissa Goldman for their invaluable support and their comments and feedback on an earlier version of this essay.

NOTES

1. Wassim Jabi, ed., "Editor's Preface: Reinventing the Discourse," in Reinventing the Discourse: ACADIA Conference Proceedings, 2001, xii–xiv.
2. Walter Bagehot, *Physics and Politics*. (New York: D. Appleton and company, 1902), 62.
3. Borkin worked on developing ARCH: Model, an early application of building information modeling, and led computational design education at the University of Michigan.
4. Flemming developed research on generative design and other computer applications, led computational design education at Michigan University, and was a member of ACADIA's steering committee.
5. In addition to his wide-ranging scholarly work on computational design, Kalay was ACADIA's fifth president and has co-founded and directed the Berkeley Center for New Media at the University of California, Berkeley.
6. McIntosh worked on developing ARCH:Model at the University of Michigan, led computational design education at Arizona State University, and was ACADIA's tenth president.
7. Denise Scott Brown, "Room at the Top? Sexism and the Star System in Architecture," in Gender Space Architecture, ed. Iain Borden, Barbara Penner, and Jane Rendell (Routledge, 2000), 265.
8. Brochure for "Architectures Non Standard," 2003, 2017W022 32, The Centre Pompidou Archives.
9. Frederic Migayrou, ed., *Architectures Non Standard* (Paris: Centre Pompidou, 2003).
10. Mario Carpo, ed., *The Digital Turn in Architecture 1992-2012*, AD Reader (Chichester: Wiley, 2013).
11. "Archeology of the Digital Projects," AI2018.Rg6.SRG3.DiGi. S1.005/10-6, The Canadian Centre for Architecture Archive, Montreal, Canada.
12. Scott Brown, "Room at the Top? Sexism and the Star System in Architecture," 260.
13. Branko Kolarevic, "Digital Architectures," in Eternity, Infinity and Virtuality in Architecture: ACADIA Conference Proceedings, ed. Guillermo P. Vasquez de Velasco and Mark J. Clayton, 2000, 251.

14. Mario Carpo in Martin Bressani et al., "L'architecture à l'heure Du Numérique, Des Algorithmes Au Projet: Un Débat Entre Martin Bressani, Mario Carpo, Reinhold Martin et Theodora Vardouli, Mené Par Antoine Picon," *Perspective*, December 30, 2019, 114. (Translated by author).
15. For more on gender, race and class biases in academic conferences, see Emily F. Henderson and James Burford, "Thoughtful Gatherings: Gendering Conferences as Spaces of Learning, Knowledge Production and Community," *Gender and Education* 32, no. 1 (January 2, 2020): 1–10; and Jo Stanley, "Pain(t) for Healing: The Academic Conference and the Classed/Embodied Self." *Community*, vol. 32, 2020, 169–82.
16. Shelby Doyle, Melissa Goldman, and Biayna Bogosian, "Reflections on the Past 40+ Years of ACADIA," in Realignments: Toward Critical Computation: ACADIA Conference Proceedings, ed. Dörfler et al., 2001, 654.
17. Ann Laura Stoler, *Along the Archival Grain: Epistemic Anxieties and Colonial Common Sense*, Course Book (Princeton, NJ: Princeton University Press, 2010), 51.
18. Charles Eastman, "Twenty Years of ACADIA," in Reinventing the Discourse: ACADIA Conference Proceedings, ed. Wassim Jabi, 2001, 3–4.
19. Elizabeth Bollinger, "Position Paper for ACADIA 2001," in Reinventing the Discourse: ACADIA Conference Proceedings, ed. Wassim Jabi, 2001, 8.
20. "Architecture at ASU Timeline," The Design School, Arizona State University Website, accessed October 10, 2023, https://timeline.design.asu.edu/.
21. John McIntosh, "A Short Narrative of My Episodic Life," Arizona State University Website, January 2005, accessed October 10, 2023, https://search.asu.edu/profile/66068.
22. "University of Michigan," *Acadia Newsletter*, no. 5 (1984): 37; and Yehuda Kalay, "The Impact of CAD On Architectural Design Education in the United States," in Teaching and Research Experience with CAAD: eCAADe Conference Proceedings, 1986, 348–55.
23. McIntosh, "A Short Narrative of My Episodic Life."
24. For example, see Patricia G. McIntosh, "A Computational Tutor for Architectural Design," *Computers, Environment and Urban Systems* 12, no. 4 (January 1, 1988): 213–19; and Patricia G. McIntosh, "The Internet as Communication Medium and Online Laboratory for Architecture Research," in Computerised Craftsmanship: eCAADe Conference Proceedings, 1998, 151–57.
25. "A MacStudio at the University of Oregon," *Acadia Newsletter* 6, no. 4 (1987): 8.
26. Mark Van Norman, "Computer Applications in Design School Education," and Donald E. Bergeson, "CAD in the Studio at the University of Illinois, Urbana-Champaign," *Acadia Newsletter* 5, no. 2 (1986): 8,9.
27. Charles F. Morgan, "Conceptual Design on a Microcomputer," in Architectural Education, Research, and Practice in the Next Decade: ACADIA Conference Proceedings, ed. James A. Turner, 1986, 89–102.
28. Robert Brehl, "Business Join College for High-Tech Training," *Toronto Star*, March 22, 1995.
29. Elizabeth Bollinger, "Research at Houston," *Acadia Newsletter* 3, no. 3 (1984): 2–3.
30. Bob Davis, "Prime Computer Claims It Is on the Road to Recovery, but Major Problems Remain," *The Wall Street Journal*, June 7, 1984; and Paula Kepos, "Computervision Corporation," in International Directory of Company Histories, vol. 10 (Detroit, MI: St. James Press, 1995), 240–42,
31. Glenn Goldman and Michael Zdepski, eds., "Acknowledgments," in Reality and Virtual Reality: ACADIA Conference Proceedings, 1991.
32. Norm Miller, "Silicon Graphics Computer Systems Animation Market Segment: FY '98 Business Plan,'" Alias|Wavefront records, Box 11, "silicon graphic software 1988," The Charles Babbage Institute Archives.
33. "Media Market Lesson Guide," Alias|Wavefront record, Box 12, The Charles Babbage Institute Archives.
34. Yehuda Kalay, "What Is Acadia's Mission? Is It Ready to Live up to It?," *Acadia Newsletter* 5, no. 1 (1986): 3–4.
35. Pamela J. Hill, "The Virtual Dinosaur Project," *Acadia Newsletter* 14, no. 3 (1995): 13–14.
36. Julio Bermudez et al., "Data Representation Architecture: Visualization Design Methods, Theory and Technology Applied to Anesthesiology," in Eternity, Infinity and Virtuality in Architecture: ACADIA Conference Proceedings, ed. Guillermo P. Vasquez de Velasco and Mark J. Clayton, 2000, 91–102.
37. Theodore W. Hall, "Space Stations, Computers and Architectural Design," in Integrating Computers into the Architectural Curriculum: ACADIA Conference Proceedings, ed. Barbara J. Novitski, 1987, 7–18.
38. Mark D. Gross, "Grids in Design and CAD," in Reality and Virtual Reality: ACADIA Conference Proceedings, ed. Glenn Goldman and Michael Zdepski, 1991, 33–44.
39. Ellen Yi-Luen Do and Mark D. Gross, "Drawing Analogies: Finding Visual References By Sketching," in Computing in Design: ACADIA Conference Proceedings, ed. Loukas N. Kalisperis, 1995, 35–52; and Mark D. Gross, "The Electronic Cocktail Napkin" *Design Studies* 17, no. 1 (January 1, 1996): 53–69.
40. For example, see Bharati Jog, "An Interface Between CAD and Energy Analysis System," in Integrating Computers into the Architectural Curriculum: ACADIA Conference Proceedings, ed. Barbara J. Novitski, 1987, 87–94.

41. For example, see Anton C. Harfmann and Stuart S. Chen, "Component Based Computer Aided Learning for Students of Architecture and Civil Engineering," in New Ideas and Directions for the 1990's: ACADIA Conference Proceedings, ed. Chris Yessios, 1989, 193–208; and Pio Luigi Brusasco et al., "Computer Supported Design Studio," in Media and Design Process: ACADIA Conference Proceedings, ed. Osman Ataman and Julio Bermúdez, 1999, 393–408.
42. Theodora Vardouli and Olga Touloumi, "Introduction: Toward a Polyglot Space," in Computer Architectures: Constructing the Common Ground, Routledge Research in Design, Technology (Milton Park, Abingdon, Oxon: New York, NY : Routledge, 2020), 5.

IMAGE CREDITS

Figure 1: Image by the author.

All other images courtesy of the ACADIA Digital Archive.

Hanan Kataw is an architect and an architectural historian. She is a PhD candidate in Architecture at Harvard University. She holds a bachelor's degree in architecture engineering from The University of Jordan and a Master of Arts in Architectural History from the Bartlett School of Architecture, University College London. Her doctoral research looks at discourse-making practices in the Western discipline of architecture, focusing on the rise of the digital discourses of the 1990s and examining the social and institutional systems and power relations that conditioned and shaped these discourses.

Word Webs: Bridging the Gap between Theory and Practice

Hayri Dortdivanlioglu
Georgia Institute of Technology

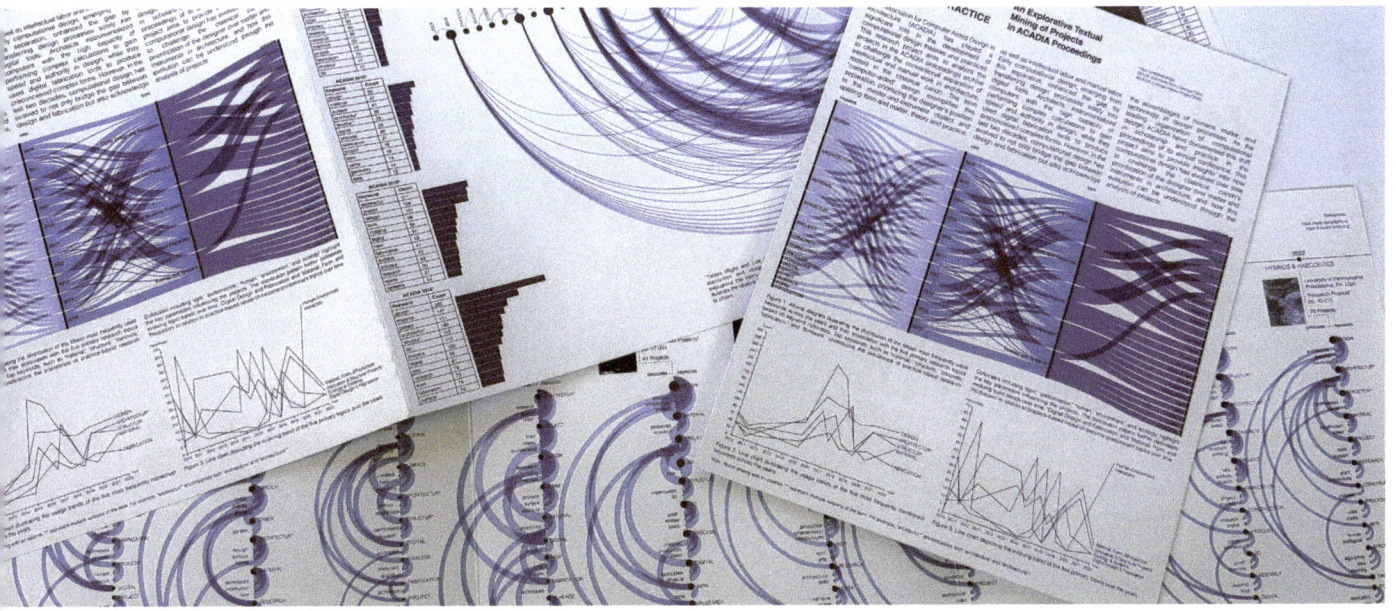

An Explorative Textual Mining of Projects in ACADIA Proceedings

The Association for Computer Aided Design in Architecture (ACADIA) has played a significant role in the development of computational design theories and practices. This research project aims to analyze the projects in the ACADIA proceedings archive to challenge the conventional separation of intellectual and manual work in architecture, rooted in the classical canon. The term "computer-aided" design exemplifies this separation, prioritizing the designer's position in the master-and-instrument dialect and splitting form and matter, mind and body, theory and practice, as well as intellectual labor and manual labor. Early computational design, emerging from this separation, enhanced the gap by transferring design processes solely into digital tools.

Architects instrumentalized computers with the high capacity of performing complex calculations to gain speed and authority in design, while they used digital fabrication tools to produce preconceived complex forms. However, in the last two decades, computational design has evolved to not only bridge the gap between design and fabrication, but also acknowledge the assemblages of humans, matter, and technology in design processes. As the leading organization of computational design, ACADIA has documented this shift in scholarship and practice in the proceedings of its annual conference. This project aims to provide insights into how computational design has evolved over time to challenge the classical canon's prioritization of the designer over matter and instruments in architecture, and how this evolution can be understood through the analysis of projects at the intersection of theory and practice.

1 Printed trifolds displaying the results of this project were distributed at the 43rd Annual Conference of the Association for Computer Aided Design in Architecture 2023 in Denver, Colorado, USA.

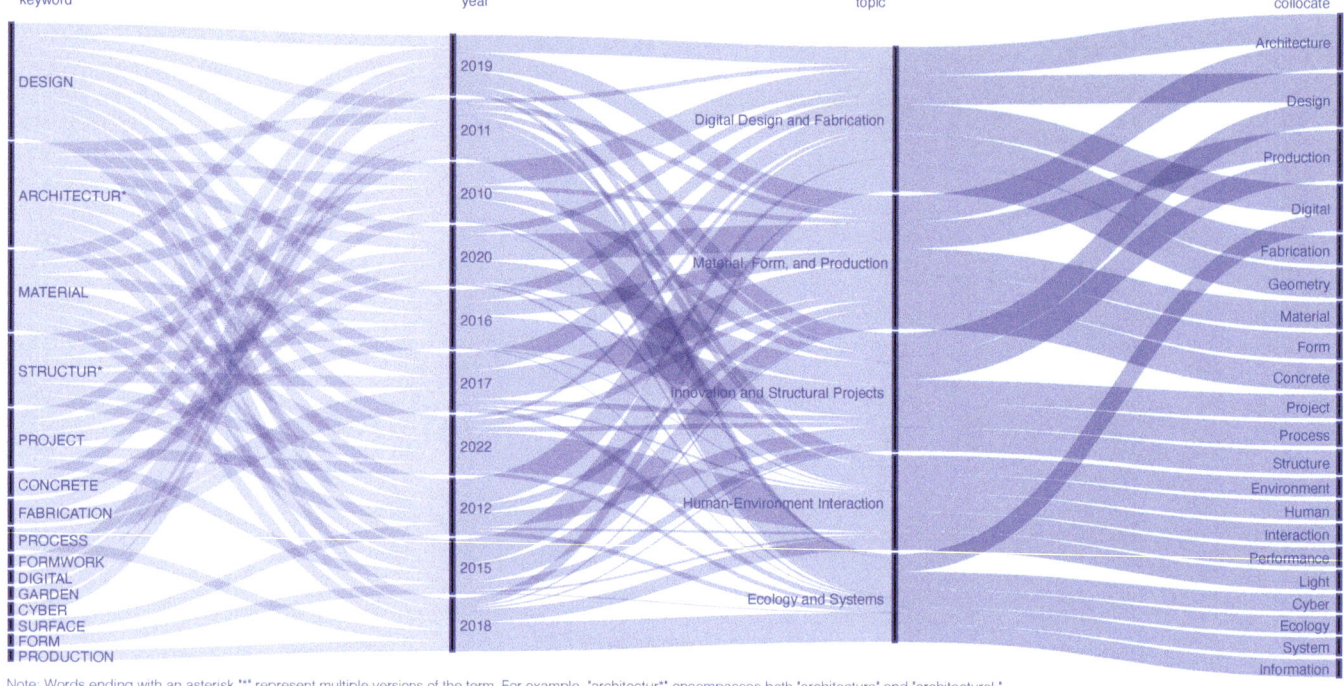

2   Alluvial diagram illustrating the distribution of the fifteen most frequently used keywords across the years and their association with the five primary research topics based on keyword collocates. Top keywords, such as 'material,' 'structure,' 'concrete,' 'fabrication,' and 'formwork,' underscore the prevalence of practice-based research. Collocates including 'light,' 'performance,' 'human,' 'environment,' and 'ecology' highlight the key parameters influencing the projects. The distribution pattern further delineates evolving topic trends over time. 'Digital Design and Fabrication' and 'Material, Form, and Production' in relation to practice-based research become predominant topics over time.

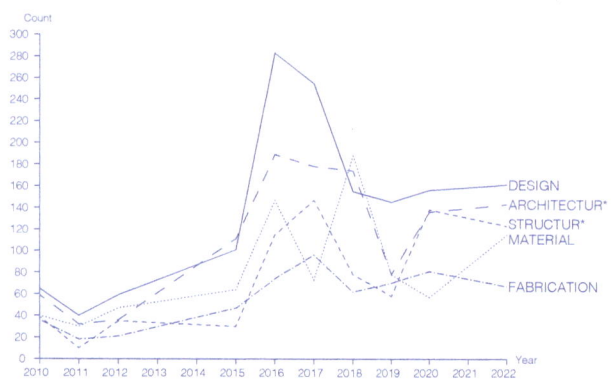

3   Line chart illustrating the usage trends of the five most frequently mentioned keywords across the years.

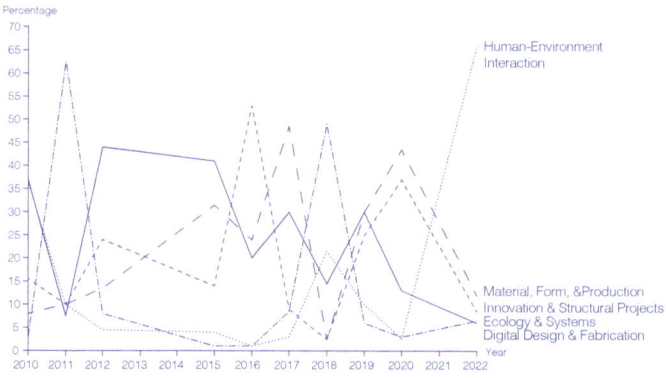

4   Line chart depicting the evolving trend of the five primary topics over the years.

This study delves into an analysis of ten volumes and chapters, titled "Projects" from the ACADIA proceedings, spanning from 2006 onwards. Its aim is to discern key terms and trace their evolving patterns, signaling shifting trends over the years. Utilizing Voyant Tools—a web-based tool for textual analysis—the project employs text mining techniques. The outcome, grounded in quantitative keyword analysis, is visualized using comparative diagrams and graphs (Figure 1). The analysis encompasses three main phases:

1. Document Preparation: Entries labeled "projects" are extracted from the proceedings. To ensure analytical accuracy, any extraneous text—such as conference titles, chapter headings, author bios, and the like—is excised from the PDF files. This meticulous curation ensures that superfluous content does not skew the analysis.

2. Data Collection: Each curated PDF, which compiles projects on an annual basis, is uploaded to Voyant Tools. The software sifts through the content,

5   Tables showing the distribution and usage count of the top keywords throughout the years, accompanied by bar graphs that illustrate the relative frequency of each keyword compared to others.

spotlighting the most recurrent keywords, their collocates, and frequency distributions. This data is subsequently exported to Excel, where I collated the keywords, along with their counts and top three collocates.

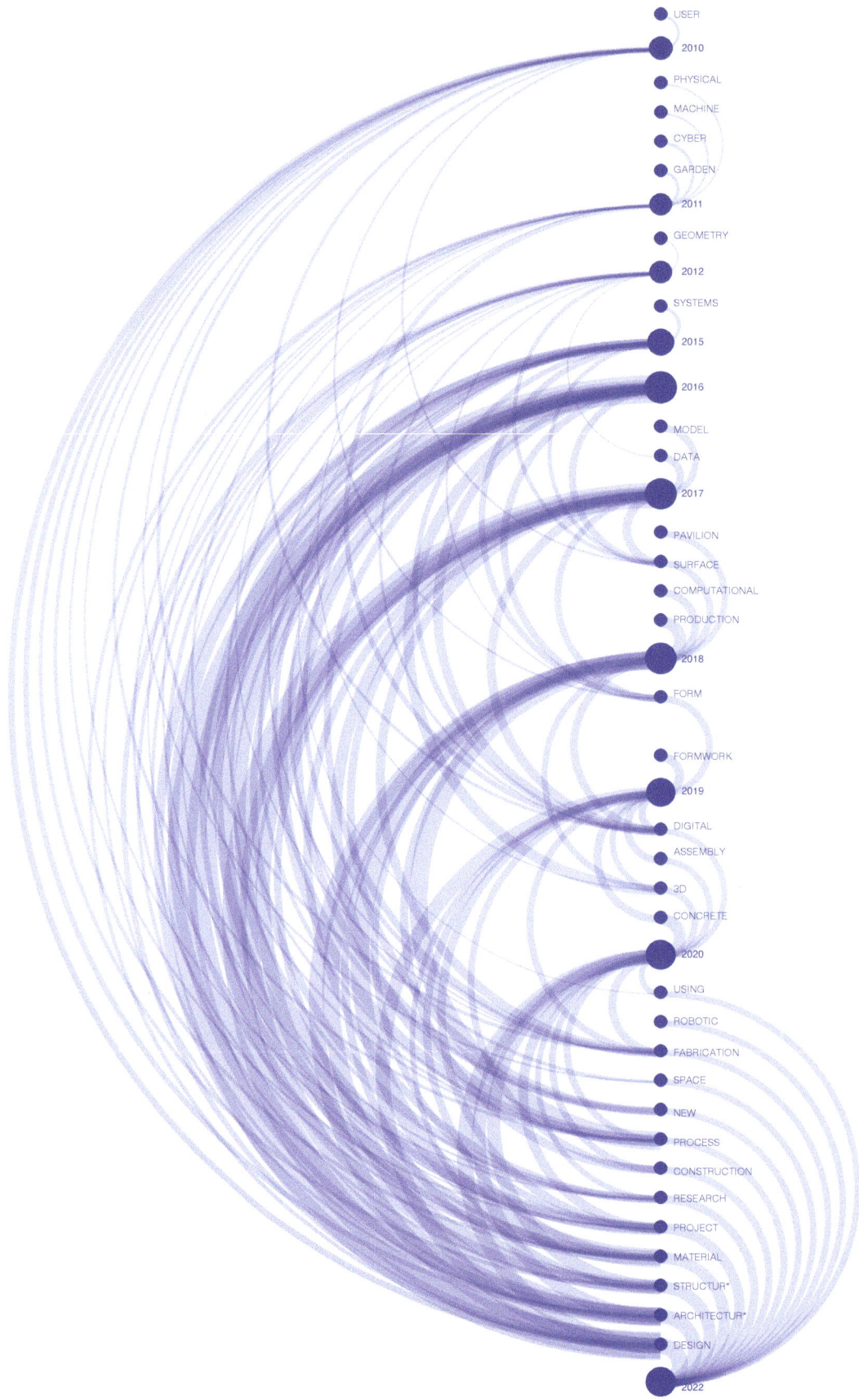

6   Network diagram representing the cumulative presence of the top thirteen keywords from ten ACADIA proceedings, charted across the years. Darker connections indicate higher keyword usage frequency, while the size of each circle reflects its proportional count relative to others.

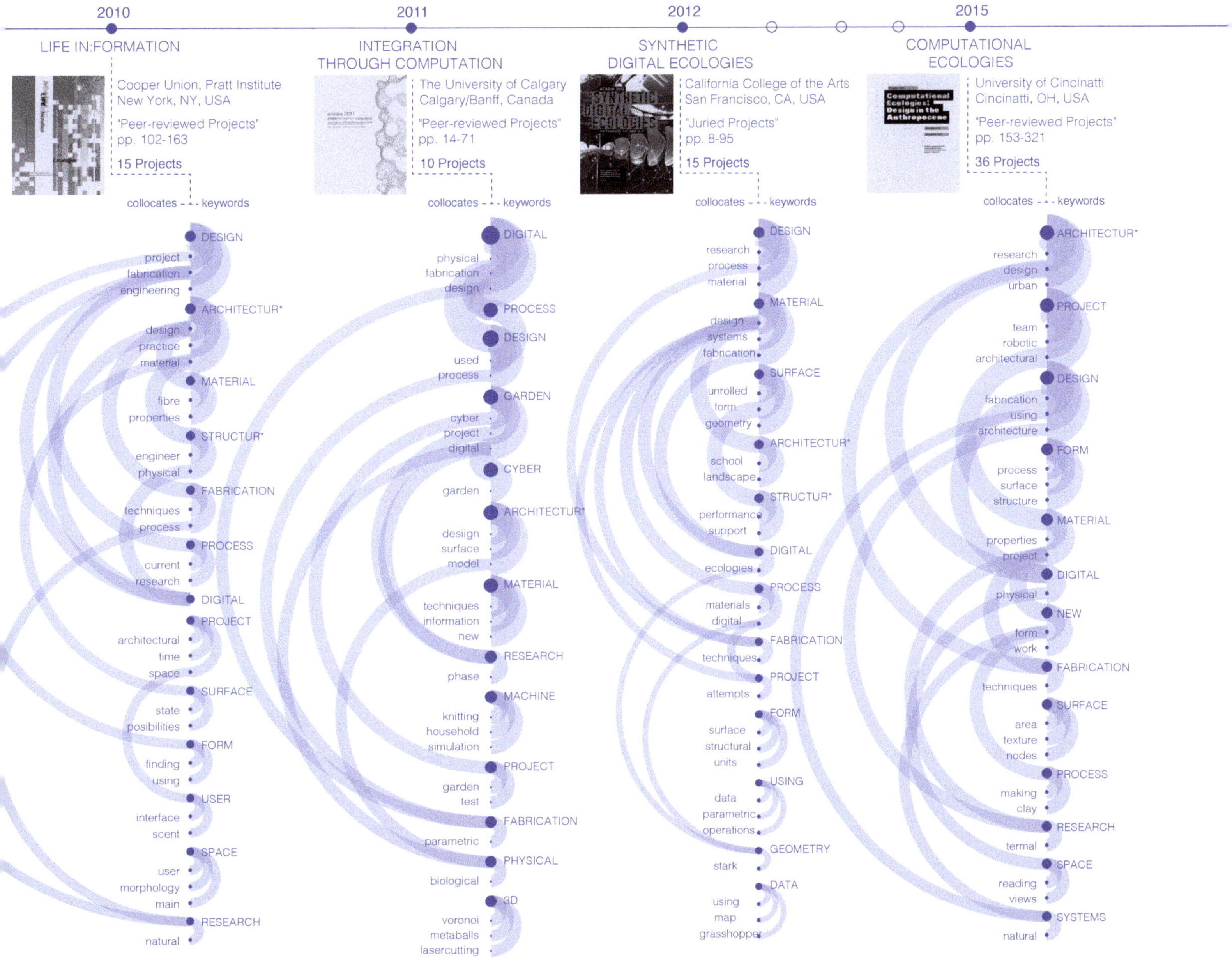

7   The timeline at the top displays the ten ACADIA conferences featuring a chapter or volume specifically dedicated to projects, enumerating the year, location, number of projects within each proceeding, and the citations for the analyzed chapters within this explorative text mining project.

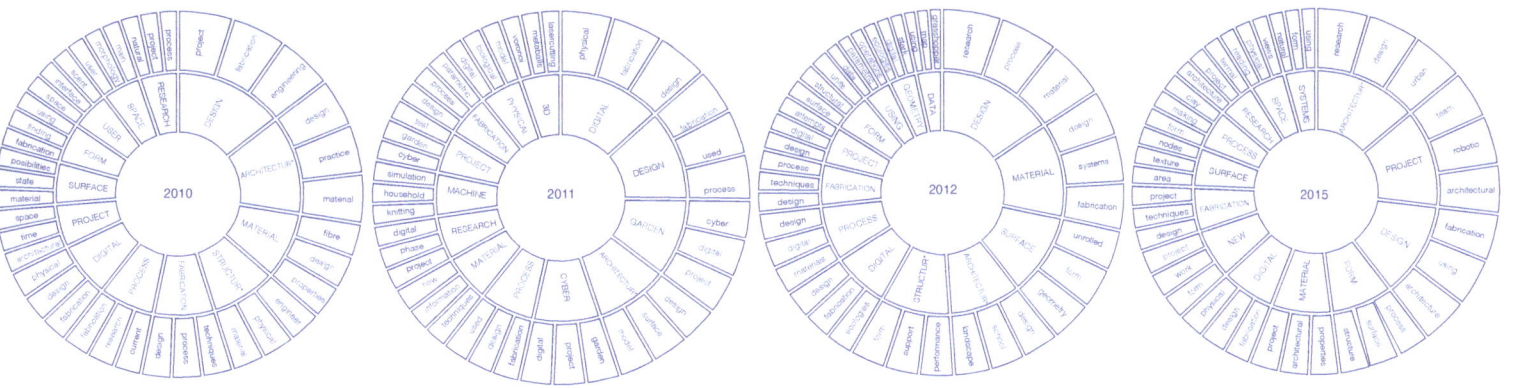

8   The sunburst diagram reveals the hierarchical relationships between keywords and their collocates, with dimensions proportional to their respective usage counts.location, number of projects within each proceeding, and the citations for the analyzed chapters within this explorative text mining project.

225   **ACADIA 2023**

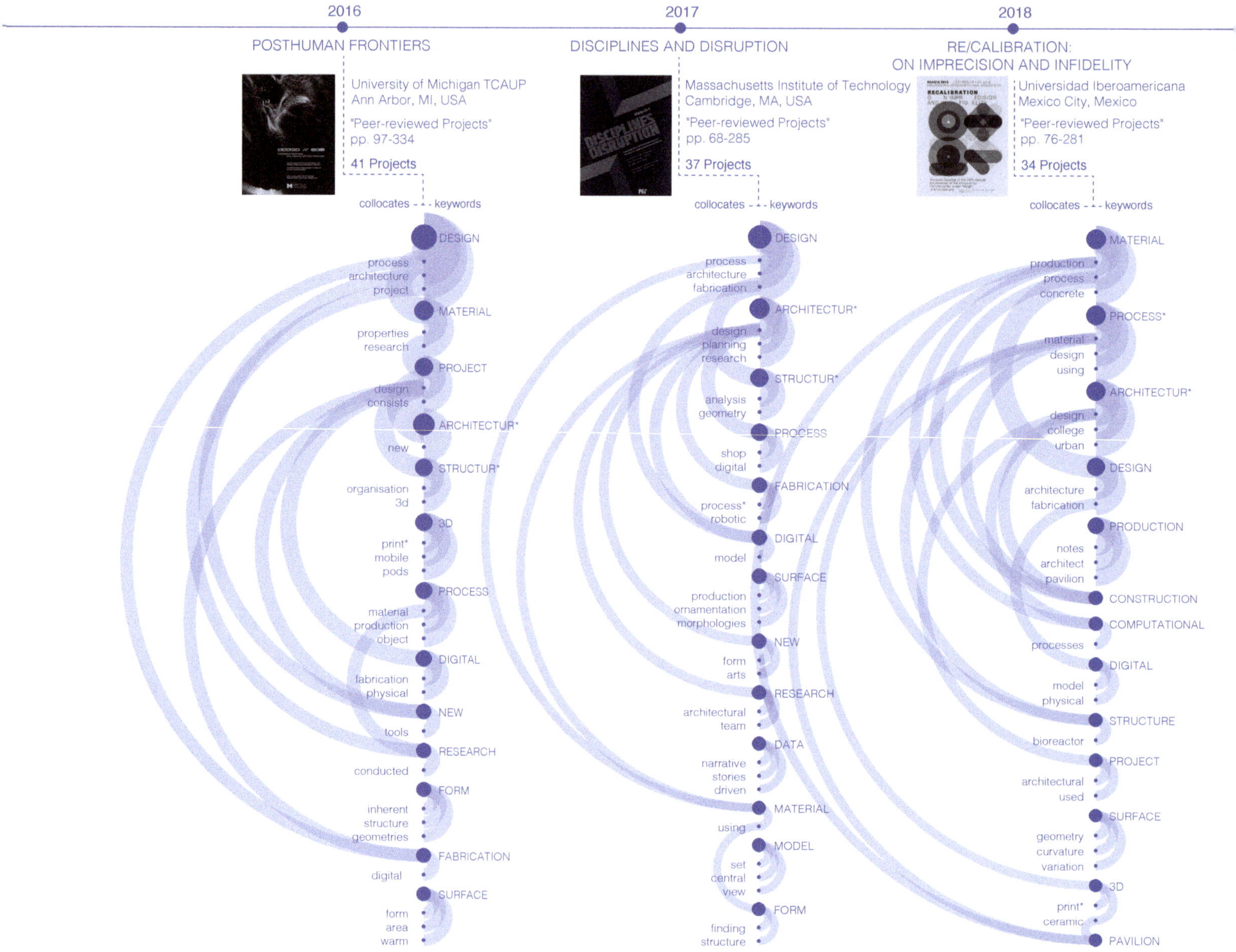

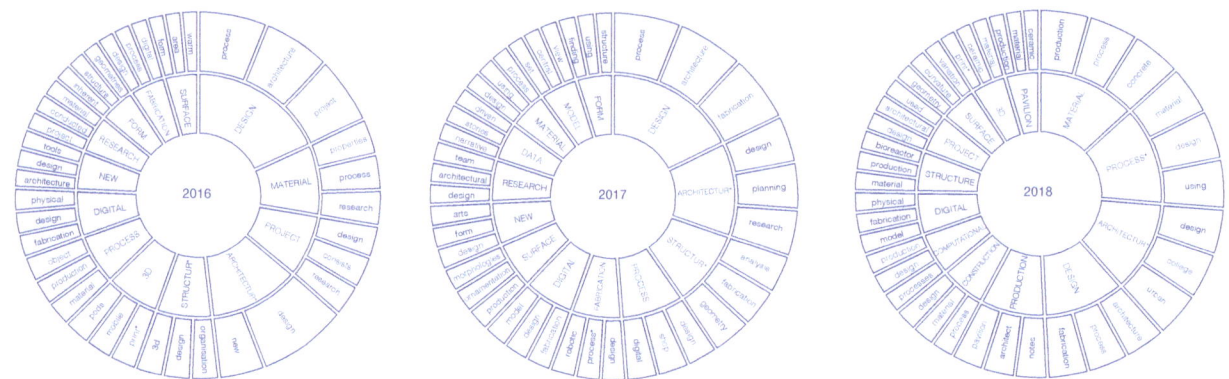

The network diagrams of each proceedings visually elucidate the relationships between keywords and their collocates. The keywords are arranged in descending order from top to bottom, while the thickness of the connection mirrors the relative count of connections between keywords and their respective collocates.

FELLOWSHIP HABITS OF THE ANTHROPOCENE 226

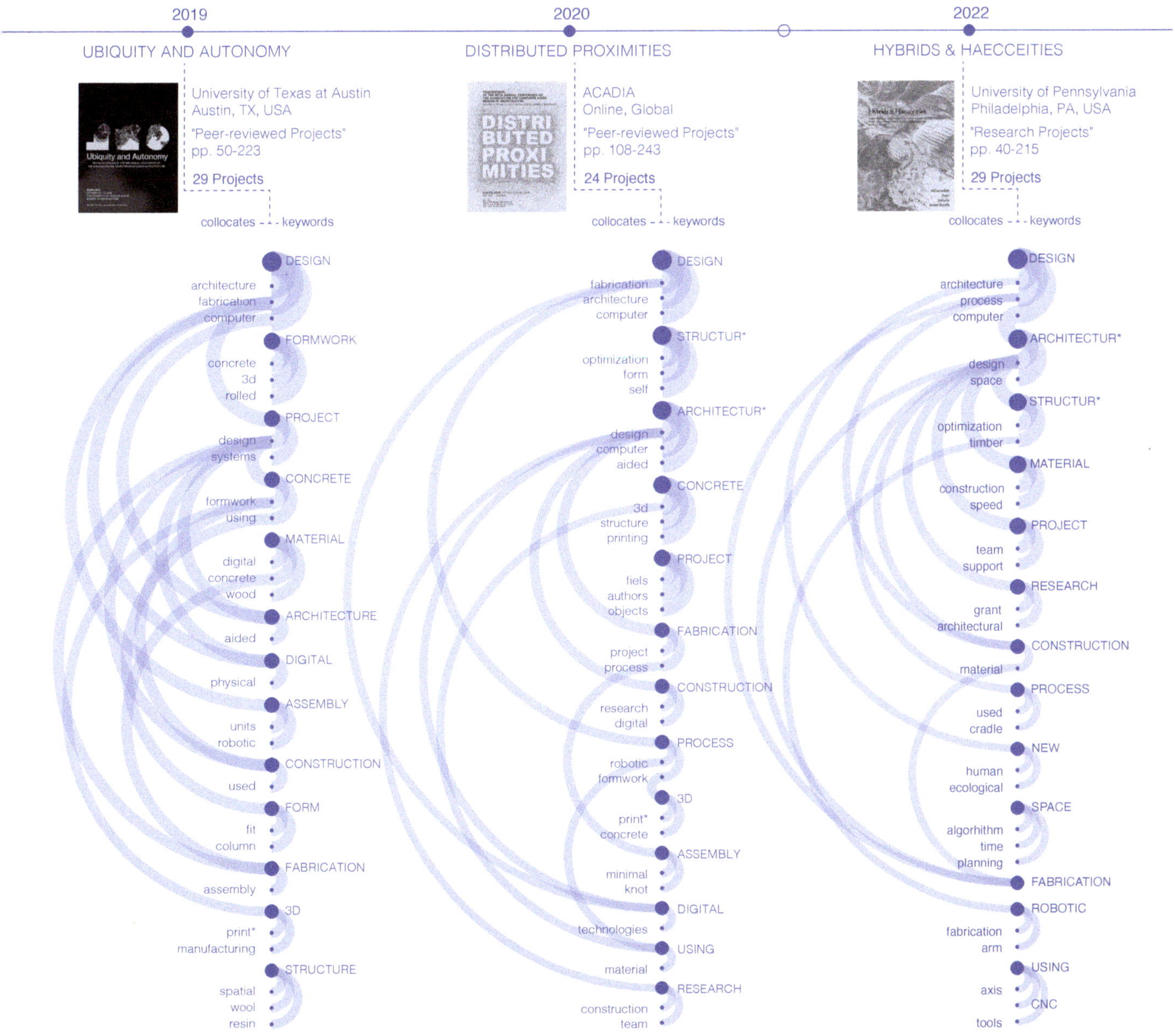

9   Continuing the timeline and network diagram for the years 2019-2022.

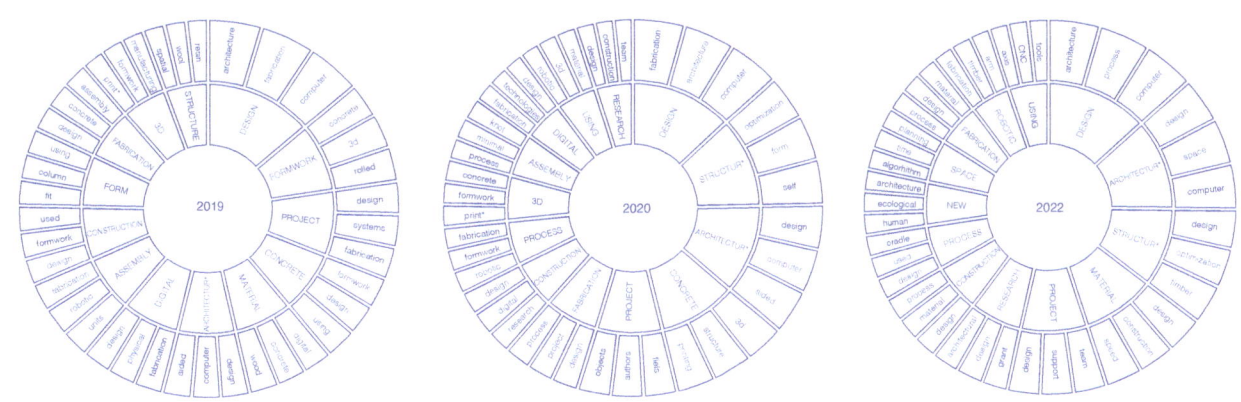

10   The sunburst diagram for the years 2019-2022.

227   ACADIA 2023

3. Data Arrangement and Visualization: The collected data is methodically restructured for compatibility with RawGraphs.io, a versatile open-source tool for data visualization. This platform necessitates specific data configurations to enable accurate reading and processing. Upon crafting the preliminary graphs, I refined the visuals to enhance coherence and legibility.

Since 2010, the "projects" section in ACADIA proceedings has become increasingly prominent, often occupying an entire chapter or volume. Despite the diversity in conference themes and host institutions, research examining the materiality in computational design has consistently been a prevailing topic. "Digital design and fabrication" and "material, form, and production" consistently emerge as the top subjects, with "material," "structur*," (words ending with an asterisk (*) represent multiple versions of the term) and "fabrication" frequently topping the keyword list (Figure 2-5). These trends suggest a connection between theory and practice, emphasizing the significance of materiality and the exploration of design through its interaction with form, fabrication techniques, and the environment (Figure 6-10). While these initial conclusions are based solely on a quantitative analysis of the text, it is crucial to corroborate these findings with traditional content analysis techniques, which offer a more nuanced understanding of semantic structures by delving deeper into contextual subtleties, allowing for the interpretation of underlying themes and research content.

ACKNOWLEDGMENTS

This project is supported by the ACADIA Cultural History Fellowship 2023. I would like to express my gratitude to Dr. Shelby Elizabeth Doyle, Dr. Biayna Bogosian, and Melissa Golman for their support and invaluable feedback on this project.

REFERENCES

Ahrens, Chandler, Axel Schmitzberger, and Michael Wen-Sen Su, eds. 2010. *Life in:Formation: On Responsive Information and Variations in Architecture: Catalogue of the 30th Annual Conference of the Association for Computer Aided Design in Architecture*. New York, N.Y: ACADIA.

Akbarzadeh, Masoud, Dorit Aviv, Hina Jamelle, and Robert Stuart-Smith, eds. 2022. *Hybrids & Haecceities: Projects Catalog of the 42nd Annual Conference of the Association for Computer Aided Design in Architecture*. Philadelphia, PA: ACADIA.

Anzalone, Phillip, Marcella Del Signore, and Andrew John Wit, eds. 2018. *Recalibration: On Imprecision and Infidelity: Proceedings Catalog of the 38th Annual Conference of the Association for Computer Aided Design in Architecture*. Mexico City: ACADIA.

Bieg, Kory, Danelle Briscoe, and Clay Odom, eds. 2019. *Ubiquity and Autonomy: Projects Catalog of the 39th Annual Conference of the Association for Computer Aided Design in Architecture*. Austin, TX: ACADIA.

Combs, Lonn, and Chris Perry, eds. 2015. *Computational Ecologies : Design in the Anthropocene Exhibition Catalog of the 35th Annual Conference of the Association for Computer Aided Design in Architecture*. New York, NY: ACADIA.

Gattegno, Nataly, and Brian Price, eds. 2012. *Synthetic Digital Ecologies : Project Catalogue of the 32nd Annual Conference of the Association for Computer Aided Design in Architecture*. New York, NY: ACADIA.

Johnson, Jason, Joshua Taron, Vera Parlac, and Branko Kolarevic, eds. 2011. *Integration Through Computation: Project Catalog of the 31st Annual Conference of the Association for Computer Aided Design in Architecture*. Portland, OR: ACADIA.

Nagakura, Takehiko, Skylar Tibbits, Caitlin Mueller, Mariana Ibañez, Joel Lamere, and Cristina Parreño Alonso, eds. 2017. *Disciplines Disruption:Projects Catalog of the 37th Annual Conference of the Association for Computer Aided Design in Architecture*. Mass.: ACADIA.

Velikov, Kathy, and Association for Computer Aided Design in Architecture, eds. 2016. *Posthuman Frontiers: Data, Designers, and Cognitive, Machines: Proceedings of the 36th Annual Conference of the Association for Computer Aided Design in Architecture*. Ann Arbor, Michigan: ACADIA.

Yablonina, Maria, Adam Marcus, Doyle, Matias Del Campo, Viola Ago, and Brian Slocum, eds. 2020. *Distributed Proximities: Projects Catalog of the 40th Annual Conference of the Association for Computer Aided Design in Architecture*. Online: ACADIA.

IMAGE CREDITS

All images by the author.

Hayri Dortdivanlioglu is a Ph.D. candidate in architecture and a Fulbright Scholar at the Georgia Institute of Technology. His dissertation research revisits Vitruvian theory and challenges canonic dichotomy between practice and theory in architecture through a counter-canonical reading of Vitruvius's foundational treatise, *De Architectura*. In a broader sense, his research interest includes the interaction between technology and design, architectural theories, mapping, and data visualization. Besides his concentration in architecture, Dortdivanlioglu received the Science, Technology, and Society certificate from Ivan Allen College of Liberal Arts at Georgia Tech.

An Open Living Archive for ACADIA

Constantinos Miltiadis
Aalto University

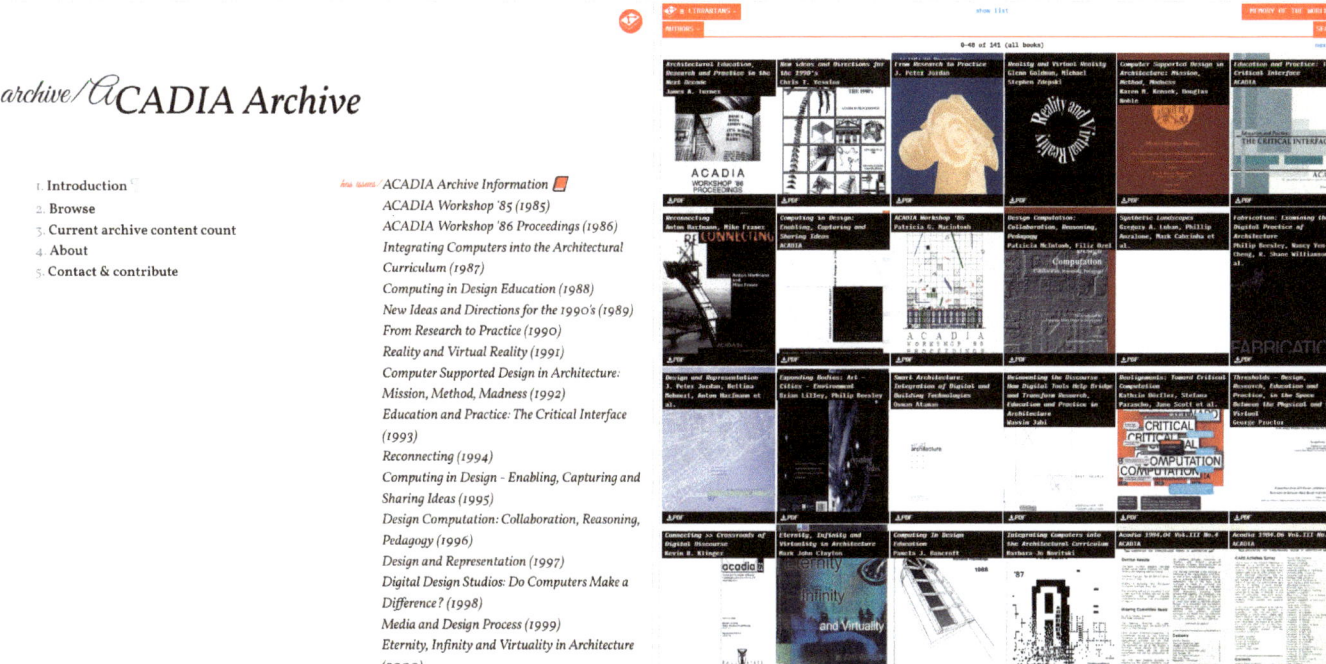

1   Screenshots of the archive landing page (left), and of the archive library (right).

What is computation today? And why archive?

ACADIA was founded in the early 1980s with a mission, like similar initiatives (e.g. eCAADe, CAAD Futures, etc.), to disseminate knowledge on computation in architectural design, planning, and education, as well as to contribute, through computation, in shaping "humane physical environments." Four decades later, the question 'What is computation?' is so ubiquitous and pervasive that it becomes elusive. Those of us old enough to remember would recall generations of pioneers eager to introduce new tools, methods, etc. to the community, as well as the resistance against 'the digital' in architecture. Nevertheless, from our present viewpoint computation seems to have won. Computing is everywhere, not just within academic research or the profession's 'avant-garde,' but in virtually all architectural practices. If there is even an outside to computation in architecture today, it would be difficult to pinpoint.

However, what we architects tend to remiss –both in discourses and classrooms– is that computation has a history, and is not just a set of practices and discourses locked in the present. All too often we observe the discourses pertaining to architectural computation shifting to the 'new' and being taken up by their times' current technologies, tools, affordances, and the hypes and speculations that these drive. Inevitably, the cycle repeats when, again, newer innovations take up the spotlight, followed by new paradigms that disrupt and supersede the previous ones. While some of these paradigms live on by feeding into their successors, others are abandoned and largely forgotten like dead ends in the branching evolution of architecture computation –for historians, perhaps, to discover at a later time. Eventually, the cost of these cycles of disruption in architectural computing practices and discourses

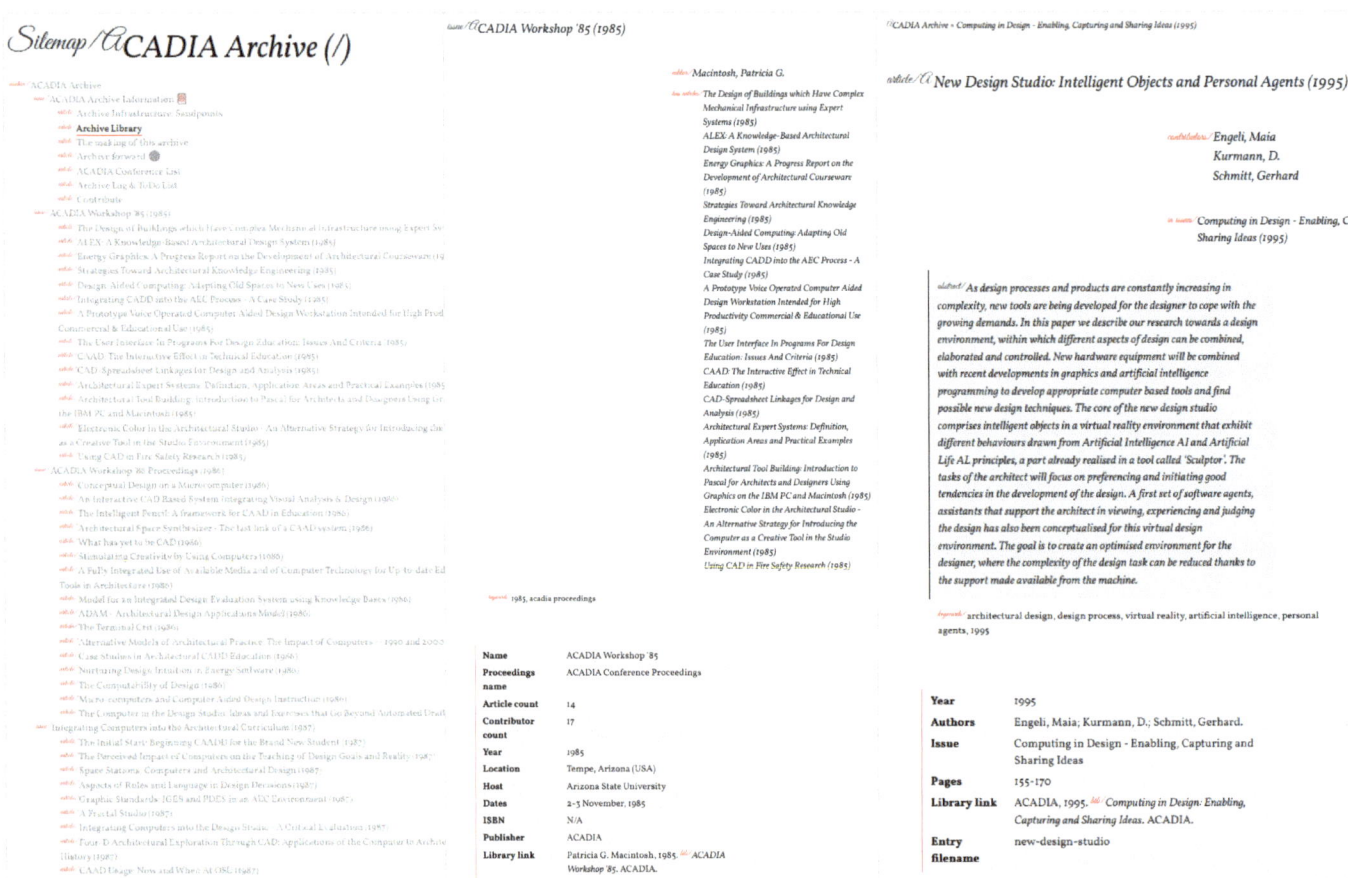

2 Screenshots of (left to right) the archive sitemap listing all content; the entry for the 1985 Acadia Workshop listing contributions, key information and a library link to the proceedings volume; and an article from the 1995 conference listing co-authors, key metadata, and library link to its proceedings volume.

is our own history. Here, we shall not conflate history with a line tracing a causal genealogy of victors that justify the present, but rather a larger body of knowledge: a space of contributions that influence one another, that reflect visions from different points in time and speculations on potentialities, even technologies, perhaps not available to us today. Moreover, this is a history of people striving to contribute to a scientific community.

Indeed, computation comes with a history, and by now this history is quite considerable. More importantly for us, as our generations' 'computationally-minded' researchers and practitioners, this history is our community's heritage. Creating an open living archive is a step closer to acknowledging this heritage.

An open-source and open-access archive for ACADIA

My proposal for the ACADIA Cultural History project was to create an open archive, using for input a list of conference contributions between 1985 and 2020, and a collection of digital proceedings publications. The archive was built using open infrastructure and open workflows implementing *Sandpoints*, an experimental publishing infrastructure developed by Marcell Mars as a theme for the static website builder *Hugo*. All entries were populated computationally via a Python program that generated entries for all 1488 articles, 2057 contributors, and 40 conference proceedings between 1985 and 2020. Each conference entry lists its editors, articles, and key metadata. Each article entry lists its contributors, abstract, and keywords (if available), and each contributor page lists their contributions and co-authors. Moreover, all entries are interconnected so one can also browse via keywords, co-authors, and backlinks. In addition, the archive's library catalog currently provides access to 22 optimized digital proceedings volumes and 119 other historical documents.

While such an archive can certainly allow for better access and traversal across the body of knowledge that constitutes ACADIA, what it can facilitate and also publish in hypertext form, are equivalents of archive-playthroughs: analyses, elaborations, mappings, and syllabuses to apprehend and disseminate reflections of this rich and openly available heritage. All are welcome!

All archive contents are open. All data, software, and infrastructure used to create it are open source. These are all provided and documented at the archive site, along with instructions for its extension and maintenance. The archive is currently hosted at: https://pages.sandpoints.org/sandpoints/acadiaarchive-46619c43/archive/acadia/ and is planned to migrate to archive.acadia.org.

ACKNOWLEDGMENTS

This work would not have been possible without the generous and unwavering support of Sandpoints creator Marcell Mars.

Constantinos Miltiadis, doctoral researcher at Aalto University, is a transdisciplinary architect and design researcher; also a programmer, media artist, curator, teacher, and librarian. He has studied architecture at NTU-Athens, and at the Chair for CAAD ETH Zurich, and pursued studies in computer music at KU Graz. He has taught creative computation and experimental VR game design for large academic courses and brief workshops, and has published contributions in fields including architecture, artistic research, and game studies. He is currently finalizing his doctoral dissertation which investigates virtual navigable environments inconstructible in the physical world, experienceable only through digital media.

Inaugural Autodesk ACADIA BIPOC Student Scholarship and Workshop

Jenny Sabin
ACADIA Vice President

Biayna Bogosian
ACADIA Board of Directors

Sabina Poole
Autodesk, Inc

Cesar Escalante
Autodesk, Inc

Zach Kron
Autodesk, Inc

1   Cesar Escalante and Zach Kron, from Autodesk, Inc., introducing project guidelines for crafting a mixed-use proposal in Denver's Sun Valley neighborhood using Autodesk Forma during the 'Achieving Sustainability Outcomes in Design' workshop, an exclusive one-day workshop for scholarship recipients.

Dedication to Fostering Diversity, Inclusivity, and Excellence

ACADIA is committed to promoting inclusivity and participation from Black, Indigenous, and People of Color (BIPOC) at ACADIA conferences and within our broader community. Together, we aim to pave the way for aspiring BIPOC computational designers, creating a vibrant pathway to success. Several years ago, ACADIA partnered with the National Organization of Minority Architects (NOMA) to create engagement opportunities for the communities. Thanks to the efforts of past Presidents Jason Kelly Johnson, Kathy Velikov, and Jenny Sabin, current President Shelby Doyle, ACADIA Board members June Grant and Biayna Bogosian, the ACADIA Diversity Committee, and generous support from Autodesk, ACADIA and Autodesk have supported grants for NOMA students and professionals to attend the annual ACADIA conference and workshops.

This year, we launched the inaugural Autodesk ACADIA BIPOC Scholarship. With generous support from Autodesk, eight students received complimentary registration to the 2023 ACADIA Conference. They also gained access to a one-day exclusive Autodesk ACADIA workshop and received a stipend for travel and accommodation. Additionally, scholars were paired with mentors from the Autodesk and ACADIA communities, fostering long-term collaboration and engagement. In the subsequent section, participants reflect on their experiences attending the events and benefiting from the scholarship.

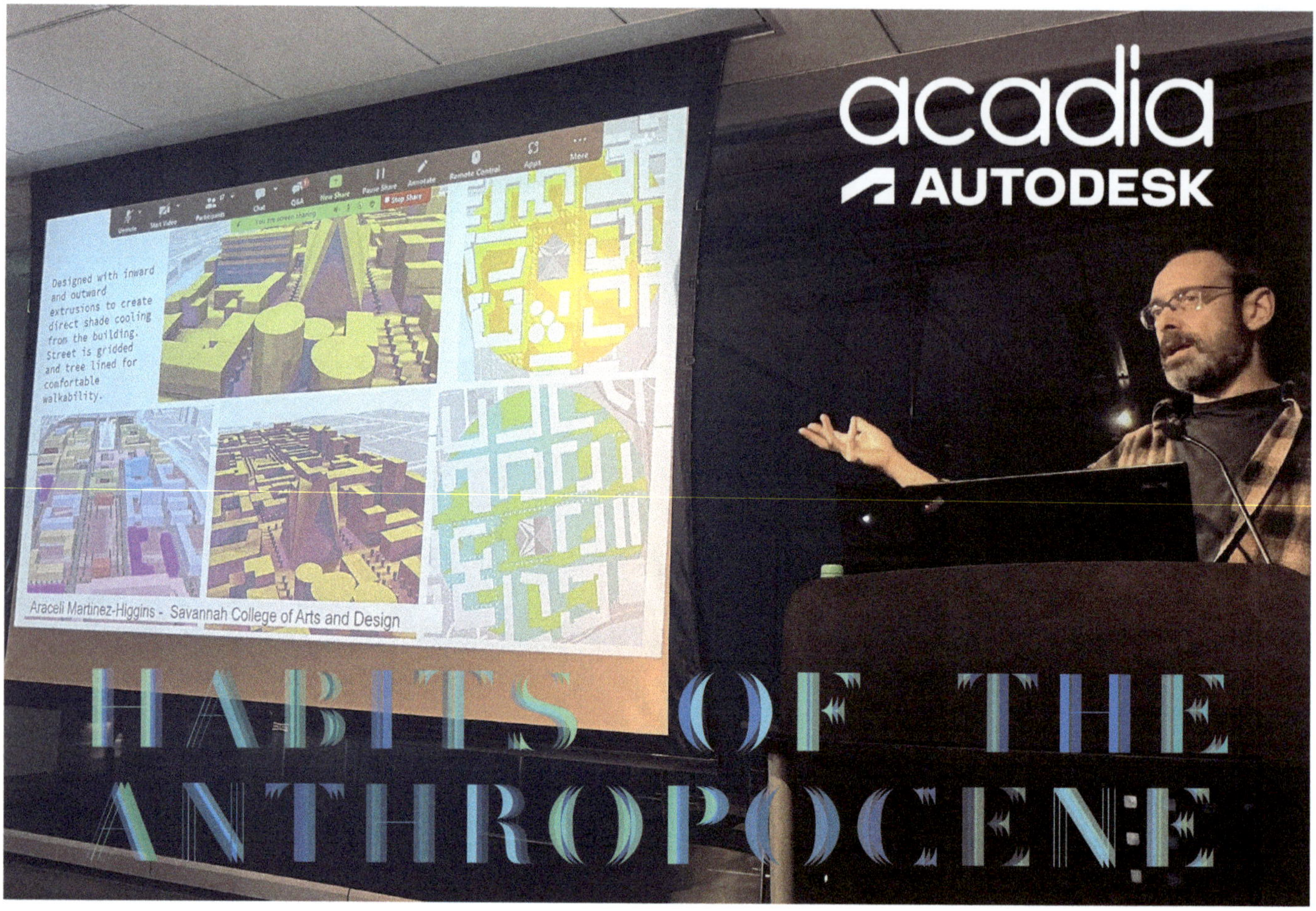

2   Zach Kron, co-instructor of the Autodesk Forma workshop alongside Cesar Escalante, unveils the outcomes of the workshop at the ACADIA Workshop Presentations, a key segment of the conference.

About the One-day Workshop

On Wednesday, October 25th, Cesar Escalante and Zach Kron, leaders of the Autodesk workshop, conducted an exclusive one-day session for the Autodesk ACADIA BIPOC scholars. The workshop, titled "Transcending Green: Achieving Sustainability Outcomes in Design," aimed to teach participants how to utilize Autodesk Forma for cloud analytics and achieve sustainability outcomes in architectural design. The session began with an overview presentation, followed by software tutorials (See Figure 1). Subsequently, participants were paired with professional mentors to develop mixed-use proposals for the Sun Valley neighborhood in central Denver (See Figure 3). The workshop covered various Forma features, including 3D sketching, along with simulation capabilities for micro-climate, energy, and noise simulations. Participants gained analytics skills to integrate environmental performance into sustainable building design. The outcomes of the workshop were shared during the ACADIA 2023 workshop presentations (See Figure 2).

3   Scholarship recipients and mentors captured throughout the workshop.

Bhavleen Kaur
Doctor of Design Candidate, Florida International University

"As an international student, I am thankful to receive the Autodesk ACADIA BIPOC scholarship, which not only provides financial assistance in attending this conference but also represents an invaluable chance to gain insights into the future of computational design and architecture. I'm eager to explore the applications of Autodesk tools in my research, which explores new ways of communicating with machines and design systems to make robotic tools more accessible."

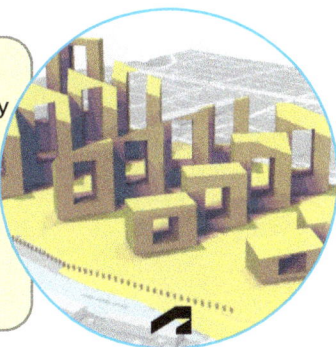

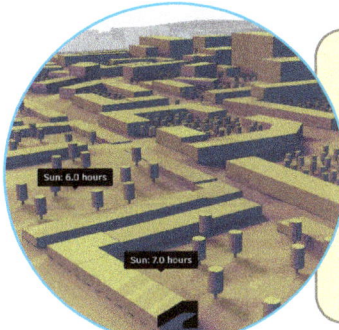

Alexander Htet Kyaw
Graduate Student, Massachusetts Institute of Technology

"Growing up in Myanmar, I had limited exposure to design and technology. As a refugee in the States, I have witnessed significant differences in access to education, infrastructure, and technologies. The Autodesk ACADIA BIPOC scholarship serves as a rare opportunity for individuals like me to participate. I'm grateful to have the opportunity to engage in critical discussions surrounding technology and computation at the ACADIA conference."

Antonio Vargas
Graduate Student, University at Buffalo

"Receiving this scholarship will no doubt have a lasting impact on my academic development as I finish my graduate studies and begin my professional career. The opportunity to share knowledge and learn from others is what I find most exciting about being a part of the Acadia community. The networking provided by the community appears to be great for anyone working within the field of computational design and architecture."

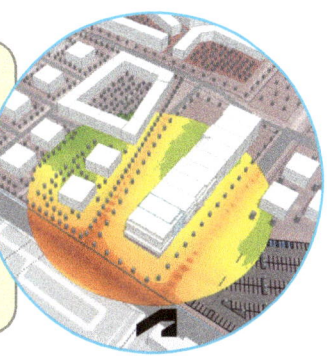

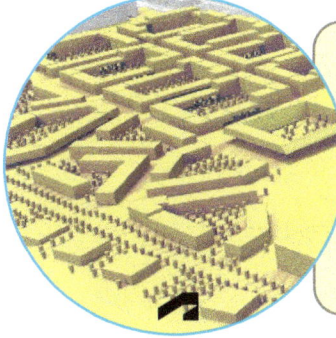

Beni Lawon
Undergraduate Student, University of Illinois at Urbana-Champaign

"Thanks to the Autodesk ACADIA Scholarship, I am looking forward to meeting the computational design community and possible future mentors. I am currently only a junior, and it is amazing that I can attend the 2023 ACADIA Conference and view the great work that people are producing."

Alireza Bayramvand
Recent Graduate, University of Michigan

"The ACADIA Autodesk BIPOC Scholarship and the Autodesk Forma workshop provide a valuable opportunity for learning, networking, and advancing my projects. I am honored to be a part of a community that advances knowledge for a better future. And I'm grateful to join this incredible community of scholarship recipients."

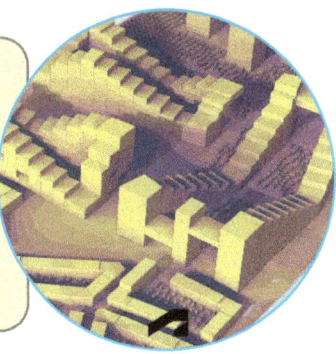

Araceli Martinez-Higgins
Undergraduate Student, Savannah College of Art and Design

"From the rich cultural blend of a Mestiza Texan, I shoulder the duty to infuse cultural and climate-specific nuances into my design. What truly ignites my enthusiasm for joining the Acadia community is the profound belief that these very communities and organizations will serve as the driving force behind the paradigm shift in architectural processes."

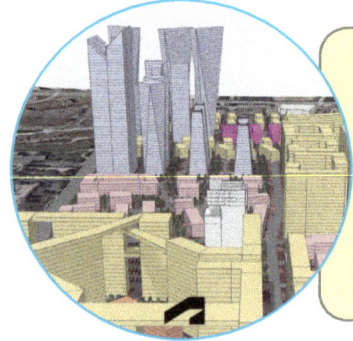

Shandon Herft
Ph.D. Student, Carnegie Mellon University

"I am really passionate about pushing the boundaries of architectural design through technological innovation. The Autodesk ACADIA BIPOC scholarship was a game-changer for my journey. Participating in the 2023 ACADIA conference, the exclusive Autodesk workshop, and learning Autodesk Forma hands-on from professional experts is a big dream come true."

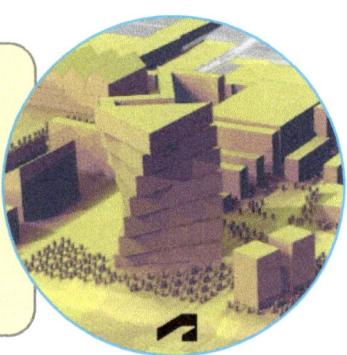

Myles Sampson
Ph.D. Student, Carnegie Mellon University

"As a first-year Ph.D. student, I could not think of a better time to attend the ACADIA Conference. In the past, costs, logistics, and scheduling have always stood in my way of attending. Receiving this scholarship will allow me to grow my academic and professional career by giving me the opportunity to attend my very first Acadia conference. Participating in this year's conference will allow me to build lifelong relationships that will strengthen my career."

4   Inaugural Autodesk ACADIA BIPOC Scholarship recipients and representatives from ACADIA and Autodesk unite at the ACADIA 2023 Annual General Meeting and banquet dinner celebration in Denver, Colorado.

Post Workshop and During the Conference

Throughout the conference, recipients of the scholarship, whose papers were accepted, successfully presented them. Additionally, all scholarship recipients actively engaged with the broader ACADIA community, participating in various events and activities (See Figure 4).

Autodesk ACADIA BIPOC Scholarship inaugural mentors, including Marc Swackhamer (University of Colorado Denver), Biayna Bogosian (Florida International University), Felecia Davis (The Pennsylvania State University), Katie MacDonald (University of Virginia), Vernelle A. A. Noel (Carnegie Mellon University), Shermeen Yousif (Florida Atlantic University), Leslie Lok (Cornell University), Sina Mostafavi (Texas Tech University), Adam Nims (Bright View

Design Group), and Tobias Hawthorn (Autodesk), volunteered to guide scholarship recipients during the Autodesk workshop. Their role involved assisting mentees in developing proposals for the Sun Valley neighborhood in central Denver using Autodesk Forma (See Figure 3). The mentors also facilitated introductions to relevant members at the conference, enabling mentees to leverage ACADIA's extensive network of academics and professionals. Additionally, mentors have maintained communication with mentees, emphasizing the enduring value of the experience.

Wall-Table-Bed

Leyuan Li
University of Colorado Denver

1   ACADIA Exhibition (Brandon Wunder, November 15, 2023).

"Wall-Table-Bed" is an exhibition installation devised for this year's ACADIA conference (Figure 1). It comprises nine movable and operable panels that create a malleable exhibition venue to showcase thirty-two posters selected through a rigorous peer-reviewed process. It also functions as a temporal device of enclosure, constructing a series of threshold conditions to engage events and activities at divergent scales and locations. The exhibition was first housed at the Jake Jabs Center during the conference and then relocated to outdoor and indoor public spaces in Denver to further its engagement with students and community stakeholders.

The installation evolved from its preemptive measure to the uncertain, unstable nature of the exhibition. Due to logistical and administrative protocols, the installation was prohibited from being constructed on-site and had to be relocated across the campus once the conference ended. These prerequisites have not only posed challenges to the fabrication process, but also required a high mobility of the installation to navigate different degrees of movement and transportation. In response to these constraints, the concept of a movable exhibition wall was further developed into a series of portable modules that could be efficiently transported and arranged according to different spatial settings (Lang, 2018). The flexible arrangements of the wall led to the deconstruction of a prescribed exhibition scene epitomized in conventional gallery spaces, which is further articulated through the differentiation of surfaces on the panel. Using dimensional lumbers as the framework, each module is clad with a smooth plywood surface on one side and removable round panels on the other. The duality of flatness—one side resembling the finish of

2   ACADIA exhibition at the CAP gallery (Brandon Wunder, November 15, 2023).

4   ACADIA exhibition at the conference (Brandon Wunder, November 15, 2023).

3   ACADIA exhibition at the CAP gallery (Brandon Wunder, November 15, 2023).

5   ACADIA exhibition at the conference (Brandon Wunder, November 15, 2023).

the inner layer and the other side exaggerating the scale of scalloped shingles—creates a false front that insulates a transient condition of threshold and a situational reading of the inside and the outside (Teyssot, 2013). This dual reading, in conjunction with the ever-changing positioning of the modules, enunciates different degrees of enclosure that allude to different ways of seeing and appreciating the exhibits (Figures 2-6).

Responding to the conference themes this year, in particular, to the uncertainty and anxiety deeply entrenched in the socio-politics of the Anthropocene, as well as to the constant separation between the human and the built environment—both heavily celebrated and manifested through the tools of digital media and artificial intelligence—the installation proposes a turn that interrogates the primitive relationship between human and the most intimate realm of space directly related to their body: *what is a room if the interior and its objects are no longer socially and spatially defined?* Taking the same dimension as a single bed, the installation module delivers its vagueness of functions through the instability of its orientation: it could be used as

a bed frame, a tabletop, a bench, and a shelf, along with the demountable panels that compose a chair. The trans-functional module, amplified through its replication in malleable conditions, accumulates to a field condition of adaptable interior objects that constantly blur the boundary between outside and inside, undefined and prescribed. In resistance to a conducive definition of a room—a term typically defined through the organization of parts performing their prescribed duties—the installation intends to challenge the normative conception of the interior, seeking alternative means to expand the contemporary definition of domesticity and interiority (Rice, 2006).

As an educational project, the installation was designed and fabricated in collaboration with undergraduate students at the University of Colorado Denver College of Architecture and Planning. During the process of transportation, each student was tasked with synchronizing with a module, interacting with their peers to produce different playful scenes on their way to the Jake Jabs Center. This series of movements (Figures 7-10), including pushing the pieces up and down the ram, as well as moving them

6   ACADIA exhibition at the CAP gallery (Brandon Wunder, November 15, 2023).

7   The transportation of the installation (Sammriddha Shrestha, October 25, 2023).

across the street, was intended for students to re-examine the lack of gravity and the loss of scale in the digital space, prompting students to grasp the heaviness and tangibility of elements in the built environment, while comprehending the vulnerability and instability of the interior. In addition, in partnership with CAADRIA (Computer-Aided Architectural Design Research in Asia), the exhibition in Denver was further developed into a series of collaborative events between ACADIA and CAADRIA, such as an online exhibition platform with RMIT University, as well as a physical exhibition in the main gallery at the University of Hong Kong. These opportunities aimed to enhance the academic connections between students and faculty worldwide, facilitating exchanges of knowledge, resources, and opportunities among the global learning community.

ACKNOWLEDGMENTS

I am grateful to my team members, Blake Brooks, Stephanie Clouse, Hannah Drummond, Trevor Motzko, and Jackson Pedrazzi, for their unconditional support during the design and construction process of the project.

REFERENCES

Lang, Peter. 2018. "La serie Misura Domus, nr./no. 517: Superstudio." *DASH | Delft Architectural Studies on Housing* 7(11): 132–135.

Rice, Charles. 2006. *The Emergence of the Interior*. London: Routledge.

Teyssot, Georges. 2013. *A Topology of Everyday Constellations*. Cambridge: The MIT Press.

8   The transportation of the installation (Sammriddha Shrestha, October 25, 2023).

9   The transportation of the installation (Sammriddha Shrestha, October 25, 2023).

10   The transportation of the installation (Sammriddha Shrestha, October 25, 2023).

IMAGE CREDITS

All photo credits go to Sammriddha Shrestha and Brandon Wunder.

Figures 1-6: © Brandon Wunder, November 15, 2023

Figures 7-10: © Sammriddha Shrestha, October 25, 2023

Leyuan Li is a Chinese architect and educator whose professional and academic work focuses on interior and urban realms in the articulation of spaces and societies. Li is an Assistant Professor of Architecture at the University of Colorado Denver. He has held academic appointments at the University of Houston and Rice University. He is the founder of Office for Roundtable, a collaborative practice that explores architectural and interior types in relation to environmental and social issues. Recent projects have been exhibited at Citygroup Gallery in New York City and the 9th Bi-City Biennale of Urbanism/Architecture in Shenzhen, Guangdong Province, China.

Notes on a Visual Identity

Luke Bulman
Office of Luke Bulman
New York

How We Think About, Develop, and Implement Visual Identities

1 Whiteout on the Ekström Ice Shelf, Weddell Sea, Antarctica, March 15, 2007.

In developing the visual identity for "ACADIA 2023: Habits of the Anthropocene," our focus was on capturing the essence of extreme environmental conditions and their parallels with the challenges of the Anthropocene era. The project drew inspiration from the disorienting whiteout conditions in snowstorms, where the lack of visible shadows and horizon lines creates navigational challenges (figure 1.) This concept serves as a metaphor for the Anthropocene, a period where traditional methods of orientation and understanding are increasingly inadequate, necessitating the development of new approaches and tools.

Our objective was to create a visual representation that echoes the need for new perspectives in this era. We began with a basic form and applied a process reminiscent of a whiteout, methodically reducing its details (figure 2.) This reductive approach allowed the form to communicate effectively while maintaining a degree of ambiguity in its recognizability. The challenge was to balance clarity in communication with an element of abstract representation, reflecting the complexity and uncertainty of the Anthropocene.

To ensure versatility across various media, the forms were designed with different thicknesses. This adaptability was crucial for their application in both digital and print formats. We also incorporated a range of color sets to enhance the visual impact and to convey different aspects of the Anthropocene. The choice of colors was deliberate, aimed at evoking specific themes related to environmental and human impacts (Figure 3.).

The color schemes were instrumental in portraying various dimensions of the Anthropocene. Each combination brought out a unique perspective, aligning with the project's thematic goals. The selection process was thoughtful, ensuring that each color set not only complemented the design but also added depth to the narrative (figure 4.)

As the project evolved, we adapted these forms for use in different contexts, including screen-based media and printed materials. The forms had to be effective at various sizes and weights, maintaining their integrity and impact across different platforms. This required a focus on functional design, ensuring that the visual identity was not only aesthetically appealing, but also practical and applicable in diverse settings.

In the end, the visual identity represents a deliberate exploration of the intersection between extreme environmental conditions and the challenges of our time. It is a visual narrative that seeks to provoke and encourage a deeper engagement with the issues of the Anthropocene. We aim for this visual identity to reflect the current state of affairs, but also to serve as a suggestion of the adaptations that will be asked of us going forward.

IMAGE CREDITS

Figure 1: Dr. Hans Grobe. March 15, 2007. Creative Commons CC-BY-SA-2.5.

Figure 4, The Garden of Earthly Delights, detail. Hieronymus Bosch. c. 1490. Public domain.

All other drawings and images by the author.

Luke Bulman is a graphic designer in Brooklyn, New York. He is a faculty member at Yale School of Architecture.

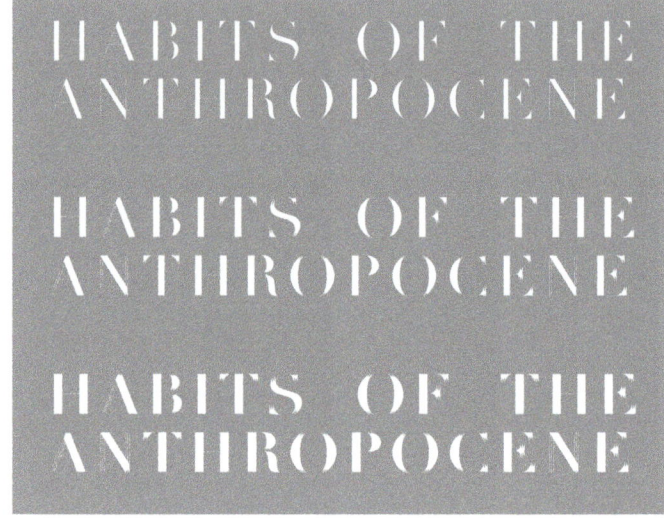

2

3

4

2. Reducing and then offsetting the base form creates a variety of weights

3. Color sets produce a variety of associative readings

4. Combining the text form with an image

An Ocean of Coffee, A Sea of Red: ACADIA Conferences are Worth It

Sarah Miller
College of Architecture
& Planning, University of
Colorado, Denver

1

What does it take to run the ACADIA conference? The answer, unsurprisingly, is coffee. Volunteers brewed fifty gallons of it over the course of three days this year in Denver. You will also need a lot of iced green tea, diet coke, and chocolate. The theme this year is caffeine -- leave the instant decaf and herbal teas at Costco, thank you.

But before you start the coffee maker, you will need to assemble swag bags. Once the swag arrived, it took hours to fill the bags -- dozens of cardboard boxes emptying as volunteers slowly lost ground to the "sea of red" overtaking every square inch of the storage room.

Speaking of taking up space -- you will need someone with more Google Drive space than me. ACADIA presentations are using up 44% of my 150-GB Google Drive. Google threatens (in red) that I have just 6% storage space left before I stop receiving emails. Oh, my -- how did this happen? There were a total of 109 presentations for this year's conference -- including 52 papers, 32 projects, and 12 Field Note sessions -- that were compiled into master presentations for 18 sessions, plus 8 keynotes and awards. The first step is to badger authors relentlessly, asking (read: threatening politely) them to submit their files. Next, find the file, check for updated versions, download and extract the compressed file, download and install missing fonts, and copy the individual file into the master file. Check slide transition settings, embedded videos, font sizing, names, titles, et cetera, and, lastly, accept any and all changes up until the literal last minute.

You will also need Cynthia Fishman. If you can't find her, cancel the conference. Joking! Sort of. If you can't find her, you will just need to locate a site coordinator who will walk 42 miles over the course of the week, make a half-dozen trips to Costco (sometimes pushing 4 carts at once), plan 6 days of meals (including coordinating with caterers, setting up tables, and delivering uneaten meals to the Denver Rescue Mission), and single-handedly coordinating and training over 30 volunteers.

This is really what it takes to run the ACADIA conference: volunteers -- enthusiastic, adaptable, engaged volunteers. This year in Denver, the difference between an event that is volunteer-run and one in which people are paid, was clear. This year, an organic, ever-evolving event infrastructure arose to problem solve in real-time with grace and ease because volunteers wanted to make the conference a success. After the conclusion of the event, volunteers expressed that they felt very fortunate to have been a part of the conference. I know that I feel the same.

2

At first, it was difficult to get students to volunteer -- even with the promise of free conference attendance. We realized that students didn't understand what a conference really was, let alone ACADIA, which means that continuing to create this kind of event is valuable work. As we look back to the isolation of COVID-era online events, we know that being together, in person, matters. Our hesitation to create events in person comes because an in-person conference requires significant resources of time and effort (see first half of this editorial), but there is an intense desire, even need, for humans to be together. Events like this create positive change.

For the first time in ACADIA conference history, a majority (51%) of attendees were female, compared to 45% in 2021, and 29% in 2018-19. Architecture is still a male-majority industry (NCARB, 2022), but most of the people surrounding me behind the scenes were women. The majority of ACADIA conference chairs, board of directors, and committee members are also women. The ACADIA female presence is shifting conference culture toward collaboration and inclusivity. In Denver this year, there was a strong emphasis on bio-design, but the subtext to that is the idea that we need to come together to do things differently, from using friendlier materials (like mycelium) to designing our buildings with community in mind -- not just people, but the planet. This is the role of conference within society -- to come together to make things better than they were before.

3

Yet, there is more than one way to create togetherness. The COVID-19 pandemic taught us that digital connections create opportunities to decentralize power and knowledge. While our volunteers were brewing coffee for in-person attendees, an immense amount of work also went into managing the livestream for 419 remote attendees -- a significant portion of which were students. Expanding the reach of the conference in this way allows for the content to spread, moving through the community, rather than being held by the fortunate few attending the event in person. This year, the keynotes are available online for free. The conversation becomes richer because more people can be a part of it.

I know what it felt like for me to be a part of ACADIA. That human satisfaction one feels from being included, from being surrounded by people that value you and the work you are doing. The joy of learning, of collaborating, and of creating. This kind of feeling can only arise fully when we come together for a common purpose, which is why ACADIA conferences will continue to be a healthier habit of the Anthropocene.

REFERENCES

NCARB. 2022. "Demographics." Ncarb.Org. 2022. www.ncarb.org/nbtn2022/demographics

IMAGE CREDITS

Figures 1, 2: © Assia Crawford
Figures 3, 4, 6 © Dania Morelli
Figure 5: © Ashtyn Franks

Sarah Miller

Sarah Miller received a Bachelor of Science in Architecture from the College of Architecture and Planning at the University of Colorado, Denver. She currently works as a research assistant at the LoDo Lab conducting experiments with bio-textiles.

CU Denver and Impact

Marc Swackhamer
Professor and Chair of the
Architecture Department

College of Architecture
& Planning, University of
Colorado, Denver

In the Architecture Department at the University of Colorado Denver, we enroll about six-hundred total students, four-hundred-fifty of whom are undergraduate students in our Bachelor of Science program and one-hundred-fifty of whom are graduate students in our Master of Architecture program, which is the only accredited architecture degree in Colorado, or within about a four-hundred-fifty-mile radius.

As host of the 2023 ACADIA Conference, we are honored to share a bit about our school's "why," or its purpose, developed by our faculty of about twenty full-time scholars, another thirty practicing Denver architects who contribute to our vibrant program, our staff, our alumni, and our students. This "why" represents where we aspire to go over the next five years.

Our shared vision starts with the premise that in a rapidly changing world, where challenges emerge with ever-increasing frequency and severity, the education of an architect must remain adaptive. In the face of these challenges, we aim for our students to develop the capacity to ask bold questions, take risks, think independently, and approach the work of architecture with curiosity. In doing so, our students grow to be agile, flexible, and visually adept thinkers and makers who contribute to addressing global challenges over a lifetime of active, inquisitive learning.

The following five strategies, or aspirations, serve to guide us through the next five years of this work:

What global challenges will intensify in the coming three years? Thirty years? How can design contribute to addressing these challenges? At CU Denver, we passionately address the systemic, messy, and emergent planetary issues we face as a society, and identify ways that architecture can have an impact.

How do we help prepare students for these challenges? We seek to advance the intellectual quality of the school by prioritizing education over vocation. We foreground questioning, risk-taking, synthetic thinking, and analytical judgment. In short, we succeed when architecture school imbues curiosity.

How will our students learn? How will our curriculum adapt? What and how we teach evolves continuously, through self-reflection, evaluation and systematic revision measured against tangible results. We proudly grade ourselves as critically as we grade our students.

How will we foster intellectual, material, and cultural experimentation? We will advance architecture by exploring new frontiers, creating new knowledge, and exposing our students to emerging developments in the discipline. We support an ethic of generously sharing, collaborating on, and debating research and scholarship.

How will we impact the national and global conversation around architecture? How will we ensure that all this work matters? Here, we commit to sharing what we learn and to inviting the highest caliber, most diverse thinkers to join us (like over the next three days with this community of ACADIA scholars).

In particular, GOAL FOUR above, which focuses on faculty research and creative work provides a clear and compelling understanding of CU Denver's personality, its unique strengths, and its future direction.

Our faculty research profile can be divided into five realms, each of which characterizes the varied ways of thinking and questioning you'll find in our program.

In "How we See," our research focuses on the conceptualization of seeing in alternative, unexpected ways through media like video, cinema, collage, or seriality. Here we ask our students: How can you learn from curious observation and the critical analysis of what you see in the mundane, everyday world around you?

In our "How we Draw" research, faculty plumb the act of drawing and its potential to reframe and question one's intuition. Through this research, we ask students, how can you approach drawing as an act of revelation, a curious interrogation that culminates in discovery?

In the category of "How we Make," discovery emerges through a critical approach to making that is, above all else, a way of thinking. Through critical making, we ask students: How can you challenge industry habits through a mastery of craft with materials, in both known, but also disruptive and unsanctioned ways?

In the territory of "How we Expand" research, we focus on the role intersectional thinking plays in resilient and adaptive approaches to architecture. Through observing and participating in this type of expansive research, students connect with diverse outside voices to address wicked, messy, and difficult societal problems.

Finally, in our "How we Reflect" research, critical curation and storytelling bring a direct understanding and relevance to historical trajectories in architecture through the manifold lenses of preservation, the vernacular, diverse and global traditions of the discipline, and varied histories of the built environment. Here, we ask students, can you reference tradition, critically and authentically, to not just celebrate, but also question its value?

Within and around this scholarship, students cultivate independent thinking skills as they mature and claim agency over their educational trajectories. While each faculty member at CU Denver privileges a distinct pathway, what is consistent in this scholarship is a profound sense of curiosity about the world.

This curiosity makes CU Denver an ideal place to host the 2023 ACADIA Conference, where a passion for leveraging technology as a force for disruption, advancement, radical inclusivity, and profound curiosity is shared by all.

HABITS OF THE ANTHROPOCENE
CONFERENCE CHAIRS

CONFERENCE CHAIRS

Assia Crawford's creative practice research focuses on the development of biological material alternatives and digital fabrication practices for a post-Anthropocene era. Her work sits on the intersection of architecture, science, and critical theory, and employs experimental and speculative design to address ecological challenges faced by communities at a time of environmental uncertainty. Assia is an ARB registered architect and has previously held positions as the architect for the Hub for Biotechnology in the Built Environment (HBBE) and artist-in-residence at the Wellcome Centre for Mitochondrial Research. Assia is an editor of the Biotechnology Design Journal, and runs Wild Futures Lab, a research and teaching bio-design fabrication wet lab. Her current projects include a monograph entitled Designer's Guide to Lab Practice (Routledge 2023) and an interdisciplinary research project that is entitled Bio-remediator Myco-Fabrics for the Built Environment and Beyond.

Marc Swackhamer's research practice, HouMinn, is a partnership with Blair Satterfield from the University of British Columbia. Their work challenges broadly accepted approaches to design agency through focus on interdisciplinary partnerships, unconventional making, material misuse, and the role of decay in architecture. HouMinn has won national Design Awards from Architect Magazine, ID Magazine, and Core77. Marc's interdisciplinary design collaborative, MinnLab, won the Minneapolis "Creative City Challenge" and a Minnesota American Society of Landscape Architects Deign Award. With Blaine Brownell, from the University of North Carolina Charlotte, he co-authored the book Hypernatural: Architecture's New Relationship with Nature. Marc recently launched a post-disciplinary design research laboratory at the University of Colorado Denver called LoDo Lab. He is Chair of the Architecture Department and Professor. He studied at the University of Cincinnati and Rice University.

Richard Beckett is an Architect and Associate Professor in Architecture at the Bartlett, UCL where he is Director of RC7 on the BPro Architectural Design Master's programme and leads Studio 3 on the Landscape Architecture course. His research is focused on design, operating at the intersection of computation, biofabrication, and microbial ecologies in buildings and cities. His research on Probiotic Design won the RIBA Presidents Research Award in 2021. He has built numerous projects and has been exhibited internationally including Archilab – Naturalising Architecture, The Pompidou Centre and Nature – Cooper Hewitt Smithsonian Design Museum. He is currently the Principal Investigator on a 3 year, EPSRC funded research project; 'Probiotic interventions to reduce the emergence and persistence of pathogens in built environments'.

Jamie Vanucchi is an an Assistant Professor and Director of Undergraduate Studies. Jamie's teaching and research test the capacity of design and design research to address our most pressing 21st-century problems. She is interested in "strong sites", landscapes driven by change in the form of powerful constructive and destructive processes, and design that intentionally intersects with those processes and unfolds in time. Current projects include the study of floodplains as unique, disturbance-driven landscapes and potential community assets, the restoration of floodplain buyouts, designed forests for climate mitigation, and framing design research as a distinct mode of knowledge production that is complementary to science and especially needed now due to the novelty and uncertainty of climate-changed futures. Her research is funded by NIFA, Cornell's Atkinson's Center for Sustainability, The Landscape Architecture Foundation, and Cornell Council of the Arts. Jamie has a small design-build practice and she is a partner with the Great Lakes Design Labs and LoDo Lab at CU Denver.

Nancy Diniz is a registered architect and educator. Her practice lies in the intersection of computational design and biological systems. She is co-founder of bioMATTERS, @biomatters.llc, a design studio focusing on 3D printed and robotically manufactured biomaterials. Nancy is Course Leader of the Masters in Biodesign at Central Saint Martins UAL @mabiodesign in London. She has exhibited, published, and curated symposia and exhibitions widely on the topics of 'living and grown design', bio and digital fabrication, data driven design, and virtual reality/augmented reality (VR/AR). Her work has been exhibited at Material Matters, Dutch Design Week, NY Design Week, 'Biodesign Here Now' London Design Festival, MAAT Museum, GAA Foundation, London Design Biennale, Lisbon Architecture Triennale, Istanbul Design Biennial, SYGGRAPH and ISEA, among others. She is the recipient of numerous grants and fellowships namely NEW INC, NYSCA /Storefront, MacDowell Colony, EYEBEAM, Seoul Art Space Geumcheon, Korea and FCT Portugal. Nancy is co-editor of the book 'Data, Matter, Design: Strategies in Computational Design' (Routledge 2020). She is chief editor and co-chair of the upcoming symposium 'Bio-Calibrated: Tools and Techniques of Biodesign Practices' Nov 30-1 Dec 2023 hosted by Central Saint Martins UAL.

Thora Arnardottir is a Research Associate at the Hub for Biotechnology in the Built Environment (HBBE), where she manages the Macro Bio-Design Lab, and conducts research centred on the Living Construction theme. She is also an Associate Lecturer at Central Saint Martins on the MA Biodesign program. Thora is a biodesigner and researcher with a background in architecture and a passion for pursuing analogy with nature by integrating living processes into our fabrication practices. She did her PhD "Bacterial Sculpting" at Newcastle University, where her research focused on fabrication techniques with bacterial biomineralization and the integration of biological systems in the built environment. She combines biotic agency with innovative crafting techniques to explore the possibilities of living materials and bio-fabrication. As a co-founder of the experimental research group BioBabes and a founder and director of Unruly Matters Ltd, Thora engages in interdisciplinary investigations at the intersection of design, science, and biology. Her key interests include biomaterials, design-led investigations, and the transformative potential of integrating biology and architecture.

Leyuan Li is a Chinese architect, educator, and researcher whose professional and academic work focuses on interior and urban realms in the articulation of underrepresented identities, situations, and societies. He has practiced architecture internationally at OMA, SOM, and Affordable Housing Lab. Li is the founder of Office for Roundtable, a collaborative practice that explores architectural and interior types in relation to environmental and social issues. Recent built works seek to interrogate the rapidly changing urban environment in China through the exploration of interior forms, and have been featured in Art and Design Magazine (China), Architecture and Urbanism (China), and Frame Magazine, among others. Li is currently a Visiting Assistant Professor of Architecture with an Emphasis on Issues of Justice, Equity, Diversity, and Inclusion at the University of Colorado Denver. He has taught at Rice University's School of Architecture and the University of Houston, and has been invited to lectures and reviews at Nanjing University, Syracuse University, and the Rhode Island School of Design. Li's work has been published in journals and books, including PLAT, New York Review of Architecture, and Drawing Codes (AR+D, 2023), and has been exhibited at the UCCA Center for Contemporary Art in Beijing, OCAT Museum in Shanghai, Citygroup Gallery in New York City, and the 9th Bi-City Biennale of Architecture and Urbanism in Shenzhen.

Cynthia Fishman, AIA | BSpec | NCARB | LEED AP | ACUE | Fitwel Ambassador (she/her) has an extensive background of 15 years in sustainability and the practice of architecture as a licensed architect. She is the Director and founder of the Biomimicry Design Alliance, a research and consulting firm in Denver, Colorado, that makes biomimicry accessible to the design community. She received her Bachelor of Architecture from Rice University in Houston, Texas as well as an Ecological Design Certificate from the Ecosa Institute in Prescott, Arizona. Cynthia was part of the first matriculating class at Arizona State University to earn a Master of Science in Biomimicry degree, which is the first in the world to offer an accredited program. Cynthia is one of the recipients of the 2019 National AIA Young Architect Award, the 2018 Engineering News Record (Mountain States Region) Top Young Professionals Award, and AIA Colorado's Leadership Award in 2015 for her outstanding contributions to the architectural profession.

Andrew Adamatzky is Professor of Unconventional Computing and head of the Unconventional Computing Group at UWE, Bristol, UK. His research interests include non-standard and nature-inspired computation, theoretical computer science, artificial intelligence and crowd dynamics, mathematical biology and psychology, and non-linear sciences. His recent work has included development of logical and arithmetical circuits in excitable chemical media, slime mould, and liquid crystal figures; and also, development of intelligent massively parallel actuator arrays, formal languages and complexity of cellular automata models, novel types of information processing in memristive devices, design of parallel hybrid computers from living slime mould, P. polycephalum and from living Fungi. He authored seven research monographs (published in Springer, Elsevier, World Scientific): "Identification of Cellular Automata", "Computing in Nonlinear media and Automata Collectives", "Reaction-Diffusion Computers", "Dynamics of Crowd Minds", "Physarum Machines", "Reaction-Diffusion Automata", "Bioevaluation of World Transport Networks", edited 14 monographs (published in the MIT Press, Elsevier, Springer, World Scientific), authored over 300 papers in peer-reviewed international journals, founded the Unconventional Computing Lab at UWE, Bristol, founded two international journals: Int J Cellular Automata and Int J Unconventional Computing, and one book series "Emergency, Complexity, Computation." News stories about Adamatzky research are published in New Scientist, Scientific American, Wired, Technology Reviews, The Guardian, New York Times, etc. He was amongst key figures in the documentary movies `The Creeping Garden' (2014, UK) and `The Blob' (2019, France).

Joern Langhorst, Associate Professor of Landscape Architecture at the University of Colorado Denver, was educated in Landscape Architecture, Architecture and Urban Planning in Germany and the UK, and has taught in Landscape Architecture, Architecture, Urban and Regional Planning and Urban Design in the US and abroad. His practice has focused on projects in highly contested situations, such as redevelopment and remediation in post-industrial cities, brownfield sites, and post-disaster recovery, and is consulting on these issues nationally and internationally. His research and teaching are exploring the processes and actors that make and unmake place, space and landscape, focusing on places of incisive and radical change, such as post-colonial, post-industrial and post-disaster cities. His approaches involve multiple perspectives and disciplines, and establish a methodology he calls "landscape forensics". He examines how concepts such as social and environmental justice, resilience, and sustainability are conceived and implemented, arguing for a "right to landscape". Langhorst scrutinizes the role of emergent technologies, alternative processes, and the relationships between traditional and new actors and agents, and foregrounds contestation and conflict as unavoidable processes central to landscape and place change.

SESSION CHAIRS

Katie MacDonald is Director of the Before Building Laboratory, where she leads material research and development. MacDonald pioneers new biomaterial assemblies, with the aim of creating building material systems that sequester carbon and reduce construction's environmental impacts. Current projects focus on rapidly renewable biomaterials, including wood, bamboo, grass, hemp, and various invasive plant species. Research accolades include the R+D Award from Architect Magazine in 2022, Best in Digital Fabrication in The Architect's Newspaper Best of Design Awards in 2022, and Best in Research in The Architect's Newspaper Best of Design Awards in 2021. MacDonald was named Educator of the Year in Metropolis Magazine's Planet Positive Awards in 2023 and was awarded the University of Virginia Outstanding Researcher Award in the 2022 UVA Research Achievement Awards.

MacDonald is Cofounder of After Architecture, an architecture firm named to convey the built environment's impact on cultures and ecologies. After Architecture was awarded the Architectural League Prize for Young Architects + Designers in 2023, named to Cultured Magazine's Young Architects List in 2021, "Next Progressive" by Architect Magazine in 2019, and "Curbed Young Gun" by Curbed National in 2014. Recent works include a memorial in Washington D.C., and installations for the Oslo Architecture Triennale, the Knoxville Museum of Art, and Exhibit Columbus as 2022-2023 University Design Research Fellow.

MacDonald creates venues for scholarly exchange including the Biomaterial Building Exposition, which put developments in biomaterial construction on view at the University of Virginia in 2022, and Projecting Fellows, a virtual symposium which brought together fellows from American architecture schools to explore the vehicle of the fellowship project in 2021. She is a member of the Association for Computer-Aided Design in Architecture's Board of Directors.

Vernelle A. A. Noel, Ph.D. is the Lucian and Rita Caste Assistant Professor in Architecture and Urban Design at the Carnegie Mellon University School of Architecture. She is a computational design scholar, architect, artist, and Director of the Situated Computation + Design Lab. She investigates traditional and digital practices, and their intersections with society. Using interdisciplinary approaches, she builds new frameworks, methodologies, and tools to explore social, cultural, and political aspects of computation and emerging technologies for new reconfigurations of practice, pedagogy, and publics. Her work has been supported by the Graham Foundation, the Mozilla Foundation, and ideas2innovation (i2i), among others. She is a recipient of the DigitalFUTURES Young Award for exceptional research and scholarship in the field of critical computational design, and gave a TEDx Talk titled, "The Power of Making: Craft, Computation, and Carnival." Dr. Noel holds a Ph.D. from The Pennsylvania State University, a Master of Science in Architecture Studies from MIT, a Bachelor of Architecture from Howard University, and a Diploma in Civil Engineering from Trinidad & Tobago. Noel has held positions at Georgia Institute of Technology, the University of Stuttgart, the University of Florida, Penn State University, MIT, the Singapore University of Technology & Design, and has practiced as an architect in the US, India, and Trinidad & Tobago. Noel is currently a board member of The Association for Computer-Aided Design in Architecture (ACADIA).

Dana Cupkova holds Associate Professorship at the Carnegie Mellon School of Architecture and is a Co-founder and Director of EPIPHYTE Lab, an architectural design and research collaborative. From 2005 to 2012 she was a Visiting Assistant Professor in the Cornell University Department of Architecture. From 2014 to 2018 she served on the ACADIA Board of Directors and currently she is on the Editorial Board for the IJAC. Professor Cupkova is Track Chair of SoA's Masters of Science in Sustainable Design (MSSD) program.

Cupkova's design work engages the built environment at the intersection of ecology, computationally driven processes, and systems analysis. In her research, she interrogates the relationship between design-space and ecology as it engages computational methods, thermodynamic processes, and experimentation with geometrically driven performance logic. Her work has been supported by the New York State Council on the Arts, the AIA NY Center for Architecture Foundation, the Cornell University Faculty Innovation in Teaching Grant, the Architectural League of New York, the AIA Urban and Regional Solution Grant, the Pennsylvania Infrastructure Technology Alliance Grant, CMU's Manufacturing Futures Infinitive and others. Cupkova's design work has been published internationally in professional venues such as Dwell, The Architectural Review, Green Building & Design, The Cornell Journal of Architecture, Architect's Newspaper, International Journal of Architectural Computing and presented at many academic conferences. In May 2018 Epiphyte Lab has been recognized as the Next Progressives design practice by ARCHITECT Magazine, The Journal of The American Institute of Architects.

Dana Cupkova teaches in the core design curriculum, serving as a coordinator for the undergraduate and graduate core design studio Environment, Form and Feedback, as well teaching advanced option studios, graduate design-research MSSD thesis and graduate-level research seminars. Cupkova received the professional degree of Engineer Architect from the Faculty of Architecture and Urban Design at the Slovak University of Technology in Bratislava; she completed her thesis at the Academy of Fine Arts Vienna and holds a Master of Architecture degree from the School of the Arts and Architecture at UCLA, where she was awarded the Unrestricted University Fellowship, the Mimi Perloff Award, and the Kate Neal Kinley Memorial Fellowship for outstanding design work. Cupkova was a founder and design director of DCm-STUDIO, an architectural design practice in New York City, and has extensive international professional experience in Europe, the United States, and Southeast Asia. She was previously in practice with Smith-Miller+Hawkinson Architects, RUR Architecture in New York City, and TR Hamzah & Yeang in Malaysia.

Melissa Goldman has an excitement for making at all scales. Her work combines an interest in exploiting material properties, hacking tools, and playing with robots, CNC routers, and 3D printers, and she teaches seminars on digital fabrication and design robotics. She joined UVA in 2011, and is in charge of the FabLab, including the Milton Air Field Hangar facility, and mentors a crew of TAs who teach a series of Shops Short Courses open to all in the University. Her work connects her to other makers across Grounds, Charlottesville, and beyond, collaborating with multiple departments and professional fabricators. She is a co-founder of UVA's MakerGrounds, the network of shops, labs, and makerspaces open to the UVA community. In 2012-2013, Melissa co-directed The Stan Winston Arts Festival of the Moving Creature at UVA, a yearlong interdisciplinary course that designed and built large puppeted creatures with Hollywood professionals, culminating in a parade and festival. From that year, she helped to produce a short film, "The Creatures are Coming," that debuted at the Virginia Film Festival. More recently, Melissa has developed ongoing research on ferrostructures and robotic fabrication. This work was awarded the 2017 Acadia Research Award.

Melissa has her Masters of Architecture degree from Columbia, where she was bit by the digital fabrication bug, and her BA in English from Harvard, where she immersed herself in theatrical set and puppet design. When she is not running from the student zombies, she serves on the UVA Staff Senate, plays the cello, and officiates roller derby.

Nancy Diniz is a registered architect and educator. Her practice lies in the intersection of computational design and biological systems. She is co-founder of bioMATTERS, @biomatters. llc, a design studio focusing on 3D printed and robotically manufactured biomaterials . Nancy is Course Leader of the Masters in Biodesign at Central Saint Martins UAL @mabiodesign in London. She has exhibited, published, and curated symposia and exhibitions widely on the topics of 'living and grown design', bio and digital fabrication, data driven design, and virtual reality/augmented reality (VR/AR). Her work has been exhibited at Material Matters, Dutch Design Week, NY Design Week, 'Biodesign Here Now' London Design Festival, MAAT Museum, GAA Foundation, London Design Biennale, Lisbon Architecture Triennale, Istanbul Design Biennial, SYGGRAPH and ISEA, among others. She is the recipient of numerous grants and fellowships namely NEW INC, NYSCA /Storefront, MacDowell Colony, EYEBEAM, Seoul Art Space Geumcheon, Korea and FCT Portugal. Nancy is co-editor of the book 'Data, Matter, Design: Strategies in Computational Design' (Routledge 2020). She is chief editor and co-chair of the upcoming symposium 'Bio-Calibrated: Tools and Techniques of Biodesign Practices' Nov 30-1 Dec 2023 hosted by Central Saint Martins UAL.

Jonathan Dessi-Olive is a researcher, designer, and educator. Presently he is an Assistant Professor in Department of Architecture at the University of North Carolina at Charlotte, where he teaches architecture design studios, structures, and construction seminars. He is also the director of the MYCO MATTERS LAB, a design and research practice that focuses on applications of fungi-based materials in architectural design and construction. Prior to joining UNCC, Jonathan was an assistant professor at Kansas State University, and he was the inaugural Ventulett NEXT Fellow at the Georgia Institute of Technology School of Architecture.

Jonathan's research takes a critical approach to technology while integrating history and theory of architecture, contemporary construction, and computational design. Recent contributions include large-scale biofabrication with mycelium composite materials, large-scale monolithic mycelium structures, computational design methodologies for architectural acoustics, large-scale inflatable tensegrity structures, constructing monolithic structures with emerging bio-materials such as mycelium, and methodologies for thin-shell vault structures in the United States, Europe, and East Africa.

Jonathan's research has been published through the International Association of Shell and Spatial Structures (IASS), the Acoustical Society of America (ASA), the Symposium for Simulation in Architecture and Urban Design (SimAUD), and the Conference for Nonconventional Materials and Technologies (NOCMAT). His design and construction work has been exhibited in public venues such as the Venice Architecture Biennale, TEDxPenn, the Center for Architecture in New York City, and The University of Virginia.

Katharina Hoerath has built a successful career spanning award-winning retail projects for renowned brands like Jimmy Choo, Urban Retreat, and Harry's of London, along with innovative office designs, including Bond Collective. Her dedication lies in creating impactful spaces that not only inspire but also leave a lasting impression. As a visionary in the industry, Katharina firmly believes in the transformative power of architecture in shaping communities. Her commitment to excellence extends beyond aesthetics, as she is equally passionate about fostering inclusive and enriched learning environments that embrace diversity. Through her teaching roles at the University of Gloucestershire and Parsons School of Design, she actively contributes to the growth of the new generation of architects.

Katharina places significant emphasis on research in materiality, sustainability, and digital technologies. Her work often involves pushing boundaries and testing concepts through art installations, such as the Arcadia Earth Museum project, to encourage social interactions and promote growth in individuals and communities alike.

Mary Polites's research explores the potential of digitally fabricated adaptive infrastructures to support the growth of natural systems within the context of architecture and indoor spaces. Her work ecognizes the importance of living systems in our life through food production, improvement of air quality, and influence on mental health. Rather than seeing nature as a decorative artifact, this work proposes system-based design solutions that act as infrastructure necessary for living systems to integrate into our built environment.

Mary Polites is an educator, architect, and researcher focusing on the integration of architectural design and ecological systems. She is co-director of MAPS (Methods for the Architecture of Patterns and Systems), a design collective specializing in developing innovative design solutions for human and natural systems at all scales. Mary has extensive international experience leading studios, lectures, and seminars related to computational tools and environmental design. Her book "The Rise of Biodesign" analyzes contemporary methodologies developed by Chinese top research institutions to innovate from nature in design.

Alex Li is founder and director of AYL, a research practice working at the intersection of architecture, computation, and material cultures. Li's experimental research explores the real-time capacity of computational tools to develop material techniques that are sensitive to time, process, and other environmental conditions. His research has taken various forms ranging from machines, mock-ups, furniture, buildings, images, and texts, all converging under three distinct yet interrelated themes: material properties, construction standards, and tectonic assemblies. His most recent exhibition, Particulate Signals, investigates the standardized protocols of concrete-handling—from formwork to labor practice—through the lens of calculability, predictability, and reproducibility.

Li has held teaching positions at Harvard University and Syracuse University. He was the 2021-2023 Irving Innovation Fellow at the Harvard University Graduate School of Design, where his research and teaching focused on historical and contemporary material techniques in architecture. Together with Sean Canty, he co-directed the "All About This One Thing" (AATOT) program as part of the graduate core curriculum. At Syracuse, he teaches undergraduate design studios and graduate design seminar. He has given lectures and served on juries at many institutions including Harvard, Cornell, SCI-Arc, the University of Toronto, RISD, CU Denver, Washington University in St. Louis, Wentworth Institute of Technology, and Northeastern University.

Prior to establishing his own practice, Li worked internationally in the United States, Canada, Japan, and China, including Diller Scofidio + Renfro, Höweler + Yoon, and Shigeru Ban Architects. He was a project manager at MILLIØNS where he led architecture and art installation projects in New York, Los Angeles, Boston, Taipei, and France. This includes leading the renovation of I.M. Pei's Everson Museum where he collaborated with ceramicists, conservationists, and contractors to develop material research and adaptive reuse strategies specific to the building scale. Li received a Master of Architecture I AP with Distinction from Harvard GSD, where he was the recipient of the Clifford Wong Housing Prize and the Architecture Research Grant. He also holds a Bachelor of Architectural Studies with Distinction from the University of Waterloo, Canada, where he received the President's Scholarship and the First in Class Award.

Leighton Beaman is a designer, writer and educator. His design work, research and writing focus on the history, discourse, and speculative future of spatial material culture and its implications for environmental responsibility, and socially conscious design practices. Leighton is an Associate Professor of Practice at Cornell University, focusing on spatial material culture, advanced technologies for design and fabrication, as well as environmental and social responsibility in design. Prior to his appointment at Cornell, he taught at Harvard University, Rhode Island School of Design, the University of Virginia, and the University of Texas.

Leighton is the Co-founder of General Architecture Collaborative (GAC), a design-based nonprofit working in East Africa and North America. GAC was named a design Game Changer by Metropolis Magazine in 2020, and Small Practice of the Year by the Architects Newspaper in 2021. GAC and has received a number of awards and recognitions for their work, including from the American Institute of Architects, Society of American Reistered Architects, Dezeen, Architizer, EDRA, and the Architectural League of NY. Their work has been featured at installations and exhibitions at the Venice Biennale, Yale University, Pinakothek de Morderne, Goethe Institute, the University of Texas, and the Seoul Biennale.

He is also the Founder of Alterior Office, a research-based design studio working across scales, systems, and processes. The work of Alterior Office has been featured in exhibitions and installations at the American Institute of Architects, Harvard University, Rhode Island School of Design Art Museum, NYCxDESIGN, the Boston Society of Architects, University of Virginia, the University of Cincinnati, and the American Academy in Rome.

As a writer, Leighton has contributed to a number of publications including Architectural Record, Cite, II Journal, IntAR Journal, Issue, and the Technology Architecture + Design Journal. He is currently a guest editor for the International Journal of Architectural Computing.

Leighton has been named a MacDowell Fellow, an American Institute of Architects Emerging Practitioner, a University of Virginia Teaching Fellow in Architecture, and was recently a visiting artist at the American Academy in Rome.

The Association for Computer Aided Design in Architecture (ACADIA) is an international network of digital design researchers and professionals that facilitates critical investigations into the role of computation in architecture, planning, and building science, encouraging innovation in design creativity, sustainability, and education.

The Association for Computer Aided Design in Architecture was founded in 1981 by some of the pioneers in the field of design computation, including Bill Mitchell, Chuck Eastman, and Chris Yessios. Since then, ACADIA has hosted over 40 conferences across North America, and has grown into a strong network of academics and professionals in the design computation field.

Incorporated in the state of Delaware as a not-for-profit corporation, ACADIA is an all-volunteer organization governed by elected officers, an elected Board of Directors, and appointed ex-officio officers.

PRESIDENT
Shelby Doyle, Iowa State University
president@acadia.org

VICE-PRESIDENT
Jenny E. Sabin, Cornell University
vp@acadia.org

SECRETARY
Katie MacDonald
secretary@acadia.org

TREASURER
Phillip Anzalone, New York City College of Technology
treasurer@acadia.org

MEMBERSHIP OFFICER
Vernelle A. A. Noel
membership@acadia.org

TECHNOLOGY OFFICER
Jose Luis Garcia del Castillo López
webmaster@acadia.org

DEVELOPMENT OFFICER
Sina Mostafavi
development@acadia.org

COMMUNICATIONS OFFICER
Melissa Goldman
communications@acadia.org

IJAC ACADIA OFFICER
Dana Cupkova
ijac-officer@acadia.org

CONFERENCE AND WEBSITE PRODUCTION ASSISTANT
Cameron Nelson

BOARD OF DIRECTORS (Term: Jan 1, 2024 - Dec 31, 2024)
Biayna Bogosian, Florida International University
Felecia Davis, The Pennsylvania State University
Melissa Goldman, University of Virginia
Katie MacDonald, University of Virginia
Vernelle A. A. Noel, Georgia Institute of Technology
Robert Stuart-Smith, University of Pennsylvania (alternate)
Stefana Parascho, École Polytechnique Fédérale de Lausanne (alternate)
Shermeen Yousif, Florida Atlantic University (alternate)

BOARD OF DIRECTORS (Term: Jan 1, 2023 - Dec 31, 2023)
Kathrin Dorfler, Technical University of Munich
Behnaz Farahi, California State University, Long Beach
Leslie Lok, Cornell University
Sina Mostafavi, Texas Tech University
Maria Yablonina, University of Toronto
Daniel Bolojan, Florida Atlantic University (alternate)
Leighton Beaman, Cornell University (alternate)

CONFERENCE CHAIRS
Assia Crawford, University of Colorado Denver
Thora Arnardottir, Newcastle University
Marc Swackhamer, University of Colorado Denver
Leyuan Li, University of Colorado Denver
Richard Beckett, University College London
Nancy Diniz, Central Saint Martins, University of the Arts London
Andrew Adamatzky, University of the West of England Bristol
Jamie Vanucchi, Cornell University
Cynthia Fishman, University of Colorado Denver
Joern Langhorst, University of Colorado Denver

LEAD EDITOR
Assia Crawford, University of Colorado Denver

ASSISTING
Nancy Diniz, Central Saint Martins, University of the Arts London

SUPPORTING
Richard Beckett, University College London
Jamie Vanucchi, Cornell University
Marc Swackhamer, University of Colorado Denver

OTHER MEMBERS OF THE PEER REVIEW
Leyuan Li, University of Colorado Denver

ASSISTANT TO THE EDITOR AND LAYOUT
Dilan Ozkan, Newcastle University

COPY EDITING
Lynne Campbell

GRAPHIC DESIGN
Luke Bulman

PRINTING LOGISTICS
Cynthia Fishman

PLATINUM SPONSORS

AUTODESK

BRONZE SPONSOR

Perkins&Will

AndersonMasonDale Architects

MD Massive Dimension

SPONSORS

ICON HDR rk20 rowland+broughton ORO EDITIONS

ARKTURA ABB Page/

MEDIA PARTNER

The Architect's Newspaper

12048UKWH00031BB/1729
UKHW060214240426
Ingram Content Group UK Ltd.
Pitfield, Milton Keynes, MK11 3LW, UK
www.ingramcontent.com/pod-product-compliance